DATE DUE

OCT 1 0 1996	
APR 1 6 1997	
May 2	
NOV - 7 1997	
MAR 1 8 1998	
NOV 1 5 1998	
DEC - 5 1999	
FEB - 3 2000	
MAR 1 2 2001	
APR 1 6 2001	
Northwest com due Nov 18/01	
FEB 2 1 2002	
MAR 2 7 2003	

BRODART

Cat. No. 23-221

THEORY AND ASSESSMENT OF

STRESSFUL LIFE EVENTS

International Universities Press
Stress and Health Series

Edited by
Leo Goldberger, Ph.D.

Monograph 6

Theory and Assessment of Stressful Life Events

edited by

Thomas W. Miller, Ph.D.

International Universities Press, Inc.
Madison   Connecticut

Library of Congress Cataloging-in-Publication Data

Theory and assessment of stressful life events / edited by Thomas W.
  Miller.
    p. cm.—(Stress and health series)
    Includes bibliographical references and index.
    ISBN 0-8236-6521-6
    1. Life change events—Psychological aspects. 2. Psychic trauma.
  3. Post-traumatic stress disorder. 4. Stress (Psychology)
  5. Psychoneuroimmunology. I. Miller, Thomas W., 1943-
  II. Series.
  RC455.4.L53T48 1996
  616.89—dc20   95-40591
                                               CIP

Manufactured in the United States of America

Contents

PART II: ASSESSMENT AND METHODOLOGICAL ISSUES

Contributors

Christine M. Adler, Ph.D., Staff Psychologist, Department of Veterans Affairs Medical Center, Mountain Home, Tennessee.

Albert N. Allain, Jr., M.S., Psychology Technician, Veterans Affairs Medical Center, New Orleans, Louisiana.

Nancy E. Betz, Ph.D., Professor, Department of Psychology, Ohio State University, Columbus, Ohio.

Yael Caspi-Yavin, M.A., M.P.H., Research Associate, Harvard Program in Refugee Trauma, Harvard School of Public Health, Boston, Massachusetts.

Joseph W. Critelli, Ph.D., Professor, Department of Psychology, University of North Texas, Denton, Texas.

Juliana S. Ee, Ph.D., Professor, Department of Psychology, Harvard University, Boston, Massachusetts.

Sherry A. Falsetti, Ph.D., Instructor, National Crime Victims Research and Treatment Center at the Medical University of South Carolina, Charleston, South Carolina.

John R. Freedy, Ph.D., Assistant Professor, National Crime Victims Research and Treatment Center at the Medical University of South Carolina, Charleston, South Carolina.

Joel J. Hillhouse, Ph.D., Assistant Professor, Department of Psychology, East Tennessee State University, Johnson City, Tennessee.

Dean G. Kilpatrick, Ph.D., Professor and Director of the National Crime Victims Research and Treatment Center at the Medical University of South Carolina, Charleston, South Carolina.

Robert F. Kraus, M.D., Professor and Chair, Department of Psychiatry, College of Medicine, University of Kentucky, Lexington, Kentucky.

Gabriele S. Leverich, M.S.W., Section on Psychobiology, Biological Psychiatry Branch, National Institute of Mental Health, Bethesda, Maryland.

J. Stephen McDaniel, M.D., Assistant Professor of Psychiatry, Department of Psychiatry and Behavioral Sciences, Emory University School of Medicine, Atlanta, Georgia.

Thomas W. Miller, Ph.D., A.B.P.P., Professor and Chief, Psychology Service, Department of Veterans Affairs and University of Kentucky Medical Centers, Lexington, Kentucky.

Richard F. Mollica, M.D., Director, Harvard Program and Refugee Trauma, Harvard School of Public Health, and Clinical Director, Indochinese Psychiatry Clinic, St. Elizabeth's Hospital, Brighton, Massachusetts.

Carol S. North, M.D., Assistant Professor, Department of Psychiatry, Washington University School of Medicine, St. Louis, Missouri.

Robert M. Post, M.D., Chief, Biological Psychiatry Branch, National Institute of Mental Health, Bethesda, Maryland.

Heidi S. Resnick, Ph.D., Associate Professor National Crime Victims Research and Treatment Center at the Medical College of South Carolina, Charleston, South Carolina.

Elizabeth M. Smith, Ph.D., Associate Professor, Department of Psychiatry, Washington University School of Medicine, St. Louis, Missouri.

Mark A. Smith, M.D., Ph.D., Medical Officer, Unit on Neurochemistry, Biological Psychiatry Branch, National Institute of Mental Health, Bethesda, Maryland.

Patricia Sutker, Ph.D., Chief, Psychology Service, Veterans Affairs Medical Center, New Orleans, Louisiana, and Professor Tulane University, New Orleans, Louisiana.

Madeline Uddo, Ph.D., Clinical Psychologist, Veterans Affairs Medical Center, New Orleans, Louisiana, and Assistant Professor, Tulane University School of Medicine, New Orleans, Louisiana.

Susan R. B. Weiss, Ph.D., Chief, Unit on Behavioral Biology, Biological Psychiatry Branch, National Institute of Mental Health, Bethesda, Maryland.

Sharon L. Younkin, Ph.D., Director of Counseling, Eckerd College, St. Petersburg, Florida.

Preface

This second volume of *Stressful Life Events* is designed to expand and update the theoretician, clinician, and researcher on the latest information related to our understanding of stressful life events and their impact on our lives. Theoretical formulations and hypotheses, issues and implications related to the validity and reliability of life stress measurement and its applications to both medical and mental health related concerns are addressed here. Furthermore, special attention is given to the individuals and how that individual functions within various life settings. This book views the person as both the producer of stress and a reactor to stress, and attempts to identify a variety of sources of stressful life experiences from within and beyond the individual's life space.

The chapters herein are directed toward the myriad of health care theoreticians, practitioners, and researchers, and attempts together a representative sample of the authorities in each of the areas presented. Many of the individuals have pioneered extremely fruitful clinical research activities and their understanding of certain ethnogenic mainstream concepts have become important ingredients in defining, analyzing, and treating stress-related disorders. There are several rich perspectives that effectively integrate the variety of generalizations about functional and dysfunctional aspects of stress.

Matthew J. Friedman, M.D., Ph.D.

Introduction: Stressful Life Events—Critical Issues in Theory and Assessment

Thomas W. Miller, Ph.D., A.B.P.P.

The effects of stressful life events on the health of individuals are made up of a multiplicity of highly complex factors, all of which must be considered in assessment and treatment. The growing body of information and clinical findings (Figley, 1985; Miller, 1989; Green, 1990; Friedman, 1993; Horowitz, Field, and Classen, 1993; Dohrenwend, Raphael, Schwartz, Stueve, and Skodol, 1993) has expanded our theoretical understanding of trauma and stress from a purely psychological context to a biopsychosocial model in which many different factors contribute to the etiology, onset, and impact on health of life stress events.

Within these assembled chapters are critically important topics that focus on the impact of psychotraumatology from the trauma itself to the symptomatology that may result. There emerges a dose–effect relationship in which the risk of developing posttraumatic stress syndrome (PTSD) increases with intensity and duration of the trauma. A continuum of sorts emerges which recognizes that modifying effects of predisposing vulnerability, the combination of learning theory, various personality characteristics, the presence of support systems, the locus of control, and the psychoneuroimmunological aspects of adjustment must be considered.

Several questions emerge that must be explored in order to help us understand critical issues in stressful life events. These include:

1. How is trauma and its symptoms diagnosed?
2. How do we assess the impact of life stress events?
3. How do humans process trauma from life stress?
4. Are there ethnocultural variants related to stressful life events?
5. Which treatment models are most helpful for traumatized persons?
6. What research is needed in the 1990s to aid clinicians in their work?

Friedman (1993) has noted that the biological research suggests that patients with PTSD display marked abnormalities and sympathetic nervous system arousal and hypothalamic pituitary adrenal cortical function in the indigenous opioid system and in the physiology of sleep and dreaming. We need to work toward a biopsychosocial model in which many different factors contribute to our understanding of traumatization and stress.

HOW IS TRAUMA AND ITS SYMPTOMS DIAGNOSED?

Over the past decade, we have viewed the impact of life stress events to mainly encompass the diagnostic entity that has come to be known as posttraumatic stress disorder. More recent inquiry into this question suggests that it may be more important to look at the impact of stressful life events on health as a spectrum disorder rather than a single disorder in and of itself. To understand stressful life events as a spectrum disorder involves looking at the components and processing of anxiety, depression, somatization, and dissociation. Its components can include panic disorder, agoraphobia, obsessive–compulsive disorder, generalized anxiety, hypochondriasis, somatization, and components of hysterical neurosis and multiple personality disorder. Its etiology may be nested in DSM-III-R Axis II diagnoses suggesting personality disturbance as a predisposer to a major psychiatric disorder in the multiaxial system (APA, 1987).

In viewing this as a spectrum disorder (Figure i), we recognize that anxiety and depression are widely present in individuals with traumatic stress. The precise description is important for several reasons. The etiology and onset may be discernible from certain other psychological disturbances, most notably generalized anxiety disorder or major depressive disorder. Features relating to reexperiencing trauma, including the assessment of the degree to which an individual ruminates and the ruminations' effect on daily functioning, is extremely important. Furthermore, numbing of responsiveness is assessed as a core ingredient in traumatization. This feature may be intertwined with aspects of anxiety and depressive components and is most similar diagnostically to the lack of interest or anhedonia and withdrawal often found in patients with clinical depression. The distinguishing features of the numbing found in traumatic stress often relate more to the unremitting severity, intensity, and chronicity of the symptoms which often derive from situations or feelings reminiscent of the traumatic event.

Of importance to the numbing and restricted range of emotional experiences found in traumatized individuals is the role of anger. For many, anger is a frequently expressed emotion that creates multiple interpersonal problems. For some, the control of anger and the accompanying fear of loss of control are major preoccupations that cause considerable distress and frequently lead to social withdrawal and isolation.

The startle response seen in traumatized individuals may be similar to that found in generalized anxiety disorder. The exaggerated startle response may reflect psychophysiological arousal which is noticeably worsened in the presence of specific situational reminders and triggers.

Finally, the presence of dual diagnosis has been important in understanding the complexity of the impact of trauma on the individual's functioning. The presence of coexisting Axis I or Axis

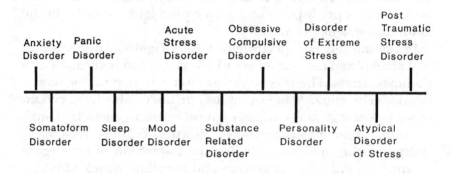

Figure i. Spectrum Disorder

II disorders has considerable clinical relevance in influencing formulation of the patient's problem in both an etiological and treatment perspective. Frequently traumatized individuals can meet the criteria for major depression, substance abuse or dependence, and various components of anxiety disorders including panic disorder. The identification of coexisting disorders at the onset of treatment can influence decision making regarding the sequence and timing of specific interventions and strategies that can be potentially helpful in optimizing treatment outcome.

HOW DO WE ASSESS THE IMPACT OF STRESSFUL LIFE EVENTS?

Numerous approaches have been utilized in the assessment of traumatization and life stress, including structured clinical interviews, diagnostic interview scales, psychometric measures, and psychophysiological measures.

THE STRUCTURED CLINICAL INTERVIEW (SCID)

At this point, the structured clinical interview for the DSM series is the one most frequently utilized to evaluate the presence or absence of psychiatric criteria. The SCID provides a comprehensive evaluation of Axis I and Axis II diagnoses. The PTSD module is concise and relatively easy to administer and score, while addressing the major diagnostic features of the disorder. Several clinical research studies have spoken to its validity and reliability, with Kulka, Schlenger, Fairbank, Hough, Jordan, Marmar, and Weiss (1990) finding the SCID diagnosis to be strongly correlated with other indices of PTSD. While this measure is highly respected for its reliability and validity, its limitation is that it yields only dichotomous information about each system and as a result, disorder severity and changes in symptom level cannot easily be detected.

TSI Life Events Questionnaire (Mac Ian and Perlman, 1992). The Traumatic Stress Institute has developed a 19-item questionnaire entitled the TSI Life Event Questionnaire. This self-report measure embraces a broad range of stressful life experiences and asks the client to rate the level of distress on a high/low dimension for both the point at which it occurred and the present. Examples of stressful life experience include: domestic violence, neglect, physical abuse, sexual abuse, natural disasters, threatening illness, litigation, rape, war and military experiences, and other traumatic events.

The PTSD Interview (Watson, Clark, and Tellegen, 1991) yields both dichotomous and continuous scores that address some of the limitations of the SCID and the DIS. Reports of high test–retest reliability, internal stability, and specificity recommend the instrument as favorable for use in diagnosing PTSD. It differs, however, from other clinical instruments in that it asks the subjects to make their own ratings of symptom severity rather than requiring this of the clinician.

PSYCHOMETRIC MEASURES

There are several psychometric measures that have been developed which hold potential for assisting in the diagnostic aspects of traumatization and stress. These include some of the following.

The Impact of Events Scale—Revised (Horowitz et al., 1993). The Impact of Events Scale focuses on the assessment of intrusions and avoidance–numbing responses. Perhaps the single most widely used instrument for assessing the psychological consequences of exposure to traumatic events, this scale has good internal consistency and test–retest reliability. Studies have found that the Impact of Events Scale correlates well with other indices of PTSD but that the limitation of this measure focuses on the fact that it does not measure other aspects of the disorder apart from intrusion and avoidant components.

The P-K Scale of the MMPI (Keane, Malloy, and Fairbank, 1984). The P-K Scale consists of 49 items that differentiate PTSD from non-PTSD patients. With the publication of the Minnesota Multiphasic Inventory (MMPI-2), Lyons and Keane (1992) describe the use of the P-K Scale within the context of the improved overall instrument.

The Mississippi Scale (Keane, Caddell, and Taylor, 1988). The Mississippi Scale is made up of a series of scales, and includes combat and civilian versions. It is a 35-item instrument that has high internal consistency, test–retest reliability, sensitivity, and specificity. The instrument has performed effectively in both clinical settings as well as research settings, indicating a general utility for measuring PTSD across settings.

The PEN Inventory (Hammarberg, 1992). The PEN Inventory is a relatively new diagnostic measure which appears to have good internal consistency, high test-retest reliability, and sensitivity. It is seen as a potentially good questionnaire to measure PTSD symptomatology.

Clinician-Administered PTSD Scale (CAPS-II). The Clinician Administered Post-Traumatic Stress Disorder Scale, Second Edition (Blake, Weathers, Nagy, and Friedman, 1990) is a structured clinical interview designed to assess the 17 symptoms of posttraumatic stress disorder outlined in DSM-III-R (APA, 1987). It is based on the original Clinically Administered Post-Traumatic Stress Disorder Scale, and has been refined to provide a more accurate means of evaluating the frequency and intensity of dimensions of each symptom, the impact of the symptoms on patients' social and occupational functioning, and the overall severity of the symptom complex.

The Structured Event Probe and Narrative Rating (SEPRATE) (Dohrenwend et al., 1993). SEPRATE provides an innovative methodology of life events measurement which reduces the problem of intracategory variability in assessing important characteristics of the events. It does this without confounding the events with health outcomes and without compromising the separate and distinct measurement of each of the components of the life stress process. The SEPRATE clinical interview includes an events checklist and probes to obtain detailed information on the number, dates, and types of events experienced by each respondent.

PSYCHOPHYSIOLOGY AND PTSD

The efforts of clinicians and researchers alike to assess biological markers of psychological disorders has focused considerable attention and interest on psychobiology and psychophysiological assessment (Friedman, 1993). Currently it is considered to be the best and most specific biological diagnostic test for traumatic stress. This diagnostic technique is based on the fact that traumatization and the stimuli deriving therefrom elicit sympathetic hyperarousal. Techniques utilized in psychophysiology are sensitive and powerful when one uses the general stimuli combat veterans associate with war or victims of natural disasters associate with an earthquake, say. It has been found to be even more discriminatory when the provocative stimulus consists of an individualized autobiographical traumatic anecdote (Pitman, 1988). Blanchard, Mold, and Pallmeyer (1982) found that reactivity predicts a diagnosis of PTSD while using auditory and audiovisual cues. Furthermore, Pitman (1988) observed the same reactivity when using personal scripts of traumatic events that were then read to subjects. These studies further observed a robust physiological component by combining the presentation of a physiologically meaningful cue while measuring psychologically and psychophysiologically relevant responses.

GENE EXPRESSION AND PSYCHONEUROIMMUNOLOGY

Within the past decade, significant advances have been made in establishing direct evidence for brain immune system interrelationships which serve a function in adaptation for both the human body's central nervous system and the immune system's ability to discriminate between self and nonself. Furthermore, various receptors for neurotransmitters, neuropeptides, and neurohormones on the cells of the immune system have been identified and recognized as critically important in both the processing and adaptation of the individual to life stress events (McDaniel, chapter 1).

Also emerging are preclinical models of behavioral sensitization and electrophysiological kindling which hold the potential to provide useful and necessary knowledge in conceptualizing various aspects of the neurobiology of traumatized individuals. The impact of triggering life stress experiences and the resultant anxiety and depression has led to the uncovering of neurobiological mechanisms that have helped to conceptualize the long-term results of stressful life events. Sensitization and kindling may also be useful analogies in considering the lasting impact of stressors on PTSD and other disorders, including major affective disorders. Emerging from such research efforts is an improved understanding of the nature of the neurobiological changes underlying the longitudinal course of major affective disorders and traumatizing experiences.

The Dexamethasone Suppression Test (DST) has been well recognized for its use in diagnosing major depressive disorders. Clinical researchers are finding that patients with traumatic stress disorder tend to have normal DST's and could therefore be classified as suppressors, whereas patients with traumatic stress disorder and major depressive disorder may well be seen as nonsuppressors. Sodium lactate or yohimbine infusion and sodium amytyl interviews have also been helpful in diagnosing traumatic stress in patients.

In the first chapter, Stephen McDaniel of the Department of Psychiatry, Emory University, explores the interactions between the central nervous system and the immune system. This chapter provides an overview of studies which have investigated the psychoneuroimmunology of stress. Stressful life events and their impact on the immune system are reviewed as well as literature which has examined the psychoneuroimmunological aspects of specific psychiatric disorders.

On the cutting edge of theoretical exploration of the impact of stressful life events is the work of Robert Post, Chief of the Biological Psychiatry Branch, National Institute of Mental Health. Examined within chapter 2 is the impact of psychosocial stress on gene expression. Two preclinical models, behavioral sensitization and electrophysiological kindling are hypothesized as providing useful and necessary bridging in our effort to conceptualize various aspects of neurobiology as it affects traumatization and resulting psychopathology. Both sensitization and kindling may also be useful analogies in considering the lasting yet evolving impact of stressors in traumatization.

The theoretical framework supporting a rapidly evolving science that is examining the multidirectional influence of life stress events and their impact on human functioning is explored by Drs. Miller and Kraus in chapter 3. Clinical models to assist in understanding the process of experiencing stressful life events and the subsequent accommodation of stress are examined within several theoretical models. Each model has applicability to our understanding of traumatization and the processing of traumatization. Insight into the impact of traumatization on disease development and its progression emerge through the transduction of psychosocial stress into neurobiological functioning.

The integration of the areas of psychology, neuroscience, immunology, and endocrinology is the focus of the work of Adler and Hillhouse. Chapter 4 addresses the impact of stressors, both acute and chronic, psychological variables such as depression and social support, stress and illness as in cancer, AIDS, and other infectious diseases, and psychological interventions. With increased understanding, the authors note, comes the possibility of more effective prevention and interventions.

Stress and physical illness and the efforts to develop an integrative model are the focus of Critelli and Ee in chapter 5. Critical issues related to measurement, contamination, and the search for more effective and comprehensive ways of measuring the spectrum of stress phenomena as it relates to physical illness are explored. The contention of the authors is that solutions to both issues, the current controversies over contamination and the search for strategies of comprehensive measurement rely on a reexamination of theory in which the stress construct is imbedded.

The role of personality variables in moderating the relationship between stress and psychological and/or physical illness have been of considerable interest to clinicians and researchers alike. Drs. Younkin and Betz focus on one personality variable which has received considerable attention as a stress buffer. Psychological hardiness as introduced by Kobeasa is seen as a composite of commitment, challenge, and control. The conceptual utility of the measure described by the author is supported by both evidence of a direct contribution of hardiness to the prediction of symptomatology beyond that accounted by stress, and by significant differences between high stress/high hardiness versus high stress/low hardiness subjects on constructs such as self-esteem, autonomy, depression and symptom level. A reconceptualization and measurement of psychological hardiness may be an important ingredient in understanding important constitutional predispositions in the accommodation of trauma and stress.

Drs. Uddo, Allain, and Sutker review theoretical issues relevant to measurement of extraordinary stress and its sequelae across diverse domains of functioning. The most obvious of the assessment domains is the encompassing of the evaluation of the psychological impact and response parameters of exposure to extreme stress. Clinical and research assessment of traumatization is directed toward the evaluation of the severity and nature of the stressing events. A description of multiple, sometimes overlapping and often phasic psychological responses indicative of traumatization and the measurement of relevant person–environment characteristics that affect symptom expression and are important in considering a response to treatment.

Current measures in the assessment of stressful life events are explored with special attention to three basic objectives: (1) the identification of experiences involving traumatization and stress and the subsequent symptoms which emerge; (2) consideration of the presence of coexisting psychological features; and (3) the specificity with respect to diagnostic and statistical evaluation criteria. Summarized by the author are several currently utilized measures in the assessment of stressful life events. Recommendations for future research and the development of measures that will more effectively assess trauma are discussed.

Recognizing that posttraumatic stress disorder has its roots in wartime experiences, Drs. Resnick, Falsetti, Kilpatrick, and Freedy of the Crime Victims Research and Treatment Center of the Medical University of South Carolina focus primarily on the assessment of civilian stressor events that often result in posttraumatic stress disorder. Issues in stressor event measurement are examined as are newly developed traumatization self-report assessment measures. The authors argue that the stressor event history is critical to gaining a better understanding of the impact of the traumatization and other significant mental and physical health outcomes that result from stressful life experiences with the civilian population.

The assessment of events and their related symptoms in torture and refugee trauma are examined by Dr. Mollica and colleague Yeal Caspi-Yavin of the Harvard Program in Refugee Trauma. Recognizing that the medical and psychiatric aspects and treatment of survivors of torture and mass trauma is a unique field of study. The authors examine both a historical and contemporary review of the impact of traumatization as evidenced by victims of torture. They note that in the torture field until recent studies, scientific investigations of the psychological symptoms of torture survivors consisted primarily of the reporting of symptoms without any systematic reference to standardization related to psychiatric diagnosis. They note that the problem of establishing reliable and valid measurements which capture the reality of the torture and trauma experience and related disease processes reveals the complex relationship between a concept of traumatization and the indicators of stressful life experiences and symptoms. Criteria emerging in DSM-IV aid in addressing a better understanding of the human reaction and its impact on the horror experienced by survivors of torture and mass trauma.

Drs. North and Smith of the Department of Psychiatry, Washington University, discuss sampling methods and practical issues in the field of quick response disaster research. Noting that disaster research consisted of limited, often unsystematic observation of small samples of convenience case reports and anecdotal findings, these authors discuss innovative methodological techniques that have been developed specifically for disaster research experience.

The impact of stressful life experiences is one of the most critical clinical, societal, and research challenges facing the mental health community in the decade of the nineties. It is to the individuals who have suffered and survived traumatization that our efforts to further our knowledge and understanding of traumatization and its process are dedicated. It is hoped that this work will generate the next wave of hypotheses to be tested, diagnostic issues to be considered, and treatment interventions to be offered.

REFERENCES

American Psychiatric Association (1987), *Diagnostic and Statistical Manual of Mental Disorders*, 3rd ed. rev. (DSM-III-R). Washington, DC: American Psychiatric Press.

Blake, W., Weathers, P., Nagy, R., & Friedman, M. (1993), *Clinician-Administered PTSD Scale (CAPS)*. Boston: National Center for PTSD, Behavioral Sciences Division.

Blanchard, E. B., Mold, L. C., & Pallmeyer, T. P. (1982), A psychological study of PTSD in Vietnam veterans. *Psychiatric Quart.*, 54:220–229.

Dohrenwend, B. S., Raphael, K., Schwartz, S., Stueve, A., & Skodol, A. (1993), Structured event probe and narrative rating method for measuring stressful life events. In: *Handbook of Stress*, 2nd ed., ed. L. Goldberger & S. Breznitz. New York: Free Press.

Figley, C. (1985), Introduction. In: *Trauma and Its Wake.* New York: Brunner/Mazel, pp. xvii–xxvi.

Friedman, M. (1993), Neurological alterations associated with post-traumatic stress disorder. National Center for PTSD, Clinical Laboratory and Education Division, Teleconference Report, July.

Green, B. (1990), Defining trauma: Terminology and generic stress dimensions. *J. Appl. Soc. Psychol.*, 20:1632–1642.

Hammarberg, J. (1992), *The PEN Inventory.* Typescript.

Horowitz, M. J., Field, N. P., & Classen, C. C. (1993), Stress response syndromes and their treatment. In: *Handbook of Stress*, 2nd ed., ed. L. Goldberger & S. Breznitz. New York: Free Press.

Keane, T. M., Caddell, J. M., & Taylor, K. L. (1988), The Mississippi Scale for Combat-Related PTSD: Three studies in reliability and validity. *J. Consult. & Clin. Psychol.*, 56:85–90.

———— Malloy, P. F., & Fairbank, J. A. (1984), Empirical development of an MMPI subscale for the assessment of combat-related posttraumatic stress disorder. *J. Consult. & Clin. Psychol.*, 52:888–891.

Kulka, R. A., Schlenger, W. E., Fairbank, J. A., Hough, R. L., Jordan, B. K., Marmar, C. R., & Weiss, D. S. (1990), *Contractual Report of Findings from the National Vietnam Veterans Readjustment Society.* Research Triangle Park, NC: Research Triangle Institute.

Lyons, J. A., & Keane, T. (1992), Posttraumatic stress disorder and MMPI-2. *Develop. & Behav. Med.*, 8:349–356.

Mac Ian, P. S., & Perlman, L. A. (1992), Development and use of the TSI life event questionnaire. *Treat. Abuse Today: Internat. News J. Abuse*, 2:9–11.

Miller, T. W., Ed. (1989), *Stressful Life Events.* Madison, CT: International Universities Press.

Pitman, R. K. (1988), Post-traumatic stress disorder, conditioning, and network theory. *Psychiatric Ann.*, 18:182–189.

Watson, D., Clark, L. A., & Tellegen, A. (1991), Development and validation of brief measures of positive and negative affect: The PANAS Scales. *J. Personal. & Soc. Psychol.*, 54:1063–1070.

Part I

Overview

Chapter 1
Stressful Life Events and Psychoneuroimmunology

J. Stephen McDaniel, M.D.

Interest in the interactions between the central nervous system (CNS) and the immune system dates back to Aristotle, who hypothesized a connection between mood and physical health. Similarly, basic writings of Indian medicine that date back two millennia contain concepts of natural and acquired immunity (Shubla, Solomon, and Dosli, 1979). These writings tell of approaching treatment by restoration of a balance of life forces and by an integrated relationship to the environment. Moreover, around 200 A.D., Galen wrote that melancholy women were more susceptible to breast cancer than sanguine women (Dunn, 1989). Over the past several decades, increasing evidence has supported the long held hypothesis that psychological factors such as stress may play a role in health and illness. The field of investigation which examines this and other related hypotheses was first referred to as psychoimmunology (Solomon and Moos, 1964), and subsequently renamed psychoneuroimmunology by Ader (1981). Pelletier and Herzing (1988) have proposed a commonly accepted definition of psychoneuroimmunology as: "the study of the intricate interaction of consciousness (psycho), brain, and central nervous system (neuro), and the body's defense against external infection and apparent cell division (immunology)" (p. 29).

3

This chapter will provide an overview of studies which have investigated the psychoneuroimmunological aspects of stress. Current literature will be reviewed with regard to the documented interconnections of the CNS and the brain. Stressful life events and their possible effects on the immune system will be reviewed, as well as literature which has examined psychoneuroimmunological aspects of specific psychiatric disorders.

OVERVIEW OF THE IMMUNE SYSTEM

The human immune system is a complex surveillance apparatus that functions to determine self from nonself. The inherent capacity of the body to distinguish between a foreign substance and that which belongs to the body is conveyed or attributed to lymphocytes. Lymphocytes comprise two cell lines of immunocompetent cells, one concerned with humoral immunity (B lymphocytes) and the other with cell-mediated immunity (T lymphocytes). These two types of immunity are interrelated. Humoral immunity is involved in the primary and secondary response to an invading antigen. Humoral immunity is rendered by B lymphocytes which produce antibodies that circulate systemically. There are five major classes of antibodies or immunoglobulins produced by B lymphocytes: IgG, IgM, IgA, IgE, and IgD. These antibodies are produced during an immune response, and are present in plasma. They primarily protect the body from invasion by encapsulated bacteria and bacterial toxins.

Cell-mediated immunity involves the direct intervention of T lymphocytes in an immune response, rather than indirectly via antibodies. These lymphocytes offer surveillance against viral and fungal infections, reject grafts of foreign tissue, and cause delayed hypersensitivity reactions. Cellular immunity is principally mediated by three subgroups of T lymphocytes: helper T cell (CD4), cytotoxic T cells, and suppressor T cells (CD8). Helper T cells augment both cellular and humoral responses through the production of lymphokines; cytotoxic T cells directly attack and destroy target antigen cells; and suppressor T cells autoregulate the immune response through negative feedback.

In recent years a population of non-B, non-T lymphocyte has been identified. These cells, known as natural killer (NK) cells, play a significant role in host surveillance against neoplastic growth, metastases, and some viral infections (Herberman and Ortaldo, 1981). In contrast to other lymphocytes, these cells do not require prior antigen recognition to become active. Natural killer cell activity (NKA) has recently been widely utilized as a measure of psychoneuroimmunological responses.

Methods of Studying Immune Changes

Psychoneuroimmunological research utilizes a variety of quantitative and functional measures for assessing immunological status. A common quantitative measure is to count total white blood cells, lymphocytes, or immunoglobulins in blood samples. These enumerative investigations are frequently used in combination with other measures. Phenotypic examination of relative percentages of subsets of immunologically active cells, such as helper T cells or suppressor T cells, can give a more informative indication of immunocompetence. Because a number of factors including nutritional status, exercise, and diurnal variation may influence peripheral blood counts, these variables must be carefully controlled in immune studies (Geiser, 1989).

Functional measures of immunity go beyond quantifying immunological components by examining how the immune system reacts to various agents. Two such functional techniques, lymphocyte mitogen stimulation and NKA, assess cell-mediated immunity. Both techniques measure in vitro function. Lymphocyte mitogen stimulation specifically measures the proliferate response of lymphocytes to a variety of mitogens or stimulants

(Schleifer, Keller, and Stein, 1985). Lymphocytes are isolated from the blood of subjects and cultured with these stimulants to measure levels of lymphocyte activity or activation. More recently, NKA has been widely used as a measure of cellular immune response. Measuring NKA assesses the ability of NK cells to destroy target tumor cells. This procedure requires a cytotoxicity assay which measures the release of chromium 51 from target cells labeled by growing them in the presence of chromium 51.

BRAIN–IMMUNE SYSTEM RELATIONSHIP

In recent years, major advances have been made in establishing direct evidence for a brain–immune system interrelationship. In serving functions of adaptation and defense, both the CNS and the immune system discriminate between self and nonself, and incorporate principles of recognition, memory, and transmission of information. Evidence for such a communication system includes anatomical confirmation of CNS innervation of immune organs as well as reports documenting behavioral effects on immune response and tumor acquisition in experimental animals. Gorman and Kertzner (1990) have reviewed a number of studies involving experimental animals and human autopsy specimens that have shown direct sympathetic nervous system innervation of the spleen, thymus, and lymph nodes. Cholinergic innervation of the thymus gland has now been documented, and investigators have described noradrenergic innervation of lymphoid tissue in a variety of mammalian species, including humans (Bullock and Moore, 1980). Further, receptors for various neurotransmitters, neurohormones, and neuropeptides are found on cells of the immune system. Noradrenergic receptors have been found on lymphocytes, and appear to be exclusively β-2 adrenergic receptors, which are similar to those found in the smooth muscles of the bronchi and lungs (Brodde, Engel, Hoyer, Bock, and Weber, 1981). In addition to the noradrenergic receptors, there is now

evidence for the presence on lymphocytes of receptors for go-
nadal steroids, endorphins, enkephalins, corticotropin, vasointes-
tinal peptide, cholecystokinin, neurotensin, acetylcholine, and
serotonin (Stoudemire and McDaniel, in press). There has also
been recent evidence that lymphocytes may synthesize some neurohormones de novo.

Just as cells of the peripheral immune system seem to be influenced by circulating factors of CNS origin, a reciprocal relationship is demonstrated by the brain's susceptibility to lymphokines,
substances produced by lymphocytes. Interleukin-1, the most
widely studied lymphokine, has been shown to play a major role
in the initiation of events leading to T-cell responses. Interleukin-
1 has now been shown to directly stimulate the hypothalamus to
produce corticotropin-releasing-factor (CRF) (Berkenbosch, van
Oers, del Rey, Tilders, and Besedovsky, 1987). It is this stimulation
of CRF which is believed to be a physiologically important part
of a possible inhibitory feedback loop which functions to regulate
the immune response. Corticotropin-releasing-factor increases secretion of adrenocorticotrophic hormone (ACTH) which in turn
increases secretion of cortisol by the adrenal glands, which then
serves to inhibit immune function. Moreover, glucocorticoids
have a well-known immunosuppressive effect including the reduction of circulating T-cell subsets (Cupps and Fauci, 1982). This
inhibitory feedback loop has been of particular interest over the
past decade to researchers studying mood disorders (Gold, Goodwin, and Chrousos, 1988). Because of the overactivity of the hypothalamic–pituitary–adrenal axis among some populations of
depressed patients, the role of increased hypothalamic CRF production has been documented and continues to be investigated
with respect to possible psychoneuroimmunologic implications.

A number of experiments dating back to the 1950s provide
further evidence for reciprocal relationships between the CNS
and the immune system. These investigations demonstrated that
lesions of the anterior hypothalamus in experimental animals
blocked the development of lethal anaphylactic "shock" reactions (Stein, Schleifer, and Keller, 1987). Similar experiments
have shown that anterior hypothalamic lesions reduce cellular

immune responses (Keller, Stein, Camerino, Schleifer, and Sherman, 1980). Firing rates of neurons in the ventromedial hypothalamus have been shown to increase during immune responses (Besedovsky, del Rey, and Sorkin, 1983).

With regard to the functional significance of this evidence, Ader and Cohen (1975) conducted one of the best known studies documenting the susceptibility of immune response to classical conditioning. These investigators paired the administration of a saccharin solution to rats (the conditioned stimulus [CS]) with intraperitoneal injections of the immunosuppressive agent cyclophosphamide (the unconditioned stimulus [UCS]). The rats were then immunized three days later with sheep red blood cells, and then given either saccharin solution (CS), cyclophosphamide (UCS), or placebo. At the height of the immune response to the sheep red blood cell immunization, animals which had been reinjected with the saccharin solution (CS) showed reduced antibody response when compared to the placebo group, though not as low as the animals which were injected with cyclophosphamide (UCS), suggesting behavioral control over immune responses. Further, there is an increasing body of research with experimental animals that has documented acute stress to be immunosuppressive, with chronic stress having more variable effects on immune function. Taken as a whole, these findings illustrate the complexities of the body's psychoneuroimmunological relationships.

PSYCHOSOCIAL FACTORS AND HEALTH

Before addressing the issue of how stressful life events impact the immune system, it is important to consider the more general concept of how psychological and psychosocial factors may affect health. Although this area has been well studied, findings have been suggestive, but inconclusive.

Several researchers have examined how psychiatric and psychosocial factors may affect general health. For example, Avery and Winokur (1976) found that inadequately treated depression has been associated with increased mortality, including nonsuicidal mortality, and increased frequency of myocardial infarction. Likewise, conjugal bereavement has been linked to increased mortality in the widowed (Helsing, Szklo, and Comstock, 1981); separated and divorced members of both sexes have been shown to have higher rates of general illness than married individuals (House, Landis, and Umberson, 1988).

Some studies of stress and specific illness have suggested a linkage between emotional health and medical morbidity. Meyer and Haggerty (1962) found a higher incidence of streptococcus infection and illness rate in families reporting higher levels of stress at baseline. Luborsky, Mintz, Brightman, and Katcher (1976) reported that nurses with higher levels of "unhappiness" had more episodes of herpetic infections over the course of a year, but did not find that daily diaries predicted specific herpetic outbreaks. Kasl, Evans, and Niederman (1979) studied Epstein-Barr virus (EBV) seroconverters among military cadets and found that several psychosocial factors significantly increased the risk of clinical infectious mononucleosis among seroconverters: higher motivation, poorer academic performance, and having fathers who were overachievers. Finally, Cohen-Cole, Cozen, Stevens, Kirk, Gaiten, Hain, and Freeman (1981) found that subjects with trenchmouth, an acute infection involving oral bacteria that are not normally pathogenic, reported a higher number of negative life events in the year preceding study and exhibited a greater degree of state anxiety, general emotional distress, and depressive symptoms than did a control group matched for age, sex, and dental hygiene.

Although these studies do not prove a psychoneuroimmunological basis for disease states, they bring into question the role of psychosocial factors and disease onset and outcome. Being aware of these investigations and of the many years of anecdotal evidence of stressful life events and health status, provides a theoretical foundation for pursuing more specific psychoneuroimmunological studies.

STRESS-ASSOCIATED CHANGES IN THE IMMUNE SYSTEM

The most extensively replicated findings in the psychoneuroimmunology literature describe the association between stress and alterations of in vitro immune function. Historically, psychosocial stress has been measured as a function of major stressful life events (e.g., death of a loved one, divorce); however, newer theories suggest that stress is a more complicated concept and is probably more directly linked to an individual's cognitive appraisal of stressful stimuli rather than a more general sociocultural appraisal of stressful events. Nonetheless, many studies have demonstrated that psychosocial stress may alter immune system function. Most studies in this area can be classified as examinations of bereavement, examination stress, other psychosocial stress, or artificial stress. Each of these areas will be discussed in the following sections.

BEREAVEMENT

Bartrop, Luckhurst, Lazarus, Kiloh, and Penny (1977) first reported the association of bereavement with immunosuppression. These investigators compared bereaved subjects (n = 26) with a control group (n = 26, hospital staff), first two weeks after the death of their spouse and again six weeks later. Although no differences between the two groups were established two weeks after death, at eight weeks after death, the bereaved individuals showed significantly reduced T lymphocyte mitogen responses.

Schleifer, Keller, Camerino, Thornton, and Stein (1983) reported similar results in their study of 15 men who were studied before and serially after the death of their wives from metastatic breast cancer. Linn, Linn, and Jensen (1984) studied 49 bereaved subjects and controls using the Hopkins Symptom Checklist to evaluate the severity of depressive symptoms. They found reduced lymphocyte mitogen responses only in those subjects with high scores on the depression subscale. In contrast to these studies

TABLE 1.1
Studies of Bereavement

Study	n (EG)	n (CG)	Immune Measure	Results
Bartrop et al. (1977)	26	26	Mitogen Stimulation	↓lymphocyte mitogen response at 6 wks greater than 3 wks
Schleifer et al. (1983)	15	13	Mitogen Stimulation	↓lymphocyte mitogen response in first 2 months after death of spouse
Linn et al. (1984)	49	49	Mitogen Stimulation	Elevated depression scores correlated with reduced lymphocyte mitogen response
Monjan (1984)	17	17	Mitogen Stimulation	No differences in lymphocyte mitogen responses compared to controls
Irwin et al. (1988)	20 (conjugal bereavement, n = 9; anticipatory bereavement, n = 11)	8	NKA, Plasma cortisol	Conjugal bereavement: ↓NKA, ↑plasma cortisol Anticipatory bereavement: ↓NKA, normal plasma cortisol

Abbreviations: CG: control group. EG: experimental group. NKA: Natural Killer Cell Activity; wks: weeks
Modified from Schulz and Schulz (1992); McDaniel (1992).

which found an association between bereavement and immuno-suppression, Monjan (1984) studied 17 widowed men and matched controls one and three months after the death of their wives. No changes were found in mitogen stimulation responses between time points in the bereaved group, and no differences were found when the bereaved group was compared to the control group.

Irwin, Daniels, Risch, Bloom, and Weiner (1988) studied NKA in bereaved subjects and found reduced NKA in association with bereavement. In one sample, NKA was studied in three groups of subjects: (1) women whose husbands had recently died of lung cancer (< 6 months); (2) women whose husbands were terminally ill with metastatic lung cancer; and (3) women with healthy husbands. Their findings showed decreased NKA in women undergoing conjugal bereavement (both bereaved and anticipatory bereaved) compared to normal control subjects. Interestingly, plasma cortisol levels, elevations of which have been associated with immunosuppression, were elevated in the group of women whose husbands had recently died.

With the exception of the work by Monjan (1984), studies of immune parameters in bereaved individuals have suggested in vitro evidence of immune suppression. Unfortunately, these studies did not consider psychological differences in the experience of the bereaved, such as social support or coping, two potentially important variables in one's experience of a stressful life event. Nonetheless, these studies are frequently referenced and remain much of the foundation for other psychoneuroimmunological investigations.

EXAMINATION STRESS

Numerous studies have examined the relationship between stress during exam preparation and changes in immune parameters. A reduction in mitogen stimulation responses was found by Dorian, Garfinkel, Brown, Shore, Gladman, and Keystone (1982) in their study of psychiatric residents about to undergo fellowship examinations. Workman and La Via (1987) studied 15 medical students before an exam and compared them to a control group (15 trainee nurses or medical students). They found mitogen responses to be significantly reduced in the experimental group when they compared the groups one day before and one week after an exam. Halvorsen and Vassend (1987) found no differences in mitogen responses in students (n = 9) before an exam compared to matched controls given no exam (n = 9); however, they found a reduced mitogen response within the examined group at the time of the exam versus six weeks previously. In various samples of medical students before exams, the group of Kiecolt-Glaser and Glaser (Kiecolt-Glaser, Garner, Speicher, Penn, Holliday, and Glaser, 1984; Kiecolt-Glaser, Glaser, Strain, Stout, Tarr, Holliday, and Speicher, 1986; Glaser, Rice, Speicher, Stout, and Kiecolt-Glaser, 1986) found lowered NKA at the time of the exam compared to four weeks previously.

Investigators have used a variety of measures of immunity in subjects undergoing examination stress. Jemmott, Borysenko, Borysenko, McClelland, Chapman, Meyer, and Benson (1983) reported a lowering of secretory immunoglobulin A (s-IgA) secretion in a group of dental students (n = 9) compared to controls during periods of high academic stress. Kiecolt-Glaser et al. (1984) also measured s-IgA concentration in saliva of students during examination stress but found no differences between sample points. Glaser, Mehl, Penn, Speicher, and Kiecolt-Glaser (1986) found an increase in the concentration of serum immunoglobulins (IgM, IgG, IgA) in 40 medical students at the time of an exam compared to 6 weeks previously. They also found higher concentrations of specific antibodies against herpes simplex viruses (HSV) at the time of the exam which they interpreted as a reduced surveillance over latent virus infections. In contrast, Fittschen, Shulz, Shulz, Raedler, and Kerekjarto (1990) found no rise in antibody titers against HSV at the time of an exam compared to 4 weeks previously in 61 medical students. Nevertheless, this research group demonstrated that for those students who largely experienced the exam as a challenge, a lowered antibody titer against HSV was present.

Some investigators have found changes in the concentrations

TABLE 1.2
Studies of Examination Stress

Study	n (EG)	n (CG)	Immune Measure	Results
Dorian et al. (1982)	8	16	Mitogen Stimulation, NKA	↓ lymphocyte mitogen response; normal NKA
Jemmott et al. (1983)	64	—	S-IgA	↓ s-IgA levels in sub-group of n = 9
Baker et al. (1984)	24	27	CD4, CD8, WBC	↑ percentage of CD4 cells in first year students
Kiecolt-Glaser, Garner, Speicher; et al. (1984); Kiecolt-Glaser, Speicher, Holliday, et al. (1984)	75 / 42	—	NKA, S-IgA	↓ NKA at exam compared to 4 wks previously. No differences in s-IgA between sample points
Kiecolt-Glaser, (1986)	34	—	CD4, CD8, NKA	↓ NKA; ↓ concentrations of CD4 and NK cells
Glaser, Rice, Speicher, et al. (1986); Glaser, Mehl, Pennetal (1986);	40	—	NKA, NK cells, IgG, IgM, IgA	↓ NKA; ↓ concentrations of NK cells; ↑ IgM, IgG, IgA
Halvorsen and Vassend (1987)	9	9	Mitogen Stimulation	↓ lymphocyte mitogen responses in EG at exam time compared to 6 wks previously
Workman and La Via (1987)	15	15	Mitogen Stimulation	↓ lymphocyte mitogen responses compared to control group
Fittschen et al. (1990)	61	—	HSV	No rise in HSV antibody titers; however, ↓ HSV antibody titer in those who saw exam a challenge

Abbreviations: CD4: Helper cells. CD8: Suppresor cells. CG: Control group. EG: Experimental group. HSV: Herpse Simplex virus. Ig: Immunoglobulin. s-IgA: Secretory Immnoglobulin A. NK: Natural Killer. NKA: Natural Killer Cell Activity. WBC: White blood cells; wks: weeks.
Adapted from Shultz and Shulz (1992); McDaniel (1992).

of peripheral lymphocytes in studies of examination stress. Baker, Byrom, Irani, Brewerton, Hobbs, Wood, and Nagvekar (1984) have reported an increased percentage of CD4 cells in first-year students compared to more advanced students. Kiecolt-Glaser et al. (1986) found lowered concentrations of CD4 cells and NK cells (Glaser, Mehl, Penn, et al., 1986) in students before an exam. Similarly, Halvorsen and Vassend (1987) found a reduced percentage of CD4 and CD8 cells in a subpopulation of lymphocytes at examination time.

While immune alterations were clearly found in many of these studies of examination stress, the heterogeneity of the samples and varying time spans are problematic. Because external control groups were often neglected, internal comparisons were made between the exam periods and presumed stress-free exam periods. These variables coupled with small sample sizes prevent generalizations.

OTHER PSYCHOSOCIAL OR ARTIFICIAL STRESS

Although bereavement and examination stress remain the most thoroughly investigated stressful life events in psychoneuroimmunology, other psychosocial stressors, such as abortion, unemployment, and caregiver stress have also been studied. Naor, Assael, Pecht, Trainin, and Samuel (1983) examined immune measures in a group of women who had experienced spontaneous abortions or induced abortions. The women were divided into two groups according to whether they had come to terms with their loss (n = 36) or not (n = 41). Lymphocyte mitogen responses were significantly lower in the latter group compared to the former group or a group of surgical controls (n = 10). The most pronounced differences were found in those subjects rated as being the most depressed.

Kiecolt-Glaser, Glaser, Dyer, Shuttleworth, Ogrocki, and Speicher (1987) examined family caregivers (n = 34) of persons with Alzheimer's disease in order to study whether the stress of caring for chronically ill patients can result in immunological changes in caregivers. They compared these subjects to normal controls (n = 34) and found reduced percentages of T lymphocytes in the peripheral blood of caregivers, as well as a lowered CD4-CD8 ratio.

The effects of partner separation and marital satisfaction with regard to immunological parameters also have been studied (Kiecolt-Glaser, Fisher, Ogrocki, Stout, Speicher, and Glaser [1987]; Kiecolt-Glaser, Kennedy, Malkoff, Fisher, and Speicher [1988]. Kiecolt-Glaser, Fisher, et al. (1987) found divorced women (n = 38) to have reduced lymphocyte mitogen responses and higher levels of EBV antibodies than married women (n = 38). They also found differences in the distribution of CD4, CD8, and NK cells when these groups were classified according to marital satisfaction and maintained bonding to the former partner. Comparable results were found in women who had been separated for less than a year (n = 16) compared to married women (n = 16). In studying divorced men, Kiecolt-Glaser and her colleagues (1988) found an increased antibody concentration against EBV and HSV in a group of men divorced for up to three years (n = 32) as compared to a group of married men (n = 32). They found no difference with respect to the distribution of peripheral lymphocytes. A subgroup of men who had initiated their own divorce (n = 14) had a lower concentration of antibodies against EBV compared to noninitiators.

The stressful effects of unemployment were studied by Arnetz, Wasserman, Petrini, Brenner, Levi, Eneroth, Salovaara, Hjelm, Salovaara, Theorell, and Petterson (1987) who examined unemployed women (n = 17) compared to women with secure jobs (n = 8) at three points in time in a prospective design. Although lymphocyte subpopulations showed no differences between groups, the unemployed women showed reduced lymphocyte mitogen responses.

Linn, Linn, and Klimas (1988) examined surgery as a stressful life event. They studied a group of men who underwent surgery for hernia repair (n = 24) 3 days before surgery, 3 days after surgery, and 30 days after surgery. These men were compared to a control group of age-matched hospital workers. From the surgery group, two groups were formed from a median split with regard to two measures: the amount of life stress and the psychophysio-logical reactivity in the cold pressor test. For the first two sample points the high life stress group had reduced lymphocyte mitogen responses and a lowered lymphocyte count compared to the low life stress and control groups.

Chronic occupational stress was prospectively examined on four occasions in accountants (n = 21) (Dorian, Garfinkel, Key-stone, Gorczyinski, Darby, and Garner, 1985) and compared to controls (n = 12). The chronic stress of accountants was reflected in the higher values on diverse psychological scales measuring distress when compared to controls. Results from this study are conflicting, however, with NKA being higher in accountants than controls at time 1 and 2 but lower at time 4.

Stone, Cos, Valdimarsdottir, Jandorf, and Neale (1987) mea-sured mood states and antigen specific s-IgA in saliva of 30 male students at 25 collection points. They observed a large difference between s-IgA antibody levels of high-negative-mood days as com-pared to low-negative-mood days and conversely s-IgA antibody levels were higher on days with high positive mood relative to days with low positive mood.

Kemeny, Cohen, and Zegans (1989) measured stressful life ex-periences, mood, and CD4-CD8 ratios for six months in 36 pa-tients with recurrent genital HSV. Subjects with a high level of negative life experiences during this period had a lower level of both CD4 and CD8 cells, and those subjects with a high level of negative mood (depression, hostility, anxiety) had a lower propor-tion of CD8 cells in their peripheral blood.

Some investigators have studied changes in immunological measures following experimental stressors. Landmann, Muller, Perini, Wesp, Erne, and Buhler (1984) found an increase in NK cells and B-lymphocytes after a short cognitive test in 15 subjects. Ursin, Mykletun, Tonder, Vaaernes, Relling, Isaksen, and Muri-son (1984) found increases in IgM during 5 days of fear-inducing tasks with navy students. Girgis, Shea, and Husband (1988) exam-ined whether the process of blood collection leads to changes in immunological parameters. Their subjects reported a high degree of state anxiety prior to blood samples being taken on the first

TABLE 1.3

Studies of Psychosocial Stress and Artificial Stressors

Study	n (EG)	n (CG)	Stress	Immune Measure	Results
Naor et al. (1983)	36	41/10	Abortion	Mitogen stimulation	↓ lymphocyte mitogen responses in women choosing elective abortion compared to spontaneous abortion or surgical controls
Landmann et al. (1984)	15	—	Cognitive testing	NK cells, B lymphocytes	↑ NK cells and B lymphocytes
Ursin et al. (1984)	40	—	Fear-inducing tasks	IgA, IgG, TgM	↑ IgM antibody levels
Dorian et al. (1985)	21	12	Occupational stress	Mitogen stimulation NKA, CD4-CD8, IL-2	↑ NKA at t1 and t2 but ↓ NKA at t4; ↓ CD4-CD8 at t1 and t2 but ↑ at t3 and t4; IL-2 ↓ at t2-t4
Stone et al. (1987)	30	—	Mood states	s-IgA	↑ s-IgA antibody levels on high-positive mood days compared to low
Arnetz et al. (1987)	9	8	Unemployment	Mitogen stimulation, Lymphocyte populations	↓ lymphocyte mitogen responses in unemployed subjects compared to employed; no differences in lymphocyte subpopulations
Kiecolt-Glaser, Glaser, Dyer, et al. (1987)	32	32	Caregiver stress	T cells, EBV, CD4-CD8	↓ CD4-CD8 and ↓ percentage of T lymphocytes in caregivers compared to controls

TABLE 1.3
Studies of Psychosocial Stress and Artificial Stressors

Study	n (EG)	n (CG)	Stress	Immune Measure	Results
Kiecolt-Glaser, Fisher, Ogrocki, et al. (1987)	38	38	Divorce/Marital separation (women)	Mitogen stimulation CD4-CD8, EBV	↓ lymphocyte mitogen responses in divorced women and separated women compared to married controls; ↑EBV antibodies in divorced women
Kiecolt-Glaser et al. (1988)	32	32	Divorce (men)	EBV, HSV, CD4-CD8	↑ EBV, HSV antibodies in divorced men compared to married controls; no differences in distribution of lymphocytes
Linn et al. (1988)	24	24	Hernia surgery	Mitogen stimulation	High life stress group had ↓ lymphocyte mitogen response compared to low life stress and control group
Girgis et al. (1988)	47	——	Venipuncture	Mitogen stimulation NKA	Parallel to reduction in state anxiety, ↑NKA and lymphocyte mitogen responses after first blood drawn
Kemeny et al. (1989)	19	——	Recurrent genital HSV	CD4-CD8	High levels of negative life events correlated with reductions in CD4 and CD8 cells

Abbreviations: CD4: Helper cells. CD8: Suppressor cells. CG: Control group. EBV: Epstein Barr Virus. EG: Experimental group. HSV: Herpes Simplex Virus. Ig: Immunoglobulin. IL-2: Interleukin-2. NK: Natural Killer cell. NKA: Natural Killer Cell Activity. s-IgA: Secretory Immunoglobulin A. t: time.
Modified from Shultz and Shultz (1992); McDaniel (1992).

occasion. After three blood samples were collected, they found that, parallel to reduction in state anxiety, there was a significant increase in T lymphocytes, CD4 cells, and in NKA. These authors postulated that the acute stress of the first blood collection was responsible for the early diminished measures.

These studies broaden the implications of research done with bereaved individuals and persons experiencing examination stress. They take into account a broader range of life experiences which may be perceived as stressful life events. Further, they provide evidence of immune alterations in the setting of experimental or artificial stress, previously unexamined conditions.

STUDIES UTILIZING PSYCHOLOGICAL INTERVENTIONS

With mounting evidence of the association of stressful life events and immune changes, several investigators have designed studies to examine the effects of interventions designed to reduce stress. In Keicolt-Glaser et al.'s (1986) study of examination stress, they divided students into two groups prior to exam time. Students were assigned to a group either with or without relaxation training. The relaxation training was intended to relieve examination stress and potentially protect these students from immune changes. However, no differences in the percentages of CD8 cells or NKA were found between groups. The frequency of the exercises was nevertheless shown to be a predictor of the percentage of CD4 cells within the relaxation group.

Kiecolt-Glaser, Glaser, Willinger, Stout, Messick, Sheppard, Ricker, Romisher, Briner, Bonnel, and Donnerberg (1985) compared two intervention groups (relaxation, n = 15, and social contact, n = 15) with a nonintervention group (n = 15) in a home for the elderly. After random assignment, subjects underwent one month of intervention which consisted of three 45-minute meetings per week. An increase in NKA and a decrease in HSV antibodies were found in the relaxation group. No differences were found in mitogen stimulation tests.

Pennebaker, Kiecolt-Glaser, and Glaser (1988) examined whether writing about personal traumas (on four consecutive days, 20 minutes per day) could be related to mitogen stimulation. Fifty students were randomly assigned to the trauma group or a control group. The trauma group was asked to report on their own traumatic experiences while the control group was asked to write about trivial, nonstressful themes. Peripheral blood was studied before the study, on the last day of the study, and again six weeks later. Although no significant differences were found in immunological parameters, the participants of the trauma group were found to visit the student health center significantly less frequently than the control group in the 6 weeks following the study. Interestingly, on the day after they wrote their essays, a subgroup of the trauma group, those subjects who had not previously spoken about their traumas, were found to have a significantly higher capacity for mitogen lymphocyte proliferation than other group members who had previously spoken of their traumas.

Dillon, Minschoff, and Baker (1985) designed a study to evaluate whether the viewing of humorous films affected the concentration of s-IgA in saliva. Students (n = 10) were asked to give saliva samples before and after viewing two films of 30 minutes duration. Half the group viewed a humorous film followed by an educational one and the other half vice versa. The concentration of s-IgA in saliva was significantly higher after viewing the humorous film than after viewing the educational film.

Fawzy, Cousins, Fawzy, Kemeny, Elashoff, and Morton (1990) and Fawzy, Kemeny, Fawzy, Elashoff, Morton, Cousins, and Fahey (1990) have reported the results of a 6-week structured, psychiatric group intervention for postsurgical patients with malignant melanoma. Those patients randomized to the group intervention (n = 38) showed reduced psychological distress and enhanced longer-term coping compared to the control group which received only routine oncology care without psychological intervention. At 6-month follow-up, those subjects in the intervention group also showed increases in the percentage of large granular lymphocytes and NK cells, as well as increased NKA.

Antoni, Schneiderman, Fletcher, Goldstein, Ironson, and Laperrier (1990) have reported on the benefits of behavioral interventions such as aerobic exercise training on both the psychological and immunological functioning among high-risk human immunodeficiency virus (HIV) seronegative and early-stage HIV seropositive patients. They studied asymptomatic gay males (n = 50) who did not yet know their HIV status, but would learn their status as a result of the study. They randomly assigned these men to either an aerobic exercise training program or a control condition. After 5 weeks of training, at a point 72 hours before serostatus notification, psychometric, fitness, and immunological data were collected on all subjects. Psychometric and immunological measures were again collected one-week postnotification. Seropositive controls showed significant increases in anxiety and depression, as well as decrements in NK cell number following notification, whereas seropositive exercisers showed no similar changes and in fact, resembled both seronegative groups.

All of these studies which examine the effects of stressful life events on immune functioning raise as many questions as answers. It remains unsettled whether in vitro immune changes actually correlate with in vivo alterations or disease morbidity. There are numerous anecdotal reports and retrospective studies of increased disease morbidity and stress; however, those studies which have specifically examined immune measures to document in vitro immune impairment have not found that secondary disease is related to this impairment. Although intervention studies show some evidence that psychological interventions may enhance or protect immune function, the mechanisms by which these changes occur remain elusive. Further studies should utilize not only a nontreatment group, but a sham control group, where staff and study subjects can meet in a nonstructured psychosocial intervention to further decipher the role of general social interactions from structured interventions.

TABLE 1.4
Intervention Studies

Study	n (EG)	n (CG)	Intervention	Immune Measure	Results
Kiecolt-Glaser et al. (1985)	15/15	15	Relaxation/Social Contact	Mitogen stimulation, NKA, HSV	↑NKA, ↓HSV in relaxation groups; no differences in lymphocyte mitogen response
Dillon et al. (1985)	9	—	Viewing humorous film	s-IgA	↑concentration of IgA antibodies after viewing humorous film compared to educational film
Kiecolt-Glaser et al. (1986)	17	17	Relaxation training in examination stress group	CD4, CD8, NKA	No significant differences between relaxation vs. nonrelaxation training group
Pennebaker et al. (1988)	20	22	Writing about personal emotional traumas	Mitogen stimulation	No significant difference between trauma group vs. control group
Fawzy et al. (1990)	35 (subjects with malignant melanoma)	26	Structured group psychotherapy	NKA, lymphocyte populations	↑NKA and ↑percentage of large granular lymphocytes at 6 months following intervention in experimental group
Antoni et al. (1990)	25	25	Aerobic exercise	NK cells	Seropositive control showed ↓NK cell number compared to exercise group

Abbreviations: CD4: Helper cells. CD8: Suppressor cells. CG: Control group. HSV: Herpes Simplex virus. NKA: Natural Killer Cell Activity. s-IgA: Secretory Immunoglobulin A.
Modified from Shulz and Shulz (1992).

PSYCHIATRIC DIAGNOSES AND IMMUNE FUNCTION

Many of the same researchers who have examined immunological parameters in stressful life events have also examined such parameters in patients with diagnosed psychiatric disorders. Investigating possible immune changes in depressed patients is a natural progression from the previous decades of work which established abnormalities of the hypothalamic–pituitary–adrenal axis in depressed individuals. Similarly, many years ago researchers examined immunological measures in patients with schizophrenia in a search for infectious or autoimmune etiologies, and more recently with regard to the potential stress of the illness itself. Moreover, in recent years, some investigators have focused on studying anxiety disorders to ascertain possible immune changes related to experiencing diagnosable anxiety symptoms.

DEPRESSION

A majority of studies in the field of psychoneuroimmunology have examined the relationship of depression and immunity. While their overall findings remain inconclusive, a review of these studies provides a greater understanding of the interconnections of the CNS, the endocrine system, and the immune system. These studies are listed chronologically in Table 1.5. Most investigators have utilized lymphocyte mitogen stimulation and/or NKA in studying psychiatric disorders. Like those studies of stressful life events, some researchers have also designed enumerative studies to examine quantitative lymphocyte changes.

The first report that evaluated the immune system in depression was published by Cappel, Gregoire, Thiry, and Sprechers (1978) who looked at lymphocyte mitogen stimulation in 21 patients with psychotic depression compared to 21 normal controls. Although results of this study showed no difference in the two samples, many other researchers have designed similar studies and have found alterations in immunity, including decreased lymphocyte mitogen stimulation and decreased NKA (see Table 1.5). After more than two decades of research, conflicting data remain. In the largest study to date, Schleifer, Keller, Bond, Cohen, and Stein (1989) examined 91 unmedicated subjects with major depression and found no mean differences in NKA or lymphocyte mitogen responses when compared to matched normal controls. In contrast to age-related increases in mitogen responses in the controls, however, the depressed patients did not show increased lymphocyte responses with advancing age. Further, severity of depression was significantly associated with suppression of mitogen proliferative responses independent of age. These findings suggest that alterations in immunity in depressive disorders, rather than being a specific biologic correlate in all cases, may occur in association with other variables that characterize depression, such as age and symptom severity (Stein, Miller, and Trestman, 1991).

SCHIZOPHRENIA

Some of the earliest literature in psychoimmunology examined the immune aspects of schizophrenia. Although numerous studies have investigated the potential role that autoimmune and viral abnormalities may play in schizophrenia, the findings have been inconsistent. Studies have examined mitogen stimulation responses in patients with schizophrenia conceptualizing psychosis and chronic psychiatric illness as stress. However, all have found normal lymphocyte mitogen responses in patients with schizophrenia when compared to controls. Examinations of NKA have produced a variety of results that have been difficult to replicate.

The most recent studies of NKA in subjects with schizophrenia conducted by Caldwell, Irwin, and Lorh (1991) and McDaniel, Jewart, Eccard, Pollard, Caudle, Stepetic, Risby, Lewine, and Risch (1992) found no differences in mean NKA in unmedicated subjects with schizophrenia compared with controls. Similarly, McDaniel et al. (1992) examined a small sample of

J. STEPHEN McDANIEL

TABLE 1.5
Immunologic Studies of Depressive Disorder

Study	Diagnosis	Hospital Status	HRSD (severity)	n Patients	n Controls	Age & Sex Match	Immune Measures	Results
Cappel et al. (1978)	PD	H	—	21	22	No	M	No difference between patients and controls
Sengar et al. (1982)	BP remitted	A	—	15	19	No	E, M	No difference between patients and controls
Kronfol et al. (1983)	MDD	H?	16.3	26	20	No	M	↓ lymphocyte mitogen responses
Schleifer et al. (1984)	MDD	H	28.0	18	18	Yes	E, M	↓ lymphocyte mitogen responses
Kronfol and House (1985)	MDD-E	H?	—	26	20	No	M	↓ lymphocyte mitogen responses
Schleifer et al. (1985)	MDD	A	18.9	15	15	Yes	E, M	No difference between patients and controls
Albrecht et al. (1985)	MDD-E, NE, BP	A (18) H (9)	19.8	27	13	No	E	No difference between patients and controls
Syvalahti et al. (1985)	MDD-E, NE	A	19.7	18	15	No	E, M	↓ lymphocyte response to some mitogens
Kronfol et al. (1986)	MDD	H?	—	33	20	No	M	↓ lymphocyte mitogen responses
Calabrese et al. (1986)	MDD	H?	>20	10	11	No	E, M	↓ lymphocyte mitogen responses
Mohl et al. (1987)	MDD, BP	H	—	10	10	No	N	No difference between patients and controls
Darko et al. (1988)	MDD	H	23	20	20	Yes	E	↑ CD4/CD8

TABLE 1.5 (continued)
Immunologic Studies of Depressive Disorder

Study	Diagnosis	Hospital Status	HRSD (severity)	n Patients	n Controls	Age & Sex Match	Immune Measures	Immune Results
Evans et al. (1988)	MD	H	20	14	7	No	E	↓ NKA
Urch et al. (1988)	MD, BP	H	22	29	27	Yes	N	↓ NKA
Altshuler et al. (1989)	MDD	H	23	8	8	Yes	M	↑lymphocyte response to some mitogens
Darko et al. (1989)	MDD	H	23	20	20	Yes	M	No difference between patients and controls
Kronfol and House (1989)	MDD	H	—	40	37	No	E, M	↓lymphocyte response to some mitogens
Kronfol et al. (1989)	MDD	A (2) H (10)	19.5	12	12	Yes	N	↓ NKA
Nerozzi et al. (1989)	MDD	H	38	22	22	Yes	N	↓ NKA
Schleifer et al. (1989)	MDD-UP	A (61) H (30)	25.9	91	91	Yes	E, M, N	No difference between patients and controls
Irwin, Daniels, Risch, et al. (1990)	MDD	H	20.2	18	50	Yes	E, N	↓ NKA
Irwin, Patterson, Smith, et al. (1990)	MDD	H	19	36	36	Yes	N	↓ NKA
Darko et al. (1991)	MDD	H	18	23	23	Yes	M	No difference between patients and controls
Miller et al. (1991)	MDD	A	20.5	34	21	No	N	No difference between patients and controls

Abbreviations: HRSD: Hamilton Rating Scale for Depression. PD: Psychotic depression. MDD: Major depressive disorder. MDD-E: Major depressive disorder, endogenous subtype. NE: Nonendogenous subtype. MD: Major depression. MDD-UP: Major depressive disorder, unipolar subtype. H: Hospitalized. A: Ambulatory. M: Mitogen-induced lymphocyte proliferation. E: Enumeration of immune cells. N: Natural killer cell activity. Modified from Miller and Stein (1992).

unmedicated patients with schizoaffective disorder, depressed type, compared with normal controls. Again, they found no mean differences in NKA in the studied population. Two other studies have yielded conflicting data on NKA in this population: Urch, Muller, Aschauer, and Zeilinski (1986) studied 37 medicated subjects with schizophrenia and found reduced NKA compared to controls; Wang (1987) found increased NKA in a group of 40 subjects with schizophrenia compared to controls. In the later study, the medication status of the subjects is unknown. This is a potential confounding variable for both of these studies as neuroleptic medications have been implicated in the suppression of lymphocyte mitogen stimulation and a decrease in NKA (Ferguson, Schmidtke, and Simon, 1975; Delisi, Ortaldo, Maluish, and Wyatt, 1983).

ANXIETY DISORDERS

Research have also studied immune alterations in patients with anxiety disorders, questioning the stressful effects of subjective anxiety. Earlier studies found inconsistent results when examining mitogen stimulation responses (Surman, Williams, Sheehan, Strom, Jones, and Coleman, 1986; Schleifer, Keller, Scott, and Vecchione, 1990). However, two groups of investigators who examined NKA in patients with panic disorder have found a correlation with immune responses. McDaniel, Risby, Jewart, Eccard, Caudle, Stepetic, Manning, and Risch (1991) reported on a group of 14 subjects with panic disorder with agoraphobia and found increased NKA compared with matched normal controls. In their study of patients with major depression and comorbid panic disorder (n = 28), Andreoli, Keller, Rabaeus, Zaugg, Garrone, and Taban (1992) found significantly greater numbers of T cells and increased lymphocyte mitogen responses compared to depressed patients without comorbid panic disorder or normal controls. These findings suggest in vitro increases in immune parameters in patients with panic disorder, but no current data support enhanced in vivo immune function, or clearly explains such changes in immune measures.

TABLE 1.6
Immunologic Studies in Schizophrenia and Schizoaffective Disorder

Study	Diagnosis	Hospital Status	n Patients	n Controls	Immune Measures	Results
Delisi et al. 1983	Schizophrenia	H	27	17	N	No difference between patients and controls
Schleifer et al. (1985)	Schizophrenia	H	16	16	M	No difference between patient and controls
Schindler et al. (1986)	Schizophrenia	H?	30	30	N	No difference between patient and controls
Kronfol and House (1988)	Schizophrenia	H	22	37	M	No difference between patient and controls
Urch et al. (1986)	Schizophrenia	H?	31	27	N	↓ NKA
Wang et al. (1987)	Schizophrenia	H?	40	42	N	↑ NKA
Caldwell et al. (1991)	Schizophrenia	H	8	8	N	No difference between patients and controls
McDaniel et al. (1992)	Schizophrenia	H	15	15	N	No difference between patients and controls
McDaniel et al. (1992)	Schizoaffective Disorder, Depressed Type	H	7	7	N	No difference between patients and controls

Abbreviations: H: Hospitalized. M: Mitogen stimulation. N: Natural Killer Cell assay. NKA: Natural Killer Cell Activity. Modified from McDaniel (1992).

CONCLUSIONS

The field of psychoneuroimmunology continues to be an exciting research area attracting the interest of multidisciplinary clinicians and a growing public awareness of the interactions between the mind and the immune system. Clinicians, however, must view previous studies with healthy skepticism and professional curiosity. In vitro evidence of immune alterations does not necessarily correlate with in vivo immune parameters or changes in medical morbidity. Nonetheless, further understanding of how stressful life events effect immune functioning can occur only with further research. Only through a more clear demonstration of an association between psychiatric conditions, such as depression and/or stress and the immune system, can research accurately establish a relation between behavioral states, physical health, and illness.

REFERENCES

Ader, R. (1981), *Psychoneuroimmunology*. New York: Academic Press.
——— Cohen, N. (1975), Behaviorally conditioned immunosuppression. *Psychosom. Med.*, 37:333–340.
Albrecht, J., Helderman, J., Schlesser, M., & Rush, A. J. (1985), A controlled study of cellular immune function in affective disorders before and during somatic therapy. *Psychiatry Res.*, 15:185–193.
Altshuler, L. L., Plaeger-Marshall, S., Richeimer, S., Daniels, M., & Baxter, L. R. (1989), Lymphocyte function in major depression. *Acta Psychiat. Scand.*, 80:132–136.
Andreoli, A., Keller, S. E., Rabaeus, M., Zaugg, L., Garrone, G., & Taban, C. (1992), Immunity, depression, and panic disorder comorbidity. *Biol. Psychiatry*, 31:896–908.
Antoni, M. H., Schneiderman, N., Fletcher, M. A., Goldstein, D., Ironson, G., & Laperriere, A. (1990), Psychoneuroimmunology and HIV-1. *J. Consult. Clin. Psychol.*, 58:38–49.
Arnetz, B. B., Wasserman, J., Petrini, B., Brenner, S. O., Levi, L., Eneroth, P., Salovaara, H., Hjelm, R., Salovaara, L., Theorell, T., & Petterson, I. L. (1987), Immune function in unemployed women. *Psychosom. Med.*, 49:3–12.

Avery, D., & Winokur, G. (1976), Mortality in depressed patients treated with electroconvulsive therapy and antidepressants. *Arch. Gen. Psychiatry*, 33:1029–1037.

Baker, G. H. B., Byrom, N. A., Irani, M. S., Brewerton, D. A., Hobbs, J. R., Wood, R. J., & Nagvekar, N. M. (1984), Stress, cortisol, and lymphocyte populations. *Lancet*, 1:574–575.

Bartrop, R. W., Luckhurst, E., Lazarus, L., Kiloh, L. G., & Penny, R. (1977), Depressed lymphocyte function after bereavement. *Lancet*, 1:834–836.

Berkenbosch, F., van Oers, J., del Rey, A., Tilders, F., & Besedovsky, H. (1987), Corticotropin-releasing-factor-producing neurons in the rat activated by interleukin-1. *Science*, 238:524–526.

Besedovsky, H. O., del Rey, A., & Sorkin, E. (1983), The immune response evokes changes in brain noradrenergic neurons. *Science*, 221:564–566.

Brodde, O. E., Engel, G., Hoyer, D., Bock, K. D., & Weber, F. (1981), The beta-adrenergic receptor in human lymphocytes: Subclassification by the use of a new radioligand, +125 iodocyanopindolol. *Life Sci.*, 29:2189–2198.

Bullock, J., & Moore, R. Y. (1980), Nucleus ambiguous projections to the thymus gland: Possible pathways for regulation of the immune response and the neuroendocrine network. *Anat. Rec.*, 196:25A.

Calabrese, J. R., Skwerer, R. G., Barna, B., Gulledge, A. D., Valenzuela, R., Butkus, A., Subichin, S., & Krupp, N. E. (1986), Depression, immunocompetence, and prostaglandins of the E series. *Psychiatry Res.*, 17:41–47.

Caldwell, C. L., Irwin, M., & Lorh, J. (1991), Reduced natural killer cell activity in depression but not in schizophrenia. *Biol. Psychiatry*, 30:1131–1138.

Cappel, R., Gregoire, F., Thiry, L., & Sprechers, S. (1978), Antibody and cell-mediated immunity to herpes simplex virus in psychotic depression. *J. Clin. Psychiatry*, 39:266–268.

Cohen-Cole, K. S., Cozen, R., Stevens, A., Kirk, K., Gaiten, E., Hain, J., & Freeman, A. (1981), Psychosocial, endocrine, and immune factors in acute necrotizing ulcerative gingivitis ("trenchmouth"). *Psychosom. Med.*, 43:91–107.

Cupps, T. R., & Fauci, A. S. (1982), Corticosteroid-mediated immunoregulation in man. *Immunol. Rev.*, 65:134–155.

Darko, D. F., Gillin, J. C., Risch, S. C., Bullish, K., Golshan, S., Tasevska, Z., & Hamburger, R. N. (1989), Mitogen-stimulated lymphocyte proliferation and pituitary hormones in major depression. *Biol. Psychiatry*, 26:145–155.

——— Lucas, A. H., Gillin, J. C., Risch, S. C., Golshan, S., Hamburger, R. N., Silverman, M. B., & Janowsky, D. S. (1988), Cellular immunity and the hypothalamic-pituitary axis in major affective disorder: A preliminary study. *Psychiatry Res.*, 25:1–9.

——— Wilson, N. W., Gillin, J. C., & Golshan, S. (1991), A critical appraisal of mitogen-induced lymphocyte proliferation in depressed patients. *Amer. J. Psychiatry*, 148:337–344.

Delisi, L. E., Ortaldo, J. R., Maluish, A. E., & Wyatt, R. J. (1983), Deficient natural killer cell activity and macrophage functioning in schizophrenic patients. *J. Neuro. Trans.*, 58:99–106.

Dillon, K. M., Minschoff, B., & Baker, K. H. (1985), Positive emotional states and enhancement of the immune system. *Internat. J. Psychiat. Med.*, 15:13–18.

Dorian, B., Garfinkel, P., Brown, G., Shore, A., Gladman, D., & Keystone, E. (1982), Aberrations in lymphocyte subpopulations and function during psychological stress. *Clin. Exp. Immunol.*, 50:132–138.

—— —— Keystone, E., Gorczyinski, R., Darby, P., & Garner, D. (1985), Occupational stress and immunity. *Psychosom. Med.*, 47:77.

Dunn, A. J. (1989), Psychoneuroimmunology for the psychoneuroendocrinologist: A review of animal studies of nervous system-immune system interactions. *Psychoneuroendocrinol.*, 14:251–274.

Evans, D. L., Pedersen, C. A., & Folds, J. D. (1988), Major depression and immunity: Preliminary evidence of decreased natural killer cell populations. *Prog. Neuropsychopharmacol. Biol. Psychiatry*, 12:739–748.

Fawzy, F. I., Cousins, N., Fawzy, N. W., Kemeny, M. E., Elashoff, R., & Morton, D. (1990), A structured psychiatric intervention for cancer patients: I. Changes over time in methods of coping and affective disturbance. *Arch. Gen. Psychiatry*, 47:720–725.

—— Kemeny, M. E., Fawzy, N. W., Elashoff, R., Morton, D., Cousins, N., & Fahey, J. L. (1990), A structured psychiatric intervention for cancer patients: II. Changes over time in immunological measures. *Arch. Gen. Psychiatry*, 47:729–735.

Ferguson, R. M., Schmidtke, J. R., & Simon, R. L. (1975), Concurrent inhibition by chlorpromazine of concanavalin A induced lymphocyte aggregation and mitogens. *Nature*, 256:744–745.

Fittschen, B., Schulz, K. H., Schulz, H., Raedler, A., & Kerekjarto, M. (1990), Changes in immunological parameters in healthy subjects under examination stress. *Internat. J. Neurosci.*, 51:3–4.

Geiser, D. S. (1989), Psychosocial influences on human immunity. *Clin. Psychol. Rev.*, 9:689–715.

Girgis, A., Shea, J. A., & Husband, F. (1988), Immune and psychological responses to acute venipuncture stress. *Med. Sci. Res.*, 16:351–352.

Glaser, R., Mehl, V. S., Penn, G., Speicher, C. E., & Kiecolt-Glaser, J. K. (1986), Stress-associated changes in plasma immunoglobulin levels. *Internat. J. Psychosom.*, 233:41–42.

—— Rice, J., Speicher, C. E., Stout, J. C., & Kiecolt-Glaser, J. K. (1986), Stress depresses interferon production by leukocytes concomitant with decrease in natural killer cell activity. *Behav. Neurosci.*, 100:675–678.

Gold, P. W., Goodwin, F. K., & Chrousos, G. P. (1988), Clinical and biochemical manifestations of depression, II: Relation to neurobiology of stress. *New Eng. J. Med.*, 319:413–420.

Gorman, J. M., & Kertzner, R. (1990), Psychoneuroimmunology and HIV infection. *J. Neuropsychiatry & Clin. Neurosci.*, 2:241–252.

Halvorsen, R., & Vassend, O. (1987), Effects of examination stress on some cellular immunity functions. *J. Psychosom. Res.*, 31:693–701.

Helsing, K. J., Szklo, M., & Comstock, G. W. (1981), Factors associated with mortality after widowhood. *Amer. J. Pub. Health*, 71:802–809.

Herberman, R. B., & Ortaldo, J. R. (1981), Natural killer cells: Their role in defenses against disease. *Science*, 214:24–30.

House, J. S., Landis, K. R., & Umberson, D. (1988), Social relationships and health. *Science*, 241:540–545.

Irwin, M., Caldwell, C., Smith, T. L., Brown, S., Schuckit, M. A., & Gillin, J. C. (1990), Major depressive disorder, alcoholism, and reduced natural killer cell cytotoxicity. *Arch. Gen. Psychiatry*, 46:81–87.

—— Daniels, M., Risch, S. C., Bloom, E., & Weiner, H. (1988), Plasma cortisol and natural killer cell activity during bereavement. *Biol. Psychiatry*, 24:173–178.

—— Patterson, T., Smith, T. L., Caldwell, C., Brown, S. A., Gillin, J. C., & Grant, I. (1990), Reduction of immune function in life stress and depression. *Biol. Psychiatry*, 27:22–30.

Jemmott, J. B., Borysenko, J. Z., Borysenko, M., McClelland, D., Chapman, R., Meyer, D., & Benson, H. (1983), Academic stress, power motivation, and decrease in secretion rate of salivary secretory immunoglobulin A. *Lancet*, 2:1400–1402.

Kasl, S. V., Evans, A. S., & Niederman, J. C. (1979), Psychosocial risk factors in the development of infectious mononucleosis. *Psychosom. Med.*, 41:445–466.

Keller, S. E., Stein, M., Camerino, M. S., Schleifer, S. J., & Sherman, J. (1980), Suppression of lymphocyte stimulation by anterior hypothalamic lesions in the guinea pig. *Cell Immunol.*, 52:334–340.

Kemeny, M. E., Cohen, F., & Zegans, L. S. (1989), Psychological and immunological predictors of genital herpes recurrence. *Psychosom. Med.*, 51:195–208.

Kiecolt-Glaser, J. K., Fisher, L., Ogrocki, P., Stout, J. C., Speicher, C. E., & Glaser, R. (1987), Marital quality, marital disruption, and immune function. *Psychosom. Med.*, 49:13–34.

—— Garner, W., Speicher, C., Penn, G. M., Holliday, B. S., & Glaser, R. (1984), Psychosocial modifiers of immunocompetence in medical students. *Psychosom. Med.*, 46:7–14.

—— Glaser, R., Dyer, C., Shuttleworth, E. C., Ogrocki, P., & Speicher, C. E. (1987), Chronic stress and immunity in family caregivers of Alzheimer's disease victims. *Psychosom. Med.*, 49:523–535.

—— —— Strain, E. C., Stout, J. C., Tarr, K. L., Holliday, J. E., & Speicher, C. E. (1986), Modulation of cellular immunity in medical students. *J. Behav. Med.*, 9:5–21.

—— —— Willinger, D., Stout, J., Messick, G., Sheppard, S., Ricker, D., Romisher, S. C., Briner, W., Bonnell, G., & Donnerberg, R. (1985), Psychosocial enhancement of immunocompetence in a geriatric population. *Health Psychol.*, 4:25–41.

—— Kennedy, S., Malkoff, S., Fisher, L., & Speicher, C. E. (1988), Marital discord and immunity in males. *Psychosom. Med.*, 50:213–229.

—— Speicher, C. E., Holliday, J. E., & Glaser, R. (1984), Stress and the transformation of lymphocytes by Epstein-barr virus. *J. Behav. Med.*, 7:1–12.

Kronfol, Z., & House, J. D. (1985), Depression, hypothalamic-pituitary-adrenal-cortical activity, and lymphocyte function. *Psychopharmacol. Bull.*, 21:476–478.

—— —— (1988), Immune function in mania. *Biol. Psychiatry*, 24:341–343.

—— —— (1989), Lymphocyte mitogenesis, immunoglobulin and complement levels in depressed patients and normal controls. *Acta Psychiat. Scand.*, 80:142–147.

———— ———— Silva, J., Greden, J., & Carrol, B. (1986), Depression, urinary free cortisol secretion and lymphocyte function. *Brit. J. Psychiatry*, 148:70–73.

———— Nair, M., Goodson, J., Goel, K., Haksett, R., & Schwartz, S. (1989), Natural killer cell activity in depressive illness: Preliminary report. *Biol. Psychiatry*, 26:753–756.

———— Silva, J., Greden, J., Dembinski, S., Gardner, R., & Carroll, B. (1983), Lymphocyte function in major depressive disorder. *Life Sci.*, 33:241–247.

Landmann, R. M. A., Muller, F. B., Perini, C., Wesp, M., Erne, P., & Buhler, F. (1984), Changes in immunoregulatory cells induced by psychological and physical stress: Relationship to plasma catecholamines. *Clin. Exp. Immunol.*, 58:127–135.

Linn, B. S., Linn, M. W., & Klimas, N. G. (1988), Effects of psychophysical stress on surgical outcome. *Psychosom. Med.*, 50:230–244.

Linn, M. W., Linn, B. S., & Jensen, J. (1984), Stressful events, dysphoric mood, and immune responsiveness. *Psychol. Rep.*, 54:219–222.

Luborsky, L., Mintz, J., Brightman, V. J., & Katcher, A. H. (1976), Herpes simplex virus and moods: A longitudinal study. *J. Psychosom. Res.*, 20:543–548.

McDaniel, J. S. (1992), Psychoimmunology: Implications for future research. *South Med. J.*, 85:388–396.

———— Jewart, R. D., Eccard, M. B., Pollard, W. E., Caudle, J., Stepetic, M., Risby, E. D., Lewine, R., & Risch, S. C. (1992), Natural killer cell activity in schizophrenia and schizoaffective disorder: A pilot study. *Schizophr. Res.*, 8:125–128.

———— Risby, E. D., Jewart, R. D., Eccard, M. B., Caudle, J., Stepetic, M., Manning, D. E., & Risch, S. C. (1991), Immune function in panic disorder with agoraphobia. *Psychosom. Med.*, 53:243.

Meyer, R. J., & Haggerty, R. J. (1962), Streptococcal infections in families: Factors altering individual susceptibility. *Pediatrics*, 29:539–549.

Miller, A. H., Asnis, G. M., Lackner, C., Halbreich, U., & Norin, A. J. (1991), Depression, natural killer cell activity, and cortisol secretion. *Biol. Psychiatry*, 29:878–886.

Mohl, P. C., Huang, L., Bowden, C., Fischbach, M., Vogtsberger, K., & Talal, N. (1987), Natural killer cell activity in major depression. *Amer. J. Psychiatry*, 144:1619.

Monjan, A. A. (1984), Effects of acute and chronic stress upon lymphocyte blastogenesis in mice and humans. In: *Stress, Immunity, & Aging.* New York: Marcel Dekker, pp. 81–108.

Naor, S., Assael, M., Pecht, M., Trainin, N., & Samuel, D. (1983), Correlation between emotional reaction to loss of an unborn child and lymphocyte response to mitogenic stimulation in women. *Israel J. Psychiat. Relat. Sc.*, 20:231–239.

Nerozzi, D., Santoni, A., Bersani, G., Magnani, A., Bressan, A., Pasini, A., Antonozzi, I., & Frajese, G. (1989), Reduced natural killer cell activity in major depression: Neuroendocrine implications. *Psychoneuroendocrinol.*, 14:295–301.

Pelletier, K. R., & Herzing, D. L. (1988), Psychoneuroimmunology: Toward a mind-body model: A critical review. *Advances*, 5:27–56.

Pennebaker, J. W., Kiecolt-Glaser, J. K., & Glaser, R. (1988), Disclosure of traumas and immune function: Health implications for psychotherapy. *J. Consult. Psychol.*, 56:239–245.

Schindler, L., Leroux, M., Beck, J., Moises, H. W., & Kirchner, H. (1986), Studies of cellular immunity, serum interferon titers, and natural killer cell activity in schizophrenic patients. *Acta Psychiat. Scand.*, 73:651–657.

Schleifer, S. J., Keller, S. E., Bond, R. N., Cohen, J., & Stein, M. (1989), Major depressive disorder and immunity: Role of age, sex, severity and hospitalization. *Arch. Gen. Psychiatry*, 14:295–301.

———— ———— Camerino, M., Thornton, J. C., & Stein, M. (1983), Suppression of lymphocyte stimulation following bereavement. *JAMA*, 250:374–377.

———— ———— Meyerson, A. T., Raskin, M. J., Davis, K. L., & Stein, M. (1984), Lymphocyte function in major depressive disorder. *Arch. Gen. Psychiatry*, 41:484–486.

———— ———— Scott, B. J., & Vecchione, J. (1990), Lymphocyte function in panic disorder. *Biol. Psychiatry*, 27:66A.

———— ———— Siris, S. G., Davis, K. L., & Stein, M. (1985), Depression and immunity: Lymphocyte stimulation in ambulatory depressed patients, hospitalized schizophrenic patients, and patients hospitalized for herniorrhaphy. *Arch. Gen. Psychiatry*, 42:129–133.

———— ———— Stein, M. (1985), Stress effects on immunity. *Psychiat. J. Univ. Ottawa*, 10:125–131.

Sengar, D. P. S., Waters, B. G. H., Dunne, J. V., & Bouer, I. M. (1982), Lymphocyte subpopulations and mitogenic responses of lymphocytes in manic–depressive disorders. *Biol. Psychiatry*, 17:1017–1022.

Shubla, H. C., Solomon, G. F., & Dosli, R. P. (1979), Psychoimmunology. *J. Hol. Health*, 4:125–131.

Shulz, K. H., & Schulz, K. H. (1992), Overview of psychoneuroimmunological stress- and intervention studies in humans with emphasis on the uses of immunological parameters. *Psycho-oncol.*, 1:51–70.

Solomon, G. F., & Moos, R. H. (1964), Emotions, immunity, and disease. A speculative theoretical integration. *Arch. Gen. Psychiatry*, 11:657–674.

Stein, M., Miller, A. H., & Trestman, R. L. (1991), Depression, the immune system, and health and illness. *Arch. Gen. Psychiatry*, 48:171–177.

———— Schliefer, S. J., & Keller, S. E. (1987), Psychoimmunology in clinical psychiatry. *Psychiatry Update*, 6:210–234.

Stone, A. A., Cos, D. S., Valdimarsdottir, H., Jandorf, L., & Neale, J. M. (1987), Evidence that secretory IgA antibody is associated with daily mood. *J. Pers. Soc. Psychol.*, 52:988–993.

Stoudemire, A., & McDaniel, J. S. (in press), History and current theoretical concepts in psychosomatic medicine. In: *Comprehensive Textbook of Psychiatry*, Vol. 6, ed. H. I. Kaplan & B. J. Saddock. Baltimore: William & Wilkins.

Surman, O. S., Williams, J., Sheehan, D. V., Strom, T. B., Jones, K. J., & Coleman, J. (1986), Immunological response to stress in agoraphobia and panic attacks. *Biol. Psychiatry*, 21:768–774.

Syvalaht, E., Eskola, J., Ruuskanen, O., & Laine, T. (1985), Nonsuppression of cortisol in depression and immune function. *Prog. Neuropsychopharmacol. Biol. Psychiatry*, 9:413–422.

Urch, A., Muller, C., Aschauer, H., & Zeilinski, C. C. (1988), Lytic effector cell function in schizophrenia and depression. *J. Neuroimmuno.*, 18:291–301.

Ursin, H., Mykletun, R., Tonder, O., Vaaernes, R., Relling, G., Isaksen, R., & Murison, R. (1984), Psychological stress factors and concentrations of immunoglobulins and complement components in humans. *Scand. J. Psychol.*, 25:340–347.

Wang, Q. D. (1987), Preliminary study on natural killer cell activity in peripheral blood lymphocytes of schizophrenic patients. *Chinese J. Neuro Psychiatry*, 20:215–225.

Workman, E. A., & La Via, M. F. (1987), T-lymphocyte polyclonal proliferation: Effects of stress and stress response style on medical students taking national board examinations. *Clin. Immunol. Immunopath.*, 43:308–313.

Chapter 2
Impact of Psychosocial Stress on Gene Expression: Implications for PTSD and Recurrent Affective Disorder

ROBERT M. POST, M.D., SUSAN R. B. WEISS, Ph.D.,
MARK A. SMITH, M.D., Ph.D., and
GABRIELE S. LEVERICH, M.S.W.

Two preclinical models, behavioral sensitization and electrophysiological kindling, may provide useful and indirect bridging analogies to help conceptualize various aspects of the neurobiology of the course of affective disorders and posttraumatic stress disorder (PTSD). This article focuses on accumulating clinical data that suggest the applicability of these models to triggering of affective episodes by psychosocial stressors and also on new neurobiological mechanisms that have been uncovered that may help conceptualize the long-term impact of stressors. Sensitization and kindling may also be useful analogies in considering the lasting yet evolving impact of stressors in PTSD. While the implications of these models for PTSD will be considered only briefly in this chapter (as the major focus will be on recurrent affective disorders), a preliminary perspective will be developed for PTSD as well. A more detailed consideration of the implications of these models for PTSD can be found elsewhere (Post, Weiss, and Smith, in press).

Unipolar and bipolar affective disorders tend not only to be recurrent, but also progressive in the sense that successive episodes occur with a shorter well interval or increased rapidity of cycling. Some 70 percent of first onset unipolar affective episodes are recurrent, and almost all of the bipolar disorders are recurrent. In a series of large N studies reviewed elsewhere (Post, Rubinow, and Ballenger, 1984; Goodwin and Jamison, 1990), the median course of illness tends to be one characterized by long well intervals between initial episodes of affective disorders, but, with successive recurrences, a progressive shortening of this well interval occurs. Though some patients may show a stable frequency of cycling over time, rapid cycling from the outset, or the more rare variant of "burnout," the tendency for progression appears to be modal across the majority of studies where the interval between successive episodes is systematically observed and recorded. These observations have helped to refocus neurobiological theorizing beyond the acute episode to the longitudinal course of affective illness and its tendency for recurrence and progression. Increasing evidence is also now available that the first episode of affective disorder, whether it is manic or depressive, is more likely to be associated with major psychosocial stressors than are episodes occurring later in the course of the illness (Tables 2.1, 2.2) suggesting a pattern not only of cycle acceleration but increasing autonomy. Similarly, by definition, stressful life events are involved in the initiation of PTSD, but symptomatic consequences may eventually begin to take on a life of their own, independent of stressor recurrence.

Recent discoveries in neurobiology indicate how electrical, chemical, and psychosocial stressors can affect gene expression and thus present a way in which acute events can have long-lasting impact on the subsequent reactivity of the organism. These data on psychosocial stressors and their potential long-term impact are paralleled by a greatly enhanced understanding of the macro- and molecular biology of sensitization and kindling, thus allowing for more precise conceptualizations of processes that might be

TABLE 2.1

Phenomena in Course of Affective Disorders Modeled by Kindling and Behavioral Sensitization

Descriptors	Kindling (K)	Sensitization (S)	Phenomena
Stressor Vulnerability	++	++	Initial stressors early in development may be without effect but predispose to greater reactivity upon rechallenge
Stressor Precipitation	++	++	Later stress may precipitate full-blown episode
Conditioning May Be Involved	– –	++	Stressors may become more symbolic
Episode Autonomy	++	– –	Initially precipitated episodes may occur spontaneously
Cross-Sensitization with Stimulants	– –	++	Comorbidity with drug abuse may work in both directions: affective illness ⇄ drug abuse
Vulnerability to Relapse	++	++	S and K demonstrate long-term increases in responsivity
Episodes May:			
1. become more severe	++	– –	S and K both show behavioral evolution in severity or stages
2. show more rapid onsets	++	++	Hyperactivity and stereotypy show more rapid onsets
Anatomical and Biochemical Substrates Evolve	++	± –	K memory-trace evolves from unilateral to bilateral
IEGs Involved	++	++	Immediate Early Genes (IEGs) such as c-fos induced
Alterations in Gene Expression Occur	++	++	IEGs may change gene expression, especially of peptides over long-time domains
Change in Synaptic Microstructure Occurs	++	– –	Neuronal sprouting and cell loss indicate structural changes
Pharmacology Differs as Function or Stage of Evolution	++	++	K differs as a function of stage; S differs as a function of development versus expression

TABLE 2.2

Psychosocial Precipitants: Greater Likelihood with First Compared with Subsequent Affective Episodes

Clinical Observations (++)

1. Kraepelin (1921)
2. Brew (1933)
3. Stern (1944)
4. Weitbrecht (1960)
5. Kornhuber (1965)
6. Ihda and Muller-Fahlbusch (1968)
7. Erlanger-Wyler (1973)

Studies (++)

1. Astrup, Fossum, and Holmboe (1959)
2. Matussek et al. (1965)
3. Angst (1966)
4. Okuma and Shimoyama (1972) (M-D)
5. Glassner et al. (1979) (M-D)
6. Ambelas (1979) (M)
7. Gutierrez et al. (1981)

Studies (cont'd) (++)

8. Perris (1984)
9. Bidzinska (1984)
10. Dolan et al. (1985)
11. Ambelas (1987) (M)
12. Ezquiaga et al. (1987)
13. Ghaziuddin et al. (1990)
14. Cassano et al. (1989)
15. Mendlewicz et al., personal communication (1990)
16. Swann et al. (1990)
17. Thase, personal communication (1990)
18. Brown, personal communication (1991)

Inconsistent (±, −)

1. Kennedy et al. (1983)
2. Glassner and Haldipur (1983) (M-D)

pertinent to the longitudinal course of affective disorders and PTSD.

THE KINDLING ANALOGY FOR EVOLUTION FROM TRIGGER TO SPONTANEOUS AFFECTIVE EPISODES

As previously discussed (Post et al., 1984, 1986) the kindling model provides an interesting, but nonhomologous paradigm (i.e., kindled seizures do not clinically resemble affective illness [Post and Weiss, 1989a, 1994]) in which events that are initially triggered begin to occur spontaneously. Following the development of amygdala-kindled seizures (which begin to occur to a stimulation current that was previously subconvulsant [Goddard, McIntyre, and Leech, 1969]), a sufficient number of repetitions of full-blown seizures will eventually result in the animal showing spontaneous epilepsy; that is, seizures in the absence of electrophysiological triggers (Wada, Sato, and Corcoran, 1974; Racine, 1978; Pinel, 1981). Thus, in this hard-wired electrophysiological model of amygdala-kindled seizures, there is an evolution from seizures that are triggered by exogenous stimulation to ones that occur autonomously without such stimuli. Though we believe that the processes underlying the evolution of kindled seizures to spontaneous seizures are substantially different from those underlying the progression from stress-engendered to spontaneous episodes in the affective disorders, the model presents a clear-cut example of the shift from episodes that are triggered to those that occur autonomously.

Earlier, we have also discussed the potential relevance of the kindling model in helping to conceptualize processes and mechanisms underlying the initial emergence of robust behavioral phenomena in response to a stimulus that was previously subthreshold (Post, Rubinow, and Ballenger, 1986; Post, Weiss, Clark, Nakajima, and Ketter, 1991). In a parallel fashion, but in different neurochemical systems, repeated stressors (matching events) may come to evoke more robust behavioral consequences than are apparent after the initial stress or loss. Although kindling represents a nonhomologous model of affective illness which can be compressed into a time frame of daily evocation of electrical events, it is known that it can also be elicited by more intermittent stimuli and its persistence (over months to years) fits a time frame pertinent to the affective disorders. Nonetheless, processes involved in sensitization may be more directly analogous to those occurring in the affective disorders because of the behavioral rather than convulsive endpoints observed.

PROGRESSION OF RESPONSE TO STIMULANTS AND STRESSORS

Psychomotor stimulant-induced and stress sensitization share many elements in common and, in some instances, each can produce cross-sensitization to the other (Antelman, Eichler, Black, and Kocan, 1980; Antelman, 1988; Kalivas, Duffy, Abhold, and Dilts, 1988; Kalivas and Duffy, 1989; Piazza, Deminiere, Le Moal, and Simon, 1990; Sorg and Kalivas, 1991). Stimulant-induced behavioral sensitization also provides a homologous model for the evolution of manic symptoms because many of the progressive components of stimulant-induced mood and behavior mimic the transition from mild and euphoric mania to more severe and dysphoric mania (Post and Weiss, 1989b) and, ultimately, to full-blown schizophreniform paranoid psychoses (Post, 1975). Whereas the mechanisms underlying stimulant-induced behavioral sensitization have not been entirely elucidated, there is increasing recognition that activation of neurotransmitter pathways not only produces acute events associated with rapid alterations in neural firing and short-term neuronal adaptations (Robinson and Becker, 1986; White, Henry, Hu, Jeziarski, and Ackerman, 1992), but also a series of events that has much longer-lasting consequences for the organism. Specifically, the process of neuronal transmission also sets in motion intracellular changes at the level of gene transcription (Nakajima, Daval, Gleiter, Deckert, Post, and Marangos, 1989; Draisci and Iadarola, 1989; Graybiel, Moratalla, and Robertson, 1990; Young, Porrino, and Iadarola, 1991). A series of oncogenes, such as the proto-oncogene c-fos, are induced that are, themselves, transcription factors for the induction of other mRNAs with effects over long time domains (days to months) (Morgan, Cohen, Hempstead, and Curran, 1989; Morgan and Curran, 1989a,b; Dragunow, Currie, Faull, Robertson, and Jansen, 1989; Crabtree, 1989). The transcription factors, such as c-fos and c-jun, are called immediate early genes (IEGs) because of the rapid onset and duration of their effects (minutes to hours). These oncogenes by virtue of their acute effects may provide the basis for a spatiotemporal cascade of events that result in more enduring neurotransmitter, receptor, and peptide changes that might provide the biochemical and anatomical basis for long-term synaptic adaptations and memory that could last indefinitely.

Effect of Stress, Stimulants, and Kindling on Gene Transcription

In our laboratory, Nakajima and associates (Nakajima, Daval, et al., 1989; Nakajima, Post, et al., 1989; Daval, Nakajima, Gleiter, Post, and Marangos, 1989) as well as others (Draisci and Iadarola, 1989; Ceccatelli, Villar, Goldstein, and Hokfelt, 1989; Bullitt, 1989; Smith, Weiss, Abedin, Post, and Gold, 1991) have demonstrated that stresses, even relatively minor ones, are capable of inducing the transcription factor IEG c-fos. This can be measured by direct assessment of the Fos protein itself with antibodies (Draisci and Iadarola, 1989; Ceccatelli, Villar, Goldstein, and Hokfelt, 1989) or with northern blot analysis to assess levels of mRNA in discrete tissues (Daval et al., 1989) or by in situ hybridization where a radioactive probe binds to the mRNA for c-fos in undisturbed structures in brain slices (Nakajima, Daval, et al., 1989; Daval et al., 1989) (Figure 2.1). This latter technique has the advantage of providing exquisite anatomical resolution of the areas involved in the c-fos induction (Nakajima, Post, et al., 1989; Daval et al., 1989) (Figure 2.1). c-Fos induction following an electroconvulsive seizure in the mouse (Nakajima, Post, et al., 1989b) is illustrated in Figure 2.1A compared with an unkindled animal (Figure 2.1D). The sham ECS control animal which receives the stress of the placement of the clips on his ears has slight but prominent induction of c-fos in the hippocampus. Even more remarkable is the induction of c-fos by the minor stress of a saline injection (Figure 2.1C).

It is now apparent that a variety of neurochemical systems can induce c-fos in addition to their more direct and classical neurotransmitter functions. Thus, c-fos can be induced by activation of noradrenergic (alpha$_1$, B) (Arenander, de Vellis, and Herschman, 1989; Gubits, Smith, Fairhurst, and Yu, 1989), dopamine (D$_1$) (Robertson, Peterson, Murphy, and Robertson, 1989; Young et al., 1991), acetylcholine (M$_1$) (Greenberg, Ziff, and Greene, 1986), glutamate (NMDA) (Sonnenberg, Mitchelmore, McGregor-Leon, Hempstead, Morgan, and Curran, 1989), opiate, VIP, and nerve growth factor (Curran and Morgan, 1985) receptors, in addition to activation by the second messengers calcium or cyclic-AMP (Morgan and Curran, 1988, 1989b).

An important feature of c-fos induction is that it occurs in specific anatomical pathways involved in biochemical and physiological systems that are activated. For example, the stress associated with water deprivation increases c-fos in areas of the hypothalamus known to be associated with fluid and electrolyte metabolism (Sagar, Sharp, and Curran, 1988). Stress involving nociceptive pathways similarly activates appropriate substrates in spinal cord and other areas involved in pain (Draisci and Iadarola, 1989). Sagar and associates (Sagar et al., 1988; Sharp, Gonzalez, Sharp, and Sagar, 1989) have shown a close parallelism between electrically stimulated cerebellar pathways mapped for metabolic activity

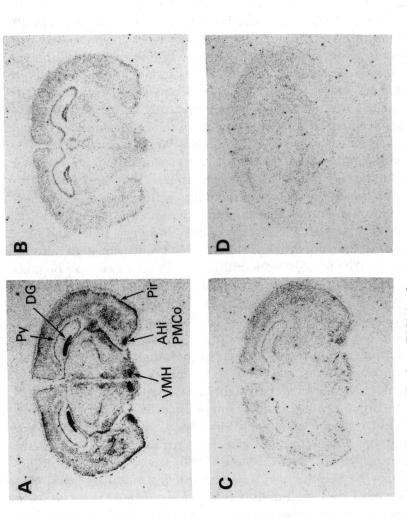

Figure 2.1. *In situ* hybridization of c-fos mRNA in the mouse.
A: following acute ECT; B: sham ECT (ear-clip control); C: saline injection; D: no treatment. Py, pyramidal cells of hippocampus; DG, dentate gyrus; Pir, piriform cortex; AHi, amygdalohippocampal area; PMCo, posteromedial cortical amygdaloid nucleus; VMH, ventromedial hypothalamic nucleus (see Nakajima et al., 1989b, for details).

by 2-deoxyglucose and those associated with c-fos induction. Some caveats and exceptions are noted, however (Labiner, Butler, Cao, Hosford, Shin, and McNamara, 1993). Moreover, in our laboratory Nakajima, Daval, Morgan, Post, and Marangos (1989) and Clark, Post, Weiss, Cain, and Nakajima (1991), Clark, Weiss, and Post (1991), and Clark, Post, Weiss, and Nakajima (1992) have demonstrated that different seizure types are associated with different patterns of c-fos induction. For example, caffeine-induced seizures induce c-fos largely in striatum and olfactory bulb (Nakajima, Daval, et al., 1989a), whereas those associated with amygdala-kindling are more predominantly limbic, with particular involvement of the dentate gyrus of the hippocampus (Dragunow and Robertson, 1987; Clark, Post, Weiss, Cain, et al., 1991). Cocaine-kindled seizures show a pattern involving both striatal and limbic substrates (Clark et al., 1992). Together, these data indicate the ability of c-fos induction to reflect activation of selective pathways in the central nervous system (Nakajima, Post, et al., 1989; Post, Weiss, Nakajima, Clark, and Pert, 1990) and help to address the potential problem of the apparent generality of nonspecificity of c-fos inducibility. Further specificity can be built in by the magnitude and temporal patterning of the expression of multiple transcription factors as discussed below.

Most pertinent to the thesis of this chapter, however, is the possibility that, in addition to providing an anatomical marker of pathway involvement, the transient induction of c-fos (lasting several hours) may also itself be an initial step in a cascade of neurobiological events that might have long-lasting consequences for the organism. Whereas the long-term effects of c-fos induction have not yet been adequately elucidated, preliminary data from Sonnenberg, Rauscher, Morgan, and Curran (1989), Morgan and Curran (1989a,b), and Crabtree (1989) suggest that c-fos induction may be the first step in the induction or suppression of a variety of factors, including peptides, as reflected in the increase in mRNA for prepro-enkephalin that follows fos induction. In a correlative fashion it appears that c-fos induction is sequentially followed by changes in a variety of neurotransmitters, receptors, peptides and proteins, including nerve growth factors and other substances in the cell (Figure 2.2).

In addition, in the development of amygdala-kindled seizures one can observe the anatomical spread of the seizure process (Clark, Post, Weiss, and Cain, et al., 1991), and not only is there the induction of the immediate early gene c-fos and related transcription factors, but also a series of longer-lasting effects on neuropeptides that include alterations in somatostatin (Kato, Higuchi, and Friesen, 1983; Nadi, Pless, and Pintor, 1989; Shinoda, Schwartz, and Nadi, 1989), TRH (Meyerhoff, Bates, and Kubek, 1990; Rosen, Cain, Weiss, and Post, 1992; Rosen, Abramowitz, and Post, 1993), enkephalin (Naranjo, Iadarola, and Costa, 1986; Lee, Zhao, Xie, McGinty, Mitchell, and Hong, 1989; Gall, Lauterborn, Isackson, and White, 1990; Rosen et al., 1992), and CRH (Smith, Weiss, Abedin, Post, and Gold, 1991) (Figures 2.1, 2.3B). There also appear to be long-term decreases in dynorphin (Gall et al., 1990; Rosen et al., 1992). Though the causal links between c-fos and other neuropeptide alterations remain to be directly demonstrated, their sequential temporal induction (Crabtree, 1989; Mocchetti, De Bernardi, Szekely, Alho, Brooker, and Costa, 1989) in areas where c-fos is initially induced (Rosen et al., 1992, 1993) is highly suggestive. It is likely that induction of c-fos, fos-related antigens (fras), and other transcription factors such as zif/268 may provide a large series of third messenger systems (Goodman, 1990) that then are associated with subsequent changes in gene transcription, providing longer-lasting fourth and fifth messenger systems as a result of prior synaptic activation (Figures 2.2, 2.3B).

Figure 2.2 illustrates, in a highly schematized fashion, that the classical time frames for pre- and postsynaptic events usually considered in neurotransmission may be only one acute phase in a variety of other intracellular mechanisms that can occur associated with intermediate and long-term neural adaptations. In the decade of the 1980s attention focused largely on transient changes in receptor density as an adaptation to repeated neurotransmitter exposure. The current schema suggests, however, that, in addition to these relatively transient changes, a variety of

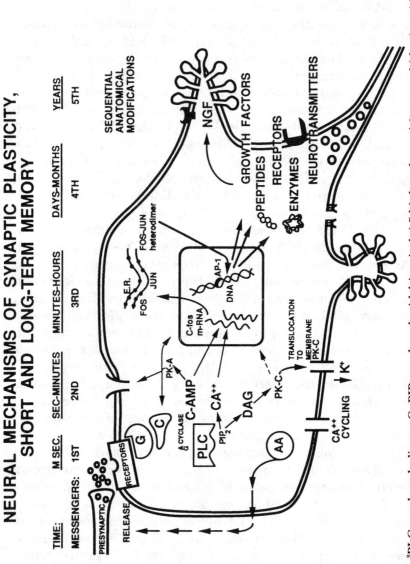

Figure 2.2. [3]PLC = phospholipase C, PIP$_2$ = phosphatidyl inositol 4,5-biphosphate, AA = arachidonic acid, DAG = diacylglycerol, PK-C = protein kinase C, PK-C = protein kinase C, AP-1 = activator protein-1 (binding site on DNA), E.R. = endoplasmic reticulum, PK-A = protein kinase A, NGF = nerve growth factor.

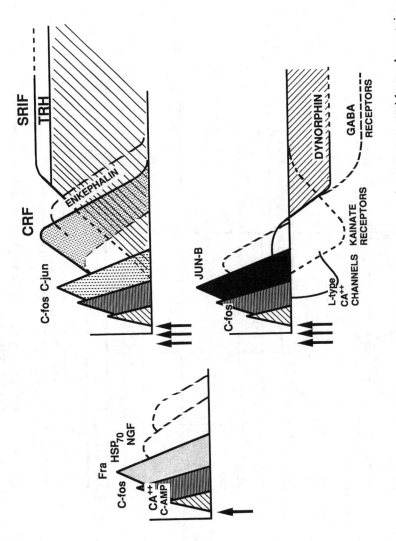

Figure 2.3A. Spatiotemporal induction of oncogenes transcriptionally activates long-term peptide and protein changes.

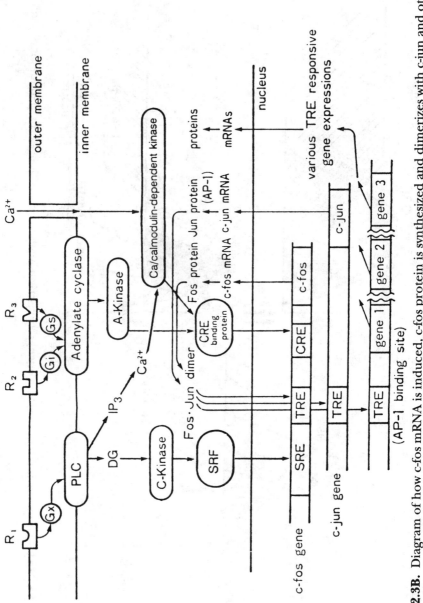

Figure 2.3B. Diagram of how c-fos mRNA is induced, c-fos protein is synthesized and dimerizes with c-jun and other transcription factors to effect changes in late gene expression.

other longer-term mechanisms may be brought into play by second messenger systems (Worley, Baraban, and Snyder, 1987) and changes in protein phosphorylation (that may be involved in long-term potentiation [LTP] and other types of intermediate memory) as well as the induction of a variety of proto-oncogenes and transcription factors (Table 2.3) (Morgan and Curran, 1989a; Crabtree, 1989; Sagar et al., 1988; Sonnenberg, Mitchelmore, et al., 1989; Goodman, 1990; Cole, Worley, and Baraban, 1990). As illustrated in Figure 2.2 once mRNA for c-fos is induced, c-fos protein is synthesized on the ribosomes of the endoplasmic reticulum. c-fos can dimerize with itself (homodimer) or form heterodimers with other oncogenes such as c-jun, which are translocated back into the nucleus and bind at an AP-1 DNA binding site which, itself, is involved in the initiation of transcription of other proteins, peptides, and growth factors. Fos and jun interact in a "leucine zipper" motif and together the binding to DNA in a "scissors grip" fashion (Vinson, Sigler, and McKnight, 1989) is much enhanced compared with either proto-oncogene alone.

Fos is only one of many proto-oncogenes (Morgan and Curran, 1990) and the ratio of fos to jun and other fos-related antigens (Fras) changes over time (Morgan and Curran, 1989a,b). This suggests that the on cogene "milieu" conditioned by prior activation may markedly affect the subsequent alterations in gene transcription to be directed depending on the prior experience of the organism. In this fashion, specificity and selectivity of responsiveness could be fully regulated depending on the prior number, intensity, and "meaning" of prior experiences (Figures 2.4, 2.5). Moreover, whereas c-jun appears to be a positive transcription factor, jun-B appears to be one that has negative or repressive functions, further suggesting that the relative ratio of cellular transcription factors can differentially affect the cellular output at the level of long-term changes in gene transcription.

In addition to the leucine zipper motif, other oncogenes interact with DNA by other motifs such as zinc finger (zif/268 [NGFI-A]) or steroid/thyroid receptor homology (NGFI-B) (Vinson, Sigler, and McKnight, 1989; Morgan and Curran, 1990) (Tables

TABLE 2.3

Greater Likelihood of Life Events Associated with First Compared with Subsequent Episodes

Author	N	Mania Dep.	# of Episodes	1st	Recurrent	P	Assessment
Matussek et al. (1965)	242 135 82 119	Dep	1 2 3 4	44%	34% 24% 19%		Stressors (138 psychologic; 58 somatic) had to clearly precede onset of episode
Angst (1966)	103	Dep	1 ≥4	60%	38%		No inventory
Okuma & Shimoyama (1972)	134 134 134	M-D	1 2 3	45%	26% 13%		Any Event (3 months prior)
Glassner et al. (1979)		M-D	1 recent	75%	56%		Rated stressful by patient and on Holmes & Rahe Scale (1 yr prior; usually 2–24 days) Role loss critical in patients and controls
Ambelas (1979)	14 67	M Surgical controls	1 ≥2	50%	28% (6.6%)	p<.01	Paykel Life Events (4 wks prior); $1/3$ cases *bereavement*

TABLE 2.3 (continued)

Study	N	Dx	Criterion	%	%	p	Stressors
							Social and somatic stressors
Gutierrez et al. (1981)	43	Dep	1	55.8%			Late onset > early onset
	35		2		40%		
	18		3		38.8%	p<.05	
	47		≥4		29.7%		
Perris (1984)	37	Dep	1	62%	50% Negative	p<.02	Semistructured interview; 56-Item inventory; (3 months prior)
	112		≥2	43%	19% Conflict	p<.001	
Dolan et al. (1985)	21	Dep	1	62%			Bedford College—Life Events and Difficulties Schedule (6 mos. prior) (Brown, Harris, 1978)
	57		≥2	29%		p<.05	
Ezquiaga et al. (1987)	52	Dep	1 or 2	50%			Semistructured interview (Brown, Harris) No effect of chronic stress
	45		≥3	16%		p<.01	
Ambela (1979)	50	M	1	66%			Paykel Life Events (4 weeks prior)
	40		≥2	20%		p<.001	
Ghaziuddin et al. (1990)	33	Dep	1	91%			Paykel Life Events (6 mos. prior)
	40		≥2	50%		p<.05	
Cassano et al. (1989)	94	Dep	1	66.0%			Paykel Life Events
	173		≥2	49.4%		p<.05	

| COCAINE | | EFFECT | | | | | | | | |
Number of Injections	Dose mg/kg i.p.	Behavioral Sensitization Duration	Activity Context Dep.	Activity Indep.	Stereotypy Context Dep.	Stereotypy Indep.	Saline Conditioning	Sensitization Neuroleptic Independent	Seizure Kindling	Death
(↑↑↑↑)	COC₈₅								++	++
x10 days	COC₈₀ subcut. (K. Gale)	++	++		++			++		
(↑↑↑↑↑↑↑↑)	COC₁₀	++ months	++	0			++			
(↑↑)	COC₄₀	+	0	++	++	++	±			
(↑)	COC₄₀	++ days	++	0	0	0	0	0		
(↑↑↑)	COC₂₀	0	0	0	0	+				
(↑↑↑)	COC₁₀	0	0	0	0	0				
(↑)	COC₁₀	0								

Figure 2.4. Size and number of arrows indicate dose of cocaine and number of administrations. COC = cocaine and dose in mg/kg administered once daily i.p., except in the study of Gale, when doses were subcutaneous. 0 = no effect; ± = equivocal; + = moderate effect; ++ = marked or definite effect. Effects of cocaine increase are more persistent with dose and number of repetitions. They also become less dependent on environmental context and conditioning. The highest doses may be associated with seizures, kindling, and their associated lethality. Thus,

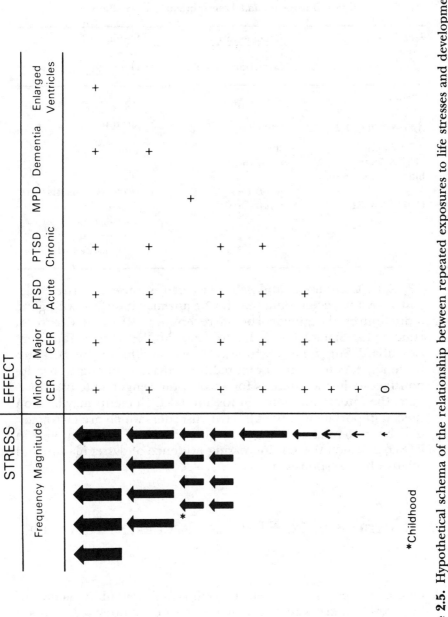

Figure 2.5. Hypothetical schema of the relationship between repeated exposures to life stresses and development of behavioral pathology. CER = conditioned emotional response; PTSD = post-traumatic stress disorder; MPD = multiple personality disorder.

TABLE 2.4
Proto-Oncogenes and Transcription Factors (Baraban)

Zinc Finger	Leucine Zipper Heterodimers-AP1	Steroid & Thyroid Receptor Homology**
*zif/268 $\begin{bmatrix} \text{NGFI-A} \\ \text{krox-24 erg-1} \end{bmatrix}$	c-fos	NGFI-B
Krox-20 erg-2	fras	(nur/77)
*LTP selective; block with MK801	c-jun (+)	
	jun-B (−)	** Glucocorticoid (HSP-90)
COPPER FIST	jun-D	Estrogen
		EProgesterone
		EVitamin D_3
		ERetinoic acid-(T_3)

2.3, 2.4). Complexity and selectivity of response is further suggested by the recent data that fos or jun may interfere with gene induction by the glucocorticoid receptor (GRE) and vice versa (Lucibello, Slater, Jooss, Beato, and Muller, 1990; Yang-Yen, Chambard, Sun, Smeal, Schmidt, Drovin, and Karin, 1990). Thus, there appears to be the potential for cross-talk among transcription factors just as there is for second messenger systems. Moreover, the interaction between fos and GRE elements may take on special importance in the affective disorders which are characterized by state-related changes in glucocorticoid function, and in PTSD, in which there is increasing evidence of dysregulation and relative hyporesponsivity.

RELATIONSHIP TO PTSD AND RECURRENT AFFECTIVE ILLNESS

One is in a position, therefore, to draw a fragmentary picture of how psychosocial stressors may come to exert long-term effects on an organism. As in cocaine sensitization (Figure 2.4), the type, magnitude, and frequency of repetition of the stressor may be critical to its long-term effects (Figure 2.5). Elsewhere, my colleagues and I have reviewed data indicating that with cocaine-induced behavioral sensitization, the dose of cocaine (perhaps in parallel with magnitude of stressors) interacts with the number of repetitions of cocaine administration (parallel with stressor repetitions) to produce an outcome matrix that affects the resulting magnitude and duration of subsequent behavioral responses (Post, Weiss, and Pert, 1988a,b). For example, repeated low doses of cocaine produce longer-lasting sensitization than a single high dose. Acute intermittent doses produce more robust sensitization than more chronic modes of administration.

The quality of the stressor appears to make an impact on neural systems implicated both on the basis of the type and location of short-term biochemical changes as well as in terms of the type, location, mixture, and interaction of oncogenes and transcription factors, with potentially diverse consequences for subsequent coding of proteins and peptides. The biological consequences of stresses dealing with the impact of threats to self-esteem and psychosocial loss (Table 2.5) may have very different behavioral and neurobiological consequences from those involved in the threat of bodily injury, which may be more pertinent to syndromes such as PTSD. Hence, some of the mechanisms described here at the level of gene transcription, postulated for long-term consequences of stressors, may be pertinent to the development of PTSD following severe single or recurrent stressors and involved in physical or sexual abuse. Again, depending on stressor severity, number of repetitions, chronicity versus intermittency, controllability, and timing in development of the individual, the consequences may be more or less long-lasting and profound on behavior and function (Figures 2.4, 2.5).

PTSD appears to be multiphasic with acute reactions paving the way for longer-term alterations including reexperiencing phenomena, hyperarousal, avoidance, and numbing. Thus, chronic alterations in baseline functioning occur from which more phasic or paroxysmal reactions (such as flashbacks and nightmares) erupt. This may be triggered by appropriate environmental cues, but may also become progressive and more autonomous.

TABLE 2.5
Diversity of Cellular Response to Extracellular Signals: Provision for Context

Neurotransmitters subtypes	Immediate Early Genes	Target Gene Regulation
Peptide Cotransmitters Multiplicity of G Proteins & Second Messengers	Gene Types & Subtypes Heterodimers Homodimers Oxidation/Reduction Phosphorylation DNA Binding Motifs Cooperativity +/− Regulation Transcriptional Cross talk	Pathway and Synapse Specific for Changes in: Biochemistry Physiology Structure and Cell Life & Death

Conditioned increases in c-fos have also been demonstrated following stressors or their conditioned cues (Daval et al., 1989; Nakajima, Daval, et al., 1989; Nakajima, Post, et al., 1989; Ceccatelli et al., 1989; Bullitt, 1989; Draisci and Iadarola, 1989; Smith et al., 1991; Deutch, Lee, Gillham, Cameron, Goldstein, and Iadarola, 1991). This opens the conceptual path for considering both conditioned and unconditioned changes (Campeau, Hayward, Hope, Rosen, Nestler, and Davis, 1991; Pezzone, Lee, Hoffman, and Rabin, 1992; Brown, Robertson, and Fibiger, 1992; Smith, Banerjee, Gold, and Glowa, 1992) in reactivity in PTSD.

DIFFERENTIAL IMPACT OF PSYCHOSOCIAL STRESSORS IN FIRST COMPARED WITH SUBSEQUENT EPISODES OF AFFECTIVE ILLNESS

Stressors related to separation, loss, and self-esteem that are associated with the onset of depressive episodes may not play an important pathophysiological role in the triggering of an affective episode (Tables 2.1, 2.2) but, because of the neurobiological encoding of memorylike functions related to these stressors, provide a long-term vulnerability to subsequent recurrences and perhaps a mechanism for retriggering of episodes with lesser degrees of psychosocial stress. In this fashion, one might conceptualize how less psychosocial stress or loss (and perhaps increasing vulnerability to more *symbolic* or conditioned stressors and losses) may come to play a role in the triggering of affective episodes (Figure 2.3A). As in the kindling model, with sufficient repetitions of episodes, specific triggers may no longer be required to induce a full-blown syndrome.

Early investigators (Kraepelin, 1921; Stern, 1944; Weitbrecht, 1960; Erlanger-Wyler, 1973) observed a greater role of psychosocial stressor in the onset of the initial episode of affective disorder compared with subsequent episodes in the course of illness (Table 2.1). More recently, systematic data (Table 2.2) have accumulated that explicitly test and confirm the notion highlighted by Kraepelin that there is a greater role for psychosocial stressors in initial, compared with subsequent, episodes.

Kraepelin stated:

The attacks begin not infrequently after the illness or death of near relatives. . . . We must regard all alleged [psychic] injuries as possibly sparks for the discharge of individual attacks, but the real cause of the malady must be sought in permanent internal changes, which are innate. . . . In spite of the removal of the discharging cause, the attack follows its independent development. But, finally, the appearance of wholly similar attacks on wholly dissimilar occasions *or quite without external occasion* shows that even there where there has been external influence, it must not be regarded as a necessary presupposition for the appearance of the attack.

As summarized in Table 2.2 these studies (Matussek, Halbach, and Troger, 1965; Angst, 1966; Okuma and Shimoyama, 1972; Glassner, Haldipur, and Dessauersmith, 1979; Ambelas, 1979, 1987; Gutierrez, De Diego, Barroso, and Martin, 1981; Perris, 1984; Dolan, Calloway, Fonagy, De Souza, and Wakeling, 1985;

Ezquiaga, Gutierrez, and Lopez, 1987; Ghaziuddin, Ghaziuddin, and Stein, 1990; Cassano, Akiskal, Musetti, Perugi, Soriani, and Mignani, 1989) and others (Swann, Secunda, Stokes, Croughan, Davis, Koslow, and Maas, 1990; Mendlewicz, 1990, personal communication; M. Thase, 1991, personal communication; G. Brown, 1991, personal communication) are noteworthy in that they have used a wide variety of measures of the impact of social stressors, ranging from global assessments to detailed systematic ones, such as the Paykel Life Event Scale (Ambelas, 1979, 1987; Ghaziuddin et al., 1990; Mendlewicz, 1990, personal communication), the contextual assessment pioneered by Brown and his collaborators (Brown and Harris, 1978; Dolan et al., 1985; Ezquiaga et al., 1987), or similar in-depth assessment of role loss (Glassner et al., 1979). In the study of G. Brown (1991, personal communication) a differential role for psychosocial stressors in the first compared with subsequent episodes was observed only when severe endogenous or agitated depressions and not when more minor and neurotic depressions were included in the sample. The recent NIMH Collaborative Study presented data consistent with the current formulation and used a combined census of self and observer ratings of the impact of psychosocial stressors and their potential role in a given affective episode (Swann et al., 1990). Those with an "environment-sensitive" episode had significantly fewer prior episodes (3.7 ± 4.2, n = 28) than those with autonomous episodes (13.4 ± 27.4. n = 35, $p < .05$). Bidzinska (1984), as well as Ghaziuddin et al. (1990), Perris (1984), and Cassano et al. (1989), also found an increased number of stressors in initial compared with subsequent depressions.

It is remarkable that this variety of studies (with the exception of Kennedy, Thompson, Stancer, Roy, and Persad [1983] and Glassner and Haldipur [1983]), with their greatly varying methodologies and assessment instruments, are all consistent in the demonstration of either a greater number of psychosocial stressors involved in the first compared with subsequent episodes of major affective disorder or that psychosocial stressors appear to have less of an impact on episodes occurring later in the course of illness, after many recurrences, compared with the initial episode.

Though the majority of these studies are retrospective in nature, the recent prospective study of depressive recurrences by Mendlewicz and colleagues (personal communication, 1990) is also supportive of this interpretation. In their study, they found more psychosocial stressors (8.7) associated with the emergence of a depressive episode in a normal control group (i.e., those who had never experienced a prior depression) compared with those with a prior history of unipolar depression (3.9; i.e., the recurrent depressive group). In the control group events were of the more undesirable, negative, and uncontrollable variety compared with those who remained well. Psychosocial stress was thus associated with an initial episode of depression in the normal volunteers, but less implicated in the recurrences.

Therefore, if we accept the observation in the literature (Kraepelin, 1921; Stern, 1944; Weitbrecht, 1960; Erlanger-Wyler, 1973) and the conclusions summarized in the studies in Table 2.2 and others, psychobiological theories must deal with this transition from episodes that are triggered by psychosocial stresses to ones that are less likely to be triggered in this fashion (Figure 2.6A), even though these later episodes are occurring in the context of increasing vulnerability to recurrence.

Inherent in this concept is the notion that there are two types of sensitization mechanisms, one related to the stressor (relating to vulnerability) and another occurring with the manifestation of an affective episode itself (see Figure 2.6B). Hence, consequently, it is possible that episodes leave a neurobiological memory trace and predispose to further episodes (i.e., "episodes beget episodes"). Cocaine-induced behavioral sensitization perhaps is an interesting model for this process. In this paradigm animals respond to repetition of the same dose of cocaine with increases in stimulant-induced motor activity, but only when cocaine is administered in the same environmental context in which it was previously administered (Post et al., 1988a,b; Post, Lockfeld, Squillace, and Contel, 1981; Weiss, Post, Pert, Woodward, and Murman, 1989). These data suggest that a learning or conditioning component is involved in the behavioral sensitization.

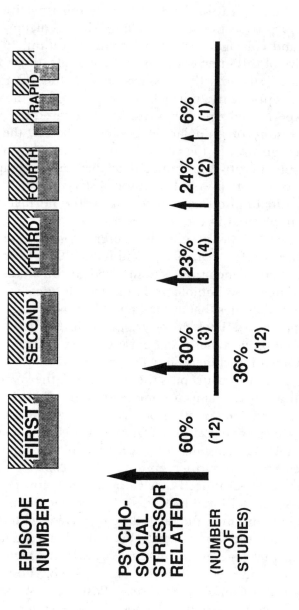

Figure 2.6A. Precipitants of affective illness: Greater relationship to first compared to subsequent episodes.

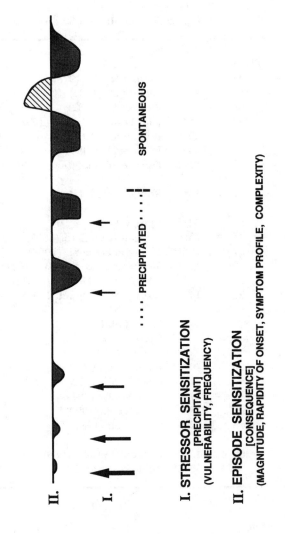

Figure 2.6B. Two types of sensitization in affective illness.

TABLE 2.6
Prophylaxis of Unipolar Depression: Controlled Studies

	% Relapse		
Nonselective	Placebo	Rx	
Amitriptyline (1)	31	0**	Coppen et al. (1978)
Amitriptyline (3)	88	43*	Glen et al. (1984)
Imipramine (1)	100	67	Kane et al. (1982)
Imipramine (1)	23	12*	Jakovljevic & Mewett (1991)
Imipramine (2)	85	29**	Prien et al. (1973)
Imipramine (2)	71	44*	Prien et al. (1984)
Imipramine (3)	78	21***	Frank et al. (1990)
NE Selective			
Maprotiline (1)	32	16**	Rouillon et al. (1989)
5HT Selective			
Zimeldine (1$^{1}/_{2}$)	84	32***	Bjork (1983)
Sertraline (1)	46	13***	Doogan & Caillard (1992)
Fluoxetine (1)	57	26***	Montgomery et al. (1988)
Paroxetine (1)	39	15**	Montgomery & Dunbar (1991)
			Jakovljevic & Mewett (1991)
Paroxetine (1)	23	14	Jakovljevic & Mewett (1991)
5HT$_{1A}$			
Buspirone ( )		*	Fabre (1991)
Lithium			
Lithium (1)	84	29***	Schou (1979)
Lithium (1)	100	29***	Kane et al. (1982)
Lithium (2)	85	41*	Prien et al. (1973)
Lithium (2)	71	57*	Prien et al. (1984)
Lithium (2)	[58]	[8*]	Souza et al. (1990)
Lithium (3)	88	42*	Glen et al. (1984)
MAOI			
Phenelzine (1)	65	13*	Georgotas et al. (1989)
Phenelzine (2)	75	10***	Robinson et al. (1991)

*p < .05
**p < .01
***p < .001
[ ] Indicates probability of recurrence

Most pertinent to the current argument for recurrent affective illness is that repeated experiences of the behavioral pathology associated with cocaine-induced hyperactivity can engage neural mechanisms that lead to increased rather than decreased responsivity in a very long-lasting fashion (Post, Rubinow, and Ballenger,

1984; Post, Weiss and Pert, 1988a,b; Post and Weiss, 1989a,b). An analogous endogenous process could also occur in recurrent depressive or manic episodes in which the experience of an episode itself (whether or not it is psychosocially triggered) may predispose to another occurrence. In this regard, it is of considerable interest that cocaine-induced hyperactivity is associated with induction of c-fos, in this instance by a dopamine (D_1) receptor mechanism (Draisci and Iadarola, 1989; Robertson et al., 1989; Graybiel et al. 1990), although it remains to be demonstrated whether c-fos induction is critical to sensitization. In an analogous fashion the acute neurotransmitter perturbations of an affective episode potentially involving not only D_1 mechanisms, but also acetylcholine, catecholamines, indoleamines, and a variety of other systems (Curran and Morgan, 1985; Greenberg, Ziff, and Greene, 1986; Gubits et al., 1989; Robertson et al., 1989; Sonnenberg et al., 1989b) could, in addition to their acute and intermediate effects on the organism, also leave behind a long-term residue (Figure 2.2) based on the downstream consequences of having activated c-fos and related proto-oncogenes leading to a cascade of long-term neuropeptide, receptor, and enzyme adaptations. Since stress induces changes in neurotrophic factors (Smith et al, 1993), mechanisms far enduring synoptic and cellular changes can now be easily envisioned.

EVOLVING ANATOMY AND PHARMACOLOGY OF MEMORY TRACES

It is also likely that in some instances long-term neurobiological responses to stress may be encoded not only in biochemical processes, but also in microanatomical ones. In *aplysia*, Kandel and associates (1983; Glanzman, Kandel, and Schacher, 1990) have identified anatomical changes at the synapse associated with conditioned mechanisms in an organism as primitive as a snail. Nelson and Alkon (1990) have documented changes in mRNAs with associative learning in *hermissenda*. In addition, rapid changes in neuronal sprouting have been observed after endocrine manipulations (McEwen, Angulo, Cameron, Chao, Daniels, Gannon, Gould, Meaney, Aitken, Van Berkel, Bhatnagar, and Sapolsky, 1992) and after long-term potentiation (LTP).

Even more relevant to the current argument are the recent observations of Steven Rose and his collaborators (Patterson, Gilbert, and Rose, 1990; Anokhin, Mileusnic, Shamakina, and Rose, 1991; Rose, 1991) following single-trial passive avoidance learning in the chick. These investigators found that long-lasting one-trial learning occurs when a chick is allowed to peck at an attractive, shiny water tube that contains a bitter substance (i.e., it subsequently avoids that tube indefinitely). This avoidance learning is encoded in a spatiotemporally arranged cascade of biochemical and microanatomical effects. These changes include early neurotransmitter and receptor alterations, translocation of protein kinase C, changes in glycogen synthesis, transient induction of the proto-oncogenes c-fos and c-jun, and a variety of other longer-lasting changes that can be identified on a microscopic and electron microscopic level, including changes in spine density, synapse number and density, and the like.

These biochemical and microanatomical changes occur with learning that is presumably minimally stressful. All the same, data of John, Tang, Brill, Young, and Ono (1986) suggest that the types of memory traces induced in learning may involve changes in metabolic activity of tens of millions of cells in the brain of the cat, suggesting that the processes (outlined in Figure 2.2) could similarly be occurring in millions of cells as well as in different spatiotemporal domains. If learning is occurring in the context of overwhelming stress it is not difficult to imagine that the changes would be amplified hundreds or thousands of times, potentially involving metabolic changes in virtually all of the 12 billion nerve cells in the brain. Under emerging circumstances the changes may be quantitatively more profound and qualitatively more advanced. Although LTP and kindling share many characteristics in common (Cain, Boon, and Hargreaves, 1992; Racine, Moore, and Wicks, 1991), they also differ considerably in their phenomenology, physiological input on the animal, pharmacology, and permanence, with kindling representing a process that is more than just multiple or enhanced LTP.

We suggest that a similar transition occurs in normal learning to that involved in PTSD, in which quantitative and qualitatively greater responses are called forth at every level of the pre- and postsynaptic network, as illustrated in Figure 2.2. Normal neurotransmitter release is implicated by peptide release. Second and third messengers (immediate early genes [IEGs]) are amplified accordingly and a panoply of late effector genes are induced.

In this fashion it may be possible to conceptualize PTSD as a dual process of (1) a "hard wired" kindled memory trace occuring (2) in the context of massive stress sensitization. Each process in PTSD (kindlinglike memory and stress sensitization) would have its impact on gene expression and, ultimately, on the micro- if not macroanatomy of the brain. In kindling there is recent recognition of both cell sprouting and cell loss (Sutula, Xiao-Xian, Cavazos, and Scott, 1988; Cavazos and Sutula, 1990; Cavazos, Golarai, and Sutula, 1991). The endocrine milieu associated with acute or chronic massive stress can also interact to produce its own adaptive and maladaptive (Post and Weiss, 1994) changes, including tropic influences and cell death (McEwen, Angulo, Cameron, Chao, Daniels, Gannon, Gould, Meaney, Aitken, Van Berkel, Bhatnagar, and Sapolsky, 1988; Sapolsky and Pulsinelli, 1985; Gould, Woolley, and McEwen, 1991), such that the two processes of kindlinglike memory changes and sensitization together may exert a profound stamp on the biochemistry, circuitry, and anatomy of brain, a "double branding" that can leave relatively permanent neural scars.

In the paradigm of Rose and associates lesion studies additionally suggest that the gross anatomical location of the putative "memory trace" involved in this learning may migrate over time from subtrates in the left dorsal part of the brain to those on the right and finally to ventral parts of the brain first on the right and then back on the left (Rose, 1991).

These data are convergent with recent data in the rhesus monkey (Mishkin and Appenzeller, 1987; Squire and Zola-Morgan,

1991) demonstrating that memory consolidation processes differ by type of memory process engaged, number of learning trials, and also migrate with the passage of time. Whereas a single high dose of cocaine (40 mg/kg) engenders context-dependent sensitization that is dependent on the presence of the nucleus accumbens and amygdala, three injections of high dose cocaine result in sensitization that occurs even in the absence of the amygdala (Post, Weiss, and Pert, 1991; Weiss and colleagues and Fontana, unpublished data). These data also suggest an evolution in the macroanatomical structures underlying single versus repeated induction of behavioral sensitization, just as there is an evolution in structures subserving "representational" versus "habit" memory (Mishkin and Appenzeller, 1987). In kindling, as noted above, c-fos induction is initially unilateral (ipsilateral to the side of the stimulation), but becomes bilateral (Clark et al., 1992). Clark et al. (unpublished data) have recently observed an animal in the late phases of kindling following a spontaneous seizure in which c-fos induction was observed unilaterally, but on the contralateral side, suggesting a different site of origin of the triggered and the spontaneous seizure.

Should related mechanisms at the level of changes in gene expression prove relevant to the neurobiology of PTSD and affective disorder, they may additionally suggest that, depending on the stage of temporal evolution in the longitudinal course of affective disorders, the neurochemical and microanatomical mechanisms may not only differ markedly, but their macroneuroanatomical substrates may differ as well. If this proves to be the case it would support a reconceptualization of the neurobiology of PTSD and affective disorder as sequentially evolving processes, not as static ones. This would have implications for therapeutic (Post et al., 1986) as well as clinical mechanistic studies, suggesting that the neurobiology of PTSD and affective disorder is a moving target that may change with the course of illness. Therapeutic interventions may differ vastly as a function of course of illness as well.

Different neurotransmitter systems are involved in the initiation (induction) versus maintenance (expression) phase of LTP,

kindling, and behavioral sensitization, and different pharmacological manipulations are, respectively, effective (Post et al., 1986;
Post et al., 1991; Pinel, 1983). This may be particularly critical in
the therapeutics of PTSD in which approaches to the acute
trauma and associated stress response may be vastly different from
those appropriate in the late phases of the illness.

Again, these conceptual vignettes are not presented with the
idea that there are direct homologies from kindling to PTSD or
the affective disorders, but only with the notion that the kind of
long-lasting processes and their underlying mechanisms expli-
cated may provide a highly preliminary blueprint for parallel alterations in different systems that might occur with a
spatiotemporal unfolding pertinent to stress reactivity and vulnerability. They highlight the potential complexity of the problem
and reveal that new and major advances within the neurobiology
of stress and cocaine sensitization, as well as kindling and related
models of long-term plasticity, are beginning to provide potential
candidate systems for molecular mechanisms underlying the biochemical and anatomical subtrates of memory and long-term responsivity of an organism. Though these findings may only be
directly relevant to PTSD and the affective disorders, they highlight principles that may be ultimately applicable to the long-term
course and treatment.

IMPLICATIONS FOR THERAPEUTICS OF RECURRENT AFFECTIVE DISORDERS: IMPORTANCE OF PROPHYLAXIS

What are the potential implications of such long-lasting changes
in both stress responsivity and episode sensitization if one assumes
for the moment that the changes outlined above occur and the
details will ultimately be documented? The current formulation
emphasizes that modern neuroscience can now incorporate on a
more mechanistic basis older psychoanalytic and dynamic theories regarding a critical role of stress and loss in the etiopathogen-
esis of affective disorder in some patients. In those patients late

in the course of affective disorder, in whom obvious psychosocial stressors are no longer as readily apparent as they were earlier in the course, the neurobiological "memory" for this vulnerability to stressors may provide a long-lasting trait or vulnerability marker for the individual. Just as acute seizures (presumably acting via the induction of immediate or early genes) (Dragunow and Robertson, 1987; Nakajima, Daval, Morgan, et al., 1989; Daval et al., 1989; Dragunow et al., 1989; Post, Weiss, Nakajima, et al., 1990; Clark, Post, Weiss, Cain, and Nakajima, 1991; Clark, Weiss, and Post, 1991; Clark et al., 1992) are capable of producing long-lasting alterations in neuropeptides (Kato et al., 1983; Naranjo et al., 1986; Nadi et al., 1989; Lee et al., 1989; Gall et al., 1990; Shinoda et al., 1989; Meyerhoff et al., 1990), and even in neural structure characterized by sprouting (Sutula et al., 1988) or even cell loss (Cavazos and Sutula, 1990), it is postulated that psychosocial stressors, under appropriate circumstances, are likewise able to lead to long-lasting changes in gene expression, including longer-lasting alterations in neuropeptides (as summarized in Figure 2.3B) and even in neuronal microstructure, as demonstrated in other models of learning and memory (Kandel, 1983; Glanzman, Kandel, and Schacher, 1990; Nelson and Alkon, 1990; Patterson et al., 1990). Although there is ample evidence for cortisol hypersecretion in depression (perhaps driven by increased secretion of CRF) (Nemeroff, Widerlov, and Bissette, 1984; Gold, Loriaux, Roy, Kling, Calabrese, Kellner, Nieman, Post, Pickar, and Galluci, 1986), there is also accumulating evidence for decreases in CSF somatostatin (see reviews of Post, Weiss, and Rubinow [1988]; Rubinow, Davis, and Post [1991]) (Figure 2.7). These changes and many others may reflect episode-related alterations in gene transcription (either triggered by stressor or not) that ultimately deserve more direct therapeutic targeting. Some of these changes may be related to the primary pathological process and require blocking strategies whereas others may be endogenous secondary or compensating processes that should be enhanced in therapeutic endeavors (Post and Weiss, 1992) (Figure 2.8).

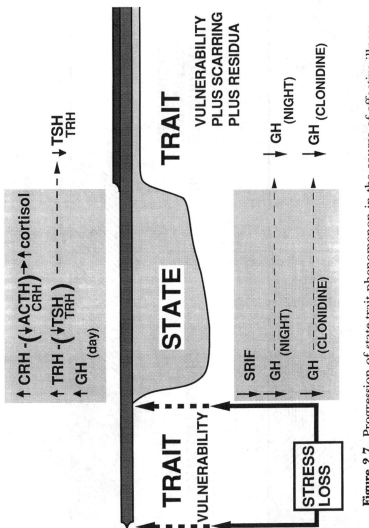

Figure 2.7. Progression of state-trait phenomenon in the course of affective illness.

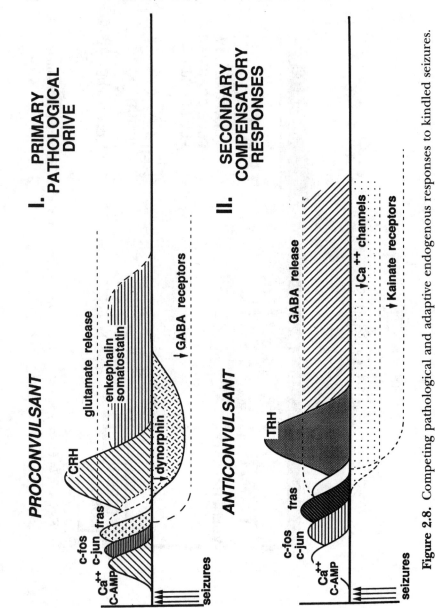

Figure 2.8. Competing pathological and adaptive endogenous responses to kindled seizures.

As we have postulated that the psychopharmacology of affective disorder may differ as a function of the stage and evolution of the disorder (Post et al., 1986; Post, Weiss, and Rubinow, 1988) (Figure 2.9) (as it does in other models of learning and memory), it is possible that psychosocial and psychotherapeutic interventions may also require alterations as a function of the stage of illness evolution. More specifically, though psychodynamic psychotherapy (utilizing "representational" or limbic memory systems [Miskin and Appenzeller, 1987]) may be appropriate for early and minor stress-related dysphorias and initial episodes of major depression, with repeated episodes and, ultimately, with the emergence of spontaneity (major episodes in the absence of psychosocial stressors), use of more cognitive and behavioral therapies may be more appropriate. If the illness is on "automatic," in part due to many repetitions of episodes, cognitive and behavioral therapies dealing with this automaticity (targeting "habit" or potentially striatal memory mechanisms [Mishkin and Appenzeller, 1987]) may be more fruitful than dynamic therapies that might play a more essential role with early episodes.

A critical role for psychotherapeutic and pharmacotherapeutic prophylaxis is also suggested by the current formulation. To the extent that "episodes beget episodes," and repetition of triggered episodes may lead to recurrence of untriggered ones (Table 2.1), the importance of prevention is reemphasized (Figure 2.10). Biological mechanisms underlying stressor sensitization and episode sensitization may be conceptualized as having the potential to carry lifelong vulnerability. These neurobiological possibilities square with the clinical data that even several decades of successful lithium prophylaxis does not appear to ensure freedom from episode recurrence once the drug is discontinued (Schou, 1973; Goodwin and Jamison, 1990; Post, 1990; Suppes, Baldessarini, Faedda, Tohen, 1991; Post et al., 1992). If having an episode incurs a greater risk of having subsequent episodes this variable should be factored into recommendations for earlier initiation and longer maintenance of pharmacoprophylaxis (Post, 1990). Some evidence suggests that having more episodes prior to initiating lithium prophylaxis results in a poorer long-term response to

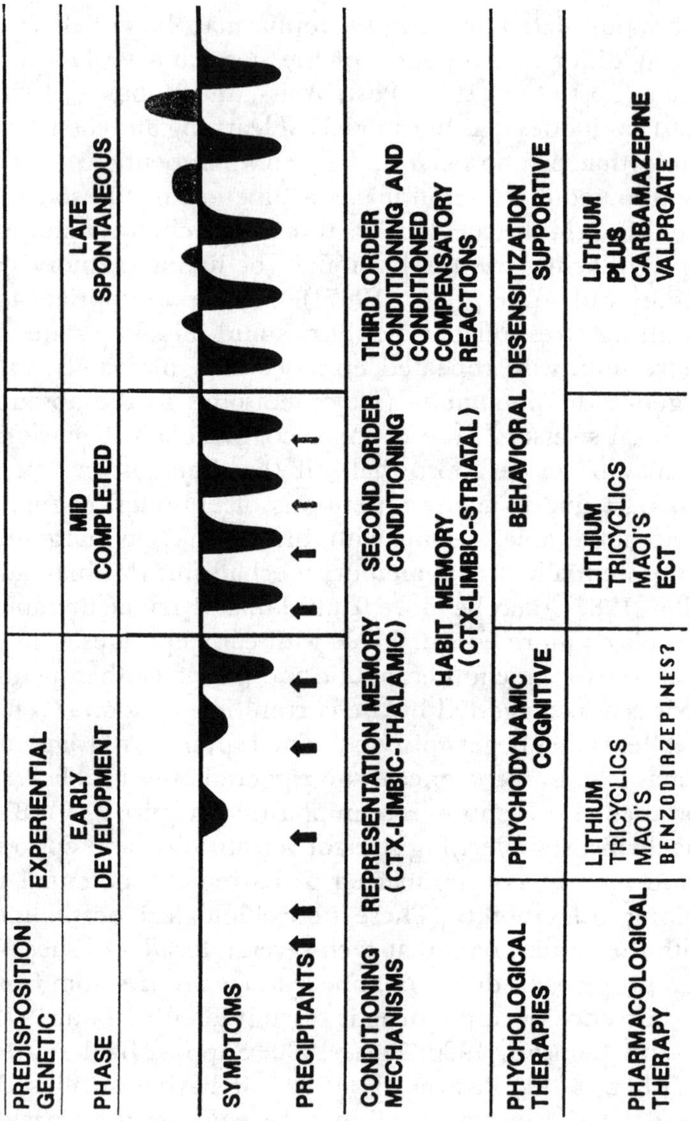

Figure 2.9. Sequential evolution and sensitization in affective illness.

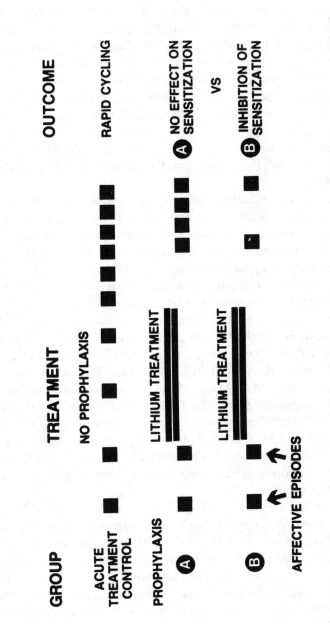

Figure 2.10. Testable hypothesis: Pharmacoprophylaxis will alter frequency of subsequent untreated episodes.

lithium therapy (Gelenberg, Kane, Keller, Lavori, Rosenbaum, Cole, and Lavelle, 1989; O'Connell, Mayo, Flatow, Cuthbertson, and O'Brien, 1991; Vestergaard, 1991; Goldberg, Harrow, Campbell, and Jobe, 1993). Moreover, in addition to the liabilities of episode recurrence with the discontinuation of effective prophylaxis (Suppes et al., 1991), we have identified a small series of initially lithium-responsive patients who have shown refractoriness to lithium once they have restarted treatment following a discontinuation-induced episode (Post, Leverich, Altshuler, and Mikalauskas, 1992; Post, Leverich, Pazzaglia, Mikalauskas, and Denicoff, 1993).

It remains a possibility, therefore, that episodes may not only engender vulnerability to recurrence, but their recurrence may also trigger new mechanisms that overwhelm or circumvent a previously effective treatment strategy (Post and Weiss, 1992; Post, Leverich, Pazzaglia, Mikalauskas, and Denicoff, 1993). Similar chemotherapeutic resistant processes have been described with the transition from primary site to metastatic malignancies which, interestingly, often involve the induction or suppression of additional oncogenesis (Takahashi, Nau, Chiba, Birrer, Rosenberg, Vinocour, Levitt, Pass, Gazdan, and Minna, 1989; Kumar, Sukumar, and Barbacid, 1990; Baker, Markowitz, Fearon, Willson, and Vogelstein, 1990; Weinberg, 1991). The rationale for maintenance of long-term prophylaxis in bioplar disorders to prevent "malignant" transformation to rapid cycling or drug resistance is supported by a modicum of clinical data that needs to be better documented and is now also bolstered by the initial insights into potential neurobiological mechanisms that may convey these long-lasting vulnerabilities.

In a parallel fashion the highly recurrent nature of unipolar affective disorder in some patients is increasingly being recognized (Grof, Angst, and Haines, 1974; Post, Rubinow, and Ballenger, 1986; Goodwin and Jamison, 1990). The long-term prophylactic studies with imipramine (Frank, Kupfer, Perel, Cornes, Jarrett, Mallenger, Thase, McEachran, and Grochocinski, 1990), fluoxetine (Montgomery, Dufour, Brion, Gailledreau, Laqueille, Ferrey, Parant-Lucena, Singer, and Danion, 1988), and maprotiline (Rouillon, Miller, Serrurier, and Gerard, 1991) high-light, not only the unexpectedly high frequency and rapidity of unipolar depressive recurrences within a year following successful treatment of an acute episode (when drug is discontinued with placebo [Montgomery et al., 1988; Frank et al., 1990]), but also emphasize the great utility of prophylaxis in substantially and sig-nificantly inhibiting these recurrences (when drug is blindly con-tinued). The current formulation—that having had an episode leaves behind neurobiologial residues that make a patient more vulnerable to subsequent episodes—raises the question of whether earlier institution and maintenance of prophylaxis in unipolar episodes would also prevent the potential for increas-ingly rapid recurrences, drug refractoriness (virtually unstudied), and chronic depression.

Whereas most of the neurobiological concomitants of affective disorders have focused on state-related alterations in classical neu-rotransmitter endocrine and peptide substances, there is increas-ing recognition that some variables may remain abnormal into the well-interval between episodes (Figure 2.3B). In particular, it appears that a number of patients who maintain a blunted TSH response to TRH (Loosen and Prange, 1982; Extein, Potash, Gold, and Cowdry, 1984; Langer, Koinig, Hatzinger, Schonbeck, Resch, Aschauer, Keshavan, and Sieghart, 1986) continue to dem-onstrate sleep abnormalities (Avery, Wildschidtz, and Rafaelsen, 1982; Rush, Erman, Giles, Schlesser, Carpenter, Vasavada, and Roffwang, 1986), to show abnormal responses in the hypothala-mic-pituitary-adrenal axis (Gurguis, Meador-Woodruff, Haskett, and Greden, 1990; Holsboer, 1989; Holsboer, personal communi-cation), and to demonstrate blunted sleep-related growth hor-mone secretion (Steiger, von Bardeleben, Herth, and Holsboer, 1989; Jarrett, Miewald, and Kupfer, 1990). It remains to be docu-mented which of these changes is reliable and which changes are markers of long-term vulnerability to recurrence as opposed to neurobiological "scars" representing markers of having experi-enced an episode of affective disorder. In either case the current discussion provides a framework for considering mechanisms re-lated to alterations in gene expression by which these changes might arise.

In the evolution of carcinogenesis it is known that there is a long sequence of activation of some oncogenes and loss of other suppressor oncogenes (interacting with environmental influences, endocrine, and hormonal changes associated with development of the organism) that are requisite to the development and progression of tumors (Kumar et al., 1990; Yoshida, Tsujino, Yasui, Kameda, Sano, Nakayama, Toge, and Tahara, 1990; Weinberg, 1991; Adams and Cory, 1991; Marx, 1993). This process highlights the potential roles of genetic predisposition, environmental (experiential) factors, and developmental processes (endocrine maturation, etc.) and their interactions (Kumar et al., 1990) in illness evolution. Therapeutic approaches to cancer chemotherapy are also, in part, driven by the stage of evolution of this process. Some of the principles uncovered in the development of oncogenesis (Figure 2.11) should be reexamined for their relevance to the evolution and unfolding of affective illness and its treatment, including the importance of prophylaxis, early intervention, combination therapies, and targeted therapeutic approaches as a function of stage of evolution of the process. Similar provisions may apply as well in psychotherapeutic (Herman, 1992) and neurobiological (Post et al., 1994) approaches to PTSD, especially in light of new data on early precursors (physical abuse in childhood) of later onset PTSD in Vietnam veterans (Bremner, Southwick, Johnson, Yehuda, and Charney, 1993).

The clinical data and biological vignettes that are presented in this chapter are obviously fragmentary and incomplete, providing only rough landscapes that must be brought into more detailed focus. Nonetheless, they are presented in order to anticipate the more detailed exposition of the precise neurobiological mechanisms involved in different types of learning and memory and the careful evaluation of their relevance for the longitudinal course of affective disorders and PTSD. Although these developments are eagerly awaited, it may nonetheless be pertinent to begin to formulate questions regarding the nature of the neurobiological changes underlying the longitudinal course of affective disorders and PTSD so that appropriate mechanistic-based studies

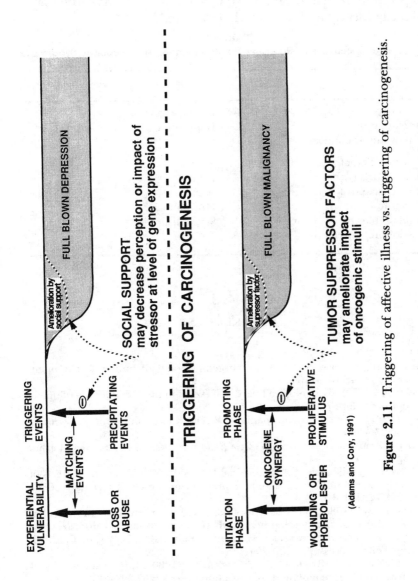

Figure 2.11. Triggering of affective illness vs. triggering of carcinogenesis.

and psychological and pharmacological interventions can be preliminarily formulated, designed, and tested.

TABLE 2.7

Qualitative Specificity of Stressors for Precipitation of Psychiatric Syndromes

Stressor	Disorder
↑Sleep Loss	Mania seizures
↑Loss (threat of);	Depression
social or family context	
☐ External Threat	Anxiety
↑Internal Threat	Panic
Self or Dyscontrol	
▲ Threat to	Posttraumatic
Bodily Integrity	Stress disorder
(loss of life; horrific)	

REFERENCES

Adams, J. M., & Cory, S. (1991), Transgenic model of tumor development. *Science*, 254:1161–1166.

Ambelas, A. (1979), Psychologically stressful events in the precipitation of manic episodes. *Brit. J. Psychiatry*, 135:15–21.

—— (1987), Life events and mania. A special relationship. *Brit. J. Psychiatry*, 150:235–240.

Angst, J. (1966), *Atiologie und Nosologie Endogener Depressiver Psychosen.* Berlin: Springer-Verlag.

Anokhin, K. V., Mileusnic, R., Shamakina, I. Y., & Rose, S. P. (1991), Effects of early experience on c-fos gene expression in the chick forebrain. *Brain Res.*, 544:101–107.

Antelman, S. M. (1988), Stressor-induced sensitization to subsequent stress: Implications for the development and treatment of clinical disorders. In: *Sensitization in the Nervous System*, ed. P. W. Kalivas & C. D. Barnes. Caldwell, NJ: Telford Press, pp. 227–254.

—— Eichler, A. J., Black, C. A., & Kocan, D. (1980), Interchangeability of stress and amphetamine in sensitization. *Science*, 207:329–331.

Arenander, A. T., de Vellis, J., & Herschman, H. R. (1989), Induction of c-fos and TIS genes in cultured rat astrocytes by neurotransmitters. *J. Neurosci. Res.*, 24:107–114.

Astrup, C., Fossum, A., & Holmboe, R. (1959), A follow-up study of 270 patients with acute affective psychoses. *Acta Psychiat. Scand.*, 34:7–62.

Avery, D., Wildschidtz, G., & Rafaelsen, O. (1982), REM latency and temperature in affective disorder before and after treatment. *Biol. Psychiatry*, 17:463–470.

Baker, S. J., Markowitz, S., Fearon, E. R., Willson, J. K. V., & Vogelstein, B. (1990), Suppression of human colorectal carcinoma cell growth by wild-type p53. *Science*, 249:912–915.

Bidzinska, E. J. (1984), Stress factors in affective diseases. *Brit. J. Psychiatry*, 144:161–166.

Bjork, K. (1983), The efficacy of zimeldine in preventing depressive episodes in recurrent major depressive disorders—a double-blind placebo-controlled study. *Acta Psychiat. Scand. Suppl.*, 308:182–189.

Bremner, J. D., Southwick, S. M., Johnson, D. R., Yehuda, R., & Charney, D. S. (1993), Childhood physical abuse and combat-related posttraumatic stress disorder in Vietnam veterans. *Amer. J. Psychiatry*, 150:235–239.

Brew, M. F. (1933), Precipitating factors in manic-depressive psychosis. *Psychiat. Quart.*, 7:401–418.

Brown, E. E., Robertson, G. S., & Fibiger, H. C. (1992), Evidence for conditional neuronal activation following exposure to a cocaine-paired environment: Role of forebrain limbic structures. *J. Neurosci.*, 12:4112–4121.

Brown, G. W., & Harris, T. O. (1978), *Social Origins of Depression*. London: Tavistock.

Bullitt, E. (1989), Induction of c-fos-like protein within the lumbar spinal cord and thalamus of the rat following peripheral stimulation. *Brain Res.*, 493:391–397.

Cain, D. P., Boon, F., & Hargreaves, E. L. (1992), Evidence for different neurochemical contributions to long-term potentiation and to kindling and kindling-induced potentiation: Role of NMDA and urethane-sensitive mechanisms. *Exp. Neurol.*, 116:330–338.

Campeau, S., Hayward, M. D., Hope, B. T., Rosen, J. B., Nestler, E. J., & Davis, M. (1991), Induction of the c-fos proto-oncogene in rat amygdala during unconditioned and conditioned fear. *Brain Res.*, 565:349–352.

Cassano, G.B., Akiskal, H. S., Musetti, L., Perugi, G., Soriani, A., & Mignani, V. (1989), Psychopathology, temperament, and past course in primary major depressions. 2. Toward a redefinition of bipolarity with a new semistructured interview for depression. *Psychopathology*, 22:278–288.

Cavazos, J. E., Golarai, G., & Sutula, T. P. (1991), Mossy fiber synaptic reorganization induced by kindling: Time course of development, progression, and permanence. *J. Neurosci.*, 11:2795–2803.

——— Sutula, T. P. (1990), Progressive neuronal loss induced by kindling: A possible mechanism for mossy fiber synaptic reorganization and hippocampal sclerosis. *Brain Res.*, 527:1–6.

Ceccatelli, S., Villar, M. J., Goldstein, M., & Hokfelt, T. (1989), Expression of c-Fos immunoreactivity in transmitter-characterized neurons after stress. *Proc. Natl. Acad. Sci. U.S.A.*, 86:9569–9573.

Clark, M., Post, R. M., Weiss, S. R. B., & Nakajima, T. (1992), Expression of c-fos mRNA in acute and kindled cocaine seizures in rats. *Brain Res.*, 582:101–106.

———— ———— ———— Cain, C. J., & Nakajima, T. (1991), Regional expression of c-fos mRNA in rat brain during the evolution of amygdala-kindled seizures. *Mol. Brain Res.*, 11:55–64.

———— Weiss, S. R. B., & Post, R. M. (1991), Expression of c-fos mRNA in rat brain after intracerebroventricular administration of corticotropin-releasing hormone. *Neurosci. Lett.*, 132:235–238.

Cole, A. J., Worley, P. F., & Baraban, J. M. (1990), Dopaminergic regulation of transcription factor mRNAs in striatal neurons *in vivo. Abstracts, Soc. for Neurosci.*, 16:800.

Coppen, A., Ghose, K., Montgomery, S., Rama Rao, V. A., Bailey, J., & Jorgensen, A. (1978), Continuation therapy with amitriptyline in depression. *Brit. J. Psychiatry*, 133:28–33.

Crabtree, G. R. (1989), Contingent genetic regulatory events in T lymphocyte activation. *Science*, 243:355–361.

Curran, T., & Morgan, J. I. (1985), Superinduction of c-fos by nerve growth factor in the presence of peripherally active benzodiazepines. *Science*, 229:1265–1268.

Daval, J. L., Nakajima, T., Gleiter, C. H., Post, R. M., & Marangos, P. J. (1989), Mouse brain c-fos mRNA distribution following a single electroconvulsive shock. *J. Neurochem.*, 52:1954–1957.

Deutch, A. Y., Lee, M. C., Gillham, M. H., Cameron, D. A., Goldstein, M., & Iadarola, M. J.(1991), Stress selectively increases fos protein in dopamine neurons innervating the prefrontal cortex. *Cereb. Cortex*, 1:273–292.

Dolan, R. J., Calloway, S. P., Fonagy, P., De Souza, F. V. A., & Wakeling, A. (1985), Life events, depression and hypothalamic-pituitary-adrenal axis function. *Brit. J. Psychiatry*, 147:429–433.

Doogan, D. P., & Caillard, V. (1992), Sertraline in the prevention of depression. *Brit. J. Psychiatry*, 160:217–222.

Dragunow, M., Currie, R. W., Faull, R. L., Robertson, H. A., & Jansen, K. (1989), Immediate-early genes, kindling and long-term potentiation. *Neurosci. Biobehav. Rev.*, 13:301–313.

———— Robertson, H. A. (1987), Kindling stimulation induces c-fos protein(s) in granule cells of the rat dentate gyrus. *Nature*, 329:441–442.

Draisci, G., & Iadarola, M. J. (1989), Temporal analysis of increases in c-fos, preprodynorphin and preproenkephalin mRNAs in rat spinal cord. *Brain Res. Mol. Brain Res.*, 6:31–37.

Erlanger-Wyler, M. (1973), *Exogene Auslosung bipolarer manisch-depressiver Erkrankungen mit spezieller Berucksichtigung der Manien.* Zurich: Druch.

Extein, I., Potash, A. L. C., Gold, M. S., & Cowdry, R. W. (1984), Changes in TSH response to TRH in affective illness. In: *Neurobiology of Mood Disorders*, ed. R. M. Post & J. C. Ballenger. Baltimore: Williams & Wilkins, pp. 279–310.

Ezquiaga, E., Gutierrez, J. L. A., & Lopez, A. G. (1987), Psychosocial factors and episode number in depression. *J. Affective Disord.*, 12:135–138.

Fabre, L. F. (1991), Buspirone in the treatment of major depression. Paper presented at a conference at the Fabre Clinic, Houston, Texas.

Frank, E., Kupfer, D. J., Perel, J. M., Cornes, C., Jarrett, D. B., Mallenger, A. G., Thase, M. E., McEachran, A. B., & Grochocinski, K. J. (1990), Three-year outcomes for maintenance therapies in recurrent depression. *Arch. Gen. Psychiatry*, 47:1093–1099.

Gall, C., Lauterborn, J., Isackson, P., & White, J. (1990), Seizures, neuropeptide regulation, and mRNA expression in the hippocampus. *Prog. Brain Res.*, 83:371–390.

Gelenberg, A. J., Kane, J. M., Keller, M. B., Lavori, P., Rosenbaum, J. F., Cole, K., & Lavelle, J. (1989), Comparison of standard and low serum levels of lithium for maintenance treatment of bipolar disorder. *N. Eng. J. Med.*, 321:1489–1493.

Georgotas, A., McCue, R. E., & Cooper, T. B. (1989), A placebo-controlled comparison of nortriptyline and phenelzine in maintenance therapy of elderly depressed patients. *Arch. Gen. Psychiatry*, 46:783–786.

Ghaziuddin, M., Ghaziuddin, N., & Stein, G. S. (1990), Life events and the recurrence of depression. *Can. J. Psychiatry*, 35:239–242.

Glanzman, D. L., Kandel, E. R., & Schacher, S. (1990), Target-dependent structural changes accompanying long-term synaptic facilitation in *Aplysia* neurons. *Science*, 249:799–802.

Glassner, B., & Haldipur, C. V. (1983), Life events and early and late onset of bipolar disorder. *Amer. J. Psychiatry*, 140:215–217.

————— ————— Dessauersmith, J. (1979), Role loss and working-class manic depression. *J. Nerv. Ment. Dis.*, 167:530–541.

Glen, A. I. M., Johnson, A. L., & Shepherd, M. (1984), Continuation therapy with lithium and amitriptyline in unipolar depressive illness: A randomized, double-blind, controlled trial. *Psychol. Med.*, 14:37–50.

Goddard, G. V., McIntyre, D. C., & Leech, C. K. (1969), A permanent change in brain function resulting from daily electrical stimulation. *Exp. Neurol.*, 25:295–330.

Gold, P. W., Loriaux, D. L., Roy, A., Kling, M. A., Calabrese, J. R., Kellner, C. H., Nieman, L. K., Post, R. M., Pickar, D., & Galluci, W. (1986), Responses to corticotropin-releasing hormone in the hypercortisolism of depression and Cushing's disease: Pathophysiologic and diagnostic implications. *N. Eng. J. Med.*, 314:1329–1335.

Goldberg, J. F., Harrow, M., Campbell, J., & Jobe, T. H. (1993), Kindling and relapse in bipolar affective illness. *Abstracts, 146th Annual Meeting, American Psychiatry Association*. Abstr. # 73:99–100.

Goodman, R. H. (1990), Regulation of neuropeptide gene expression. *Ann. Rev. Neurosci.*, 13:111–127.

Goodwin, F. K., & Jamison, K. R. (1990), *Manic-Depressive Illness*. New York: Oxford University Press.

Gould, E., Woolley, C. S., & McEwen, B. S. (1991), Adrenal steroids regulate postnatal development of the rat dentate gyrus: I. Effects of glucocorticoids on cell death. *J. Comp. Neurol.*, 313:479–485.

Graybiel, A. M., Moratalla, R., & Robertson, H. A. (1990), Amphetamine and cocaine induce drug-specific activation of the c-fos gene in striosome-matrix compartments and limbic subdivisions of the striatum. *Proc. Nat. Acad. Sci., U.S.A.*, 87:6912–6916.

Greenberg, M. E., Ziff, E. B., & Greene, L. A. (1986), Stimulation of neuronal acetylcholine receptors induces rapid gene transcription. *Science*, 234:80–83.

Grof, P., Angst, J., & Haines, T. (1974), The clinical course of depression: Practical issues. In: *Symposia Medica Hoest; Classification and Prediction of Outcome of Depression*, Vol. 8, ed. F. K. Schattauer. New York: Schattauer, pp. 141–148.

Gubits, R. M., Smith, T. M., Fairhurst, J. L., & Yu, H. (1989), Adrenergic receptors mediate changes in c-fos mRNA levels in brain. *Brain Res. Mol. Brain Res.*, 6:39–45.

Gurguis, G. N. M., Meador-Woodruff, J. H., Haskett, R. F., & Greden, J. F. (1990), Multiplicity of depressive episodes: Phenomenological and neuroendocrine correlates. *Biol. Psychiatry*, 27:1156–1164.

Gutierrez, J. L. A., De Diego, F. F., Barroso, R. M., & Martin, I. M. (1981), Analyse des facteurs declencheurs sur un echantillon de patients hospitalises pour depression endogene. *Ann. Med. Psychol.*, 139:759–769.

Herman, J. L. (1992), *Trauma and Recovery*. New York: Basic Books.

Holsboer, F. (1989), Psychiatric implications of altered limbic-hypothalamic-pituitary-adrenocortical activity. *Eur. Arch. Psychiatry Neurol. Sci.*, 238:302–322.

Ihda, S., & Muller-Fahlbusch, H. (1968), Zu den Entstehungssituationen wiederholter endogener depressiver Phasen. *Psychiat. Clin.*, 1:32–43.

Jakovljevic, M., & Mewett, S. (1991), Comparison between paroxetine, imipramine and placebo in preventing recurrent major depressive episodes. *Eur. Neuropsychopharmacol.*, 1:440.

Jarrett, D. B., Miewald, J. M., & Kupfer, D. J. (1990), Recurrent depression is associated with a persistent reduction in sleep-related growth hormone secretion. *Arch. Gen. Psychiatry*, 47:113–118.

John, E. R., Tang, Y., Brill, A. B., Young, R., & Ono, K. (1986), Double-labeled metabolic maps of memory. *Science*, 233:1167–1175.

Kalivas, P. W., & Duffy, P. (1989), Similar effects of daily cocaine and stress on mesocorticolimbic dopamine neurotransmission in the rat. *Biol. Psychiatry*, 25:913–928.

———— ———— Abhold, R., & Dilts, R. P. (1988), Sensitization of mesolimbic dopamine neurons by neuropeptides and stress. In: *Sensitization in the Nervous System*, ed. P. W. Kalivas & C. D. Barnes. Caldwell, NJ: Telford Press, pp. 119–143.

Kandel, E. R. (1983), From metapsychology to molecular biology: Explorations into the nature of anxiety. *Amer. J. Psychiatry*, 140:1277–1293.

Kane, J. M., Quitkin, F. M., Rifkin, A., Ramos-Lorenzi, J. R., Nayak, D. D., & Howard, A. (1982), Lithium carbonate and imipramine in the prophylaxis of unipolar and bipolar II illness. *Arch. Gen. Psychiatry*, 39:1065–1069.

Kato, N., Higuchi, T., & Friesen, H. G. (1983), Changes of immunoreactive somatostatin and beta-endorphin content in rat brain after amygdala kindling. *Life Sci.*, 32:2415–2422.

Kennedy, S., Thompson, R., Stancer, H. C., Roy, A., & Persad, E. (1983), Life events precipitating mania. *Brit. J. Psychiatry*, 142:398–403.

Kornhuber, H. (1965), Ueber ausloesung cyclothymer depressionen durch seelische erschuetterungen. *Archiv fuer Psychiatrie und Zeitschrift Neurologie*, 193:391–405.

Kraepelin, E. (1921), *Manic-Depressive Insanity and Paranoia*, tr. R. M. Barclay, ed. G. M. Robertson. Edinburgh: E. S. Livingstone.

Kumar, R., Sukumar, S., & Barbacid, M. (1990), Activation of rat oncogenes preceding the onset of neoplasia. *Science*, 248:1101–1104.

Labiner, D. M., Butler, L. S., Cao, Z., Hosford, D. A., Shin, C., & McNamara, J. O. (1993), Induction of c-fos mRNA by kindled seizures: Complex relationship with neuronal burst firing. *J. Neurosci.*, 13:744–751.

Langer, G., Koinig, G., Hatzinger, R., Schonbeck, G., Resch, F., Aschauer, H., Keshavan, M. S., & Sieghart, W. (1986), Response of thyrotropin to thyrotropin-releasing hormone as predictor of treatment outcome. Prediction of recovery and relapse in treatment with antidepressants and neuroleptics. *Arch. Gen. Psychiatry*, 43:861–868.

Lee, P. H., Zhao, D., Xie, C. W., McGinty, J. F., Mitchell, C. L., & Hong, J. S. (1989), Changes of proenkephalin and prodynorphin mRNAs and related peptides in rat brain during the development of deep prepyriform cortex kindling. *Brain Res. Mol. Brain Res.*, 6:263–273.

Loosen, P. T., & Prange, A. J., Jr. (1982), Serum thyrotropin response to thyrotropin-releasing hormone in psychiatric patients: A review. *Amer. J. Psychiatry*, 139:405–416.

Lucibello, F. C., Slater, E. P., Jooss, K. U., Beato, M., & Muller, R. (1990), Mutual transrepression of Fos and the glucocorticoid receptor: Involvement of a functional domain in Fos which is absent in Fos B. *EMBO J.*, 9:2827–2834.

Marx, J. (1993), Cellular changes on the route to metastasis. *Science*, 259:626–629.

Matussek, P., Halbach, A., & Troger, U. (1965), *Endogene Depression*. Munchen: Urban & Schwarzenberg.

McEwen, B. S., Angulo, J., Cameron, H., Chao, H. M., Daniels, D., Gannon, M. N., Gould, E., Meaney, M. J., Aitken, D. H., Van Berkel, C., Bhatnagar, S., & Sapolsky, R. M. (1988), Effect of neonatal handling on age-related impairments associated with the hippocampus. *Science*, 239:766–768.

Meyerhoff, J. L., Bates, V. E., & Kubek, M. J. (1990), Elevated TRH levels in pyriform cortex after partial and fully generalized kindled seizures. *Brain Res.*, 525:144–148.

Mishkin, M., & Appenzeller, T. (1987), The anatomy of memory. *Scientific Amer.*, 256:80–89.

Mocchetti, I., De Bernardi, M. A., Szekely, A. M., Alho, H., Brooker, G., & Costa, E. (1989), Regulation of nerve growth factor biosynthesis by beta-adrenergic receptor activation in astrocytoma cells: A potential role of c-Fos protein. *Proc. Nat. Acad. Sci., U.S.A.*, 86:3891–3895.

Montgomery, S. A., Dufour, H., Brion, S., Gailledreau, J., Laqueille, X., Ferrey, G., Parant-Lucena, N., Singer, L., & Danion, J. M. (1988), The prophylactic efficacy of fluoxetine in unipolar depression. *Brit. J. Psychiatry*, 153:69–76.

——— Dunbar, G. C. (1993), Paroxetine is better than placebo in relapse prevention and the prophylaxis of recurrent depression. *Internat. Clin. Psychopharmacol.*, 8:189–195.

Margan, J. I. & Cohen, D. R., Hempstead, J. L., & Curran, T. (1989), Mapping patterns of c-fos expression in the central nervous system after seizure. *Science*, 237:192–197.

——— Curran, T. (1988), Calcium as a modulator of the immediate-early gene cascade in neurons. *Cell Calcium*, 9:303–311.

——— ——— (1989a), Stimulus-transcription coupling in neurons: Role of cellular immediate-early genes. *Trends Neurosci.*, 12:456–462.

——— ——— (1989b), Calcium and proto-oncogene involvement in the immediate-early response in the nervous system. *Ann. NY Acad. Sci.*, 568:283–290.

——— ——— (1990), Inducible proto-oncogenes of the nervous system: Their contribution to transcription factors and neuroplasticity. *Prog. Brain Res.*, 86:287–294.

Nadi, N. S., Pless, M., & Pintor, M. (1989), The levels of somatostatin in eight brain regions of the rat during the development of kindling. *Abstracts, Soc. for Neurosci.*, 15:779, Abs. #310.16.

Nakajima, T., Daval, J. L., Morgan, P. F., Post, R. M., & Marangos, P. J. (1989a), Adenosinergic modulation of caffeine-induced c-fos mRNA expression in mouse brain. *Brain Res.*, 501:307–314.

——— ——— Gleiter, C. H., Deckert, J., Post, R. M., & Marangos, P. J. (1989), C-fos mRNA expression following electrical-induced seizure and acute nociceptive stress in mouse brain. *Epilepsy Res.*, 4:156–159.

——— Post, R. M., Weiss, S. R. B., Pert, A., & Ketter, T. A. (1989b), Perspectives on the mechanism of action of electroconvulsive therapy: Anticonvulsant, dopaminergic, and c-fos oncogene effects. *Conv. Ther.*, 5:274–295.

Naranjo, J. R., Iadarola, M. J., & Costa, E. (1986), Changes in the dynamic state of brain proenkephalin-derived peptides during amygdaloid kindling. *J. Neurosci. Res.*, 16:75–87.

Nelson, T. J., & Alkon, D. L. (1990), Specific high molecular weight mRNAs induced by associative learning in *Hermissenda*. *Proc. Nat. Acad. Sci., U.S.A.*, 87:269–273.

Nemeroff, C. F., Widerlov, E., & Bissette, G. (1984), Elevated concentrations of CSF corticotropin-releasing factor-like immunoreactivity in depressed patients. *Science*, 226:1342–1344.

O'Connell, R. A., Mayo, J. A., Flatow, L., Cuthbertson, B., & O'Brien, B. E. (1991), Outcome of bipolar disorder on long-term treatment with lithium. *Brit. J. Psychiatry*, 159:123–129.

Okuma, T., & Shimoyama, N. (1972), Course of endogenous manic-depressive psychosis, precipitating factors and premorbid personality—A statistical study. *Folia Psychiatr. Neurol. Jpn.*, 26:19–33.

Patterson, T. A., Gilbert, D. B., & Rose, S. P. (1990), Pre- and post-training lesions of the intermediate medial hyperstriatum ventrale and passive avoidance learning in the chick. *Exp. Brain Res.*, 80:189–195.

Perris, H. (1984), Life events and depression. Part 2. Results in diagnostic subgroups, and in relation to the recurrence of depression. *J. Affective Disord.*, 7:25–36.

Pezzone, M. A., Lee, W.-S., Hoffman, G. E., & Rabin, B. S. (1992), Induction of c-fos immunoreactivity in the rat forebrain by conditioned and unconditioned aversive stimuli. *Brain Res.*, 597:41–50.

Piazza, P. V., Deminiere, J. M., Le Moal, M., & Simon, H. (1990), Stress- and pharmacologically-induced behavioral sensitization increases vulnerability to acquisition of amphetamine self-administration. *Brain Res.*, 514:22–26.

Pinel, J. P. J. (1981), Kindling-induced experimental epilepsy in rats: Cortical stimulation. *Exp. Neurol.*, 72:559–569.

———— (1983), Effects of diazepam and diphenylhydantoin on elicited and spontaneous seizures in kindled rats: A double dissociation. *Pharmacol. Biochem. Behav.*, 18:61–63.

Post, R. M. (1975), Cocaine psychoses: A continuum model. *Amer. J. Psychiatry*, 32:225–231.

———— (1990), Prophylaxis of bipolar affective disorders. *Internat. Rev. Psychiatry*, 2:165–208.

———— Leverich, G., Altshuler, L., & Mikalauskas, K. (1992), Lithium discontinuation-induced refractoriness. *Amer. J. Psychiatry*, 149:1727–1729.

———— Pazzaglia, P. J., Mikalauskas, K., & Denicoff, K. (1993), Lithium tolerance and discontinuation as pathways to refractoriness. In: *Lithium in Medicine and Biology*, ed. N. J. Birch, C. Padgham, & M. S. Hughes. Lancashire, UK: Marius Press, pp. 71–84.

———— Lockfeld, A., Squillace, K. M., & Contel, N. R. (1981), Drug-environment interaction: Context dependency of cocaine-induced behavioral sensitization. *Life Sci.*, 28:755–760.

———— Rubinow, D. R., & Ballenger, J. C. (1984), Conditioning, sensitization, and kindling: Implications for the course of affective illness. In: *Neurobiology of Mood Disorders*, ed. R. M. Post & J. C. Ballenger. Baltimore: Williams & Wilkins, pp. 432–466.

———— ———— ———— (1986), Conditioning and sensitization in the longitudinal course of affective illness. *Brit. J. Psychiatry*, 149:191–201.

———— Weiss, S. R. B. (1989a), Sensitization, kindling, and anticonvulsants in mania. *J. Clin. Psychiatry*, 50:23–30.

———— ———— (1989b), Non-homologous animal models of affective illness: Clinical relevance of sensitization and kindling. In: *Animal Models of Depression*, ed. G. Koob, C. Ehlers, & D. J. Kupfer. Boston: Birkhauser Boston, pp. 30–54.

———— ———— (1992), Endogenous biochemical abnormalities in affective illness: Therapeutic vs. pathogenic. *Biol. Psychiatry*, 32:469–484.

———— ———— (1994), The neurobiology of treatment-resistant mood disorders. In: *Psychopharmacology: The Fourth Generation of Progress*, ed. F. E. Bloom & D. J. Kupfer. New York: Raven Press, pp. 2–30.

———— ———— Clark, M., Nakajima, T., & Ketter, T. A. (1991), Seizures as an evolving process: Implications for neuropsychiatric illness. In: *Epilepsy and Behavior*, ed. W. H. Theodore & O. Devinsky. New York: Alan R. Liss, pp. 361–387.

———— ———— Nakajima, T., Clark, M., & Pert, A. (1990), Mechanism-based approaches to anticonvulsant therapy. In: *Current and Future Trends in Anticonvulsant, Anxiety and Stroke Therapy*, ed. B. S. Meldrum & M. Williams. New York: Wiley-Liss, pp. 45–90.

———— ———— Pert, A. (1988a), Cocaine-induced behavioral sensitization and kindling: Implications for the emergence of psychopathology and seizures. In: *Mesocorticolimbic Dopamine System*, ed. P. W. Kalivas & C. B. Nemeroff. New York: NY Acad. Sci., pp. 292–308.

———— ———— ———— (1988b), Implications of behavioral sensitization and kindling for stress-induced behavioral change. In: *Mechanisms of Physical and Emotional Stress*, ed. G. P. Chrousos, D. L. Loriaux, & P. W. Gold. New York: Plenum Press, pp. 441–463.

———— ———— ———— (1991), Sensitization and kindling effects of chronic cocaine administration. In: *Cocaine: Pharmacology, Physiology, and Clinical Strategies*, ed. J. M. Lakoski. West Caldwell, NJ: Telford Press, pp. 115–161.

———— ———— Rubinow, D. R. (1988), Recurrent affective disorders: Lessons from limbic kindling. In: *Current Topics in Neuroendocrinology*, ed. D. Ganten & S. Fuxe. New York: Springer-Verlag, pp. 91–115.

———— ———— Smith, M. (in press), Sensitization and kindling: Implications for the evolving substrate of PTSD. In: *Neurobiology and Clinical Consequences of Stress: From Normal Adaptation to PTSD*, ed. M. J. Friedman, D. S. Charney, & A. Y. Deutch. New York: Raven Press.

Prien, R. F., Klett, C. J., & Caffey, E. M., Jr. (1973), Lithium carbonate and imipramine in prevention of affective episodes. A comparison in recurrent affective illness. *Arch. Gen. Psychiatry*, 29:420–425.

———— Kupfer, D. J., Mansky, P. A., Small, J. G., Tuason, V. B., Voss, C. B., & Johnson, W. E. (1984), Drug therapy in the prevention of the recurrences in unipolar and bipolar affective disorders. *Arch. Gen. Psychiatry*, 41:1096–1104.

Racine, R. J. (1978), Kindling: The first decade. *Neurosurgery*, 3:234–252.

———— Moore, K. A., & Wicks, S. (1991), Activation of the NMDA receptor: A correlate in the dentate gyrus field potential and its relationship to long-term potentiation and kindling. *Brain Res.*, 556:226–239.

Robertson, H. A., Peterson, M. R., Murphy, K., & Robertson, G. S. (1989), D1-dopamine receptor agonists selectively activate striatal c-fos independent of rotational behaviour. *Brain Res.*, 503:346–349.

Robinson, D. S., Lerfald, S. C., Bennett, B., Laux, D., Devereaux, E., Kayser, A., Corcella, J., & Albright, D. (1991), Continuation and maintenance treatment of major depression with the monoamine oxidase inhibitor phenelzine: A double-blind placebo-controlled discontinuation study. *Psychopharmacol. Bull.*, 27:31–39.

Robinson, T. E., & Becker, J. B. (1986), Enduring changes in brain and behavior produced by chronic amphetamine administration: A review and evaluation of animal models of amphetamine psychosis. *Brain Res. Rev.*, 11:157–198.

Rose, S. P. R. (1991), How chicks make memories: The cellular cascade from c-fos to dendritic remodeling. *Trends Neurosci.*, 14:390–397.

Rosen, J. B., Abramowitz, J., & Post, R. M. (1993), Co-localization of TRH mRNA and Fos-like immunoreactivity in limbic structures following amygdala-kindled seizure. *Mol. Cell. Neurosci.*, 4:335–342.

———— Cain, C. J., Weiss, S. R. B., & Post, R. M. (1992), Alterations in mRNA of enkephalin, dynorphin and thyrotropin releasing hormone during amygdala kindling: An in situ hybridization study. *Mol. Brain Res.*, 15:247–255.

Rouillon, F., Phillips, R., Serrurier, D., Miller, H. D., & Gerard, M. J. (1991), Prophylactic efficacy of maprotiline on unipolar depression relapse. *J. Clin. Psychiat.*, 52:423–431.

—— Lejoyeux, M., Filteau, M. D. (1992), Unwanted effects of longterm treatment. In: *Long-Term Treatment of Depression*, ed. S. A. Montgomery & F. Rouillon. New York: John Wiley & Sons, pp 81–111.

Rubinow, D. R., Davis, C. L., & Post, R. M. (1991), Somatostatin. In: *Neuropeptides and Psychiatric Disorders*, ed. C. B. Nemeroff. Washington, DC: American Psychiatric Press, pp. 30–49.

Rush, A. J., Erman, M. K., Giles, D. E., Schlesser, M. A., Carpenter, G., Vasavada, N., & Roffwang, H. P. (1986), Polysomnographic findings in recently drug-free and clinically remitted depressed patients. *Arch. Gen. Psychiatry*, 43:878–884.

Sagar, S. M., Sharp, F. R., & Curran, T. (1988), Expression of c-fos protein in brain: Metabolic mapping at the cellular level. *Science*, 240:1328–1331.

Sapolsky, R. M., & Pulsinelli, W. A. (1985), Glucocorticoids potentiate ischemic injury to neurons: Therapeutic implications. *Science*, 229:1397–1400.

Schou, M. (1973), Prophylactic lithium maintenance treatment in recurrent endogenous affective disorders. In: *Lithium: Its Role in Psychiatric Research and Treatment*, ed. S. Gershon & B. Shopsin. New York: Plenum, pp. 269–295.

—— (1979), Lithium as a prophylactic agent in unipolar affective illness. *Arch. Gen. Psychiatry*, 36:849–851.

Sharp, F. R., Gonzalez, M. F., Sharp, J. W., & Sagar, S. M. (1989), c-Fos expression and (^{14}C) 2-deoxyglucose uptake in the caudal cerebellum of the rat during motor/sensory cortex stimulation. *J. Comp. Neurol.*, 284:621–636.

Shinoda, H., Schwartz, J. P., & Nadi, N. S. (1989), Amygdaloid kindling of rats increases preprosomatostatin mRNA and somatostatin without affecting glutamic acid decarboxylase (GAD) mRNA or GAD. *Mol. Brain Res.*, 5:243–246.

Smith, M. A., Banerjee, S., Gold, P. W., & Glowa, J. (1992), Induction of c-fos mRNA in rat brain by conditioned and unconditioned stressors. *Brain Res.*, 578:135–141.

—— Makino, S., Kvetnansky, P., Post, R. M. (1993) abstract, Stress alters brain derived neurotrophic factor and neurotrophin-3m RNA levels in the hippocampus. *Society for Neuroscience Abstracts*, 19:866.

—— Weiss, S. R. B., Abedin, T., Post, R. M., & Gold, P. (1991), Effects of amygdala-kindling and electroconvulsive seizures on the expression of corticotropin releasing hormone (CRH) mRNA in the rat brain. *Mol. Cell. Neurosci.*, 2:103–116.

Sonnenberg, J. L., Mitchelmore, C., MacGregor-Leon, P. F., Hempstead, J., Morgan, J. F., & Curran, T. (1989), Glutamate receptor agonists increase the expression of Fos, Fra, and AP-1 DNA binding activity in the mammalian brain. *J. Neurosci. Res.*, 24:72–80.

—— Rauscher, F. J., III, Morgan, J. I., & Curran, T. (1989), Regulation of proenkephalin by Fos and Jun. *Science*, 246:1622–1625.

Sorg, B. A., & Kalivas, P. W. (1991), Effects of cocaine and footshock stress on extracellular dopamine levels in the ventral striatum. *Brain Res.*, 559:29–36.

Souza, F. G., Mander, A. J., & Goodwin, G. M. (1990), The efficacy of lithium in prophylaxis of unipolar depression. Evidence from its discontinuation. *Brit. J. Psychiatry*, 157:718–722.

Squire, L. R., & Zola-Morgan, S. (1991), The medial temporal lobe memory system. *Science*, 253:1380–1386.

Steiger, A., von Bardeleben, U., Herth, T., & Holsboer, F. (1989), Sleep EEG and nocturnal secretion of cortisol and growth hormone in male patients with endogenous depression before treatment and after recovery. *J. Affective Disord.*, 16:189–195.

Stern, E. S. (1944), The psychopathology of manic depressive disorder and involutional melancholia. *Brit. J. Med. Psychol.*, 20:20–32.

Suppes, T., Baldessarini, R. J., Faedda, G. L., & Tohen, M. (1991), Risk of recurrence following discontinuation of lithium treatment in bipolar disorder. *Arch. Gen. Psychiatry*, 48:1082–1088.

Sutula, T., Xiao-Xian, H., Cavazos, J., & Scott, G. (1988), Synaptic reorganization in the hippocampus induced by abnormal functional activity. *Science*, 239:1147–1150.

Swann, A. C., Secunda, S. K., Stokes, P. E., Croughan, J., Davis, J. M., Koslow, S. H., & Maas, J. W. (1990), Stress, depression, and mania: Relationship between perceived role of stressful events and clinical and biochemical characteristics. *Acta Psychiat. Scand.*, 81:389–397.

Takahashi, T., Nau, M. M., Chiba, I., Birrer, M. J., Rosenberg, R. K., Vinocour, M., Levitt, M., Pass, H., Gazdan, A. F., & Minna, I. J. (1989), p53, A frequent target for genetic abnormalities in lung cancer. *Science*, 246:491–494.

Vestergaard, P. (1991), Treatment of mania. *ACNP Abstracts 1991*.

Vinson, C. R., Sigler, P. B., & McKnight, S. L. (1989), Scissors-grip model for DNA recognition by a family of leucine zipper proteins. *Science*, 246:911–916.

Wada, J. A., Sato, M., & Corcoran, M. E. (1974), Persistent seizure susceptibility and recurrent spontaneous seizures in kindled cats. *Epilepsia*, 15:465–478.

Weinberg, R. A. (1991), A short guide to oncogenes and tumor-suppressor genes. *J.N.I.H. Res.*, 3:45–48.

Weiss, S. R. B., Post, R. M., Pert, A., Woodward, R., & Murman, D. (1989), Context-dependent cocaine sensitization: Differential effect of haloperidol on development versus expression. *Pharmacol. Biochem. Behav.*, 34:655–661.

Weitbrecht, H. J. (1960), Depressive und manische endogene psychosen. In: *Psychiatrie der Gegenwart*, Vol. 2. Berlin: Springer-Verlag.

White, F. J., Henry, D. J., Hu, X.-T., Jeziarski, M., & Ackerman, J. M. (1992), Electrophysiological effects of cocaine in the mesoaccumbens dopamine system. In: *Cocaine: Pharmacology, Physiology and Clinical Strategies*, ed. J. M. Lakoski, M. P. Galloway, & F. J. White. West Caldwell, NJ: Telford Press, pp. 261–293.

Worley, P. F., Baraban, J. M., & Snyder, S. H. (1987), Beyond receptors: Multiple second-messenger systems in brain. *Ann. Neurol.*, 21:217–229.

Yang-Yen, H. F., Chambard, J. C., Sun, Y. L., Smeal, T., Schmidt, T. J., Drovin, J., & Karin, M. (1990), Transcriptional interference between c-Jun and the glucocorticoid receptor: Mutual inhibition of DNA binding due to direct protein-protein interaction. *Cell*, 62:1205–1215.

Yoshida, K., Tsujino, T., Yasui, W., Kameda, T., Sano, T., Nakayama, H., Toge, T., & Tahara, E. (1990), Induction of growth factor-receptor and metallo-proteinase genes by epidermal growth factor and / or transforming growth factor-alpha in human gastric carcinoma cell line MKN-28. *Jpn. J. Cancer Res.*, 81:793–798.

Young, S. T., Porrino, L. J., & Iadarola, M. J. (1991), Cocaine induces striatal c-fos immunoreactive proteins via dopaminergic D1 receptors. *Proc. Nat. Acad. Sci., U.S.A.*, 88:1291–1295.

Chapter 3
Theoretical Models of Stress Adaptation

THOMAS W. MILLER, Ph.D., A.B.P.P., AND
ROBERT F. KRAUS, M.D.

There is a rapidly evolving science that is examining the multidirectional influence of life stress events and its impact on human functioning (Miller and Basoglu, 1992). Clinical models have been realized in several areas to assist in understanding the process of experiencing stressful life events and the subsequent accommodation of the stress. These areas include personality, immunology, neurology, biochemistry, and pathophysiology.

Concepts such as psychological hardiness, which explores the possible role of personality variables in moderating the relationship between stressful life experiences and psychological and physical well-being, have been explored, as has the role of cognition and the interaction with the hypothalamic–pituitary–adrenal axis.

PSYCHOLOGICAL MODELS

The impact of stressful life events on health has been the focus of considerable theory and research, stimulated, of course, by the

Acknowledgments. The authors wish to acknowledge the assistance of Tag Heister, Deborah Kessler, and Katrina Scott, Library Services; and Virginia Lynn Morehouse and Robin

development of the social readjustment rating scale (Holmes and Rahe, 1967) and subsequent use of that scale in the study of stressful life events. Horowitz (1976) built upon Freudian concepts as to the role and function of signal anxiety and defense and viewed anxiety as a motivating factor in the regulation of mental content entering consciousness. The application of such insights into the role of signal anxiety and defense resulted in the appraisal of emotional arousal and coping by such specialists as Lazarus (1964) and Janis (1967). Emotions were characterized as capable of influencing cognitive controls and perceived to affect subsequent cognitive processes resulting in various psychopathological states.

The general adaptation syndrome suggested by Hans Selye (1936) generated one of the initial efforts to map the processing of stressful life experiences by human beings based initially on animal research. It suggested that the organism being exposed to a noxious agent capable of eliciting a reaction led to a stage of alarm, the state of alarm not being maintained on a continuous basis.

The initial reaction leads to a stage of resistance, the manifestations of which provide the organism with the ability to cope with the particular stressful event. Concentrated exposure and a state of resistance can be maintained for a limited period of time based on the psychophysiology of the individual. After that period of time the acquired adaptation is lost and a third stage emerges. This latter is a stage of exhaustion which results in a failure of the organism to maintain a level of resistance and ability to cope with the stressor itself. A linkage has been realized between nonspecific stress and numerous biochemical and structural changes in human beings.

Psychological hardiness as a construct of personality has gained considerable attention as a moderating variable in the relationship between stress and psychological or physical illness. More specifically, Kobasa (1979) focused on personality characteristics

Lynn Oakley, Department of Psychiatry, University of Kentucky, for their contributions to the completion of this manuscript.

which potentially differentiate people who deteriorate physically or psychologically under stress from those who seem to be able to tolerate high levels of stress without decompensating. The variable of interest is psychological hardiness, which serves as a stress buffer and is defined within the constructs of control, commitment, and challenge. The initial attempt to assess psychological hardiness was based on a study of male executives. Based on retrospective measures of stress and illness, Kobasa (1979) compared a group of high stress/high illness executives to a group of high stress/low illness or stress-resistant executives. The statistical analysis and review yielded six scales significantly different for the groups, including commitment, control, and challenge. While research investigating psychological hardiness has been plagued by serious problems in measurement, recent reviews of the construct have concluded that although the measurement of hardiness presents several methodological difficulties, the concept itself must be given serious consideration in the growing knowledge of stress coping styles and the accommodation of stressful life events within the personality of highly stressed individuals. Younkin and Betz (chapter 6) have rethought the concept of hardiness and have generated an operationally defined definition.

Efforts by several research clinicians have led to more recent psychological hypotheses applicable to the processing of stressful life events. Among these is the trauma accommodation syndrome identified by Miller and Veltkamp (1988). This syndrome suggests that individuals who experience trauma such as war, natural disasters, or domestic violence may experience the processing of these stressors in a series of stages or phases that deal with the trauma. The initial stage is often that of a stressor itself when it usually is realized as an acute psychological trauma outside the range of normal human experience. The psychological response of the person is usually one of feeling overwhelmed and intimidated by the experience. The locus of control is more external in nature. It is not uncommon for the individual experiencing such trauma to think recurrently of the stressful experience and to focus on various aspects including vulnerability, survival, and the many losses that may have been experienced both personally and materially through the stressful life experience.

Following the acute phase of traumatization, comes a phase during which the person realizes that the physical impact has made itself known. This may include the spectrum of both physical and psychological sequelae.

Considered as well are the psychological components of loss or adjustment that must be realized by the individual in dealing with the stressful life experience. This stage is often followed by a stage of cognitive disorganization and confusion, during which denial and avoidance may manifest themselves, and where a period of grieving may be experienced. In this stage, avoidance may show itself by conscious inhibition. An effort is made on the part of the survivor to actually inhibit thoughts and feelings related to the trauma. Denial, withdrawal, and isolation are not uncommon in this stage, even though there may be the appearance of an outward adjustment. There may also be an unconscious denial wherein the victim is not aware of the efforts to avoid the psychological trauma associated with both the physical and psychological factors. The conscious inhibition phase can be revisited by exploring earlier memories through flashbacks and cognitive preoccupation. The unconscious denial usually ignores any reconsideration of the trauma itself. Where the denial is unconscious there is a tendency to show little or no allowance for revisitation to the stressor or to the previous stages of processing the trauma.

The next stage in a cognitive processing model is usually precipitated by triggering life experiences that lead to a recognition, perhaps a reevaluation, reflection, and realization of the impact of the stressor on the victim. There is often some effort toward reasoning through and reconsideration, because of factors that bring to light thoughts of the original stressor and find the victim now willing to reconsider the traumatization itself. The reasoning and reevaluation of the psychological and physical traumatization allow for reexamination of important informational aspects of the stress as well as the revisitation of previous stages realized in trauma accommodation.

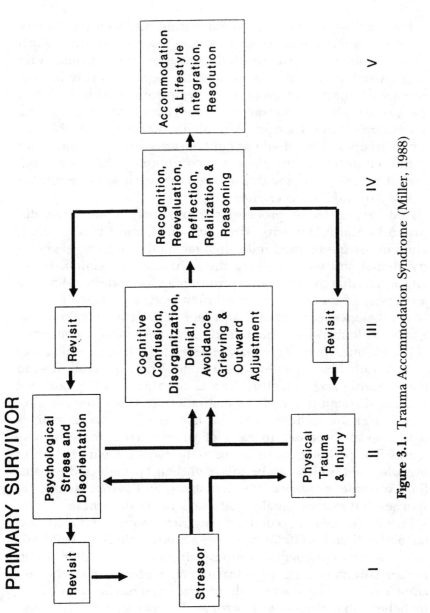

Figure 3.1. Trauma Accommodation Syndrome (Miller, 1988)

The last stage in trauma accommodation syndrome is a stage of accommodation, life-style integration, or resolution during which there may be emotional growth. In this stage, the individual who has survived the trauma may be able through supportive psycho-therapy or some other medium to begin to deal with the issues that relate to the traumatization. The survivor furthermore is able to develop coping strategies. This ability may now allow this person to accept without doubt or guilt or other associated outcomes of the trauma either the ability to accommodate the trauma as a part of his or her personality makeup, or reach some resolution of this stressful life experience.

Another model of processing traumatization has been discussed by Mardi Horowitz (Horowitz, Field, and Classen, 1993), wherein the traumatized individual moves through stages of outcry, denial, intrusion, working through, and completion. Horowitz argues that these stages provide a map for understanding the processing of trauma. The event often leads to a stage of outcry which includes fear, sadness, and rage. This stage is followed by a stage of denial where the individual refuses to face the memory of the trauma. Next, there may be a stage of intrusion which may include unbidden thoughts of the event. Those generally lead to the following stage which is seen as the therapeutic phase and working through phase of traumatization. In this phase the individual faces the reality of what has happened. Horowitz outlines pathological responses to each of these normal response segments. The pathological response to the event is feelings of being overwhelmed, which can be followed then by panic and exhaustion, extreme avoidance, flooded states, and psychosomatic responses that may eventually lead to character distortions.

Within the area of accommodating victimization and child sexual abuse, Summit (1983) proposes a model called the child sexual abuse accommodation syndrome. In this model, children who are sexually abused are often fearful and confused about the outcome of disclosure in sexual abuse. The child has been socialized to believe that this topic is wrong. The perpetrator has often convinced them that they will be rejected or suffer dreadful and perhaps life-threatening consequences if they disclose the abuse, and parents and significant others may send the child the message that they are not readily believed. In response, children often delay disclosure for extended periods despite the ongoing threat and harm they are suffering. If disclosure is met with resistance or disbelief, children may retract their allegation rather than suffer the rejection of significant others.

Summit (1983) identified five phases of the child sexual abuse accommodation syndrome to include: secrecy, helplessness, accommodation, delayed disclosure, and retraction. It is in the accommodation phase where children may suffer dissociative experiences as a result of child sexual abuse and repress recent and remote memories of the abuse itself. These accommodations are often reinforced if the child's eventual disclosure is met with disbelief, rejection, increased abuse, or threats of violence by the perpetrator. This type of accommodation creates its own syndrome of psychopathological development wherein the trauma is accommodated through a distorted cognition and maladaptive emotional functioning which evolves from the victim's experience of the severe and persistent child sexual abuse.

BIOCHEMICAL MODELS

Biochemically, stressful life events may activate the central noradrenergic neurons to release norepinephrine in the effector regions. These regions usually include the amygdala, the hippocampus, and the cerebral cortex. This activation contributes to the affective, behavioral, and cognitive effects associated with acute stress response. Furthermore, norepinephrine binds to the presynaptic alpha adrenergic receptors as a part of the feedback inhibition of the noradrenergic neurons, resulting in the termination of the noradrenergic stress response. Following stressful life experiences, decreased alpha receptor functions impair feedback inhibition and increase sensitivity to yohimbine. Effects such as these are associated with a change of events that include increased locus ceruleus reactivity, altered function in several brain region areas, including the limbic system and cortex, and the expression or exacerbation of symptoms and sequelae of posttraumatic stress disorder (PTSD).

The question of the nature of the trauma and the victim's cognitive appraisal in determining the clinical outcome has led to physiological hypotheses and biologically based theory that address the role of the sympathetic nervous system and its relationship to hyperarousal. The dysfunction of the locus ceruleus and the serotonergic mechanisms as playing a key role in the symptomatology is consistent with traumatization and stress. Kolb (1987) has advanced a theory based on neuropsychological functioning in which lower brain stem structures such as the medial hypothalamus and locus ceruleus escape from the normal inhibitory cortical control. The lower brain centers, therefore, repeatedly reactivate the perceptual, cognitive, and emotional components of traumatization. Thus the experience is linked with the notion of neuronal "kindling" in which repetitively stimulated neurons eventually fire spontaneously, which accounts for various symptoms experienced by traumatization victims, including the flashback experience.

Others, including van der Kolk (1987), have suggested that some trauma victims may actually become addicted to the traumatization they experience. This condition is mediated by endogenous opioids resulting in a surge of such opioids during the traumatization process and resulting in the symptomatology complex we have come to know as posttraumatic stress disorder. Van der Kolk and others (van der Kolk, Greenburg, Boyd, and Krystal, 1985) note that after the trauma these endogenous opioids may diminish, sending the individual into a state of endogenous opioid withdrawal. With the reexposure to some triggering life event, the individual may once again experience the initial opioid-driven acceleration, again resulting in the traumatization syndrome. The use of psychophysiological assessment may well be at the cutting edge of understanding the role of sympathetic hyperarousal as one component of traumatization and stress.

Friedman (1981) has been a strong advocate of recognizing the

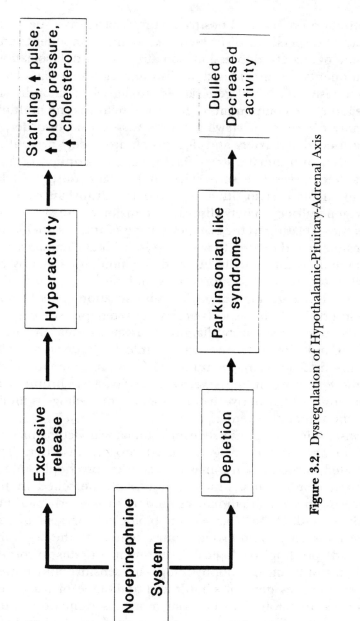

Figure 3.2. Dysregulation of Hypothalamic-Pituitary-Adrenal Axis

traumatization process and posttraumatic disorder as a spectrum disorder. The spectrum disorder looks at the components and processing of anxiety, depression, somatization, and dissociation. Its components can include panic disorder, agoraphobia, obsessive–compulsive disorder, generalized anxiety, hypochondriasis, somatization, and components of hysterical neurosis and multiple personality disorder. In viewing this as a spectrum disorder, it is recognized that anxiety and depression are widely present in individuals with traumatic stress. The precise description is most important for several reasons. The etiology and onset may be discernible from certain other psychological disturbances, most notably generalized anxiety disorder or major depressive disorder. Features relating to the reexperiencing of trauma, including the assessment and degree to which an individual ruminates and the ruminations affect daily life and functioning, is clearly an important feature. Furthermore, the numbing of responsiveness is assessed as a core ingredient in traumatization. This feature may be intertwined with aspects of anxiety and depressive components and is most similarly diagnosed as anhedonia and withdrawal found in patients with clinical depression. The distinguishing features in the numbing found in traumatic stress relate more to unremitting severity, intensity, and chronicity of the symptoms which derive from situations or feelings reminiscent of the traumatic event.

Likewise, startle response seen in traumatized victims may be similar to that found in generalized anxiety disorder. The exaggerated startle response may reflect a few psychophysiological arousal components, which is noticeably worsened in the presence of specific situational reminders in triggering events.

Friedman (1991) has focused on biological markers of psychological disorders, and brought our attention to the psychobiology and psychophysiological assessment of this disorder. Techniques utilizing psychophysiology are sensitive and powerful when one uses general stimuli and audiotape of triggering experiences. It is found to be even more discriminatory when provocative stimuli are used in individualized autobiographical traumatic anecdotes (Pitman, 1988). Blanchard (1990) and

Malloy, Fairbank, and Keane (1983) found that reactivity predicts the presence of the PTSD diagnosis while using auditory and audiovisual cues.

Finally, Friedman (1991) argues that the dexamethasone suppression test (DST) has been recognized for its use in diagnosing major depressive disorders and has applicability in the diagnosis of traumatic stress. Patients with traumatic stress disorder tend to have normal DSTs and could therefore be classified a suppressors, whereas patients with traumatic stress disorder and major depressive disorder may well be seen as nonsuppressors. Sodium lactate or yohimbine infusion and sodium amytal interviews have been suggested as helpful in the diagnosing of traumatic stress in patients.

THE PSYCHONEUROIMMUNOLOGY MODEL

The relationship between immune function and psychological states is gaining considerable attention as we move toward a better understanding of the role and function of various body systems in accommodating stress and traumatization. Stressful life events can alter a wide range of immunological activities. Psychoneuroimmunology is quickly evolving as a science that examines the multidirectional influence of psychological states on immune function as moderated by both the nervous system and the endocrine system. The role of the hypothalamic–pituitary–adrenal axis is seen as an essential component to understanding this model. A stressful psychological event stimulates the adrenal cortical output of glucocorticoids which results in immunosuppression. The recognition that the hypothalamic–pituitary–adrenal (HPA) axis plays a key role in stress response has led to subsequent study of several distinct roles played by the HPA components. Corticotropin-releasing factor (CRF) has been recognized as playing a key role in modulating roles in the brain, where it activates structures associated with the generation of fear states. Symptoms associated with traumatization such as anxiety, startle response, hypervigilance, and avoidance of traumatization triggers, seem to directly or indirectly reflect a long-lasting problem of modulating alarm and arousal.

Since many victims of traumatization manifest these hyperarousal signs, it is hypothesized that trauma produces long-lasting hyperactivity in brain alarm systems. Uncontrollable stress appears to be a useful model in realizing that conditioned alarm states and learned helplessness follow uncontrolled stress and can be long-lasting in nature. Researchers such as Irwin, Daniels, Bloom, Smith, and Weiner (1987) and Kiecolt-Glaser (Kiecolt-Glaser, Garner, Spelcher, Penn, and Glaser, 1984) have studied NK cell activity in three groups of subjects. The findings show decreased NK cell activity when compared with normal control subjects. Plasma cortisol levels, elevations of which have been associated with immunosuppression, are elevated in the group of traumatization victims. Researchers such as these have concluded that traumatization was capable of reducing NK cell activity, and this may result, in part, in the group of symptoms we have come to know as associated with traumatization and stress.

Similarly, stress-induced activation of central noradrenergic neurons releases norepinephrine in effector regions such as the amygdala, hippocampus, and cerebral cortex to contribute to the cognitive, affective, and behavioral effects associated with traumatization. In addition, norepinephrine binds to the presynaptic alpha adrenergic receptors as part of the feedback inhibition of noradrenergic neurons, resulting in the termination of the noradrenergic stress response. Friedman has suggested that current findings in the biological research suggest that patients who have experienced traumatization and show a resultant symptom cluster consistent with posttraumatic stress disorder display marked abnormalities in sympathetic nervous system arousal and hypothalamic–pituitary–adrenocortical function and in the endogenous opioid system.

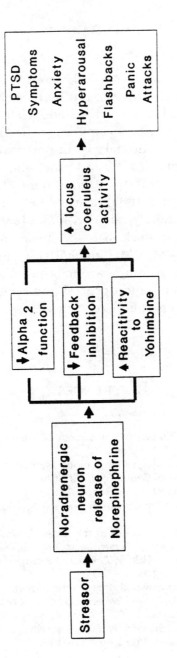

Figure 3.3. Stress Related Biochemically Based Theory

SUMMARY

There exists within our framework several models that have emerged and have applicability to our understanding of traumatization and the processing of traumatization. These have included the groundbreaking work of Hans Selye, which implicated the hypothalamic–pituitary–adrenal axis in understanding aspects of stress response to signal anxiety and processing stress (Horowitz, 1976; Horowitz et al., 1993), to the conditioned fear (Kolb, 1987), two-factor theory (Keane, 1985), learned helplessness (Seligman, 1975), inescapable shock (van der Kolk, 1989), and kindling (Friedman, 1991). The work of Irwin (Irwin and Livnat, 1987), Kiecolt-Glaser et al. (1984), McDaniel (1994), and others has generated for us realistic hypotheses which should aid in our understanding of the traumatization process and serve as the stepping stones to the next generation of clinical research activities on traumatization.

REFERENCES

Blanchard, E. B. (1990), Biofeedback treatment of essential hypertension. *Biofeedback & Self-Reg.*, 15:209–228.
Friedman, M. (1991), Neurological alterations associated with post-traumatic stress disorder. National Center for PTSD, Clinical Laboratory and Education Diversion, Teleconference Report, July.
Friedman, M. J. (1981), Post-Vietnam syndrome: Recognition and management. *Psychosomatics*, 22:931–943.
——— (1991), Biological approaches to the diagnosis and treatment of post-traumatic stress disorder. *J. Traum. Stress*, 4:67–91.
Holmes, T. H., & Rahe, R. H. (1967), The Social Readjustment Rating Scale. *J. Psychosom. Res.*, 11:213–218.
Horowitz, M. J. (1976), Intrusive and repetitive thoughts after experimental stress: A summary. *Arch. Gen. Psychiatry*, 32:1457–1463.
——— Field, N. P., & Classen, C. C. (1993), Stress response syndromes and their treatment. In: *Handbook of Stress*, 2nd ed. ed. L. Goldberger & S. Breznitz. New York: Free Press, pp. 757–774.

Irwin, J., & Livnat, S. (1967), Behavioral influences on the immune system: Stress and conditioning. *Prog. Neuropsychopharmacol. & Biolog. Psychiatry*, 11:137–143, 1987.

Irwin, M., Daniels, M., Bloom, E., Smith, T. L., & Weiner, H. (1987), Life events, depressive symptoms, and immune function. *Amer. J. Psychiatry*, 144:437–441.

Janis, I. L. (1967), Effects of fear arousal on attitude change: Recent development in theory and experimental research. In: *Advances in Experimental and Social Psychology*, Vol. 3, ed. L. Berkowitz. New York: Academic Press, 1967, pp. 87–96.

Kiecolt-Glaser, J. K., Garner, W., Spelcher, C., Penn, G., & Glaser, R. (1984), Psychosocial modifiers of immunocompetence in medical students. *Psychosom. Med.*, 46:7–14.

Kobasa, S. C. (1979), Stressful life events, personality, and health: An inquiry into hardiness. *J. Personal. & Soc. Psychol.*, 37:1–11.

Kolb, L. C. (1987), A neuropsychological hypothesis explaining post-traumatic stress disorders. *Amer. J. Psychiatry*, 144:989–995.

Lazarus, R. S. (1964), A laboratory approach to the dynamics of psychological stress. *Amer. Psychologist*, 19:400–411.

Malloy, P. F., Fairbank, J. A., & Keane, T. M. (1983), Validation of a multimethod assessment of posttraumatic stress disorders in Vietnam veterans. *J. Consult. Clin. Psychol.*, 51:488–494.

McDaniel, J. S. (1994), Stressful life events and psychoneuro-immunology. In: *Stressful Life Events*, ed. T. W. Miller. Madison, CT: International Universities Press, Inc.

Miller, T. W., & Basoglu, M. (1992), Post-traumatic stress disorder: The impact of life stress events on adjustment. *Integrat. Psychiatry*, 47:209–217.

——— Veltkamp, L. J. (1988), The abusing family in rural America. *Internat. J. Fam. Psychiatry*, 9:259–275.

——— ——— (1993), Family violence: Clinical indicators in military and post-military personnel. *Military Med.*, 86:384–395.

Pitman, R. K. (1988), Post-traumatic stress disorder, conditioning, and network theory. *Psychiatric Ann.*, 18:182–189.

Seligman, M. E. P. (1975), *Helplessness: On Depression, Development and Death*. San Francisco: Freeman.

Selye, H. (1936), A syndrome produced by diverse nocuous agents. *Nature*, 138:32.

——— Ed. (1980), *Selye's Guide to Stress Research*, Vol. 1. New York: Van Nostrand.

Summit, R. (1983), The child abuse accommodation syndrome. *Child Abuse & Neglect*, 7:177–193.

van der Kolk, B. A. (1987), The drug treatment of post-traumatic stress disorder. *J. Affect. Disord.*, 13:203–213.

——— Greenberg, M., Boyd, H., & Krystal, J. (1985), Inescapable shock, neurotransmitters, and addiction to trauma: Toward a psychobiology of post-traumatic stress. *Biolog. Psychiatry*, 20:314–325.

——— Pitman, R. K., Orr, S. P., & Greenburg, M. S. (1989), Endogenous opioids, stress induced analgesia, and post-traumatic stress disorder. *Psychopharmacol. Bull.*, 25:108–112.

Chapter 4
Stress, Health, and Immunity:
A Review of the Literature

CHRISTINE M. ADLER, Ph.D., AND JOEL J. HILLHOUSE, Ph.D.

Despite the fact that Western medicine has overwhelmingly subscribed to the notion of mind–body dualism, theories proposing a relationship between emotional and physical states have maintained a long and colorful history. While the latter has long been the basis for cultural beliefs and clinical lore, it is only recently that scientific knowledge and methodological skills have achieved a level of sophistication necessary to put these ideas to empirical test.

This field of study, which has emerged in the last 20 years, is generally referred to as psychoneuroimmunology (PNI), a term which reflects its multidisciplinary character. Integrating the areas of psychology, neuroscience, immunology, and endocrinology, PNI traces its empirical roots to Ader and Cohen's (1975) landmark work which demonstrated the classical conditioning of immunosuppression in rats. In the years which have followed, the field has experienced explosive growth, which has resulted in a wealth of information. In this chapter, we will attempt to review the major areas of human work in PNI, highlighting impact of stressors (acute vs. chronic), psychological variables (depression, social support), stress and illness (cancer, AIDS, infectious diseases), and psychological interventions. Lastly, we will address the growing area of employment stress, with particular focus on health professionals.

REVIEW OF THE IMMUNE SYSTEM

In brief, the human immune system performs a surveillance function, identifying and defending against pathogenic agents. These protective services are attributed to the lymphocytes because they possess an inherent capacity to distinguish self from nonself. The two primary types of immunological reaction are: (1) humoral or immunoglobulin-mediated and (2) cell-mediated. B-lymphocytes mature in the bone marrow, and are responsible for the rapid, antibody mediated responses that characterize humoral immunity. These antibodies circulate systemically throughout the plasma and external bodily secretions, identifying and destroying antigens. In contrast, in cell-mediated immunity, there is no production of antibodies. Rather, specialized T lymphocytes perform several critical tasks. Natural killer (NK) cells bind to and destroy target cells (such as cancer or virally infected cells) directly. Helper T lymphocytes produce a battery of chemical messengers (lymphokines) which act to augment both cellular and humoral responses. Lastly, suppressor T cells regulate immune responses through a process of negative feedback. T lymphocytes are produced in the thymus, and function primarily within the lymph and circulatory systems. An excellent and much more detailed overview of this area can be found in Borysenko (1987).

ACUTE AND CHRONIC STRESSORS

ACUTE OR COMMONPLACE STRESSORS

A relatively large body of literature has resulted from studies of the effects of more commonplace or "acute" stressors on immune system function. While the empirical study of these stressors presents some methodological advantage, there is evidence that such everyday hassles may also be better predictors of health and psychological dysfunction (Lazarus and Folkman, 1984). A popular paradigm for studying the immunological effects of acute stressors has involved student populations and academic exams.

Dorian and colleagues (Dorian, Keystone, Garfinkel, and Brown, 1982) explored the impact of oral examination on psychiatry residents compared to age- and sex-matched physician controls. Preexam results for these residents indicated higher levels of emotional distress, a reduction in mitogen-induced lymphocyte proliferation, and slightly higher numbers of T and B lymphocytes when compared to either controls or their own postexam values. Similar preexam results were obtained by Halvorsen and Vassend (1987) using undergraduate students.

Kiecolt-Glaser, Glaser, and colleagues have conducted an impressive series of studies utilizing this paradigm with first- and second-year medical students. Results have indicated that exam stress may be associated with declines in natural killer cell activity (NKA) (Kiecolt-Glaser, Garner, Speicher, Penn, and Glaser, 1984), a poorer proliferative response to mitogens (Glaser, Kiecolt-Glaser, Stout, Tarr, Speicher, and Holliday, 1985), and decreased gamma interferon production by lymphocytes (Glaser, Rice, Speicher, Stout, and Kiecolt-Glaser, 1986; Glaser, Rice, Sheridan, Fertel, Stout, Speicher, Pinsky, Kotur, Post, Beck, and Kiecolt-Glaser, 1987). These changes are thought to reflect alterations in cellular antiviral and antitumor activity. Alterations in the cellular immune response are thought to indicate poorer cellular immune system control over virus latency (Henle and Henle, 1982). Lastly, Glaser and colleagues (1987) also found that among medical students, more self-reported illnesses were associated with exam periods than with baseline.

Another approach in the study of acute stressors has involved the correlation of immunological change with naturally occurring life events. In an early report, Locke and colleagues (Locke, Hurst, Heisel, Kraus, and Williams, 1979) found that the lowest rates of NKA were associated with subjects experiencing high rates of both symptoms and life change stress. These authors hypothesized an association between coping ability and immune function, as numerous life changes alone were not associated with altered NKA. Support for the moderating effects of coping ability was obtained in a follow-up study of 117 subjects reporting variable amounts of life change stress. Results indicated that NKA was significantly reduced in subjects obtaining high depression scores, but not in those individuals with high overall life-change scores and low depression (Locke, Kraus, Leserman, Hurst, Heisel, and Williams, 1984). A recent study which examined the relationship between life events, stress, psychological coping, and immune function in 39 older adults obtained a similar pattern of results. While life events were positively correlated with self-reported physical symptoms, concomitant stress was unrelated to NKA (Mishra, Aldwin, Colby, and Oseas, 1991). These results should be interpreted with some caution as the relationship between negative affect and NKA was not reported, and there were restrictions on sample size and selection.

Although infrequent in the literature, several studies have utilized experimentally manipulated stressors to examine the effects of acute stress on immune function. Palmblad and colleagues (Palmblad, Cantell, Strander, Froberg, Karlson, Levi, Gronstrom, and Unger, 1976; Palmblad, Petrini, Wasserman, and Akerstedt, 1979) found that episodes of sleep deprivation of either 48 or 77 hours were associated with decreased phagocytic activity, and reduced lymphocyte response to stimulation by phytohemagglutinin (PHA). Utilizing a variation of the Stroops color–word conflict test, Landmann and colleagues found that this brief mental stress test could produce elevations of cortisol, and numbers of lymphocytes and circulating monocytes in a group of 15 normal individuals (Landmann, Muller, Perini, Wesp, Erne, and Buhler, 1984).

In summary, it appears that acute stressors are capable of producing transient immunological alterations, with increased NK cell numbers and reduced mitogen response being the most consistent changes noted. In a recent review, Kiecolt-Glaser, Cacioppo, Malarkey, and Glaser (1992) underscore the role of individual variability, as well as the duration and intensity of psychological stressors in determining the magnitude and breadth of immune change. The authors suggest that improved under-standing of individual differences in response to acute stressors may help identify those potentially at-risk for long-term health consequences.

CHRONIC STRESSORS

A number of studies have examined the effects of chronic stres-sors on immune function in humans. Among the diverse stressors studied are divorce-separation, caregiving for Alzheimer's disease (AD) patients, and living in close proximity to the Three Mile Island nuclear power plant. Long-term unemployment and occu-pational stress have also been considered to fall into this category, but will be separately addressed in a later section.

Divorce and separation may be conceptualized as chronic stres-sors since adjustment appears to occur over a period of several years (Weiss, 1975). An initial study by Kiecolt-Glaser and associ-ates (Kiecolt-Glaser, Fisher, Ogrocki, Stout, Speicher, and Glaser, 1987) found that recently separated–divorced women evidenced higher Epstein-Barr Virus (EBV) antibody titres, reduced respon-siveness to PHA, and significantly lower percentages of NK cells when compared to a well-matched group of married women. In-terestingly, "attachment" to the former spouse was negatively as-sociated with immune function. In a follow-up study which examined the effects of marital discord on males, some similar results emerged, as well as some new findings (Kiecolt-Glaser, Kennedy, Malkoff, Fisher, Speicher, and Glaser, 1988). The separ-ated–divorced men appeared more psychologically distressed, lonelier, and reported more recent illnesses than their matched, married controls. In addition, these men also demonstrated poorer immune function, as reflected in elevated EBV and Her-pes Simplex Virus type 1 (HSV-1) titres, and altered T helper to suppressor cell ratios. Separated–divorced men who had both initiated the separation, and were separated within the last year appeared less distressed, and reported better health than the non-initiators. This last finding may provide some support for the role of active, effective coping in modifying immunological status, and is consistent with the results of Locke and colleagues discussed previously.

Another potentially long-term stressor is that of caring for an individual with AD. Kiecolt-Glaser and colleagues (Kiecolt-Glaser, Glaser, Shuttleworth, Dyer, Ogrocki, and Speicher, 1987) found that when compared to sociodemographically matched control subjects, caregivers demonstrated significantly greater emotional distress and poorer immune functioning, as evidenced by higher EBV titres and reduced percentages of total T lymphocytes and T helper cells. Additional work by these authors provides evidence that the immune system may fail to adapt to long-term stressors, as AD caregivers evidenced down-regulations on three measures of cellular immunity when compared to controls at a 13-month follow-up assessment (Kiecolt-Glaser, Dura, Speicher, Trask, and Glaser, 1991). Consistent with this finding, caregivers also reported significantly more days of infectious illness.

The impact of living in a community which poses ongoing threats to one's well-being has also received attention as a chronic or long-term stressor. Schaeffer, McKinnon, Baum, Reynolds, Rikli, Davidson, and Fleming (1985) found that individuals living near the Three-Mile Island (TMI) nuclear power plant had fewer T lymphocytes, T helper, and T suppressor cells than did demographically matched control subjects living in another area. Further studies indicated fewer NK cells, and higher antibody titres of HSV and Cytomegalovirus (CMV) in TMI residents (McKinnon, Weisse, Reynolds, Bowles, and Baum, 1989). Thus, across a variety of subjects, situations, and immune measures, chronic stressors have been found to have deleterious effects on the immune system. It remains unclear, however, which aspect(s) of these long-term stressors may be responsible for these events (e.g., chronicity vs. negatively valued life-events, vs. ongoing absence of social support, etc.), as well as the mechanism by which these effects are accomplished (Kaplan, 1991).

PSYCHOLOGICAL VARIABLES

DEPRESSION AND BEREAVEMENT

A number of studies have reported relationships between dysphoric mood and several immune measures, with results generally taken to suggest that dysphoria has adverse effects of immunocompetence (Kaplan, 1991). In studies of clinical depression this general finding has been both replicated and further clarified. Preliminary results from several studies suggested that patients hospitalized for major depression evidenced reductions in lymphocyte response to mitogens, as well as lower numbers of B and T cells when compared to either age- and sex-matched normal controls (Kronfol, Silva, Greden, Dembinski, Gardner, and Carroll, 1983; Schleifer, Keller, Meyerson, Raskin, Davis, and Stein, 1984), or to a demographically matched nondepressed inpatient population (Schleifer, Keller, Siris, Davis, and Stein, 1985). While a more recent follow-up study conducted by Schleifer and associates (Schleifer, Keller, Bond, Cohen, and Stein, 1989) failed to find differences between depressed patients and controls in lymphocyte numbers, responsiveness, or cell activity, it did demonstrate an interaction between depression severity and age. As age and severity increased, the negative association between depression and immune function increased.

Although some studies have failed to find a relationship between depression and the immune system (Weisse, 1992), a review of this literature suggests that this has most often occurred when young patients are compared to age-matched controls, or when other depressive subtypes (e.g., bipolar) are included. Taken together, these studies suggest that altered immunity in depressed patients may be related to factors such as age, severity, and diagnostic subtype, with the most pronounced immune changes evidenced in older, hospitalized, unipolar depressives. The interested reader is referred to an excellent review of this area in Weisse (1992).

The potential immune consequences of bereavement have also received considerable attention and are intertwined with our understanding of depression and immunity. Among the earliest work in this area was a study by Bartrop and colleagues which explored the effects of spousal death on mitogen-stimulated lymphocyte proliferation (Bartrop, Lazarus, Luckhurst, Kiloh, and Penny, 1977). Results indicated that T cell function was reduced following bereavement. Utilizing a prospective design, Schleifer assessed the immune response of 16 male partners of terminal breast cancer patients both prior to and following their spouse's death (Schleifer, Keller, Camerino, Thornton, and Stein, 1983). Blastogenic responses following the patients' death were significantly suppressed compared to the subjects' own prebereavement values.

Many of these early studies failed to include assessments of mood, however, thus making it difficult to determine whether the immune alterations noted reflected the stress of normal bereavement, or of some other process (e.g., depression and loss). In consideration of this issue, Linn and colleagues (Linn, Linn, and Jensen, 1984) assessed both severity of depressive symptoms and immune changes during bereavement. Results indicated that reductions in lymphocyte responsiveness were demonstrated only by those bereaved subjects with high depression symptom scores. In an impressive series of studies involving bereaved and nonbereaved subjects, Irwin and associates have consistently demonstrated an inverse relationship between depressed mood and immune function, such that severity of depressive symptoms was predictive of decreases in NKA (Irwin, Daniels, Bloom, Smith, and Weiner, 1987; Irwin, Daniels, Smith, Bloom, and Weiner, 1987; Irwin, Daniels, and Weiner, 1987). The results of these studies have been taken by some to suggest that depression may mediate the immune alterations noted in bereavement, as well as other adverse life events (Locke et al., 1984). While it appears from the literature that either bereavement or magnitude of life events experienced may be insufficient to produce reduced immune responses in the absence of depression, the processes which may link depressive symptoms and immunologic change remain un-known.

SOCIAL SUPPORT

The effect of social support on immunity has rarely been studied in its own right, but rather its presence or absence has been noted to affect some other factor under study, such as chronic stress. Nevertheless, the association between interpersonal relationships and immune function has been among the most robust of PNI findings. Loneliness has been associated with poorer immune functioning (reduced NKA, reduced lymphocyte response to PHA, increased antibody titre to HSV-1) in medical students (Kie-colt-Glaser, Ricker, George, Messick, Speicher, Garner, and Gla-ser, 1984; Glaser, Kiecolt-Glaser, Speicher, and Holliday, 1985), as well as psychiatric inpatients (Kiecolt-Glaser et al., 1984). Simi-larly, caregivers of AD patients who initially reported low levels of social support demonstrated the greatest reductions in immune function when assessed again over one year later (Kiecolt-Glaser et al., 1991).

In contrast, the presence of positive personal relationships has generally been associated with enhanced immune responsiveness. This finding has been demonstrated in healthy medical students receiving a hepatitis B vaccine (Glaser, Kiecolt-Glaser, Bonneau, Malarkey, and Hughes, 1992), as well as in early-stage breast can-cer patients (Levy, Herberman, Maluish, Schlien, and Lippman, 1985). In a study of older adults, Thomas, Goodwin, and Goodwin (1985) reported a positive relationship between social support (as measured by the presence of frank and confiding relation-ships), and immunocompetence (lymphocyte numbers and re-sponse to PHA). Interestingly, however, these relationships were only significant for women. The previously reported studies of separation and divorce also appear to provide evidence for the potential immunomodulatory effect of personal relationships. De-spite the consistency of the findings, social support and its ab-sence are complex phenomena having both direct and indirect effects, which will require considerably more study before our understanding is complete.

STRESS AND HUMAN ILLNESS

CANCER

The role of psychosocial factors in cancer etiology, progression, and treatment response has generated a large body of literature. Frequently studied factors have included personality, stress, life events, health habits, and coping styles. While the majority of these studies have been flawed by retrospective methodology, nevertheless they have consistently revealed three general categories of psychosocial variables which appear to be associated with cancer: a history of psychic distress, social support, and personality (Bovbjerg, 1991). As the scope of this literature exceeds present space allotments, the reader is directed to several excellent reviews (Bahnson, 1980, 1981; Redd and Jacobson, 1988; Holland, 1989).

Far fewer studies have examined the relationship between psychological factors, immune functioning, and cancer. An early study of Pettingale and colleagues (Pettingale, Greer, and Tee, 1977) explored the relationship between emotional expression and immune functioning in breast cancer patients. Results indicated an association between preoperative anger suppression and elevated serum IgA levels. A later study by this same group failed to find a relationship between psychological response to diagnosis and immune measures at preoperative assessments. However, at a 3-month follow-up, breast cancer patients who were in the "denial" response group demonstrated increased levels of serum IgM compared to the other groups (Pettingale, Philalithis, Tee, and Greer, 1981). Consistent with these findings, Levy, Herberman, Lippman, and d'Angelo (1987) reported reduced NKA at 3-month follow-up in those breast cancer patients who had reported depressive, fatiguelike symptoms and lack of family support at baseline.

As most carcinogens appear to induce cancer by damaging the DNA in cells, the body's ability to repair these cells is critically related to cancer risk. A recent PNI finding of potential relevance to this area suggests that DNA repair may be affected by psychological stress. Kiecolt-Glaser and colleagues examined DNA repair (as assessed by in vitro recovery of nucleoid sedimentation following X-irradiation) in 28 newly admitted, nonmedicated, nonpsychotic psychiatric inpatients. A significant difference in DNA repair was found between high- and low-distress subject groups (as measured by MMPI-depression scale 2), with the high-distress group evidencing poorer DNA repair (Kiecolt-Glaser, Stephens, Lipetz, Speicher, and Glaser, 1985). While the findings of these studies are encouraging, further well-controlled, prospective work in this area is clearly needed.

AIDS

Recently, investigators have begun to explore psychosocial influences on the progression of HIV infection. Suggested pathways for these effects include reactivation of latent viruses, reduction of numbers and functioning of peripheral lymphocytes, and alteration in host condition at the time of infection (O'Leary, 1990). In an early study by Solomon and colleagues (Solomon, Temoshok, O'Leary, and Zich, 1987), the effects of psychosocial factors on immune functioning were assessed in 18 persons with AIDS. Results indicated that larger absolute numbers of lymphocytes were associated with lower reports of tension, depression, fatigue, and anger (as measured by the Profile of Mood States [POMS]). Lower levels of self-reported stress from illness, fatigue, and tension were also correlated with increased numbers of cytotoxic T cells. Interestingly, conflicting results were obtained by these same investigators when they followed a group of seropositive gay men for 6 months (e.g., positive correlation between anxiety, anger, loneliness, and absolute numbers of helper T cells) (Temoshok, Solomon, Jenkins, and Sweet, 1989). The authors speculated that the variance in findings may reflect different psychoimmunological relationships at different stages of the illness. Much of the current PNI work with AIDS involves the implementation of behavioral or psychological interventions, and will be discussed in the following section.

INFECTIOUS DISEASE

The influence of stress on the incidence and duration of infectious disease is of particular relevance to health. A study by Kasl, Evans, and Niederman (1979) examined psychosocial factors in the development of infectious mononucleosis (IM) in a class of 1400 West Point cadets. Cadets who became infected and developed clinical IM could be distinguished from nonsymptomatic infected cadets on a variety of psychosocial measures, including parental achievement and career motivation. Additional support for the role of psychosocial variables has come from viral studies demonstrating the relationship of extrovert–introvert personality status to virus shedding, a well as family dysfunction and susceptibility to influenza B infection (Hillhouse, Kiecolt-Glaser, and Glaser, 1991).

A series of studies have focused on the role of psychosocial factors in the recurrence of herpes symptoms (HSV-1 and HSV-2), including both oral and genital lesions. An early study by Katcher and associates (Katcher, Brightman, Luborsky, and Ship, 1973) reported that psychosocial factors such as mood, social assets, and life change accounted for 14 percent of the variance in herpes recurrence. Additional studies have found a negative association between mood and cold sore recurrences (Friedmann, Katcher, and Brightman, 1977); a positive association between psychological distress and genital herpes recurrence (Goldmeier and Johnson, 1982); and a correlation between the occurrence of increased anxiety, stressful life events, and daily hassles and the appearance of recurrent genital lesions (Schmidt, Zyzanski, Ellner, Kumar, and Arno, 1985). Vanderplate and colleagues (Vanderplate, Aral, and Magder, 1988) reported a significant relationship between disease-specific social support, stress, and HSV recurrence. At lower levels of social support, there was a positive relationship of stress to recurrence, although with higher levels of support, no such relationship was found.

Kemeny and associates (Kemeny, Cohen, Zegans, and Conant, 1989) conducted a similar prospective study of stress, life change, mood, and HSV recurrence, but included several immunological measures as well. Results indicated that while stress and mood scores were uncorrelated with HSV recurrence, they were negatively associated with helper and suppressor T lymphocyte proportions. A relationship between suppressor T cell proportions and recurrence was also indicated. The HSV literature provides a linkage between psychosocial factors and health behaviors which is crucial to this field. While many of the studies have been retrospective, and have failed to assess immune function as well as disease status, they nevertheless provide evidence that psychosocial factors may relate to the incidence of infectious disease.

Additional evidence has come from the work of Cohen, Tyrell, and Smith (1991), which has prospectively explored the relationship between stress and susceptibility to colds. Using volunteers inoculated with one of five different cold viruses or a placebo, the investigators found that across all viruses, rates of both respiratory infection and colds increased in a dose–response manner with increases in psychological stress. Consistent findings have also been obtained by Glaser et al. (1992) in a recent study of the effect of academic stress on students' ability to generate an immune response to a hepatitis B vaccine. Students who seroconverted (produced an antibody response to the vaccine) after one injection demonstrated significantly less stress and anxiety than students who did not seroconvert until after the second injection. A role for social support was identified as well. Those students reporting greater levels of support demonstrated a stronger immune response to the vaccine by the end of the injection series. Taken with the work in HSV, these studies provide strong evidence for the relevance of stress, mood, and social support to infectious illness.

PSYCHOLOGICAL INTERVENTIONS

As data linking psychosocial variables and immune modification have accumulated, investigators have been intrigued with the possibility that psychological interventions might alter or even enhance immune functioning. Psychoneuroimmunology intervention studies have utilized a variety of diverse strategies and subject populations. While some work has focused on populations with specific diseases, a few studies have attempted to improve immunity in healthy populations. The overall results of these studies will be briefly reviewed. More detailed coverage of PNI interventions can be found in Halley (1991), and Kiecolt-Glaser and Glaser (1992).

Hypnosis and relaxation have been the most commonly employed PNI interventions. Among the earliest studies are a series of experiments by Black and colleagues (Black, Humphrey, and Niven, 1963) which utilized the "double arm" technique to assess the effects of hypnotic suggestion on the delayed hypersensitivity reaction to tuberculin. The results of these and more recent similar studies have generally pointed to differences in responsiveness between arms. However, it has not been clear whether these results reflect immune modulation or simply superficial skin changes. In their review, Pelletier and Herzing (1988) report that hypnosis has been found to exert a positive influence on a number of cutaneous disorders, including contact dermatitis, viral warts, and chronic urticaria, in addition to the hypersensitivity response.

In two separate studies, Kiecolt-Glaser and associates have assessed the potential prophylactic value of a relaxation–hypnosis intervention. In the first study, 45 older adults received either progressive relaxation training, social contact alone, or no contact. Following one month of treatment, only subjects in the relaxation group demonstrated increased NK cell activity and decreased HSV antibody titres, as well as reduced psychological distress (Kiecolt-Glaser, Glaser, Williger, Stout, Mesick, Sheppard, Ricker, Romisher, Briner, Bonnell, and Donnerberg, 1985). In the second study, 34 medical students were randomly assigned to relaxation and control groups. Blood samples were taken at the beginning of their school quarter, and again during final exams, with relaxation training provided during the interval between these two points. At examination time, the relaxation group reported less anxiety and distress than did control group subjects. While no immunological differences were found between groups, among intervention subjects the frequency of relaxation practice was positively associated with percentage of T helper cells (Kiecolt-Glaser et al., 1986).

Support for a more cognitively based intervention has also been obtained. Drawing from a dynamic model of psychotherapy, Pennebaker, Kiecolt-Glaser, and Glaser (1988) assessed the immunological effects of intrapsychic confrontation and self-disclosure. A group of 25 undergraduates wrote about traumatic or upsetting personal experiences for 20 minutes on each of four consecutive days. Another group of 25 students spent the same amount of time writing about trivial experiences. Following this "intervention," the "trauma" subjects were found to have a higher blastogenic response to PHA, a reduction in illness-related health center visits, and greater reports of happiness at 3-month follow-up. When this group was split into high- and low-disclosure subgroups, those who had written about previously undisclosed experiences had an improved lymphocyte proliferative response when compared to either low-disclosure or control subjects.

The possibility of influencing the course of a serious illness through behavioral means has been of obvious and considerable interest. Within the cancer arena, many intervention studies have failed to randomly assign patients to treatment and control conditions, or have failed to control for type and stage of disease, thus making it impossible to assess the effects of any intervention. There have been some notable exceptions, however; Speigel, Bloom, Kraemer, and Gottheil (1989) studied the effects of weekly supportive group therapy sessions plus self-hypnosis for pain control on 86 women with metastatic breast cancer. The 50 women randomly assigned to the intervention group evidenced reduced pain and anxiety, and survived an average of 18 months longer than did the 36 control subjects. At 10-year follow-up, the three subjects still living were all from the intervention group.

Another excellent study in this area evaluated the effects of a 6-week, multifaceted group intervention, which included health education, training in problem solving, and stress management techniques (Fawzy, Kemeny, Fawzy, Elashoff, Morton, Cousins, and Fahey, 1990). All subjects were diagnosed with stage I or II malignant melanoma, and had received no treatment beyond initial surgical excision of the cancer. Subjects in the intervention group demonstrated reduced psychological distress, increased NKA, and increased percentage of NK cells relative to control subjects. Interestingly, the majority of these changes were not apparent at the 6-week follow-up, but emerged 6 months later.

Like cancer, human immune virus (HIV) infection is considered by many to be a chronic disease which may be amenable to modification by psychosocial interventions, particularly during the early stages of the infection. Over the past 5 years, the Miami Asymptomatic HIV-1 project has studied the relationship between behavioral, immune, and psychological factors in high-risk gay men before and after notification of serostatus (Antoni, Schneiderman, Fletcher, Goldstein, Ironson, and LaPerriere, 1990). Antoni and colleagues found that in the 5 weeks preceding notification of their HIV-1 status, seronegative subjects demonstrated a significant enhancement of several immune parameters (e.g., increased lymphocyte response to PHA), in an apparent mobilizing response to a potent stressor. In contrast, no anticipatory immune enhancement was found in seropositive subjects, possibly suggesting that their compromised immune systems were already insensitive to psychosocial factors.

A second area of study within this project focused on the effects of behavioral intervention on psychological and immune functioning in asymptomatic HIV-1 positive and negative gay men. Two experimental paradigms have been used: aerobic exercise and psychosocial stress-management groups. One study compared subjects randomly assigned to a 5-week aerobic exercise group to those in a no-contact control group both before and after notification of serostatus. Seropositive control subjects demonstrated marked increases in psychological distress at 72 hours postdiagnosis, whereas seropositive exercisers resembled seronegative groups, with no affective or immunological change (LaPerriere, Fletcher, Antoni, Ironson, Klimas, and Schneiderman, 1991). Seronegative exercisers were also found to have a net increase in T helper (CD4) cells. While seropositive individuals derived fewer immunomodulatory benefits from aerobic training, results suggest that this intervention was effective in buffering the psychological impact of news of seropositivity.

A parallel study utilized a 5-week stress management intervention (cognitive skills, relaxation training) in place of aerobic exercise. A similar pattern of results was obtained, with seropositive subjects demonstrating an increase in NK and CD4 cell numbers, as well as an attenuation of postnotification distress (Antoni et al., 1991). In contrast to these positive findings, Coates, McKusick, Kuno, and Stites (1989) failed to demonstrate any immunological change following an intensive 8-week stress-reduction intervention targeting HIV-positive subjects. The authors suggest that these results may have been influenced by greater preexisting immune impairment in the experimental group (lower T cell numbers than control group at baseline), as well as failure to achieve the affective change potentially necessary for immune modulation.

In summary, while the results of many intervention studies appear promising, further work is clearly needed. Our understanding of the consequences of behavioral interventions lags behind our knowledge of the immune effects of various stressors. In particular, as few intervention studies have included follow-ups, little is known regarding the potential duration of any immunological changes. While Kiecolt-Glaser and Glaser (1992) have hypothesized that shorter-term, narrowly focused interventions are likely to be associated with less enduring benefits, this remains to be tested. These authors also provide an important caveat for PNI intervention studies: it may be neither possible nor advisable to enhance immune functioning above normal levels in an individual whose immune system is functioning satisfactorily. Determining the immune function parameters within which psychosocial interventions may be effective remains an important avenue for future research.

EMPLOYMENT/UNEMPLOYMENT

Work is valued not only for its economic and social benefits, but for its influence on identity and self-respect, provision of purpose and direction in life, opportunities for social support, and status (Arnetz, Wasserman, Petrini, Brenner, Levi, Eneroth, Salovaara, Hjelm, Salovaara, Theorell, and Peterson, 1987). Unemployment, or job dissatisfaction, may result in loss of one or more of these advantages, and may be experienced by the individual as a chronic stressor. Kaplan (1991) has suggested that unemployment, like bereavement and divorce, is an intrinsically disvalued, and thus stressful social identity, which is likely to influence immune functioning.

Despite the fact that reactions to job loss occur on multiple levels (e.g., cognitive, behavioral) the majority of studies have focused on the psychological and social impact of unemployment. In contrast, Arnetz and colleagues (1987; Arnetz, Brenner, Levi, Hjelm, Petterson, Wasserman, Petrini, Eneroth, Kellner, Kvetnansky, and Vigas, 1991) have conducted several studies designed to explore immunological and health consequences as well. In the first study, women were divided into unemployed and employed groups, and were prospectively studied for 8 months. In addition, the unemployed group was further subdivided by randomly assigning half to a psychosocial self-help program in addition to their standard welfare support, while the other half received state support alone. Results indicated significant reduction in lymphocyte reactivity to PHA in both groups of unemployed women after 9 months of unemployment. Interestingly, the psychosocial intervention did not appear to counteract this decrease.

A large scale follow-up study by this same group examined the physical and immunological effects of different phases of the unemployment experience (from anticipation of job loss through long-term unemployment). While lymphocyte reactivity was again reduced after 9 months of unemployment, it was found to return to baseline values when unemployment lasted more than 20 months, perhaps reflecting some accommodation. Although the majority of psychological and physical changes were most pronounced during the first year of unemployment, HDL cholesterol levels remained depressed throughout the 2 years of the study. As higher HDL levels have been associated with lower rates of morbidity–mortality from ischemic heart disease, this finding suggests that chronic unemployment may be associated with a prolonged and increased risk for cardiovascular disease. In addition, the investigators postulated a role for coping style as well, as direct or problem-focused coping was found to attenuate the physical and mental stress of unemployment.

While it appears that unemployment may be correlated with health and immune changes, the stress of employment has also been linked to numerous health-related consequences. These include hypertension, coronary heart disease, respiratory symptoms, anxiety, depression, and ulcers. A review of the literature indicates that workload, role ambiguity or conflicts, poor relationships with coworkers and supervisors, and lack of participation–control are among the sources of work stress most commonly associated with these mental and physical outcomes (Israel, House, Schurman, Heaney, and Mero, 1989). While personal resources, interpersonal relationships, coping strategies, and influence–control appear to be primary variables in modifying the relationship between occupational stress and health, their effects may be direct or indirect, and are often complex (Israel et al., 1989). Personality factors such as type A behavior, hardiness, and locus of control have also recently been explored in relation to work stress and health, but findings are limited and equivocal (Taylor and Cooper, 1989).

Despite a large body of literature highlighting the emotional and physical consequences of both everyday and occupational stress, attempts to provide stress management skills in the workplace are only a recent development. As research has suggested that stress management interventions may improve the health and safety of employees, as well a reducing health care costs, such strategies are often viewed in the context of health promotion or wellness programs (Ivancevich, Matteson, Freedman, and Phillips, 1990). Initial findings from several large-scale interventions have been positive, with results indicating reductions in anxiety, depression, headaches, and health-center visits following training in relaxation, biofeedback, or cognitive modifications (Ivancevich et al., 1990). Many of the intervention studies in this area have been methodologically weak, however, and have failed to include immunological measures to corroborate observed changes in health status (e.g., reduced symptom reports). Given the rising costs of health care, and growing uncertainty as to who should pay for these services, identifying work-related sources of health impairment and promotion have potential benefit for employees and employers alike. Well-controlled, longitudinal PNI studies of occupational stress are likely to greatly enhance our understanding of this area. Preliminary studies have begun to appear in explorations of the health care professions.

STRESS IN HEALTH-CARE PROFESSIONALS

Stress research in the health field is rapidly growing, perhaps owing to the common belief that jobs which involve caring for people are particularly stressful. While the proportion of health-care workers who experience severe job-related stress is probably comparable to other professional groups, they nevertheless are subject to regular, and more frequent occurrences of moderate levels of strain than are most other professional workers (Payne and Firth-Cozens, 1987). Jobs in the health field are generally very labor intensive and are unique among other professions for the emphasis placed on relationships. In many cases, "clients" are also "products," and as such, these relationships may be a major source of both satisfaction and strain. In addition, many health-care positions require a lengthy training period, during which overload, time constraints, feelings of isolation, and difficulties dealing with death and dying are often cited as major sources of stress. While the various health professions differ in terms of sources and consequences of stress, the one stressor which is clearly common to all is feelings of overload, whether organizational or personal.

Although nurses are perhaps the best studied of all health care workers, it is only recently that well-controlled studies have begun to empirically test the commonly held belief that this is a stressful profession. A review of the literature suggests that the primary sources of nursing stress include work overload, poor communication with colleagues, repetitive experiences of separation and death, emotional demands of patients and families, and a constantly changing work environment (Hillhouse and Adler, 1991). Recently, the concept of "burnout" has been applied to the nursing literature to describe the potentially negative consequences of chronic exposure to job stressors. The burnout phenomenon is typically characterized as a syndrome of maladaptive psychological, psychophysiological, and behavioral reactions to occupational stress. Manifestations with particular relevance for PNI include depression, headaches, gastrointestinal complaints, and substance abuse.

While there has been considerable research interest regarding the relative "stressfullness" of nonspecialized versus critical care or intensive care unit (ICU) nursing, the results of empirical investigations have been inconsistent (Harris, 1989). Regardless of ICU or non-ICU affiliation, however, it is clear that nurses do report considerable job-related stress, the experience of which is intensified as the perceived severity of the stressor increases (Kelly and Cross, 1985; Vincent and Coleman, 1986). Additionally, expressions of fatigue, frustration, and withdrawal have been identified as common responses to job stress among nurses, with greater degrees of burnout manifested in those who are younger, more anxious, and less experienced (Harris, 1989).

Initial investigation with nurses has indicated links between life changes and physical and mental health. Direct correlations have been found between burnout and negative life events, while positively perceived life events are inversely related to this phenomena (Cronin-Stubbs and Rooks, 1985). Similarly, early findings suggest that social support may act as a buffering factor in stressful work environments (Milazzo, 1988), while lack of support enhances one's vulnerability to burnout (Cronin-Stubbs and Rooks, 1985). While these findings appear consistent with the results of previously reviewed PNI studies (e.g., Glaser, Kiecolt-Glaser, Stout, et al., 1985; Locke et al., 1979) their failure to include measures of immune functioning with their assessment of health-related symptoms greatly limits comparison.

A variant of nursing's "burnout syndrome" appears common to physicians as well. Known as "house-officer syndrome," or "overwork syndrome," this pattern is characterized by rumination over work problems, increased work time to compensate for decreased productivity, isolation, overseriousness, and substance abuse (Scheiber, 1987). While this represents an extreme of experience, commonly reported stressors among physicians include workload, lack of personal time, sleep deprivation, alienation from family and social networks, and time pressures. The training period appears to be a particularly stressful time, with prevalence estimates for anxiety and depression ranging from 16 to 24 percent throughout the residency years (Scheiber, 1987). Although some may experience personal or professional impairment as a result of work-related stress, a study by Linn and colleagues (Linn, Yager, Cope, and Leake, 1985) suggests that in general, physicians are as healthy and satisfied as any other professional group. Similar results have been found with the dental profession as well. While the majority of dentists report that their profession is more stressful than others, psychological and medical indices of stress and health suggest that the stress of dentistry is not substantially greater than that of other health professions (Kent, 1987).

Surgery is distinguished from medicine not only by the nature of the work, but by the stressors as well. Among surgeons, primary sources of stress are reported to be those which tax their knowledge–skills, or exceed their capacity to cope with fatigue (Payne, 1987). Studies of those choosing this profession reveal personalities characterized by intolerance of ambiguity, a high degree of self-confidence/internal locus of control, and authoritarianism. This finding suggests that medical students who choose a career in surgery do so at least in part out of a belief that they possess the resources necessary to cope with its stresses.

Several studies of work stress among surgeons are unique in this area in their inclusion of physiological measures. Studies of heartrate have indicated frequent and sustained increases; however, this appears to reflect the physical, rather than psychological demands of the work (Payne, 1987). Interestingly however, social support (e.g., consultation with a senior colleague) was found to reduce elevations of heartrate resulting from stressful decision-making situations. A consistent finding across several studies of surgeons is that of chronically raised levels of cortisol (Payne, 1987). As elevated cortisol has been linked to feelings of help-lessness and distress, this initially appears inconsistent with the personal data reported above. However, extreme confidence in one's ability to cope with stress may lead some surgeons to deny their stress response. Some support for this possibility was demonstrated by Bates (1982), who found that surgeons' reports of the frequency of their emotional distress grossly underestimated the frequencies provided by their spouses. While the chronic cortisol elevations suggest some potential long-term health costs, these have not yet been demonstrated.

Within the literature on the health professions, few attempts have been made to deal with modifications to the impact of perceived work stress on either emotional or physical health. Of the intervention studies conducted, many are limited by methodological difficulties. In a notable exception, Randolphe and associates (Randolphe, Price, and Collins, 1986) compared nurses who attended a 2-day cognitive–behavioral burnout prevention workshop to a nontreated control group. Results indicated reduction in depression, hostility, and somatic symptoms among workshop participants, but failed to assess such key factors as perceived work stress and social support. While similar preventative stress management approaches have been undertaken with resident physicians (Scheiber, 1987), conclusions are limited by absence of control groups. Future research would benefit not only from such methodological considerations, but from the inclusion of immunological and additional health measures to further clarify the results.

Conclusion

Twenty years ago the notion that psychosocial variables could affect immunological processes was generally scoffed at. However, these last two decades have witnessed an impressive array of studies in this area, demonstrating these relationships in diverse populations, and across varying methodologies and a battery of immunological and health assessments. At present, psycho–immuno relationships appear solid and robust. While the majority of scientists no longer question the existence of this interconnection, there are nevertheless numerous uncertainties as to its specific nature and importance. The crucial link between psychosocial functioning, immune processes, and health outcomes has not been unequivocally demonstrated. Much of the blame for this lies in the relative youth of the immunological field, and its concomitant general inability to specify the health implications of immunological variability. In this regard, the field of immunology could profit considerably from some of the methodology already well developed in the social sciences.

However, while we wait for immunological work to bridge this gap, there is still much that can be done. The relationship between psychological variables, immunological processes, and health is undoubtedly a complex one. This is readily apparent if we examine the diversity of results reported in this chapter. In order to tease apart these relationships we must take advantage of: (1) the increased availability of more sensitive assessments; (2) more sophisticated methodologies, such as covariate structural modeling techniques; and (3) the use of experimental research designs whenever possible. In relation to this last point, the interventions described in this chapter can also be conceptualized as experimental manipulations. When well designed, they can provide important insights into these psycho-immuno–health relationships, as well as being of potential importance in terms of producing behavior change.

Lastly, as the relationships discussed likely vary by population as well as situation, it is crucial that future work focus in on specific populations and stressors. The area of occupation stress presents an excellent opportunity here. With the assistance of employers and the health care system, we may be able to design long-term, sophisticated projects of potential benefit to both groups. With increased understanding comes the possibility of more effective prevention and interventions, perhaps resulting in lower costs and improved health as well.

References

Ader, R., & Cohen, N. (1975), Behaviorally conditioned immunosuppression. *Psychosom. Med.*, 37:333–340.

Antoni, M. H., Baggett, L., Ironson, G., LaPerriere, A., August, S., Klimas, N., Schneiderman, N., & Fletcher, M. A. (1991), Cognitive–behavioral stress management intervention buffers distress responses and elevates immunologic markers following notification of HIV-1 seropositivity. *J. Clin. & Consult. Psychol.*, 59:906–915.

———— Schneiderman, N., Fletcher, M. A., Goldstein, D. A., Ironson, G., & LaPierriere, A. (1990), Psychoneuroimmunology and HIV-1. *J. Clin. & Consult. Psychol.*, 58:1–12.

Arnetz, B. B., Brenner, S. O., Levi, L., Hjelm, R., Petterson, I. L., Wasserman, J., Petrini, B., Eneroth, P., Kellner, A., Kvetnansky, R., & Vigas, M. (1991), Neuroendocrine and immunological effects of unemployment and job insecurity. *Psychother. & Psychosom.*, 55:76–80.

———— Wasserman, J., Petrini, B., Brenner, S. O., Levi, L., Eneroth, P., Salovaara, H., Hjelm, R., Salovaara, L., Theorell, T., & Petterson, I. L. (1987), Immune function in unemployed women. *Psychosom. Med.*, 49:3–12.

Bahnson, C. B. (1980), Stress and cancer: The state of the art. Part 1. *Psychosomatics*, 21:975–981.

———— (1981), Stress and cancer: The state of the art. Part 2. *Psychosomatics*, 22:207–220.

Bartrop, R. W., Lazarus, L., Luckhurst, E., Kiloh, L. G., & Penny, R. (1977), Depressed lymphocyte function after bereavement. *Lancet*, 1:834–836.

Bates, E. (1982), Doctors and their spouses speak: Stress in medical practice. *Health & Illness*, 4:25–29.

Black, S., Humphrey, I., & Niven, W. (1963), Inhibition of immediate-type hypersensitivity response by direct suggestions under hypnosis. *Brit. Med. J.*, 1:925–929.

Borysenko, M. (1987), The immune system: An overview. *Ann. Behav. Med.*, 7:3–10.

Bovbjerg, D. H. (1991), Psychoneuroimmunology: Implications for oncology? *Cancer*, 67:828–832.

Coates, T. J., McKusick, L., Kuno, R., & Stites, D. P. (1989), Stress reduction training changed number of sexual partners but not immune function in men with HIV. *Amer. J. Pub. Health,* 79:885–887.

Cohen, S., Tyrell, D. A., & Smith, A. P. (1991), Psychological stress in humans and susceptibility to the common cold. *N. Eng. J. Med.,* 325:606–612.

Cronin-Stubbs, D., & Rooks, C. A. (1985), The stress, social support, and burnout of critical care nurses: The results of research. *Heart Lung,* 14:31–39.

Dorian, B. J., Keystone, E., Garfinkel, P. E., & Brown, G. M. (1982), Aberrations in lymphocyte subpopulations and function during psychological stress. *Clin. Exp. Immunol.,* 50:132–138.

Fawzy, F. I., Kemeny, M. E., Fawzy, N. W., Elashoff, R., Morton, D., Cousins, R., & Fahey, J. L. (1990), A structured psychiatric intervention for cancer patients. *Arch. Gen. Psychiatry,* 47:729–735.

Friedman, E., Katcher, A. H., & Brightman, V. (1977), Incidence of recurrent herpes labialis and upper respiratory infection: A prospective study of the influence of biologic, social, and psychologic predictors. *Oral Surg.,* 43:873–878.

Glaser, R., Kiecolt-Glaser, J. K., Bonneau, R., Malarkey, W., & Hughes, J. (1992), Stress-induced modulation of the immune response to recombinant hepatitis B vaccine. *Psychosom. Med.,* 54:22–29.

———— ———— Speicher, C. C., & Holliday, J. E. (1985), Stress, loneliness, and changes in herpes virus latency. *J. Behav. Med.,* 8:249–260.

———— ———— Stout, J. C., Tarr, K. L., Speicher, C. E., & Holliday, J. E. (1985), Stress-related impairments in cellular immunity. *Psychiat. Res.,* 16:233–239.

———— Rice, J., Sheridan, J., Fertel, R., Stout, J. C., Speicher, C. E., Pinsky, D., Kotur, M., Post, A., Beck, M., & Kiecolt-Glaser, J. K. (1987), Stress-related immune suppression: Health implications. *Brain Behav. & Immun.,* 1:7–20.

———— ———— Speicher, C. E., Stout, J. C., & Kiecolt-Glaser, J. K. (1986), Stress depresses interferon production concomitant with a decrease in natural killer cell activity. *Behav. Neurosci.,* 100:675–678.

Goldmeier, D., & Johnson, A. (1982), Does psychiatric illness affect the occurrence rate of genital herpes? *Brit. J. Vener. Dis.,* 54:40–43.

Halley, F. M. (1991), Self-regulation of the immune system through biobehavioral strategies. *Biofeed. & Self-Reg.,* 16:55–74.

Halvorsen, R., & Vassend, O. (1987), Effect of examination stress on some cellular immunity functions. *J. Psychosom. Res.,* 31:693–701.

Harris, R. B. (1989), Reviewing nursing stress according to a proposed coping-adaptation framework. *Adv. Nurs. Sci.,* 11:12–28.

Henle, W., & Henle, G. (1982), Epstein-Barr virus and infectious mononucleosis. In: *Human Herpesvirus Infections: Clinical Aspects,* ed. R. Glaser & T. Gottleib-Stematsky. New York: Marcel Dekker, pp. 151–161.

Hillhouse, J. J., & Adler, C. M. (1991), Stress, health, and immunity: A review of the literature and implications for the nursing profession. *Holist. Nurs. Pract.,* 5:22–31.

———— Kiecolt-Glaser, J. K., & Glaser, R. (1991), Stress-associated modulation of the immune response in humans. In: *Stress and Immunity,* ed. N. Plotnikoff, A. Murgo, R. Faith, & J. Wybran. Ann Arbor, MI: CRC Press.

Holland, J. C. (1989), Behavioral and psychosocial risk factors in cancer: Human studies. In: *Handbook of Psychooncology*, ed. J. C. Holland & J. H. Rowland. New York: Oxford University Press, pp. 236–240.

Irwin, M., Daniels, M., Bloom, E., Smith, T. L., & Weiner, H. (1987), Life events, depressive symptoms, and immune function. *Amer. J. Psychiatry*, 144:437–441.

―― ―― Smith, T. L., Bloom, E., & Weiner, H. (1987), Impaired natural killer cell activity during bereavement. *Brain Behav. & Immun.*, 1:98–104.

―― ―― Weiner, H. (1987), Immune and neuroendocrine changes during bereavement. *Psychiat. Clin. N. Amer.*, 10:449–465.

Israel, B. A., House, J. S., Schurman, S. J., Heaney, C. A., & Mero, R. P. (1989), The relation of personal resources, participation, influence, interpersonal relationships and coping strategies to occupational stress, job strains, and health: A multivariate analysis. *Work & Stress*, 3:163–194.

Ivancevich, J. M., Matteson, M. T., Freedman, S. M., & Phillips, J. S. (1990), Worksite stress management interventions. *Amer. Psychol.*, 45:252–261.

Kaplan, H. B. (1991), Social psychology of the immune system: A conceptual framework and review of the literature. *Soc. Sci. Med.*, 33:909–923.

Kasl, S. V., Evans, A. S., & Niederman, J. C. (1979), Psychosocial risk factors in the development of infectious mononucleosis. *Psychosom. Med.*, 41:445–466.

Katcher, A. H., Brightman, V., Luborsky, L., & Ship, I. (1973), Prediction of recurrent herpes labialis and systemic illness from psychological measurements. *J. Dent. Res.*, 52:49–58.

Kelly, J., & Cross, D. G. (1985), Stress, coping behaviors, and recommendations for intensive care and medical surgical ward registered nurses. *Res. Nurs. Health*, 8:321–328.

Kemeny, M. E., Cohen, F., Zegans, L. S., & Conant, M. A. (1989), Psychological and immunological predictors of genital herpes recurrence. *Psychosom. Med.*, 51:195–208.

Kent, G. (1987), Stress amongst dentists. In: *Stress in Health Professionals*, ed. R. Payne & J. Firth-Cozens. New York: John Wiley, pp. 236–249.

Kiecolt-Glaser, J. K., Cacioppo, J. T., Malarkey, W. B., & Glaser, R. (1992), Acute psychological stressors and short-term immune changes: What, why, for whom, and to what extent? *Psychosom. Med.*, 54:680–685.

―― Dura, J. R., Speicher, C. E., Trask, O. J., & Glaser, R. (1991), Spousal caregivers of dementia victims: Longitudinal changes in immunity and health. *Psychosom. Med.*, 53:345–362.

―― Fisher, L. D., Ogrocki, P., Stout, J. C., Speicher, C. E., & Glaser, R. (1987), Marital quality, marital disruption, and immune function. *Psychosom. Med.*, 49:13–34.

―― Garner, W., Speicher, C. E., Penn, G., & Glaser, R. (1984), Psychosocial modifiers of immunocompetence in medical students. *Psychosom. Med.*, 46:7–14.

―― Glaser, R. (1992), Psychoneuroimmunology: Can psychological interventions modulate immunity? *J. Clin. & Consult. Psychol.*, 60:569–575.

―― ―― Shuttleworth, E. C., Dyer, C. S., Ogrocki, P., & Speicher, C. E. (1987), Chronic stress and immunity in family caregivers of Alzheimer's disease victims. *Psychosom. Med.*, 49:523–535.

————— ————— Strain, E., Stout, J., Tarr, K., Holliday, J., & Speicher, C. E. (1986), Modulation of cellular immunity in medical students. *J. Behav. Med.*, 9:5–21.

————— ————— Williger, D., Stout, J., Mesick, G., Sheppard, S., Ricker, D., Romisher, S. C., Briner, W., Bonnell, G., & Donnerberg, R. (1985), Psychosocial enhancement of immunocompetence in a geriatric population. *Health Psychol.*, 4:25–41.

————— Kennedy, S., Malkoff, S., Fisher, L. D., Speicher, C. E., & Glaser, R. (1988), Marital discord and immunity in males. *Psychosom. Med.*, 50:213–229.

————— Ricker, D., George, J., Messick, G., Speicher, C. E., Garner, W., & Glaser, R. (1984), Urinary cortisol levels, cellular immunocompetency, and loneliness in psychiatric inpatients. *Psychosom. Med.*, 46:15–23.

————— Stephens, R. E., Lipetz, P. D., Speicher, C. E., & Glaser, R. (1985), Distress and DNA repair in human lymphocytes. *J. Behav. Med.*, 8:311–320.

Kronfol, B., Silva, J., Greden, J., Dembinski, S., Gardner, R., & Carroll, B. J. (1983), Impaired lymphocyte function in depressive illness. *Life Sci.*, 33:241–247.

Landmann, R. M., Muller, F. B., Perini, C. H., Wesp, M., Erne, P., & Buhler, F. R. (1984), Changes of immuno-regulatory cells induced by psychological and physical stress: Relationship to plasma catecholamines. *Clin. Exp. Immunol.*, 58:127–135.

LaPerriere, A., Fletcher, M. A., Antoni, M. H., Ironson, G., Klimas, N., & Schneiderman, N. (1991), Aerobic exercise training in an AIDS risk group. *Internat. J. Sports Med.*, 12:553–557.

Lazarus, R. S., & Folkman, S. (1984), *Stress, Appraisal and Coping*. New York: Springer-Verlag.

Levy, S. M., Herberman, R. B., Lippman, M., & d'Angelo, T. (1987), Correlation of stress factors with sustained depression of natural killer cell activity and predicted prognosis in patients with breast cancer. *J. Clin. Oncol.*, 5:348–353.

————— ————— Maluish, A., Schlien, B., & Lippman, M. (1985), Prognostic risk assessment in primary breast cancer by behavioral and immunological parameters. *Health Psychol.*, 4:99–113.

Linn, L. S., Yager, J., Cope, D., & Leake, B. (1985), Health status, job satisfaction, and life satisfaction among academic and clinical faculty. *JAMA*, 254:2775–2782.

Linn, M. W., Linn, B. S., & Jensen, J. (1984), Stressful events, dysphoric mood, and immune responsiveness. *Psych. Rep.*, 54:219–222.

Locke, S. E., Hurst, M. W., Heisel, J. S., Kraus, L., & Williams, R. M. (1979), The influence of stress on the immune response. Paper presented at the American Psychosomatic Society, Annual Meeting, Washington, DC.

————— Kraus, L., Leserman, J., Hurst, M. W., Heisel, J. S., & Williams, R. M. (1984), Life change stress, psychiatric symptoms, and natural killer cell activity. *Psychosom. Med.*, 46:441–453.

McKinnon, W., Weiss, C. S., Reynolds, C. P., Bowles, C. A., & Baum, A. (1989), Chronic stress, leukocyte subpopulations, and humoral response to latent viruses. *Health Psychol.*, 8:389–402.

Milazzo, N. (1988), Stress levels of ICU vs non-ICU nurses. *Dimens. Crit. Care Nurs.*, 7:52–58.

Mishra, S. I., Aldwin, C. M., Colby, B. N., & Oseas, R. S. (1991), Adaptive potential, stress, and natural killer cell activity in older adults. *Aging & Health*, 3:368–385.

O'Leary, A. (1990), Stress, emotion, and human immune function. *Psych. Bull.*, 108:363–382.

Palmblad, J., Cantell, K., Strander, H., Froberg, J., Karlson, L., Levi, M., Gronstrom, M., & Unger, P. (1976), Stressor exposure and immunological response in men: Interferon-producing capacity and phagocytosis. *J. Psychosom. Res.*, 20:193–199.

—— Petrini, B., Wasserman, J., & Akerstedt, T. (1979), Lymphocyte and granulocyte reactions during sleep deprivation. *Psychosom. Med.*, 41:273–278.

Payne, R. (1987), Stress in surgeons. In: *Stress in Health Professionals*, ed. R. Payne & J. Firth-Cozens. New York: John Wiley.

—— Firth-Cozens, J. (1987), Conclusions. In: *Stress in Health Professionals*, ed. R. Payne & J. Firth-Cozens. New York: John Wiley, pp. 385–407.

Pelletier, K. R., & Herzing, D. L. (1988), Psychoneuroimmunology: Toward a mind-body model: A critical review. *Advances*, 5:27–56.

Pennebaker, J. W., Kiecolt-Glaser, J. K., & Glaser, R. (1988), Disclosure of traumas and immune function: Health implications for psychotherapy. *J. Clin. & Consult. Psychol.*, 56:239–245.

Pettingale, K. W., Greer, S., & Tee, D. E. (1977), Serum IgA and emotional expression in breast cancer patients. *J. Psychosom. Res.*, 21:395–399.

—— Philalithis, A., Tee, D. E., & Greer, S. (1981), The biological correlates of psychological responses to breast cancer. *J. Psychosom. Res.*, 25:453–458.

Randolphe, G. L., Price, J. L., & Collins, J. R. (1986), The effects of burnout prevention training on burnout symptoms in nurses. *J. Cont. Educ. Nurs.*, 17:43–49.

Redd, W. H., & Jacobsen, P. B. (1988), Emotions and cancer: New perspectives on an old question. *Cancer*, 62:1871–1879.

Shaeffer, M. A., McKinnon, W., Baum, A., Reynolds, C. P., Rikli, P., Davidson, L. M., & Fleming, I. (1985), Immune status as a function of chronic stress at Three-Mile Island. *Psychosom. Med.*, 47:85.

Scheiber, S. C. (1987), Stress in physicians. In: *Stress in Health Professionals*, ed. R. Payne & J. Firth-Cozens. New York: John Wiley, pp. 226–235.

Schleifer, S. J., Keller, S. E., Bond, R. N., Cohen, J., & Stein, M. (1989), Major depressive disorder and immunity. *Arch. Gen. Psychiatry*, 46:81–87.

—— —— Camerino, M., Thornton, J. C., & Stein, M. (1983), Suppression of lymphocyte stimulation following bereavement. *JAMA*, 250:374–377.

—— —— Myerson, A. T., Raskin, M. J., Davis, K. L., & Stein, M. (1984), Lymphocyte function in major depressive disorder. *Arch. Gen. Psychiatry*, 41:484–486.

—— —— Siris, S. G., Davis, K. L., & Stein, M. (1985), Depression and immunity: Lymphocyte function in ambulatory depressed, hospitalized schizophrenic patients, and hospitalized herniorrhaphy patients. *Arch. Gen. Psychiatry*, 42:129–133.

Schmidt, D. D., Zyzanski, S., Ellner, J., Kumar, M. L., & Arno, J. (1985), Stress as a precipitating factor in subjects with recurrent herpes labialis. *J. Fam. Pract.*, 20:359–366.

Solomon, G. F., Temoshok, L., O'Leary, A., & Zich, J. (1987), An intensive psychoimmunological study of long surviving persons with AIDS: Preliminary work, background studies, hypotheses, and methods. *Ann. NY Acad. Sci.*, 496:647–655.

Spiegel, D., Bloom, J. R., Kraemer, H. C., & Gottheil, E. (1989), Effect of psychosocial treatment on survival of patients with metastatic breast cancer. *Lancet*, 2:888–901.

Taylor, H., & Cooper, C. L. (1989), The stress-prone personality: A review of the research in the context of occupational stress. *Stress Med.*, 5:17–27.

Temoshok, L., Solomon, G. F., Jenkins, S. R., & Sweet, D. M. (1989), Psychoimmunologic studies of men with AIDS and ARC. Paper presented at the annual meeting of the American Association for the Advancement of Science, San Francisco, CA.

Thomas, P. D., Goodwin, J. M., & Goodwin, J. S. (1985), Effect of social support on stress-related changes in cholesterol level, uric acid level, and immune function in an elderly sample. *Amer. J. Psychiatry*, 142:735–737.

Vanderplate, C., Aral, S. D., & Magder, L. (1988), The relationship among genital herpes simplex virus, stress, and social support. *Health Psychol.*, 7:159–168.

Vincent, P., & Coleman, W. F. (1986), Comparisons of major stressors perceived by ICU and non-ICU nurses. *Crit. Care Nurse*, 6:64–69.

Weiss, R. S. (1975), *Marital Separation*. New York: Basic Books.

Weisse, C. S. (1992), Depression and immunocompetence: A review of the literature. *Psych. Bull.*, 111:475–489.

Chapter 5
Stress and Physical Illness: Development of an Integrative Model

JOSEPH W. CRITELLI, Ph.D., AND JULIANA S. EE, Ph.D.

It is now considered common knowledge that stress can lead to physical illness. Yet claims of measurement contamination have arisen which, if accepted, would nullify this conclusion. At the same time, investigators are searching for more comprehensive ways of measuring the spectrum of stress phenomena in the hopes of better understanding how stress might be linked to physical illness. This chapter contends that solutions to both issues, the controversies over contamination and the search for a strategy of comprehensive measurement, rely on a reexamination of the theory which embeds the stress construct.

SELYE AND TRADITIONAL STRESS THEORY

Hans Selye, the major pioneering researcher and theoretician of stress, initially defined stress as the rate of all the wear and tear caused by life (1956). By implication, extreme demands placed

139

on the organism, such as exposure to natural disasters or temperature extremes, could increase the rate of bodily breakdown. Thus the central metaphor was an extension of the physics of solid objects (e.g., airplane wings), wherein the application of prolonged or repeated force leads to stress and strain, which can eventually damage the object's physical integrity. Although enamored of this description, Selye felt it was not satisfactory as an operational definition.

To understand Selye's "official" definition of stress, we must broach the issue of generality. Selye was impressed with the finding that many diseases share a commonality of symptoms: malaise, fatigue, lethargy, loss of appetite, weight loss, sleeplessness, fear, fever, and loss of interest in work, people, and sex. In addition, much of his research involved observing the physiological effects of applying demanding or life-threatening conditions to animals. Selye found that a wide variety of noxious agents produced what appeared to be the same reaction pattern in these animals. This pattern included, for example, adrenal stimulation, shrinkage of lymphatic organs, gastrointestinal ulcers, and loss of body weight. As a result of these observations, he defined stress as the nonspecifically induced response of the body to any demand (1956, 1983). This definition has led to a number of confusions regarding "specificity." For example, Selye maintained that stress is both specific and nonspecific. By this he meant that stress is a state or condition that causes a specific pattern of bodily responses, as described above, but that stress itself is nonspecifically caused by a wide range of noxious agents. He called the pattern of biobehavioral responses caused by stress the general adaptation syndrome (GAS). Thus stress is a hypothetical construct which is said to cause certain changes to the structure and chemical composition of the body. These changes may be signs of damage or of the body's adaptive reactions or defenses against stress. The totality of these changes make up the GAS, which develops in three stages: alarm, resistance, and exhaustion. Selye believed that virtually every organ and chemical constituent of the body participates in the GAS, with the main regulators being the brain, nerves, pituitary, thyroid, adrenals, liver, kidney, blood vessels, connective tissue, and white blood cells.

Selye distinguished between stress and the stressor, that is, the noxious agent which places an adaptational demand on the organism, causing stress. Every stressor agent has both specific and nonspecific effects on the body. There is a specifically induced (i.e., relatively unique) local adaptation syndrome (LAS) in tissue directly affected by the stressor (e.g., inflammation in tissue where microbes enter the body). As part of the LAS, chemical alarm signals sent out by directly stressed tissues may trigger the GAS. The complete response to the noxious agent includes the direct effect of the stressor on the body, internal responses which stimulate tissue defense or attack damaging substances, and responses which inhibit unnecessary defense and cause tissue surrender. Selye emphasized that specificity is always a matter of degree. Thus many, but not necessarily all stressors were thought to lead to the same GAS pattern of physiological responses, and local adaptation responses were relatively unique, but certainly not absolutely unique to each stressor. What captured Selye's attention was that generality in patterns of response would exist at all.

Selye distinguished between two types of stress. Distress refers to unpleasant or harmful stress, and, unless otherwise specified, this is the type of stress most often discussed in the research literature. Selye maintained, however, that stress could also have beneficial effects on the body, as in the stress resulting from shock therapy, participation in sports, or engaging in exhilarating and creative work. *Eustress* was his term for pleasant or beneficial stress. It is important to note that both forms of stress were thought to lead to virtually the same nonspecific pattern of responses, yet eustress was hypothesized to be curative in effect or at least to cause much less damage than distress. Selye noted that what distinguishes eustress from distress is largely determined by the attitude that we take toward the stressor.

Selye maintained that many common diseases, such as nervous and emotional disturbances, high blood pressure, ulcers, and certain rheumatic, allergic, cardiovascular, and renal diseases, are caused by errors, excesses, inadequacies, or failures in our adaptive response to stress. For example, hormonal secretions that accompany physiological mobilization can cause direct damage, as in ulceration of the gastrointestinal tract, or indirect damage from the reduction of blood lymphocytes which weakens the immune system. Buckley (1983) observed that the cardiovascular response to stress includes the activation of central sympathetic centers and stimulation of the adrenal cortex to secrete cortical steroids. He points out that stress can produce an acute hypertensive response and, following prolonged exposure, a gradual increase in blood pressure leading to sustained hypertension. The failure to adapt to environmental stressors can result in pathological changes in the cardiovascular system, especially to sustained elevations in blood pressure, which have been linked to congestive heart failure, coronary thrombosis, atherosclerosis, and kidney failure. In large part, the linkage between stress and disease has sustained the widespread interest in stress phenomena.

MODIFICATIONS TO THE TRADITIONAL THEORY

Lazarus and Folkman (1984; Lazarus, Cohen, Folkman, Kanner, and Schaefer, 1980) have been pivotal in developing more comprehensive and integrative models of stress variables. In particular they have emphasized the importance of cognitive processes as mediators of stress. In a manner similar to Selye's distinction between distress and eustress, they argue for the importance of how an individual interprets or appraises a stressful event. As with a number of current researchers, they believe that whether a person views a potentially stressful event positively, as a challenge, or negatively, as a personal threat, influences the health implications of that stressor. They acknowledge, however, that there is still not much evidence as to whether challenge appraisals differ from threat appraisals in demonstrated health outcomes.

Lazarus and Folkman have also emphasized the role of coping practices. For example, using cigarettes or alcohol to cope with stress can lead to direct tissue damage. Coping can also interfere with adaptive behaviors, as in denial leading to delay in seeking medical attention. Thus they are suggesting that cognitive and behavioral attempts to deal with the stressor, as well as physiological reactions, must be taken into account in an integrative model of stress. They acknowledge that we do not yet know how we get from an acute, short-range emergency reaction to a condition of permanently diseased tissue, but it appears that relatively stable patterns of appraisal, emotion and coping may mediate these changes.

A number of researchers (e.g., Lazarus and Folkman, 1984; Weiner, 1992) have commented that empirical support for the GAS may not be as robust as Selye assumed. Because of pragmatic limitations, studies rarely look at the full gamut of physiological responses at the same time, making it difficult to detect patterns of response specific to a particular stressor. Nevertheless, evidence has been accumulating that stressful responses are more specific to the stressor than Selye had assumed. Lacey (1967) found specific somatic patterns of autonomic end-organ reactions to different types of person–environment relationships. Mason (1971) showed that starving an animal in isolation had different physiological effects than starving it while others were being fed, and Mason (1975) also found different patterns of hormonal response to various physical stressors. Shavit, Lewis, Terman, Gale, and Liebeskind (1984) found that continuous and intermittent shock had different effects on natural killer cell functioning. Weiss (1971, 1972) reported that, when electric shocks are avoidable the organism develops fewer gastric erosions. In addition, certain specific bodily responses to noxious agents are well-known: cold produces shivering, heat incites sweating, blood loss results in hypovolemia and a drop in blood pressure, and infection leads to a specific immune response. Weiner (1992) concluded that Selye's emphasis on the GAS was overstated, as both specific and general physiological changes occur and impact health status.

Weiner (1992) argued that some of Selye's formulations may have been unduly affected by his methods of observation. For example, Selye typically employed biologically irrelevant, over-powering, or unavoidable stressors that obscured subtler varia-tions in behavioral and physiological response. In addition, the use of such stressors may have overdramatized the linkage to dis-ease. Weiner maintains that more ecologically valid, milder stres-sors lead to disease because they occur in the presence of preexisting disease or risk factors. In most cases, stressful experi-ence does not linearly or by itself produce disease. Weiner con-tends that the GAS seems to occur naturally only under dire, life-threatening conditions; if the organism is not overwhelmed by the stressor, the GAS may or may not occur.

In light of these modifications to the data underlying Selye's theory of stress, Weiner has employed the term *stressful experience* instead of stress, defining it as the experience of a potential or actual threat or challenge to the organism. The term *experience* has been emphasized to draw attention to the active, interpretive nature of stress, which was present, but somewhat implicit in Sel-ye's formulation. Stressful experiences would include experiences of natural disasters, man-made disasters, disease or illness, per-sonal events such as the birth of a child or family discord, and conditions such as disappointment and monotony. Although the technical definition has eliminated Selye's focus on the GAS, the phenomena encompassed by stressful situations/conditions and their corresponding stressful experiences seems quite consistent with Selye's notion of stressors and stress.

Both Selye and Weiner view the stress reaction in terms of patterns of biobehavioral responses. Weiner, however, has also emphasized the cyclic nature of these responses. He argues that many hormones and neurotransmitters operate in a rhythmic manner, manifesting frequency, duration, amplitude, and wave-form. Environmental challenge or change leads to an alteration in one or more of these parameters. His view of stress reactions emphasizes the study of covariances in patterns of rhythmically organized physiological systems that are intimately linked by chemical communication signals. Stressful experiences can lead to disturbances or perturbations in the rhythmic cycles of vital biological functions such as respiratory and cardiac rhythms, food intake, digestion, elimination, reproduction, sleep rhythms, menstruation, pain modulation, and mood.

In a manner similar to Selye, Weiner argues that stressful experiences can lead to personal growth, temporary perturbations, or permanent deleterious effects on the organism. Weiner goes on to distinguish between illness and disease. In disease, there is identifiable anatomical damage. But many patients seen by physicians are in ill health without having an identifiable disease. Weiner maintains that symptoms of illness are often not the consequence of disease. Instead, they are often due to changes in rhythmic functions such as sleep, body temperature, gastrointestinal motility, menstruation, or respiration. Thus ill-health results from a change in the normal rhythms of a subsystem incited by stressful experience. When this model is applied to bereavement, for example, it can be said that bereavement not only leads to grief and depression, it also disrupts the order of a person's life. Symptoms of illness include hyperventilation, functional bowel and musculoskeletal syndromes, and sleep disturbance. In contrast to illness, disease occurs when stressful experience interacts with a preexisting regulatory disturbance or with structural change. Stressful experiences do not by themselves produce disease; they act as cofactors in predisposed persons. Ill health may eventually lead to disease, but, at present, the mechanisms by which this occurs are largely unknown.

Weiner acknowledges that there are marked individual differences in response to stressful experiences. Thus an integrative model of illness and disease should include the individual's appraisal of the signals generated by the stressor, genetic predispositions, coping that enhances or reduces the impact of the stressor, social support, the meaning of the stressful experience to the individual, personality, and age (the impact of stressful situations may be greater in childhood and in old age).

The present overview of stress theory suggests that, despite many new findings that have altered the linkage between stress and nonspecifically induced biobehavioral responses, the types of situations or condition that are considered stressful have remained quite consistent and noncontroversial. In addition, the linkage between stress and health disturbance has remained intact. Maddi, Bartone, and Puccetti (1987) argue that there is an emerging concordance among many researchers (e.g., Selye, 1956; Holmes and Masuda, 1974; Antonovsky, 1979; Moos, 1979; Maddi and Kobasa, 1984) as to the core ideas of stress theory. Within this model, certain psychosocial events trigger danger signals that stimulate the sympathetic nervous system and adrenal-type hormonal arousal. Because of the rule structure of modern civilization, these psychosocial stressors, such as major life events or daily hassles, do not generally lead to an intense physical coping reaction such as fighting or running away. As a result, the mobilized reaction may persist too long or otherwise fail to resolve the stressful situation. The resulting exhaustion or strain increases the likelihood of physiological breakdown which can lead to one or more of the stress-related disorders.

STRESS AND PHYSICAL ILLNESS

A large body of evidence now either directly or indirectly supports the view that accumulations of stressful experience make physical illness more likely. Although the strength of these relationships is not high, the relationships themselves are often clinically significant. For example, Cooke and Hole (1983) estimate that one-third of psychiatric cases an be attributed to stressful life events. In addition, a widespread expectation among researchers is that a more comprehensive assessment of stress and its possible moderators may lead to better predictions of physical illness.

A brief overview of selected findings may help clarify the nature of the relationship between stress and physical illness. Weiner (1992) concluded that stressful experience has been related to a number of illnesses, including hyperventilation syndrome, irritable bowel syndrome, and fibromyositis. Many studies have shown that elevated scores on measures of stressful life events have been related to the onset of accidents, illness, and disease (Holmes and

Rahe, 1967; Dohrenwend and Dohrenwend, 1974; Roth, Wiebe, Fillingim, and Shay, 1989). Maddi, Bartone, and Puccetti (1987) concluded that there are now a number of prospective studies showing that stressful life events lead to physical illness, even when prior physical illness is held constant. In a review of the literature, Dorian and Garfinkel (1987) surmise that there is general support for the linkage between stress and immune suppression, although the suppression response may occur during the poststress, rather than the peak-stress period. (This finding is compatible with Selye's distinction between resistance and exhaustion phases of the GAS.) With regard to specific stressors, giving up a baby for adoption has been related to ill health (Condon, 1986), and the stress of divorce has been related to immune suppression (Kiecolt-Glaser, Glaser, Strain, Stout, Tarr, Holliday, and Speicher, 1986). In addition, forced unemployment is followed by a 70 percent increase in illnesses and a 200 percent increase in attendance at medical clinics (Beale and Nethercott, 1986).

Thus the evidence supporting the influence of stress on physical illness appears to be substantial. In humans, this evidence relies heavily on self-report measures of stress, particularly measures of stressful life events (Holmes and Rahe, 1967), or of daily hassles (Kanner, Coyne, Schaefer, and Lazarus, 1981), or modifications of these measures. In recent years, however, a number of researchers have come forward to argue that these self-report measures are subject to a variety of contaminants which now prevent our drawing any conclusions about the linkage between stress and physical illness.

CONTROVERSIES OVER CONTAMINATION

Three particular contamination issues have dominated the current debate on the adequacy of self-report measures of psychosocial stress. These are (1) that many stress items are so ambiguous that their endorsement cannot be reliably interpreted; (2) that a number of stress items directly refer to illness or disease, seriously compromising interpretations about stress causing illness or disease; (3) that stress inventories are contaminated with negative affectivity–neuroticism.

The first issue, that a number of stress items are too ambiguous to be interpreted, seems valid, although somewhat overstated. Several original life event items were highly ambiguous and subjective. Two items typically cited in this regard are "revision in personal habits" and "major change in social activities" from the original Holmes and Rahe (1967) checklist. These items are so vague as to be unverifiable. In addition, it would be impossible to determine the amount of adaptive demand reflected in such items. On the other hand, much of the existing literature supporting a causal relationship between stress and physical illness has omitted or revised such items (Maddi et al., 1987), so it does not appear that this issue can seriously compromise the evidence that stress leads to physical illness.

The second issue deals with item overlap in measures of stress and illness. Nearly all theories of stress acknowledge that illness or disease would constitute significant stressors in themselves. Consequently, life event measures typically include items such as "major personal injury or illness" and "hospitalization." Many stress researchers have acknowledged this problem and it has become common practice to delete illness-related items from stress inventories. It is also the case that a number of studies have made this correction and still supported the link between stress and physical health (Dohrenwend and Dohrenwend, 1978; Kobasa, Maddi, Puccetti, and Zola, 1985; Maddi et al., 1987).

It could be argued, however, that the inclusion of illness items on stress inventories is theoretically appropriate and should be continued. According to stress theory, illness would itself place demands on an individual, depleting adaptive reserves and making future illness more likely. No confound would be implicated as long as the stress and illness inventories could be elaborated to insure that the stress-illness and the later criterion-illness were not the same. This could be done with minimal complication and result in a more accurate test of stress theory.

The third controversial issue, that stress measures are contaminated by negative affectivity, is a claim made by a number of researchers (Dohrenwend, Dohrenwend, Dodson, and Shrout, 1984; Schroeder and Costa, 1984; Flannery, 1986; Wickramasekera, 1986; Nowack, 1991) and is undoubtedly the most troubling of the three issues. The argument here is that self-report measures of stress partly reflect a pervasive mood disposition of negative affectivity or neuroticism, which involves tendencies to perceive cognitive, emotional, and somatic states negatively. Those high on negative affectivity worry frequently, show negative emotions such as anger, guilt, feelings of rejection, and anxiety, and have low self-esteem (Watson and Clark, 1985). Since negative affectivity has been related to somatic complaints (Costa and McCrae, 1985) and to a number of illnesses, including coronary heart disease, asthma, and ulcers (Friedman and Booth-Kewley, 1987), purported relationships between stress and illness may actually reflect linkages between negative affectivity and illness.

Several methods have been used to make the interpretation that self-report measures of stress reflect negative affectivity. Flannery (1986) found that hassles were as strongly correlated with negative affectivity as with physical illness. Dohrenwend et al. (1984) had psychologists rate the extent to which stress items are likely to be symptoms of a psychological disorder, and they concluded that hassles and life events were confounded with psychological distress. Schroeder and Costa (1984) argued that life events are contaminated with neuroticism because some items, such as "major change in eating habits" and "sexual difficulties" are direct symptoms of psychopathology, and a number of other items represent events that could be the result of neuroticism, such as divorce or being fired from a job. Using their own judgments, they derived a list of stress items which were contaminated with neuroticism. On the other hand, Maddi et al. (1987) made separate ratings of whether stress items reflected neuroticism and came to the opposite conclusion. Employing the DSM-III definition of neuroticism, they had judges rate a stress item as reflecting neuroticism if it indicated the presence of "a mental disorder in which the predominant disturbance is a symptom or group of symptoms that is distressing and unacceptable to the individual" (p. 837). Based on this criterion, they found no items to reflect neuroticism.

If the above arguments appear confusing, this is probably not an illusion. It also suggests that it may be some time before these issues get sorted out and conclusions can be reached about the extent to which possible contamination by negative affectivity compromises the linkage between stress and physical illness. At the same time, several observations can be made. There does appear to be some overlap between stress and negative affectivity, but, in itself, this would not necessarily constitute contamination. The issue here is whether the overlap with negative affectivity is consistent or discrepant with the stress construct as currently defined (i.e., is the overlap appropriate and consistent with stress theory?). Current variations of stress theory define stress in terms of the perception, appraisal, and active interpretation of signals generated by the objective stressful event. If some individuals, because of predispositions toward negativity or other systematic tendencies, are more likely to view an environmental event as threatening or requiring active adaptation than would others, this would be entirely consistent with current definitions of stress. The emphasis on appraised stress is designed to accommodate just such individual differences, and this is a central reason for distinguishing between stressful situations and stressful experiences. Thus greater tendencies of those high in negative affectivity to experience certain events as stressful would be encompassed by stress theory and represent no necessary contamination of the stress construct.

At the same time, several qualifications must be made. If it were determined that negative affectivity led to physical illness via mechanisms that are incompatible with the patterns of physiological response described by stress theory, then this would be grounds for possible contamination. At present, however, stress theory includes references to such a wide range of physiological reactions that it would be difficult to specify any such mediating processes that would be incompatible with the theory. Although this amorphousness does represent a weakness in the current theory, this weakness does not appear to involve contamination by negative affectivity.

A related issue that may be more relevant, is that, although no contamination by negative affectivity may be involved, if further analyses indicated that the entire stress–illness relationship were being carried by those high in negative affectivity, then this should be acknowledged in the interests of presenting a more precise description of the phenomena being observed. Although this would not contradict stress theory, it would extend it by incorporating a new and important moderator variable to the causal flow.

A final qualification deals with the measurement of physical illness. Although stress theory encompasses the active, subjective appraisal of the objective stressor, it assumes that the resulting physical illness actually occurs, as opposed to representing possible hypochondriacal fantasies of those high in negative affectivity. To date, the research on negative affectivity has not shown a linkage only to fantasies or distorted perceptions of normal somatic functions (Friedman and Booth-Kewley, 1987), but if this were found to be the case then a reconsideration of the contamination issue would be appropriate. In this regard, Maddi et al. (1987) have cautioned that illness measures should only include symptoms that are definite and clear and that illness items that are readily self-diagnosed should be avoided.

Several researchers (Dohrenwend et al., 1984; Schroeder and Costa, 1984) appear to have adopted the criterion that if neurotic individuals would be more likely to endorse a stress item than would others, that, in itself, would constitute evidence of contamination. Although this criterion vaguely resembles the contrasted groups criterion for item selection in scale development, the fact that there might be slightly different endorsement rates for neurotics and others on many stress items would not indicate that these items constitute an adequate measure of neuroticism. It is likely, for example, that males and females differ on endorsement rates for a number of stress items, but this would not make the hassles scale an acceptable measure of gender. The broader issue, however, is that of theoretical consistency. From the viewpoint of stress theory, it is quite sensible that neurotics would be somewhat more likely to experience certain stressful experiences, such as divorce, being fired, or problems with parents, than would others. As such, this would not constitute contamination, but appropriate and expected overlap. Instead of discrediting stress theory, such expected findings provide a small measure of empirical support for the theory.

Schroeder and Costa (1984) have cogently argued that some stress items, such as "major change in eating habits" and "sexual difficulties" are direct symptoms of psychopathology. This point is similar to the one discussed above with reference to inclusion of illness and disease items on self-report measures of stress. To avoid contamination, such items should be eliminated if the measure of physical illness also includes the same or comparable items. When such changes have been made, however, the relationship between stress and illness has remained (Maddi et al., 1987).

In conclusion, the present evidence does not appear to seriously compromise the linkage between stress and physical illness. Nevertheless, the possibility of some types of contamination cannot be entirely ruled out, so more final decisions will require further empirical and theoretical development.

Toward an Integrative Model

Previous attempts at specifying more integrative models of stress (e.g., Lazarus and Folkman, 1984; Weiner, 1992) have emphasized the inclusion of moderator variables that, by taking individual differences into account, would contribute to the prediction of physical illness. To this end, a comprehensive model for predicting physical illness should ideally include variables such as personality, age, health and exercise habits, social support, and coping styles. The present discussion, however, will focus on comprehensiveness in the measurement of stress.

By examining the development of stress theory, it is clear that certain discriminations have been made repeatedly at a conceptual level, but have not yet been systematically incorporated into the measurement of stress. For example, many have recommended distinguishing between the objective stressor and the more subjectively perceived stressful experience (Dorian et al., 1982; Dohrenwend and Shrout, 1986; Green, 1986). This can be done in a preliminary way by having items which measure objective stressors refer to the stressor itself rather than to feelings or reactions to the stressor. Measures of objective stressors might assess frequency of occurrence for each item and then sum frequencies across items or, if items vary widely in apparent stress value, apply a nomothetic weighting to each item before summing.

It has also been customary in stress theory, although not always in stress measurement, to distinguish between eustress and distress. Selye described eustress as pleasant or beneficial (i.e., curative) and distress as unpleasant or harmful. (Although the criteria of pleasant and beneficial usually go together, Selye listed shock therapy as a counterexample.) With regard to this distinction, life events have been classified into positive and negative events and hassles have been distinguished from uplifts.

A number of contemporary theorists have emphasized the importance of how the individual appraises the stressor, with the constructs "challenge" and "threat" being the most typical appraisal dimensions. Although this is similar to the distinction between eustress and distress, it may be useful to keep these notions separate. It does not appear to be the case, for example, that unpleasant events are always perceived as threats rather than challenges.

Several researchers (Cohen, Kamarck, and Mermelstein, 1983; Schroeder and Costa, 1984) have also argued for the inclusion of a more subjective, global, and feeling-toned measure of perceived stress. Rather than the cognitive appraisal of the stressor, this measure would reflect the affective reaction to the stressor, as in feelings of being pressured and overwhelmed. This could be measured at the global level in terms of stress feelings during the past week, in terms of stress feelings in particular areas of life, such as work/school and personal relationships, or they could be measured at the level of individual life events or hassles.

The two types of psychosocial stress measures most often used in research are life events and hassles. Life events refer to major stressors that occur relatively infrequently and are typically measured over a one- or two-year time period. Hassles are minor stressors that may occur on a daily basis and are usually measured over a one- or two-week period. The appropriate time periods for measuring life events and hassles differs in accord with their typical frequencies of occurrence and with the likelihood of accurate recall. Because life events include more major occurrences such as marriage, divorce, and death of a spouse, they can be recalled accurately over a greater retrospective period. In the interests of accuracy, however, six-month periods would be preferable to longer time spans. It seems clear that both major and minor stressful events should be assessed, despite recent findings suggesting that life events may not add to the predictive ability of hassles (Kanner et al., 1981; Holahan and Holahan, 1987; Weinberger, Hiner, and Tierney, 1987; Banks and Gannon, 1988). With regard to possible predictive redundancies between life events and hassles, it may be useful to expand the listing of life events in the manner of Maddi et al. (1987).

A final category that has not been systematically employed in stress research is that of lifetime traumatic stress. Weiner (1992) suggests that highly traumatic events, especially if experienced in childhood, could have long-term effects on health status. Weiner includes a listing of natural and man-made disasters that could be used as a starting point for this measure. Items might include child sexual molestation, life-threatening illness or injury, amputation, rape, witness of violent death, and other such traumatic events.

The present attempt at integrating measures of stress includes the following: lifetime traumatic stressors, threat–challenge appraisals summed over the traumatic stressors, and stress feelings summed over traumatic stressors. Because of the nature of traumatic stress, it probably would not make sense to attempt a separation of positive and negative events. The next predictor cluster would involve positive and negative life events. Measurement would again include an objective frequency measure nomothetically weighted, threat–challenge ratings summed over all positive or negative items, and subjective stress feelings summed over all positive or negative items. The third cluster involves hassles and uplifts. The objective stressor measures of hassles and uplifts could be derived by modifying existing scales so that items refer to specific events rather than to feelings or concerns about these events. Threat–challenge appraisals and stress feelings could also be made and separately summed over hassles and uplifts. As indicated above, stress feelings could be assessed at the item level, as with threat–challenge appraisals, or more globally. At least initially, it may be more useful to assess stress feelings at the item level to make this variable more comparable in structure to threat–challenge appraisals.

The above integrative predictor system may be represented as a structural model with arrows indicating possible causal pathways, but the empirical and theoretical basis for a full specification of the model is not yet available. Causal direction can be specified for several pathways, however, as determined by the following criteria: (1) the model is based on the assumption that stress causes (contributes to) physical illness; (2) stress variables which occur earlier in time would be causes rather than effects of later variables; and (3) it would be assumed that for the triad of objective stressor–cognitive appraisal–emotional reaction, the causal flow would be from most objective to most subjective (i.e., from event to cognition to emotion). This would be consistent, for example, with cognitive theories of psychopathology such as those of Beck and Ellis.

In addition to the possibility of advancing the prediction of physical illness, the implementation of this model would allow us to answer a number of questions that would help advance the development of stress theory. Within each type of stress (traumatic, life event, hassle), does the causal flow appear to proceed from the objective stressor to the threat–challenge appraisal to stress feelings? In other words, are the path coefficients from threat–challenge to feelings greater than those from the objective event to feelings? Are the path coefficients from event to threat–challenge greater than those from event to feelings? Within each type of stress, which aspect of stress, objective event, cognitive appraisal, or subjective feeling is more highly related to physical illness? As stress feelings are assumed to be the more proximate causes, and as feelings appear to be more closely linked to illness, we would expect feelings to be more highly related to physical illness, although such an effect may be time dependent (Green, 1986).

Are threat–challenge appraisals redundant with feelings of being pressured and overwhelmed? These appear to be the two dimensions most often discussed as ways of evaluating the meaning of the stressor to the subject. But evaluations of threat may be so close in meaning to feelings of pressure that it may not be useful to distinguish between these two types of relatively subjective reaction. Consistent with the measurement of many other psychological behaviors, however, it would appear to be useful to include a more cognitive and a more emotive component to the subjective stress reaction.

Of course, we would expect negative events to impact physical illness more strongly than positive events. Although a legitimate part of stress theory, this point may have been demonstrated so frequently that, in the interests of measurement efficiency, the use of clearly positive events in predictions of physical illness may no longer be practical. Nevertheless, several qualifications may be in order. New measures of positive events that may have a better chance of having a curative rather than a minimally deleterious effect are needed. For example, situations such as psychotherapy or close relationships may involve interactions that are stressful but curative. In addition, certain life events, such as birth or marriage, that might typically be classified as "positive" are probably better thought of as complex combinations of positive and negative features, and these should be retained in predictions of physical illness. Finally, the central issues surrounding eustress are still of interest to stress theory, and these have not yet been answered. What are the differences in physiological reactions between eustress and distress that lead to their different health outcomes? Answering this question may be pivotal in identifying key physiological reactions that mediate physical illness.

If traumatic stress has long-term effects on physical illness, does this occur directly or through indirect effects on life events or hassles? Because of the long time periods and little apparent overlap between traumatic stressors and either life events or hassles, it would appear that any effect on illness from traumatic stress would be direct. On the other hand, it is possible that an effect through life events or hassles could be mediated by a variable such as low self-esteem, which could conceivably result from high levels of early traumatic stress.

It should be reiterated that there is little that is new in the present model. It simply aims at a systematic measurement of existing distinctions in the theoretical literature. Although somewhat complicated, this model provides a better test of modern stress theory than would simpler models that ignore key distinctions, such as those among lifetime traumatic stress, life events, and hassles; or between pleasant and unpleasant stressful events; or those among objective stressors, cognitively appraised stress, and emotionally toned stress reactions.

REFERENCES

Antonovsky, A. (1979), *Health, Stress, and Coping.* San Francisco: Jossey-Bass.

Banks, J. K., & Gannon, L. R. (1988), The influence of hardiness on the relationship between stressors and psychosomatic symptomatology. *Amer. J. Commun. Psychol.*, 16:25–37.

Beale, N., & Nethercott, S. (1986), Job-loss and health—The influence of age and previous morbidity. *J. Res. Coll. Gen. Pract.*, 36:261–264.

Buckley, J. P. (1983), Present status of stress research related to the development of cardiovascular diseases. In: *Selye's Guide to Stress Research*, Vol. 2, ed. H. Selye. New York: Van Nostrand Reinhold, pp. 363–374.

Cohen, S., Kamarck, T., & Mermelstein, R. (1983), A global measure of perceived stress. *J. Health & Soc. Behav.*, 24:385–396.

Condon, J. T. (1986), Psychological disability in women who relinquish a baby for adoption. *Med. J. Australia*, 144:117–119.

Cooke, D. J., & Hole, D. J. (1983), The aetiological importance of stressful life events. *Brit. J. Psychiatry*, 143:397–400.

Costa, P. T., & McCrae, R. R. (1985), Hypochondriasis, neuroticism and aging: When are somatic complaints unfounded? *Amer. Psychologist*, 40:19–28.

Dohrenwend, B. P., & Shrout, P. E. (1986), Reply to Green and Deutsch. *Amer. Psychologist*, 41:716.

Dohrenwend, B. S., & Dohrenwend, B. P. (1974), Social and cultural influences on psychopathology. *Ann. Rev. Psychology*, 25:417–452.

————— ————— (1978), Some issues on research on stressful life events. *J. Nerv. & Mental Dis.*, 166:7–15.

————— ————— Dodson, M., & Shrout, P. E. (1984), Symptoms, hassles, social supports, and life events: Problem of confounded measures. *J. Abnorm. Psychology*, 93:222–230.

Dorian, B., & Garfinkel, P. E. (1987), Stress, immunity and illness—A review. *Psycholog. Med.*, 17:393–407.

Flannery, R. B. (1986), Negative affectivity, daily hassles, and somatic illness: Preliminary inquiry concerning hassles measurement. *Ed. & Psycholog. Measurement*, 46:1001–1004.

Friedman, H., & Booth-Kewley, S. (1987), The "disease prone personality": A meta-analytic view of the construct. *Amer. Psychologist*, 42:539–555.

Green, B. L. (1986), On the confounding of "hassles" stress and outcome. *Amer. Psychologist*, 41:714–715.

Holahan, C. K., & Holahan, C. J. (1987), Life stress, hassles, and self-efficacy in aging: A replication and extension. *J. Appl. Soc. Psychology*, 17:574–592.

Holmes, T. H., & Masuda, M. (1974), Life change and illness susceptibility. In: *Stressful Life Events: Their Nature and Effects*, ed. B. S. Dohrenwend & B. P. Dohrenwend. New York: John Wiley, pp. 25–47.

————— Rahe, R. H. (1967), The social readjustment rating scale. *J. Psychosom. Res.*, 11:213–218.

Kanner, A. D., Coyne, J. C., Schaefer, C., & Lazarus, R. S. (1981), Comparison of two modes of stress measurement: Daily hassles and uplifts versus major life events. *J. Behav. Med.*, 4:1–39.

Kiecolt-Glaser, J. K., Glaser, R., Strain, E., Stout, J., Tarr, K., Holliday, J., & Speicher, C. (1986), Modulation of cellular immunity in medical students. *J. Behav. Med.*, 9:5–21.

Kobasa, S. C., Maddi, S. R., Puccetti, M. C., & Zola, M. A. (1985), Effectiveness of hardiness, exercise, and social support as resources against illness. *J. Psychosom. Res.*, 29:525–533.

Lacey, J. I. (1967), Somatic response patterning and stress: Some revisions of activation theory. In: *Psychological Stress*, ed. M. Appley & R. Trumbull. New York: Appleton-Century-Crofts, pp. 14–42.

Lazarus, R. S., Cohen, J. B., Folkman, S., Kanner, A., & Schaefer, C. (1980), Psychological stress and adaptation: Some unresolved issues. In: *Selye's Guide to Stress Research*, Vol. 1, ed. H. Selye. New York: Van Nostrand Reinhold, pp. 90–117.

——— Folkman, S. (1984), *Stress, Appraisal, and Coping.* New York: Springer-Verlag.

Maddi, S. R., Bartone, P. T., & Puccetti, M. C. (1987), Stressful events are indeed a factor in physical illness: Reply to Schroeder and Costa (1984). *J. Pers. & Soc. Psychol.,* 52:833–843.

——— Kobasa, S. C. (1984), *The Hardy Executive: Health Under Stress.* Homewood, IL: Dow Jones-Irwin.

Marx, M. B., Garrity, T. F., & Bowers, F. R. (1975), The influence of recent life experience in the health of college freshmen. *J. Psychosom. Res.,* 19:87–98.

Mason, J. W. (1971), A re-evaluation of the concept of nonspecificity in stress theory. *J. Psychiat. Res.,* 8:323–333.

——— (1975), An historical view of the stress field. *J. Human Stress,* 1:6–12, 22–35.

Moos, R. R. (1979), Social–ecological perspectives on health. In: *Health Psychology,* ed. G. C. Stone, F. Cohen, & N. E. Adler. San Francisco: Jossey-Bass, pp. 523–547.

Nowack, K. M. (1991), Psychosocial predictors of health status. *Work & Stress,* 5:117–131.

Reich, W. P., Parrella, D. P., & Filstead, W. J. (1988), Unconfounding the hassles scale: External sources versus internal responses to stress. *J. Behav. Med.,* 3:239–249.

Roth, D. L., Wiebe, D. J., Fillingim, R. B., & Shay, K. A. (1989), Life events, fitness, and hardiness, and health: A simultaneous analysis of proposed stress-resistance effects. *J. Pers. & Soc. Psychol.,* 57:136–142.

Schroeder, D. H., & Costa, P. T. (1984), Influence of life event stress on physical illness: Substantive effects of methodological flaws? *J. Pers. & Soc. Psychol.,* 46:853–863.

Selye, H. (1956), *The Stress of Life.* New York: McGraw-Hill, 1976.

——— (1983), *Selye's Guide to Stress Research,* Vol. 2. New York: Van Nostrand Reinhold.

Shavit, Y., Lewis, J. W., Terman, G. W., Gale, R. P., & Liebeskind, J. C. (1984), Opioid peptides mediate the suppressive effects of stress on natural killer cell cytoxicity. *Science,* 223:188–190.

Watson, D., & Clark, L. A. (1985), Negative affectivity: The disposition to experience aversive emotional states. *Psychol. Bull.,* 96:465–490.

Weinberger, M., Hiner, S. L., & Tierney, W. M. (1987), In support of hassles as a measure of stress in predicting health outcomes. *J. Behav. Med.,* 10:19–31.

Weiner, H. (1992), *Perturbing the Organism.* Chicago: University of Chicago Press.

Weiss, J. M. (1971), Effects of coping behavior with and without a feedback signal on stress pathology in rats. *J. Comp. Physiol. Psychol.,* 77:22–30.

——— (1972), Psychological factors in stress and disease. *Scient. Amer.,* 226:104–113.

Wickramasekera, I. (1986), A model of people at high risk to develop chronic stress-related somatic symptoms. Some predictions. *Internat. Psychol.: Res. & Pract.,* 17:437–447.

Wyler, A. R., Masuda, M., & Holmes, T. H. (1968), Seriousness of illness rating scale. *J. Psychosom. Res.,* 11:33–375.

Chapter 6
Psychological Hardiness: A Reconceptualization and Measurement

Sharon L. Younkin, Ph.D., and Nancy E. Betz, Ph.D.

A major focus of recent research in the field of personality has been the possible role of personality variables in moderating the relationships between stress and psychological and/or physical illness. The area of inquiry focuses on personality characteristics which may potentially differentiate people who deteriorate physically and/or psychologically under stress from those who seem to be able to tolerate high levels of stress without faltering.

One personality variable which has received considerable attention as a stress buffer is that of psychological hardiness, as introduced by Kobasa (1979a,b). Kobasa defined hardiness as a composite of the following constructs: commitment, challenge, and control.

Kobasa's first attempt to assess hardiness was based on a study of male executives. Based on retrospective measures of stress and illness, Kobasa (1979b) compared a group of high stress/high illness executives to a group of high stress/low illness (stress-resistant) men on 19 personality measures related to the concepts of commitment, challenge, and control. Discriminant function analysis indicated that six scales significantly differentiated the groups: alienation from self (an indicator of commitment); nihilism and external locus of control (control indicators); and powerlessness, vegetativeness, and adventurousness (indicators of the challenge dimension). Using an empirical approach to scale construction, the logical next step would have been to use these six measures as hardiness indicators. However, Kobasa's next series of studies (Kobasa, Maddi, and Courington, 1981; Kobasa, Maddi, and Kahn, 1982; Kobasa, Maddi, and Zola, 1983; Kobasa and Puccetti, 1983) used only three of these measures (alienation from self, external locus of control, and powerlessness) and two additional scales which had not significantly differentiated the groups (i.e., alienation from work and security). In fact, the only study using the six scales significant in the original discriminant analysis was that of Ganellen and Blaney (1984). Additional work by the Kobasa group further confused the issue, in that every subsequent study used new variations in the measurement of commitment, challenge, and control (Funk and Houston, 1987; Hull, Van Treuren, and Virnelli, 1987). At least five different versions, consisting of 20, 36, 50, 71, and 90 items, have appeared in published research.

In addition to the lack of stability in the Kobasa measures, additional difficulties with the current measurement of hardiness have been identified. First, a construct intended to be reflective of a unitary trait important to stress resistance, that is, "hardiness," was defined in terms of three other traits (control, commitment, and challenge). These traits had already been proposed as important in stress resistance and/or mental health and functioning by other theorists and researchers (e.g., control has been studied by Rotter [1966], and Abramson, Seligman, and Teasdale [1978], among numerous others). Carver (1989) discusses the conceptual difficulties created when personality constructs are initially postulated to be multidimensional rather than unidimensional, and psychometricians more generally discuss the desirability of unidimensional versus multidimensional approaches to trait measurement (Nunnally, 1978). Furthermore, factor analyses do not indicate any general factor or second-order dimension that would warrant inferences that "hardiness" is being measured, and measures of challenge, commitment, and control relate very differently to criterion variables. In the prediction of health outcomes, commitment and, secondarily, control, usually have been related as predicted, while challenge has tended to have negative as often as positive, relationships to health outcomes (Hull, Van Treuren, and Virnelli, 1987).

Second, the domain of possible measures of control, commitment, and challenge was composed largely of "negative indicators." For example, measures of alienation (from self and from work) were used as negative indicators of commitment. If a construct can be measured directly, use of negative indicators simply increases the conceptual "distance" between the construct and its measure and, consequently, the likelihood of invalidity of the measure. Furthermore, use of negative indicators increases the probability that the measure will reflect more general negative affectivity (Funk and Houston, 1987; Rhodewalt and Zone, 1989).

Thus, research investigating psychological hardiness has been plagued by serious problems in measurement. Many recent reviews of the construct conclude that although the measurement of hardiness presents many problems and has not been shown to be psychometrically sound, the concept itself has promise (e.g., Hull et al., 1987; Carson, 1988). Carson (1988), for example, suggests that a better research strategy for studying hardiness would focus on a more precisely measurable construct.

The basis for this study was the belief that although the concept of hardiness has logical merit and face validity, it has been very poorly defined, operationalized, and measured. Instead of a multidimensional conceptualization of hardiness we proposed and operationalized a unidimensional concept based on the lexical meaning of hardiness, that is, "the capacity for enduring hardship, privation etc." or its synonym "resilience," defined as "the ability to recover rapidly from illness, depression, adversity, or the like." This characteristic could be measured directly rather than indirectly and using positive as well as negative trait indicators.

Thus, the purposes of the present study were as follows: (1) to develop a new conceptualization and measure of the construct of psychological hardiness; (2) to examine the psychometric characteristics of the new measure, including its reliability, validity, and factor structure; (3) to investigate its relationships to other psychological characteristics potentially related to a healthy or stress-resistant personality, including self-esteem, autonomy, depression, and general psychological symptomatology; and (4) to investigate its comparative utility relative to the earlier measures of hardiness as a moderator of the stress–well-being relationship.

Method

Subjects and Procedure

Two hundred and ninety-five students (152 women and 143 men) enrolled in an introductory psychology course at a large Midwestern university served as subjects for this investigation. Subjects received course credit for their participation and were considered to have volunteered for this study in that they had a variety of experiments from which to choose. Subjects were given the instruments described below, and subjects were given a written debriefing statement upon completing the instruments.

Development of the Psychological Hardiness Scale

The Psychological Hardiness scale was developed to reflect a more direct definition of the concept of hardiness; specifically, a resilience under stress, or the capacity to endure hardship. Resilience refers to the ability to recover from adversity.

Consistent with established procedures for a construct-based approach to test construction (e.g., Nunnally, 1978; Walsh and Betz, 1990), development of the measure consisted of developing a comprehensive and precise definition of the construct of interest and writing a pool of items larger than that needed for the final instrument scale. Accordingly, 49 items representing the construct were written. Examples are: "I often find it hard to get things done when I'm upset" and "I tend to 'fall apart' pretty easily," and "I'm one of those people who just keep going no matter what happens." Responses were obtained on a 5-point Likert continuum ranging from "Strongly Disagree" (1) to "Strongly Agree" (5). Based on item–total correlations below .30, 9 items were eliminated, resulting in a 40-item scale. Eighteen of the items were positively worded, and negatively worded items were reverse scored as necessary such that higher scores indicated greater degrees of hardiness.

In order to evaluate the quality of the scale, internal consistency reliability and factorial unidimensionality, and concurrent, construct, and criterion-related validity were examined.

Cognitive Hardiness Scale (Nowack, 1990, 1991). The Cognitive Hardiness scale was administered in order to investigate the concurrent validity of the Psychological Hardiness scale. The Cognitive Hardiness scale is a 30-item scale based upon Kobasa's definition of hardiness. As such, the scale assesses: (1) commitment; (2) challenge; and (3) control. Responses are obtained using a 5-point Likert response continuum (1 = strongly agree, 2 = agree, 3 = neither agree nor disagree, 4 = disagree, 5 = strongly disagree). "My involvement in nonwork activities and hobbies provides me with a sense of meaning and purpose" is a sample item. Scores on this measure range from 30 to 150, with higher scores indicating greater levels of cognitive hardiness. The scale has shown adequate internal consistency reliability (alpha = .83). This scale has been validated in over 1000 professional working adults (Nowack, 1990). Reliability in this sample (coefficient alpha) was .86.

CONSTRUCT VALIDITY MEASURES

Rosenberg Self Esteem Inventory (RSE) (Rosenberg, 1965). The RSE is a well-known 10-item 4-point Likert scale (1 = strongly disagree, 2 = disagree, 3 = agree, 4 = strongly agree) designed to measure "global self-esteem." Scores on this measure range from 10 to 40, with higher scores indicating higher levels of self-esteem. The following is a sample item: "I feel that I'm a person of worth, at least on an equal basis with others." Sample internal consistency reliability coefficients (α) are .77 (Dobson, Goudy, Keith, and Powers, 1979) and .88 (Fleming and Courtney, 1984); test-retest correlations have been .85 for a 2-week interval (Silber and Tippett, 1985) and .82 for a 1-week interval (Fleming and Courtney, 1984). Evidence for convergent and discriminant validity is summarized in Robinson, Shaver, and Wrightsman (1991). Reliability herein (α) was .91.

Beck Depression Inventory (BDI) (Beck, 1967). The BDI consists of 21 items measuring affective, cognitive, motivational, and physiological indicators of depression. This measure utilizes a 4-point scoring system, with scores on individual items ranging from 0 to 3. Total scores range from 0 to 63, with higher scores indicating greater levels of depression. The BDI is psychometrically sound, with stability coefficients in the 70's (Steer, Beck, and Garrison, 1986). Internal consistency reliability was reported at .86, and the Spearman-Brown-corrected split-half reliability coefficient is .93 (Beck, 1967). Convergent validity correlations with clinical ratings of depression range from .60 to .90 (Steer et al., 1986; Robinson et al., 1991). Although the BDI was developed for use in psychiatric populations, a study investigating the use of the BDI in a university setting resulted in the finding that it is a valid instrument for use in a college population (Blumberry, Oliver, and McClure, 1978). Reliability herein was .89.

Autonomy Scale (Beck, Epstein, and Harrison, 1983). Autonomy was assessed utilizing the Autonomous Achievement subscale of the Sociotropy–Autonomy Scale. This subscale consists of 12 items scored on a 5-point Likert scale (1 = strongly agree, 2 = moderately agree, 3 = aren't sure or neutral, 4 = moderately disagree, 5 = strongly disagree). The following is a sample item: "The possibility of being rejected by others for standing up for my rights would not stop me." Scores on this measure range from 12 to 60, and are determined additively, with lower scores indicating greater levels of autonomy. To facilitate comparisons between this instrument and the other instruments utilized, the entire scale was reverse scored such that higher scores indicated greater levels of autonomy. This test is reported to have an alpha coefficient of .82. The value found within this sample was .80.

CRITERION-RELATED VALIDITY

Brief Symptom Inventory (Derogatis and Spencer, 1982). The Brief Symptom Inventory consists of 12 scales, 9 primary (symptom) dimensions, and 3 global indices of distress. It is a 53-item self-report symptom inventory designed to reflect the symptom patterns of psychiatric and medical patients as well as nonclinical samples. This test is designed as a modified checklist; for example, a sample item reads as follows: "nervousness or shakiness inside." This test utilizes a 5-point Likert scale (1 = not at all to 5 = extremely). Scores on this measure range from 53 to 260, with higher scores indicating greater levels of symptomatology. This instrument utilizes an additive scoring method, and has a variety of subdimensions that may be scored; however, since this investigation required only a global index of symptomatology, only the summed item totals were used.

Internal consistency reliability estimates for the BSI are acceptable, ranging from .71 to .83. Values of test–retest reliability have ranged from .68 to .91 on the primary scales and above .80 on each of the three global scales. Excellent convergent validity (derived from a comparison of the BSI with its parent instrument, the SCL-90) is also reported, with correlations ranging from .29 to .99. Evidence for concurrent validity has been provided by examining the correlations of BSI with scores on various subscales of the MMPI, with salient correlations ranging from .30 to .72. Additionally, a factor analysis based on a sample of 1002 individuals supported the a priori construction of the symptom dimensions (Derogatis and Melisaratos, 1983). This instrument has been normed and validated for use with college students (Cochran and Hale, 1985). Reliability within the present sample (alpha) was .97.

Life Stress Survey. This measure consisted of items from the Life Experiences Survey (LES; Sarason, Johnson, and Siegel, 1978) that would most likely be encountered by college students. This scale consisted of 25 items scored along a 5-point Likert scale (1 = did not experience, 2 = not at all stressful . . . 5 = extremely stressful). A sample item is as follows: "Death of a close family member." The LES has been judged as being appropriate for use with college students (Sarason et al., 1978). Total scores, obtained using cumulative scoring, ranged from 25 to 125; higher scores indicate greater levels of stress. Test–retest reliability correlations for total change scores were noted to be in the .60's (Sarason et al., 1978). The value of coefficient alpha within the present sample was .81.

Data Analysis

Descriptive data were obtained for each instrument. Gender differences on these data were analyzed with t tests. T tests were also used to investigate the differences between groups differentiated on the basis of hardiness scores. Internal consistency reliability and factor analysis were used to examine the internal structure and postulated unidimensionality of the PHS. Correlation coefficients were computed to examine predictions regarding concurrent, construct, and criterion-related validity. Finally, comparisons of high stress/high hardiness and high stress/low hardiness and hierarchical multiple regression analyses were used to examine the direct and moderating effects of hardiness on psychological health indices.

Results

Item total score correlations for the PHS ranged from .31 to .72, with the majority lying in the range of .50 to .59. Internal consistency reliability (coefficient alpha) was .92. The 40 items were factor analyzed using the principal factors method. Prior communality estimates were based on square multiple correlations. The scree plot of eigenvalues revealed one clear general factor, having an eigenvalue of 10.2 and accounting for 58 percent of the common variance and 26 percent of the total variance. The next two eigenvalues were 2.4 and 1.3. Loadings on the general factor ranged from .21 to .73, and the majority fell between .50 to .69. Only four items had loadings in the range of .21 to .29.

Table 6.1 provides descriptive statistics and gender comparisons for the major variables assessed herein. As shown, significant gender differences were indicated in depression and symptomatology, with women reporting higher levels of both depression and other symptoms. No significant gender differences on either measure of hardiness, self-esteem, or autonomy were evident.

The correlations among all of the variables of interest are shown in Table 6.2. Concurrent validity was assessed by the correlation between the Psychological Hardiness Scale and the Cognitive Hardiness Scale; this value of r was .75. Evidence for construct validity was provided by examining the relationships between hardiness and self-esteem, depression, and autonomy. The results indicated significant relationships in the directions hypothesized, that is, the measure of hardiness was associated with higher levels of self-esteem ($r = .56$) and autonomy ($r = .42$) and lower levels of depression ($r = -.59$). For comparative purposes, correlations of the Cognitive Hardiness Scale with self-esteem, autonomy, and depression were comparable, with values of .52, .37, and $-.52$, respectively. The PHS was related as postulated to both stress and illness symptoms, showing a significant negative relationship with both self-perceived stress ($r = -.32$) and illness ($r = -.64$).

In addition to computing correlations, a median split was used to divide the sample into those scoring above and below the median on the Hardiness Scale, similar to the subgrouping procedure advocated by Barling (1986). T tests comparing subjects high in hardiness to subjects low in hardiness revealed significant differences on all variables, as shown in Table 6.3. Specifically, individuals who reported high levels of hardiness were found to

TABLE 6.1

Descriptive Statistics and the Significance of Gender Differences on the Major Variables

	Males		Females		t	Total Scores	
	M	SD	M	SD		M	SD
Psychological							
Hardiness Scale	177.3	21.3	173.3	23.3	1.55	175.3	22.4
Cognitive							
Hardiness Scale	106.2	12.8	107.0	15.6	− .48	106.6	14.3
Brief Symptom							
Inventory	90.3	32.1	100.4	36.7	−2.52*	95.5	34.8
Beck Depression							
Inventory	6.1	6.2	9.0	7.9	−3.50**	7.6	7.3
Rosenberg							
Self-esteem							
Scale	32.5	5.8	31.3	6.3	1.66	31.8	6.1
Stress							
Scale	45.2	12.9	49.1	13.0	−2.5*	47.3	13.1
Autonomy							
Scale	45.8	6.5	44.9	7.3	1.11	45.4	6.7

Note: Female n = 152, Male n = 143
* = $p <$ .01, ** = $p <$ .001

have higher levels of self-esteem and autonomy, and lower levels of depression and symptomatology.

A hierarchical regression analysis was conducted to test the hypothesis that hardiness accounted for variance in symptomatology beyond that accounted for by stress; stress, hardiness, and their interaction were the independent variables and symptomatology was the dependent variable.

As shown in Table 6.4, stress was the first variable entered in the equation, yielding a significant multiple correlation of .54 (F = 119.97, $p <$ .0001, R^2 = .29). The second step added hardiness, accounting for an additional 24 percent of the variance. Finally, the interaction between hardiness and stress did not add a significant amount of explainable variance to the equation. Thus, although hardiness has a large direct influence on symptoms reported, there is no evidence here for a moderating effect.

TABLE 6.2
Pearson Correlation Coefficients Describing the Relationships Among Variables

	2	3	4	5	6	7
1. Psychological Hardiness Scale	.75	.56	−.59	−.64	−.32	.43
2. Cognitive Hardiness Scale		.52	−.52	−.53	−.21	.37
3. Rosenberg Self-Esteem Scale			−.49	−.49	−.29	.31
4. Beck Depression Inventory				.78	.54	−.24
5. Brief Symptom Inventory					.54	−.25
6. Stress Scale						−.18
7. Autonomy Scale						

Note: All correlations are significant at $p < .001$.

TABLE 6.3
t-Tests Comparing High Hardy Versus Low Hardy Subjects

Variable		High Hardy		Low Hardy		t
	Median	Mean	SD	Mean	SD	
Rosenberg Self-Esteem Scale	33	35.0	6.3	29.0	5.5	8.74**
Autonomy Scale	46	47.4	6.2	43.3	6.9	5.35**
Beck Depression Inventory	6	4.8	5.1	10.6	7.9	−7.40**
Stress Scale	46	44.5	11.8	50.2	13.8	−3.80*
Brief Symptom Inventory	87	79.4	21.8	112.3	38.0	−9.07**

Note: High Hardy $n = 151$, Low Hardy $n = 144$.
  $* = p < .001$
  $** = p < .0001$

TABLE 6.4
Hierarchical Multiple Linear Regression Models
for the Prediction of Symptomatology

Order of Entry	Predictor Variables	Beta	R^2	Overall F	P	Change in R^2	Source F	P
1	Stress	.54	.29	119.97	.0001	.29	119.97	.0001
2	Hardiness	−.52	.54	108.49	.0001	.25	154.26	.0001
	and Stress	.37					77.73	.0001
3	Hardiness	−.52	.54	112.64	.0001	001	150.75	.0001
	and Stress	.36					69.25	.0001
	Interaction	−.04					.98	.32

A second approach to examining the possible buffering effects of hardiness is shown in Table 6.5. Subjects above the median on stress were divided into two groups, that is, those above and those below the median psychological hardiness scores; high stress/ high hardiness subjects were compared to high stress/low hardiness subjects on the major variables. As shown in Table 6.5, there were significant differences between these two groups on all major variables, with the "stressed but hardy" individuals reporting significantly higher levels of self-esteem and autonomy and significantly lower levels of depression and symptoms than "stressed but less hardy" individuals.

TABLE 6.5
t-Tests of High Stress/High Hardy Versus
High Stress/Low Hardy Subjects

Variable	High Stress/High Hardy		High Stress/Low Hardy		t
	Mean	SD	Mean	SD	
Rosenberg Self-esteem Scale	34.1	6.4	27.8	5.6	6.39**
Autonomy Scale	47.7	6.3	42.1	7.1	5.13**
Beck Depression Inventory	6.9	5.8	13.1	8.2	−5.44**
Brief Symptom Inventory	89.4	25.1	124.1	37.1	−6.83**

Note: High Hardy/High Stress $n = 63$
Low Hardy/High Stress $n = 87$
** = $p < .0001$

Analyses of the reliability and validity of the cognitive hardiness scale indicated comparable levels of coefficient alpha (.86 vs. .92 for the PHS), comparable correlations with other variables postulated to be related to the construct of hardiness, and similar behavior in the prediction of stress and psychological symptoms.

However, it had also been postulated a priori that the Psychological Hardiness Scale would be found to be unidimensional, while the Cognitive Hardiness Scale would show the multidimensionality inherent in its multifaceted definition. Accordingly, the CHS was also subjected to factor analysis via the principal factors method, using squared multiple correlations as the communality estimates and the scree test to determine the number of factors to extract. Using this rule, three factors were extracted; their eigenvalues were 5.9, 1.6, and 1.1. The factors were rotated using an oblique method (Harris-Kaiser) because the three postulated components of hardiness are assumed to be intercorrelated. The factors extracted accounted for 59, 16, and 11 percent of the total variance; factor loadings are shown in Table 6.6, and all loadings equal to or above .30 are underlined.

Although a 3-factor structure would correspond to the three components postulated, the item loadings do not correspond well to the three dimensions of commitment, challenge, and control. Both of the first two factors contain items from all three subscales, and the third factor contains only two items (both "challenge" items in the Kobasa instruments). Two items (numbers 20 and 8) do not load significantly on any factor, and two others (numbers 17 and 16) load below .30. Thus, the obtained factor structure is not consistent with the a priori definition of the construct. The factor intercorrelations were as follows: Factors I and II (.47), II and III (.30) and I and III (.47).

DISCUSSION

The results of the present study provided strong evidence for both the psychometric and predictive utility of a unidimensional concept and measure of psychological hardiness. The measure developed herein was highly internally consistent (alpha was equal to .92) and factorially unidimensional. Correlations with other indices of a "healthy personality" were statistically significant and of moderate magnitude, ranging from .42 to .59 in absolute value.

TABLE 6.6
Rotated Factor Pattern of the
Cognitive Hardiness Scale

Item Number[a]	Factor I	Factor II	Factor III
24	*82*	3	−14
25	*71*	4	−12
26	*70*	8	−13
23	*57*	6	−12
7	*56*	−16	15
6	*56*	6	− 2
27	*55*	−10	15
28	*50*	−13	11
21	*48*	−27	24
15	*42*	11	25
13	*40*	2	−27
9	*38*	11	15
12	*34*	10	16
11	*33*	20	26
17	24	7	14
20	19	9	14
18	10	*62*	−12
5	− 5	*55*	− 6
22	14	*58*	−18
1	−21	*45*	21
19	*35*	*42*	− 2
3	− 8	*42*	21
14	2	*41*	− 8
30	− 5	*38*	− 3
2	−20	*31*	25
8	1	14	11
10	− 3	−24	*68*
4	−19	32	*54*
29	27	−14	*30*
16	−13	15	22

Note. Decimal places have been omitted. Values greater than or equal to .30 are set in italic.
[a]Items are presented in association with the factor on which their highest loading occurs. Within primary factors, items are ordered from highest to lowest loading.

The conceptual utility of the measure examined herein was supported by both evidence of a direct contribution of hardiness to the prediction of symptomatology, beyond that accounted for by stress, and by significant differences between high stress/high hardiness, versus high stress/low hardiness subjects on self-esteem, autonomy, depression, and symptom level. Group differences of 89.4 vs. 124.1 (symptoms) and 6.9 vs. 13.1 (depression) illustrate the practical facilitative significance of higher versus lower levels of hardiness in individuals perceiving relatively high levels of stress in their lives.

The unidimensionality of the PHS was in contrast to the findings of three factors in the Cognitive Hardiness Scale. Even if the three factors were completely consistent with the three components specified a priori, which they were not, most psychometricians (e.g., Nunnally, 1978) recommend the conceptual and interpretive preferability of unidimensional measures. That the present measure of hardiness was as reliable and valid, if not more so, than the existing multidimensional conceptualization may suggest a change in further investigations of the hardiness construct.

Although the present study suggests the possible utility of this scale for use in further research, it does not by itself answer the broader question of the place of psychological hardiness within a more general framework summarized as the healthy personality or, conversely, general maladjustment or psychopathology. As mentioned previously, Rhodewalt and Zone (1989) have suggested that nonhardiness may essentially reflect negative affectivity. More generally, the relationship of hardiness to such inclusive systems as the 5-factor model of personality (McCrae, 1991) or specific constructs such as rationality/emotional defensiveness (Swan, Carmelli, Dame, Rosenman, and Spielberger, 1991) needs further exploration. It is hoped that a conceptually concise and factorially unidimensional measure of hardiness will facilitate progress in this area.

REFERENCES

Abramson, L., Seligman, M., & Teasdale, J. (1978), Learned helplessness in humans: critique and reformulation. *J. Abnorm. Psychol.*, 87:47–74.

Barling, J. (1986), Inter-role conflict and marital functioning amongst employed fathers. *J. Occupat. Behav.*, 7:1–8.

Beck, A., Epstein, N., & Harrison, R. (1983), Cognitions, attitudes, and personality dimensions in depression. *Brit. J. Cog. Psychother.*, 1:1–16.

Beck, A. T. (1967), *Depression: Causes and Treatment.* Philadelphia: University of Pennsylvania Press.

Blumberry, W., Oliver, J., & McClure, J. (1978), Validation of the Beck Depression Inventory in a university population using psychiatric estimate as the criterion. *J. Consult. & Clin. Psychol.*, 46:150–155.

Carson, A. (1988), Personality. *Ann. Rev. Psychol.*, 40:227–248.

Carver, C. (1989), How should multifaceted personality constructs be tested? Issues illustrated by self-monitoring, attributional style, and hardiness. *J. Personal. & Soc. Psychol.*, 56:577–585.

Cochran, C., & Hale, D. (1985), College student norms on the Brief Symptom Inventory. *J. Clin. Psychol.*, 41:777–779.

Derogatis, L. R., & Melisaratos, N. (1983), The Brief Symptom Inventory: An introductory report. *Psycholog. Med.*, 13:595–605.

—————— Spencer, P. M. (1982), *The Brief Symptom Inventory (BSI), Administration, Scoring, and Procedures Manual-I.* Baltimore: Johns Hopkins University Press.

Dobson, C., Goudy, W. J., Keith, P. M., & Powers, E. (1979), Further analysis of Rosenberg's self-esteem scale. *Psycholog. Reports*, 44:639–641.

Fleming, J. S., & Courtney, B. E. (1984), The dimensionality of self-esteem. II. Hierarchical facet model for revised measurement scales. *J. Personal. & Soc. Psychol.*, 46:404–421.

Funk, S. C., & Houston, B. K. (1987), A critical analyis of the hardiness scale's validity and utility. *J. Personal. & Soc. Psychol.*, 53:572–578.

Ganellen, R., & Blaney, P. (1984), Hardiness and social support as moderators of the effects of life stress. *J. Personal. & Soc. Psychol.*, 47:156–163.

Hull, J., Van Treuren, R., & Virnelli, S. (1987), Hardiness and health: A critique and alternative approach. *J. Personal. & Soc. Psychol.*, 53:518–530.

Kobasa, S. C. (1979a), Stressful life events, personality, and health: An inquiry into hardiness. *J. Personal. & Soc. Psychol.*, 37:1–11.

—————— (1979b), Personality and resistance to illness. *Amer. J. Commun. Psychol.*, 7:413–423.

—————— Maddi, S. R., & Courington, S. (1981), Personality and constitution as mediators in the stress-illness relationship. *J. Health & Soc. Behav.*, 22:368–378.

—————— —————— Kahn, S. (1982), Hardiness and health: A prospective study. *J. Personal. & Soc. Psychol.*, 42:168–177.

—————— —————— Zola, M. A. (1983), Type A and hardiness. *J. Behav. Med.*, 6:41–51.

—————— Puccetti, M. C. (1983), Personality and social resources in stress resistance. *J. Personal. & Soc. Psychol.*, 45:839–850.

McCrae, R. R. (1991), The five-factor model and its assessment in clinical settings. *J. Personal. Assess.*, 57:399–414.

Nowack, K. M. (1990), Initial development of an inventory to assess stress and health risk. *Amer. J. Health Promot.*, 4:173–180.

—————— (1991), *Stress Assessment Profile.* Woodland Hills, CA: Organizational Performance Dimensions.

Nunnally, J. (1978), *Psychometric Theory.* New York: McGraw-Hill.

Rhodewalt, F., & Zone, J. (1989), Appraisal of life change, depression, and illness in hardy and nonhardy women. *J. Personal. & Soc. Psychol.*, 56:81–88.

Robinson, J. P., Shaver, P. R., & Wrightsman, L. S. (1991), *Measures of Personality and Social Psychological Attitudes.* San Diego, CA: Academic Press.

Rosenberg, M. (1965), *Society and the Adolescent Self-Image.* Princeton, NJ: Princeton University Press.

Rotter, J. (1966), Generalized expectancies for internal versus external control of reinforcement. *Psychological Monographs*, 80: Whole No. 609.

Sarason, I., Johnson, J., & Siegel, J. (1978), Assessing the impact of life changes: Development of the Life Experiences Survey. *J. Consult. & Clin. Psychol.*, 46:932–946.

Silber, E., & Tippett, J. (1965), Self-esteem: Clinical assessment and measurement validation. *Psycholog. Rep.*, 16:1017–1071.

Steer, R. A., Beck, A. T., & Garrison, B. (1986), Applications of the Beck Depression Inventory. In: *Assessment of Depression*, ed. N. Sartorius & A. T. Ban. Berlin: Springer-Verlag, pp. 123–142.

Swan, G. E., Carmelli, D., Dame, A., Rosenman, R. H., & Spielberger, C. D. (1991), The Rationality/Emotional Defensiveness Scale—Internal structure and stability. *J. Psychomat. Res.*, 35:545–554.

Walsh, B., & Betz, N. E. (1990), *Tests and Assessment.* Englewood Cliffs, NJ: Prentice-Hall.

Part II

Assessment and Methodological Issues

Chapter 7
Assessment of Posttraumatic Stress Disorder: A Conceptual Overview

MADELINE UDDO, Ph.D., ALBERT N. ALLAIN, JR., M.S., AND PATRICIA B. SUTKER, Ph.D.

It is now recognized that a predictable pattern of psychological symptoms conceptualized as posttraumatic stress disorder (PTSD) may occur subsequent to the experience of extraordinary or life-threatening events. Introduction of PTSD as a distinct diagnostic category in the third edition of the *Diagnostic and Statistical Manual of Mental Disorders* (DSM-III) (APA, 1980) with revisions in the DSM-III-R (APA, 1987) prompted increased scrutiny of the psychological symptoms that may develop after trauma experiences. Despite gains in knowledge of the negative psychological sequelae to exposure to extreme stress, understanding of PTSD remains incomplete, in part because clinical and research assessment protocols have lacked methodological precision, comprehensiveness, and sophistication. The aim of this chapter is to review theoretical issues relevant to measurement of extraordinary stress and its sequelae across diverse domains of functioning.

Highlighting the role of the trauma in marking disorder onset calls into play the necessity of examining both stimulus and response aspects of the disorder as well as the person who becomes afflicted. Accordingly, it is essential to develop an assessment protocol encompassing evaluation of not only the stimulus properties of the stressor and the stress response, but also pre- and posttrauma person and environment variables that potentially influence the stress response. This discussion will provide an overview of conceptual issues pertinent to assessment of these three distinct yet interactive domains. Emphasis is devoted to examination of the DSM-III-R (APA, 1987) stressor criterion, or criterion A, exploration of the multiple outcomes of exposure to extreme stress, and discussion of the significance of quantifying person and environment factors that interact to influence the complex human response to stress.

CONCEPTUALIZING AND MEASURING STRESSOR EVENTS: STIMULUS PARAMETERS

Posttraumatic stress disorder is unique among mental disorders in that an environmental stimulus, or identified stressor, is required in order for the disorder to be recognized by the current nosology. Features listed by the DSM-III-R (APA, 1987) as defining stressors that are associated with development of PTSD include events that may be seen as "outside the range of usual experiences"; "markedly distressing to almost anyone"; and "usually experienced with intense fear, terror, and helplessness" (p. 247). When examined from sociocultural and clinical perspectives, shortcomings of the DSM-III-R stressor definition become apparent. However, reformulation of the PTSD diagnostic criteria for the upcoming DSM revision has sparked considerable debate centering around determining the properties of a stimulus that qualify it as a potential catalyst for PTSD, or traumatic stressor. Within the current nomenclature, exploration of distinctions between extraordinary and more common life stressors, as well as examination of salient stressor characteristics, is of particular relevance to assessment of traumatic stress.

The current criterion A definition has been criticized because certain experiences commonly associated with PTSD unfortunately are too prevalent, albeit traumatic, in contemporary society to be considered out of the ordinary (Green, Lindy, and Grace, 1985; Kilpatrick and Resnick, 1993; March, 1993). By reason of exposure to highly stressful events, members of diverse subpopulations within American society may be seen as potentially suffering the symptoms of PTSD. For instance, during 1991, over 1.8 million violent crimes, such as murder, rape, robbery, and assault, were reported in the United States (*World Almanac*, 1992). Estimates indicate that each year between 1.5 and 2 million children are victims of physical abuse (Garmezy and Rutter, 1983), and 4 to 14 percent of the general population (Finkelhor, 1984), or as many as 56 percent of adult women (Kilpatrick, Edmunds, and Seymour, 1992) have experienced some form of sexual trauma. There remain alive 8.8 million veterans of the World War II era, 4.6 million Korean conflict era veterans, more than 3 million survivors of Vietnam combat, over 540,000 Operation Desert Storm returnees (U.S. Department of Veterans Affairs, 1992), and approximately 66,000 American prisoner-of-war (POW) survivors (Stenger, 1993). Moreover, it is estimated that as many as 2 million Americans experience the devastation of earthquake, hurricane, flood, and other natural and manmade disasters each year (Solomon, 1989). Such statistics reveal that highly stressful, potentially catastrophic events are not unusual occurrences in contemporary society. It is indefensible to argue, however, that traumas endured as a result of sexual assault, other violent crimes, or combat are incapable of initiating PTSD because these events are not statistically rare.

It also has been argued that some individuals who experience a low magnitude, commonplace stressor (e.g., marital discord, bereavement, miscarriage, financial problems) endorse symptoms of other requisite DSM-III-R PTSD diagnostic criteria, including reexperiencing, avoidance-numbing, and hyperarousal, although the identified stressor does not fulfill the current PTSD criterion A requirements (Burstein, 1985; Helzer, Robins, and McEvoy, 1987; Solomon and Canino, 1990). Limited data suggest that

PTSD may be initiated by the cumulative effects of exposure to multiple losses or chronic, low intensity stress (Horowitz, Wilner, and Alvarez, 1979; Davidson and Baum, 1986; Breslau and Davis, 1987). To add to this body of research, a multisite field trial is being conducted by the DSM-IV PTSD Advisory Committee to examine empirically rates of PTSD in cohorts who have experienced low versus high magnitude stressors (Kilpatrick and Resnick, 1993). These findings imply that there are no clear boundaries between everyday and catastrophic stress.

Data suggest that PTSD diagnosis is influenced by quantitative factors such a trauma intensity, duration, and frequency as well as by parameters such as the nature or characteristics of the traumatic event (Sutker, Uddo-Crane, and Allain, 1991). The most robust finding in the PTSD etiology literature is that PTSD is predicted most powerfully by the severity of the stress experience or magnitude of the stressor (Foy, Osato, Houskamp, and Neumann, in press). Employing specially targeted measures, often tallied cumulatively, to characterize the severity of given stressors, this dose–response relationship between trauma severity and PTSD diagnosis has been documented among war veterans, including World War II and Korean POW and combat veterans (Sutker, Galina, West, and Allain, 1990; Sutker, Allain, and Winstead, 1993); Vietnam veterans (Foy, Carroll, and Donahoe, 1987; Green, Lindy, Grace, and Glesser, 1989; Kulka, Schlenger, Fairbank, Hough, Jordan, Marmar, and Weiss, 1990) and POW survivors (Ursano, 1981); Operation Desert Storm returnees (Sutker, Uddo, Brailey, and Allain, 1993; Sutker, Uddo, Brailey, Vasterling, and Errera, 1994); as well as survivors of natural disaster (Shore, Tatum, and Vollmer, 1986; Green, 1991) and physical assault and rape (Kilpatrick, Saunders, Veronen, Best, and Von, 1987; Kilpatrick, Saunders, Amick-McMullan, Best, Veronen, and Resnick, 1989).

In addition to trauma intensity, assessment of trauma duration and frequency is essential in order to understand fully the survivor's symptomatology and therapeutic needs. That is, it has been observed that survivors of prolonged or repeated trauma exhibit a clinically distinct, more complex symptom picture than those exposed to a single traumatic event of limited duration (Horo-witz, Wilner, and Alvarez, 1979; Kiser, Ackerman, and Brown, 1988; Herman, 1992a). This clinical finding, as well as data indi-cating that a significant proportion of trauma survivors are victims of more than one trauma (Kilpatrick et al., 1992), highlights the necessity of conducting a comprehensive trauma history that sys-tematically evaluates the type and extent of exposure to traumatic lifetime events (Resnick, Kilpatrick, and Lipovsky, 1991). It has been suggested that when faced with the complicated task of as-sessing the effects of multiple or continuous lifetime traumas, rather than attempting to tease apart the sequelae of each sepa-rate trauma and tie diagnostic criteria to each event, it is more efficacious to focus on the cumulative impact of traumatization on psychological functioning (Kilpatrick, 1993). Although cur-rently employed by most research and clinical assessment ap-proaches, the former method may impose an artificial structure on the evaluation that does not necessarily provide a representa-tive picture of stress residuals in individuals who have endured multiple traumatic life events.

Of importance is the necessity of characterizing stressful events in terms of salient aspects of the trauma that are hypothesized to provoke PTSD or pinpointing those psychosocial and biological trauma components that are most deleterious in terms of psycho-logical residuals. Such elements, referred to as "within-trauma exposure characteristics" by Kilpatrick and Resnick (1993) and "event specific dimensions" by March (1993), that have been identified to increase risk for negative outcomes include endur-ing severe malnutrition and physical torture (Thygesen, Her-mann, and Willanger, 1970; Eitinger, 1975; Mollica, Wyshak, and Lavelle, 1987; Sutker, Galina, et al., 1990), encountering the gro-tesque and macabre (Green et al., 1989; Green, Grace, Lindy, Glesser, and Leonard, 1990; Sutker, Uddo, Brailey, Allain, and Errera, 1994; Sutker, Uddo, Brailey, Vasterling, and Errera, in press); sustaining physical injury (Kilpatrick et al., 1989; Pitman, Altman, and Macklin, 1989); witnessing death (Green, Grace, Lindy, Titchener, and Lindy, 1983; Green et al., 1989; Saigh,

1989; Speed, Engdahl, Schwartz, and Eberly, 1989); being exposed to unpredictable and uncontrollable stressors (Foa, Zinbarg, and Rothbaum, 1992); and experiencing human-induced trauma versus traumatic events classified as "acts of God" (Baum, 1990; Green, Grace, Lindy, Glesser, and Leonard, 1990; Janoff-Bulman, 1992).

Evaluation of the survivor's role during the trauma represents an important assessment component. That is, within the context of some traumatic events, such as war, survivors at times are not only the target, but also the agent of death and violence. Research indicating that Vietnam veterans who became perpetrators of abusive violence were at high risk for developing PTSD reveals the significance of assessing this aspect of the stressor experience (Breslau and Davis, 1987; Yehuda, Southwick, and Giller, 1992). Additionally, Herman (1992b) discussed issues related to subjective interpretation by survivors of their role during the trauma. For instance, subsequent to traumatization, some survivors, particularly of sexual trauma or captivity, may experience feelings of complicity. In these cases, such cognitions may intensify the effect of the stressor. Although findings of these research investigations reveal progress in isolating stressor properties that may be associated with enhanced vulnerability to negative sequelae, there has been meager attention to developing qualitative indices of stressor elements. A taxonomy of stressor characteristics estimating the relative likelihood of a stressor, or category of stressors, to be associated with PTSD or other negative psychological outcomes would represent an important addition to the PTSD assessment repertoire.

Subjective interpretation of a stressor greatly influences the psychological impact of the event on the individual. In the viewpoint of some researchers, an event is not stressful unless it is perceived as such, and even the most traumatic of events may not be regarded as stressful by some individuals (Lazarus, DeLongis, Folkman, and Gruen, 1985); accordingly, problems related to conducting assessments that incorporate evaluation of subjective appraisal, or meaning, of stressful events plague much of the stress literature. This controversial issue regarding differentiating objective and subjective aspects of stressor events, as well as issues related to confounding of stressor and response properties, is addressed in the DSM-IV criterion A revision. The proposed stressor definition provides equal emphasis to the stressor event and to individual response to and subjective appraisal of the event (Kilpatrick and Resnick, 1993). Thus, the revision endorses a viewpoint that measurement of objective properties of discrete stressful circumstances does not preclude efforts to understand the individual meanings of such experiences and acknowledges that stress as a concept implies effects on response systems. However, the revised nomenclature will require concomitant revisions in assessment protocols, as well as conceptualizations of traumatic stress, posing theoretical and practical challenges to individuals evaluating stress-related disorders in both clinical and research situations.

Assessing Psychological Impact of Trauma: Response Parameters

The most obvious assessment domain is that encompassing evaluation of the psychological impact, or response parameters, of exposure to extreme stress. Comprehensive assessment of stress outcomes is directed toward the goals of describing symptoms uniquely indicative of PTSD as specified by the current nomenclature, identifying other types of symptoms associated with PTSD and in addition to PTSD, including emotional, behavioral, somatic, and cognitive sequelae, and charting the course of the disorder and associated symptoms over time. Thus, to describe the complex, multifaceted human response to stress, it is essential for PTSD assessment protocols to evaluate responses longitudinally within the following domains: (1) symptoms specific to PTSD; (2) associated psychological symptoms, including mental disorders (e.g., lifetime and current psychiatric diagnoses), negative affect states (e.g., anger, anxiety, depression), and behavioral patterns (e.g., substance abuse); (3) somatic discomfort and physical distress; and (4) cognitive functioning (e.g., attention, concentration, and memory).

PTSD SYMPTOMATOLOGY

Evaluation of response to an identified stressor event begins with determining the presence or absence of the 17 diagnostic criteria for PTSD specified in the DSM-III-R (American Psychiatric Association, 1987). Posttraumatic stress disorder diagnostic criteria are divided into three distinct symptom clusters: reexperiencing, avoidance-numbing, and hyperarousal. Specifically, one of four reexperiencing symptoms, including recurring intrusive recollections of the trauma, flashbacks, nightmares, or intense psychological distress triggered by exposure to trauma-related events, is required for diagnosis. Although it has been recommended that the revised DSM-IV criteria require only two avoidance-numbing symptoms (Kilpatrick and Resnick, 1993), the current diagnostic system requires the presence of three of these symptoms in order to meet criteria. Symptoms of this cluster are experienced as avoidance of thoughts or feelings associated with the stressor, avoidance of activities or situations reminiscent of the trauma, psychogenic amnesia, loss of interest in pleasurable activities, interpersonal isolation and alienation, emotional numbing, and sense of a foreshortened future. The final cluster focuses on symptoms of increased arousal such as sleep disturbance, irritability, difficulty concentrating, hypervigilance, exaggerated startle response, and physiologic reactivity. Endorsement of at least two of these symptoms is considered indicative of PTSD. To fulfill PTSD DSM-III-R criteria, the requisite constellation of symptoms must be present for at least one month.

Within the past decade, multiaxial, multimodal PTSD assessment batteries incorporating structured clinical interview, self-report psychometric rating scales, and psychophysiological assessment have been developed to evaluate PTSD diagnostic criteria as specified by the DSM. Recent trends in the evaluation of PTSD symptomatology, reflecting advances in the understanding of

PTSD phenomenology, display increased focus on measurement of frequency, intensity, and duration of symptoms (Blake, Weathers, Nagy, Kaloupek, Klauminzer, Charney, and Keane, 1990; Falsetti, Resick, Resnick, and Kilpatrick, 1992) and attention to subthreshold yet clinically significant symptomatology (Weiss, Marmar, Schlenger, Fairbank, Jordan, Hough, and Kulka, 1992). A discussion of specific assessment instruments and their psychometric properties is beyond the scope of this review; however, this topic is the subject of several comprehensive discussions of state-of-the-art assessment methodologies employed to diagnose PTSD among diverse populations (Wolfe and Keane, 1990; Sutker, 1991; Litz, Penk, Gerardi, and Keane, in press).

ASSOCIATED PSYCHOLOGICAL SYMPTOMS

Thorough evaluation of comorbid lifetime and current psychiatric diagnoses, negative affect states, and behavior patterns represent an important complement to PTSD assessment for clinical and research purposes. Surprisingly little effort has been devoted to unraveling the intricacies of disorder cooccurrence and symptom overlap among samples of subjects exposed to identifiable stressor circumstances and approriate control subjects. Specifically, the issue of cause and effect regarding comorbidity and the sequencing of disorders among individuals suffering PTSD is as yet unresolved, and further research is needed to understand the intricate interplay of PTSD and other disorders. It is essential to determine if exposure to extreme stress is associated with or productive of cooccurring disorders among individuals with PTSD or if the presence of other disorders increases risk for developing PTSD following exposure to extreme events.

Studies have revealed that high rates of comorbid psychiatric disorders and negative mood states are associated with PTSD diagnoses among diverse traumatized samples, including war-zone veteran inpatients (Sierles, Chen, McFarland, and Taylor, 1983); outpatients (Escobar, Randolph, Puente, Spiwak, Asamen, Hill, and Hough, 1983; Sierles, Chen, Messing, Besyner, and Taylor, 1986; Green et al., 1989; Davidson, Kudler, Saunders, and Smith,

1990; Keane and Wolfe, 1990; Mellman, Randolph, Brawman-Mintzer, Flores, and Milanes, 1992); Vietnam (Centers for Disease Control, 1988; Kulka et al., 1990) and Operation Desert Storm (Sutker, Uddo, Brailey, and Allain, in pess; Sutker, Uddo, Brailey, Vasterling, and Errera, 1993); veterans living in the community, POW survivors (Kluznik, Speed, Van Valkenburg, and Magraw, 1986; Sutker, Winstead, Goist, Malow, and Allain, 1986; Sutker, Allain, and Motsinger, 1988; Sutker, Winstead, Galina, and Allain, 1990); general population-based samples (Helzer et al., 1987; Davidson, Hughes, Blazer, and George, 1991); individuals exposed to volcanic eruption (Shore, Vollmer, and Tatum, 1989); crime victims (Kilpatrick et al., 1987); and Southeast Asian refugees (Mollica, Wyshak, Lavelle, Truong, and Yang, 1990). Frequent cooccurring diagnoses identified in these studies include mood, substance abuse, and other anxiety disorders.

Additionally, evaluation of pre- and posttrauma substance use behavior patterns is of relevance. An increasing number of clinical research studies have documented frequent cooccurrence of substance use disorders and PTSD. For example, Kulka et al. (1990) found comorbidity rates ranging from 55 to 70 percent for substance use and PTSD disorders among Vietnam theater veterans undergoing inpatient treatment. Keane, Gerardi, Lyons, and Wolfe (1988) concluded that among veterans seeking treatment for PTSD, comorbidity rates with substance use disorders ranged from 60 to 80 percent. Additional evidence of the complex relationship between PTSD and substance abuse is provided by data from a national probability household sample of adult women indicating that crime victims with PTSD were 17 times more likely than nonvictims to report major substance abuse problems (Kilpatrick, 1993). These findings suggest that because individuals suffering PTSD are at high risk for substance abuse related problems, evaluation of alcohol and illicit drug use constitutes a relevant aspect of PTSD assessment.

PHYSICAL DISTRESS

Of particular interest is the common coexistence of PTSD and somatic complaints. Few studies examining somatic comorbidity in trauma populations exist in the literature even though diverse traumatized populations such as rape victims (Ellis, Atkeson, and Calhoun, 1981; Norris and Feldman-Summers, 1981); victims of childhood sexual abuse (Sedney and Brooks, 1984; Briere, 1988); individuals exposed to natural disasters (Melick, Logue, and Frederick, 1982); survivor assistance officers (Bartone, Ursano, Wright, and Ingraham, 1989); survivors of political confinement, mass violence, and torture (Goldfeld, Mollica, Pesavento, and Faraone, 1988; Mollica et al., 1990); World War II and Korean conflict POW survivors (Sutker et al., 1986, 1988, 1993; Sutker, Winstead, et al., 1990); Vietnam (Kulka et al., 1990); and Operation Desert Storm veterans with high war-zone stress (Sutker, Uddo, Brailey, Allain, and Errera, 1994; Sutker, Uddo, Brailey, Vasterling, and Errera, in press) frequently reported multiple somatic complaints, including fatigue and symptoms of gastrointestinal, neurological, cardiopulmonary, and auditory–visual disturbances. In most of these studies, measures of somatic concerns were designed for the research underway, and the instruments lacked sufficient methodological rigor and coverage of health problem domains to yield a comprehensive picture of somatic distress. Additionally, these studies failed to provide corroborative medical diagnoses or supportive laboratory data.

Review of data from four studies which focused on physical comorbidity in combat-related PTSD indicated that PTSD diagnoses are associated with subjective complaints of somatic distress. Investigation of physical health complaints in Vietnam combat veterans (Litz, Keane, Fisher, Marx, and Monaco, 1992) and Lebanon War veterans (Shalev, Bliech, and Ursano, 1990), differentiated by PTSD diagnosis, found that PTSD veterans reported increased somatic concerns, but no differences in physician-diagnosed medical disorders were found. Results of studies of the relationship between somatic complaints and PTSD symptoms in combat-stress-reaction casualties and combat control soldiers of the 1982 Lebanon War indicated that soldiers suffering from war stress reported higher levels of somatic distress than did their nondiagnosed counterparts (Solomon and Mikulincer, 1987; Solomon, Mikulincer, and Kotler, 1987). More thorough assessment of bodily ailments represents an important adjunct to PTSD assessment for clinical and research purposes. Areas of overlap between psychological disturbance and biological distress residuals and their sometimes subtle interaction among trauma victims are critical areas for future study.

Cognitive Functioning

Almost universal reports of problems with concentration, memory, and learning among trauma survivors signal the need for closer examination of neuropsychological performances among survivors of extreme stress. Cognitive functioning is particularly intriguing for study because aberrant memory, attention, and concentration are cited as integral components of PTSD (APA, 1987; Pitman, 1989), and theories of the pathogenesis of PTSD implicate neurochemical and neurobiological changes in brain structures thought to be involved in learning and memory (Kolb, 1987; van der Kolk, 1987; Everly and Horton, 1989; Wolfe and Charney, 1991). Complaints of problems with cognitive functioning have been documented among samples of trauma survivors, including former POWs (Klonoff, McDougall, Clark, Kramer, and Horgan, 1976; Sutker, Winstead, and Allain, 1987; Sutker, Galina, West, et al., 1990; Sutker, Winstead, Galina, and Allain, 1991); Southeast Asian refugees (Goldfeld et al., 1988); and Vietnam combat veterans (Boulanger, 1985).

Preliminary controlled studies of neuropsychological concomitants of PTSD suggest that PTSD may be associated with memory and attention deficits. Gil, Calev, Greenberg, Kugelmass, and Lerer (1990) compared 12 Israeli patients diagnosed with civilian or military-related PTSD to 12 patients diagnosed with affective disorder and 12 nonpatient volunteers on various neuropsychological tasks. These researchers found that whereas PTSD-diagnosed patients performed more poorly than the nonpatient volunteer sample across most measures, the PTSD group performed more poorly than the psychiatric comparison sample only on verbal abstraction and word list generation tasks. A study conducted by Uddo, Vasterling, Brailey, and Sutker (1993) showed that PTSD veterans performed more poorly than a comparison sample on a measure of verbal learning and evidenced impairments in word fluency and visual attention/tracking abilities. Findings were consistent with self-reported complaints of concentration and memory impairments among PTSD-diagnosed clinical samples.

In addition to these findings, investigations also have demonstrated attentional biases in Vietnam PTSD veterans (McNally, Luedke, Beysyner, Peterson, Bohm, and Lipps, 1987; Trandel and McNally, 1987; Zeitlin and McNally, 1991) and reported evidence of decreased hippocampal volume, assessed by magnetic resonance imaging (Bremner, Seibyl, Scott, Southwick, Delaney, Mason, Scanley, McCarthy, Charney, and Innis, 1992), and short-term memory loss (Bremner et al., 1993) in PTSD-diagnosed Vietnam veterans compared to physically healthy, matched controls. Results of these preliminary neuropsychological studies of PTSD highlight the need for continued investigation of the neuropsychological sequelae of prolonged stress exposure. The possibility of neuropsychological impairment is one with important implications for PTSD assessment. Thus, neuropsychological screening, and in many cases, full neuropsychological evaluation may be required to gain a complete picture of psychosocial functioning among individuals suffering PTSD.

Increased understanding of the chronic, phasic, and sometimes delayed nature of response to extreme stress and of the impact of trauma over time has led researchers to emphasize longitudinal assessment of PTSD and its natural course (Sutker, Uddo-Crane, and Allain, 1991; Weiss et al., 1992). Yet, in most cases PTSD assessment occurs as a static phenomenon, and therefore, may not be representative of the range of symptoms integral to the full response pattern or its more devastating and enduring sequelae. Administration of periodic assessments over time is essential to detect the delayed onset of symptoms observed in some trauma survivors and to capture the characteristic alternation between intrusion and numbing–avoidance symptomatology in PTSD initially described by Horowitz (1986) and conceptualized more recently as the "dialectic of trauma" by Herman (1992b). Studies tracking psychological manifestations of trauma over time shed light on the complexities of PTSD and yield a comprehensive and representative picture of the residuals of exposure to extreme stress.

Several research reports offer descriptive accounts of long-term psychopathology, psychological characteristics, and psychological functioning among survivors of war-related and civilian trauma. Thygesen, Hermann, and Willanger (1970) reported a 23-year follow-up of Danish Nazi concentration camp survivors, and Eitinger (1975) summarized the long-term outcome of Norwegian Jews subjected to deportation and imprisonment. Studies of World War II and Korean conflict prisoners of war by Beebe (1975) and Keehn (1980) documented elevated levels of psychological distress over time, especially among POWs held by the Japanese and Koreans. Other studies have described the long-term residuals of POW captivity at 30 (Klonoff et al., 1976), 40 (Kluznik et al., 1986; Tennant, Goulston, and Dent, 1986; Goldstein, van Kammen, Shelly, Miller, and van Kammen, 1987; Zeiss and Dickman, 1989), and more than 40 (Sutker, Allain, and Motsinger, 1988; Speed et al., 1989; Sutker and Allain, 1991; Sutker, Allain, and Winstead, 1993) years subsequent to repatriation as well as combat in veterans of World War II and the Korean conflict (Archibald and Tuddenham, 1965), and the Vietnam War (Kulka et al., 1990). The chronicity of stress responses also has been documented among incest survivors who were symptomatic up to 24 years postmolestation (Goodwin, 1985) and rape victims who met criteria for PTSD as many as 15 years subsequent to assault (Kilpatrick et al., 1987).

Increasing research work reflects planned rather than coincidental assessments of stress-related symptoms at outcome intervals established prospectively. Terr (1983) studied the Chowchilla children over 4 to 5 years subsequent to their 27-hour kidnapping ordeal, and Kilpatrick, Resick, and Veronen (1981) reported victim reactions to rape at 1, 6, and 12 months postrape. McFarlane (1988) followed Australian firefighters exposed to a disastrous bushfire at intervals of 4, 8, 11, and 29 months after the event.

Other survivor populations studied using a repeated-measures design include health assistance officers who provided services to the families of victims killed in military air disaster (Bartone et al., 1989); Israeli combat veterans (Solomon and Mikulincer, 1988); flood victims (Green, Lindy, et al., 1990); schoolchildren who witnessed a sniper attack (Nader, Pynoos, Fairbank, and Frederick, 1990); mothers and young children living near the Three Mile Island nuclear power plant at the time of the nuclear accident (Cornely and Bromet, 1986); and Cambodian adults traumatized as children (Kinzie, Sack, Angell, Clarke, and Ben, 1989; Sack, Clarke, Him, Dickason, Goff, Lanham, and Kinzie, 1993). These studies highlight the wisdom of gathering information over time to yield a comprehensive and vivid representation of stress residuals. A longitudinal perspective, perhaps even culminating in autopsy data (Karson, Garcia-Rill, Biedermann, Mrak, Husain, and Skinner, 1991), will permit the piecing together of information such that the full extent of trauma response, or its diverse toll on human life, is better understood.

In sum, the expression of negative psychological sequelae to trauma exposure may be acute or delayed for months, years, or perhaps decades subsequent to the objective occurrence of trauma events, and diverse trauma outcomes may be observed. For example, stress reactions may be of short duration with circumscribed symptoms, may be experienced as complex reactions with pervasive effects on psychological functioning (Horowitz, 1986; Herman, 1992a), and may present as persistent changes in psychological adaptation and temperament or as characterological features (Southwick, Yehuda, and Giller, 1993). Posttraumatic stress disorder subtypes have been suggested to distinguish survivors of a single trauma from those who have endured multiple and/or prolonged trauma (Herman, 1992a; Terr, 1991) or to form subclassifications in terms of the most salient clinical symptomatology exhibited such as anxiety, depression, or dissociation (Davidson and Foa, 1991). To understand the multiple outcomes associated with traumatic experiences, phasic fluctuations in symptomatology, potential reactivation of symptoms, high degree of symptom overlap, and frequent comorbidities, it is necessary to supplement assessment of PTSD symptomatology with thorough evaluation of the impact of exposure to extreme stress on emotional, behavioral, somatic, and cognitive aspects of functioning over time.

VARIABLES INFLUENCING RESPONSE TO TRAUMATIC STRESS

Increasingly, etiological models of PTSD emphasize a multivariate explanation that incorporates contributions of person and environment factors as well as stressor characteristics (Green et al., 1985; Ursano, 1987; Keane, 1989; Sutker, Uddo-Crane, and Allain 1991; Davidson and Foa, 1993; Fairbank, Schlenger, Caddell, and Woods, 1993). However, evaluation of variables that influence the response to traumatic stress has received limited empirical scrutiny. Individual differences are important for study in light of evidence that most individuals confronted with extreme stress do not react in pathological ways. Data indicate that even the highest levels of fierce military combat (Chemtob, Bauer, Nellar, Hamada, Glisson, and Stevens, 1990; Kulka et al., 1990) and the persistent, multiple, and severe trauma of POW confinement (Urano, 1981; Sutker, Bugg, and Allain, 1990) are not necessarily associated with negative psychological outcomes or psychiatric disorders in some survivors. In fact, some traumatized individuals report positive outcomes of surviving extreme stress (Egendorf, 1982; Frankl, 1984).

Because only a subsample of individuals exposed to a stressor will develop PTSD, it is apparent that factors apart from the stressor experience intervene or influence the emergence of negative psychological sequelae. In part, such findings support the notion of a diathesis–stress model of PTSD; that is, because of particular acquired or inherited vulnerabilities or predisposing factors, some susceptible individuals may be at greater risk for developing PTSD when exposed to a highly stressful environmental event

(Sutker, Davis, Uddo, and Ditta, in press). Conversely, some individuals may be protected from negative outcomes by certain individual traits or environmental circumstances. This attention to person–environment mediating variables does not negate the dose–response relationship between trauma severity and PTSD development, but instead highlights the importance of exploring individual differences in the capacity to endure extreme stress. It is suggested that, while everyone is susceptible, personal characteristics and environmental influences may alter the threshold for stress resistance. This assessment domain has important implications for studying individuals who, though having endured significant environmental stress, manage to avoid psychological symptoms and psychiatric disorders, whereas others do not.

Preliminary research has identified person and environment variables that set people at greater risk for PTSD as well as characteristics that contribute to stress resistance. Among the person–environment factors that have been discussed in the literature as possibly associated with increased vulnerability to PTSD, and hence represent variables of interest for future study, are family history of psychopathology (Davidson, Smith, and Kudler, 1989); lower education, military rank, and socioeconomic status (Ursano, 1981; Sutker, Bugg, and Allain, 1991); alexythymia (Kosten, Krystal, Giller, Frank, and Dan, 1992); avoidant coping style (Fairbank, Hansen, and Fitterling, 1991; Roth and Cohen, 1986); female gender (Shore et al., 1986; Helzer et al., 1987); resource loss (Hobfoll, 1989; Freedy, Shaw, Jarrell, and Masters, 1992); and minority race or ethnicity, family of origin socioeconomic status, previous psychiatric history, and prior traumatization (Kulka et al., 1990). Research on protective factors has focused on the adaptive value of certain person–resource characteristics such as personality hardiness (Bartone et al., 1989), social support (Burgess and Holmstrom, 1979; Wilson and Krauss, 1985), and effective coping (Fairbank et al., 1991; Wolfe, Keane, Kaloupek, Mora, and Wine, 1993).

Further empirical investigation with the aim of identifying person–environment variables that influence response to extreme stress, with special attention to distiguishing between mediator and moderator variables, will contribute to a more sophisticated understanding of individual differences in stress response. As described by Baron and Kenny (1986), although frequently confused, mediator and moderator variables represent distinct classes of variables that account for individual differences in behavior. Briefly summarized, within the context of PTSD research, a moderator model would be operative when a significant interaction between a stressor and an identified person–environment factor influences the impact of the stressor on the individual. In a mediational model, there are two causal paths feeding into the outcome variable; that is, the direct impact of the stressor on manifestation of PTSD symptomatology and the impact of a person-environment variable on psychological outcome. In complex models, variables may function in both mediator and moderator roles. Identification and measurement of potential mediating and/or moderating variables, then, is highly relevant for predicting degree of risk to mental health from extreme stress.

CONCLUSIONS AND IMPLICATIONS

In summary, clinical and research assessment of PTSD is directed toward the goals of: (1) evaluating the severity and nature of stressor events; (2) describing the multiple, sometimes overlapping, and often phasic psychological responses indicative of PTSD, with special attention to identifying associated symptomatology and charting the course of psychopathology over time; and (3) measuring relevant person-environment characteristics that affect symptom expression and response to treatment. That is, a longitudinal person–environment perspective that assesses stressor stimulus properties and stress outcome factors, is endorsed to record the effects of extraordinary stress on the intricacies of human functioning.

It has become evident that PTSD represents a heterogeneous and complex, if not controversial, disorder. If PTSD has relevance as a clinical entity, salient characteristics will surface across populations and stressor events. For these crucial similarities to be researched adequately, methodologies must be derived that are sufficiently broad from a theoretical perspective and suitably appropriate to diverse traumatized populations. Careful assessment work will allow clinicians and researchers to reach agreement on the core distinguishing symptoms of PTSD, understand subtypes and clusters of PTSD-related symptoms, and pinpoint the role of specific person and environment factors in influencing the etiology, expression, and course of stress-related residuals. It is suggested that clinical and research understanding of PTSD as a mental disorder will be only as sophisticated as assessment protocols permit.

REFERENCES

American Psychiatric Association (1980), *Diagnostic and Statistical Manual of Mental Disorders* (DSM-III), 3rd ed. Washington, DC: American Psychiatric Press.
——— (1987), *Diagnostic and Statistical Manual of Mental Disorders* (DSM-III-R), 3rd ed. rev. Washington, DC: American Psychiatric Press.
Archibald, H., & Tuddenham, R. (1965), Persistent stress reaction after combat: A twenty-year follow-up. *Arch. Gen. Psychiatry*, 12:475–481.
Baron, R. M., & Kenny, D. A. (1986), The moderator-mediator variable distinction in social psychological research: Conceptual, strategic, and statistical consideration. *J. Personal. & Soc. Psychol.*, 51:1173–1182.
Bartone, P. T., Ursano, R. J., Wright, K. M., & Ingraham, L. H. (1989), The impact of a military air disaster on the health of assistance workers: A prospective study. *J. Nerv. & Ment. Dis.*, 177:317–328.
Baum, A. (1990), Stress, intrusive imagery, and chronic distress. *Health Psychol.*, 9:653–675.
Beebe, G. W. (1975), Follow-up studies of World War II and Korean War prisoners: Morbidity, disability, and maladjustments. *Amer. J. Epidemiol.*, 101:400–422.
Blake, D. D., Weathers, F. W., Nagy, L. M., Kaloupek, D. G., Klauminzer, G., Charney, D., & Keane, T. M. (1990), A clinician rating scale for assessing current and lifetime PTSD: The CAPS-1. *Behav. Therapist*, 13:187–188.
Boulanger, G. (1985), Post-traumatic stress disorder: An old problem with a new name. In: *The Trauma of War: Stress and Recovery in Viet Nam Veterans*, ed.

M. Sonnenberg, A. S. Blank, & J. A. Talbott. Washington, DC: American Psychiatric Press, pp. 13–29.

Bremner, J. D., Scott, T. M., Delaney, R. C., Southwick, S. M., Mason, J. W., Johnson, D. R., Innis, R. B., McCarthy, G., & Charney, D. S. (1993), Deficits in short-term memory in posttraumatic stress disorder. *Amer. J. Psychol.*, 150:1015–1019.

—— Seibyl, J. P., Scott, T. M., Southwick, S. M., Delaney, R. C., Mason, J. W., Scanley, E., McCarthy, G., Charney, D. S., & Innis, R. B. (1992), Decreased hippocampal volume in posttraumatic stress disorder. *New Res. Prog. Abst.*, 145th Annual Meeting of the American Psychiatric Association. Washington, DC: American Psychiatric Association.

Breslau, N., & Davis, G. C. (1987), Posttraumatic stress disorder: The stressor criterion. *J. Nerv. & Ment. Dis.*, 175:255–264.

Briere, J. (1988), Long-term clinical correlates of childhood sexual victimization. *Ann. NY Acad. Sci.*, 528:327–334.

Burgess, A. W., & Holmstrom, L. L. (1979), Adaptive strategies and recovery from rape. *Amer. J. Psychiatry*, 136:1278–1282.

Burstein, A. (1985), Posttraumatic stress disorder. *J. Clin. Psychiatry*, 46:554.

Centers for Disease Control (1988), Health status of Vietnam veterans: Psychosocial characteristics. *JAMA*, 259:2701–2707.

Chemtob, C., Bauer, G. B., Nellar, G., Hamada, R. S., Glisson, C., & Stevens, V. (1990), Post-traumatic stress disorder among Special Forces Vietnam veterans. *Military Med.*, 155:16–20.

Cornely, P., & Bromet, E. (1986), Prevalence of behavior problems in three year old children living near Three Mile Island: A comparative analysis. *J. Child Psychol. & Psychiatry*, 27:489–498.

Davidson, L. M., & Baum, A. (1986), Chronic stress and posttraumatic stress disorder. *J. Consult. & Clin. Psychol.*, 54:303–308.

—— Foa, E. B. (1991), Refining criteria for posttraumatic stress disorder. *Hosp. & Commun. Psychiatry*, 42:259–261.

—— —— (1993), Epilogue. In: *Posttraumatic Stress Disorder: DSM-IV and Beyond*, ed. E. B. Foa & J. R. T. Davidson. Washington, DC: American Psychiatric Press.

—— Hughes, D., Blazer, D., Blazer, D., & George, L. K. (1991), Post-traumatic stress disorder in the community: An epidemiological study. *Psycholog. Med.*, 21:713–721.

—— Kudler, H. S., Saunders, W. B., & Smith, R. D. (1990), Symptom and comorbidity patterns in World War II and Vietnam veterans with PTSD. *Comprehen. Psychiatry*, 31:162–179.

—— Smith, R., & Kudler, H. (1989), Familial psychiatric illness in posttraumatic stress disorder. *Comprehen. Psychiatry*, 30:338–345.

Egendorf, A. (1982), The postwar healing of Vietnam veterans: Recent research. *Hosp. & Commun. Psychiatry*, 33:901–908.

Eitinger, L. (1975), Jewish concentration camp survivors in Norway. *Israel Ann. Psychiatry*, 13:321–334.

Ellis, E. M., Atkeson, B. M., & Calhoun, K. S. (1981), An assessment of short-term reaction to rape. *J. Abnorm. Psychol.*, 90:263–266.

Escobar, J. I., Randolph, E. T., Puente, G., Spiwak, F., Asamen, J. K., Hill, M., & Hough, R. L. (1983), Post-traumatic stress disorder in Hispanic Vietnam veterans: Clinical phenomenology and sociocultural characteristics. *J. Nerv. & Ment. Dis.*, 171:585–596.

Everly, G., & Horton, A. (1989), Neuropsychology of posttraumatic stress disorder: A pilot study. *Percept. & Motor Skills*, 68:807–810.

Fairbank, J. A., Hansen, D., & Fitterling, J. (1991), Patterns of appraisal and coping across different conditions among former prisoners of war with and without post-traumatic stress disorder. *J. Consult. & Clin. Psychol.*, 9:274–281.

—— Schlenger, W. E., Caddell, J. M., & Woods, M. G. (1993), Post-traumatic stress disorder. In: *Comprehensive Handbook of Psychopathology*, 2nd ed., ed. P. B. Sutker & H. E. Adams. New York: Plenum, pp. 145–165.

Falsetti, S. A., Resick, P. A., Resnick, H., & Kilpatrick, D. G. (1992), Posttraumatic stress disorder: The assessment of frequency and severity of symptoms in clinical and nonclinical samples. Paper presented at the 26th annual meeting of the Association for the Advancement of Behavior Therapy, Boston.

Finkelhor, D. (1984), *Child Sexual Abuse: New Theory and Research.* New York: Free Press.

Foa, E. B., Zinbarg, R., & Rothbaum, B. O. (1992), Uncontrollability and unpredictability in post-traumatic stress disorder. An animal model. *Psychol. Bull.*, 112:218–238.

Foy, D. W., Carroll, E. M., & Donahoe, C. P. (1987), Etiological factors in the development of PTSD in clinical samples of Vietnam combat veterans. *J. Clin. Psychol.*, 43:17–27.

—— Osato, S. S., Houskamp, B. M., & Neumann, D. A. (in press), PTSD etiology. In: *Post-Traumatic Stress Disorder: A Behavioral Approach to Assessment and Treatment*, ed. A. Saigh. New York: Pergamon.

Frankl, V. E. (1984), *Man's Search for Meaning*, 3rd ed. New York: Simon & Schuster.

Freedy, J. R., Shaw, D. L., Jarrell, M. P., & Masters, C. R. (1992), Towards an understanding of the psychological impact of natural disasters: An application of the conservation resources stress model. *J. Traumat. Stress*, 5:441–454.

Garmezy, N., & Rutter, M. (1983), *Stress, Coping, and Development in Children.* New York: McGraw-Hill.

Gil, T., Calev, A., Greenberg, D., Kugelmass, S., & Lerer, B. (1990), Cognitive functioning in post-traumatic stress disorder. *J. Traumat. Stress*, 3:29–45.

Goldfeld, A. E., Mollica, R. F., Pesavento, B. H., & Faraone, S. V. (1988), The physical and psychological effects of torture: Symptomatology and diagnosis. *JAMA*, 259:2725–2729.

Goldstein, G., van Kammen, W., Shelly, C., Miller, D. J., & van Kammen, D. P. (1987), Survivors of imprisonment in the Pacific theater during World War II. *Amer. J. Psychiatry*, 144:1210–1213.

Goodwin, J. (1985), Family violence: Principles of intervention and prevention. *Hosp. & Commun. Psychiatry*, 36:1074–1079.

Green, B. L. (1991), Evaluating the effects of disaster. *Psychol. Assess.: J. Consult. & Clin. Psychol.*, 3:538–546.

────── Grace, M. C., Lindy, J. D., Glesser, G. C., & Leonard, A. (1990), Risk factors for PTSD and other diagnoses in general sample of Vietnam veterans. *Amer. J. Psychiatry*, 147:729–733.

────── ────── ────── Titchener, J. L., & Lindy, J. G. (1983), Levels of functional impairment following a civilian disaster: The Beverly Hills Supper Club fire. *J. Consult. & Clin. Psychol.*, 51:573–580.

────── Lindy, J. D., & Grace, M. C. (1985), Posttraumatic stress disorder: Toward DSM-IV. *J. Nerv. & Ment. Dis.*, 173:406–411.

────── ────── ────── Glesser, G. C. (1989), Multiple diagnosis in posttraumatic stress disorder: The role of war stressors. *J. Nerv. & Ment. Dis.*, 177:329–335.

────── ────── ────── ────── Leonard, A., Korol, M., & Winget, C. (1990), Buffalo Creek survivors in the second decade: Stability of stress symptoms. *Amer. J. Orthopsychiatry*, 20:43–54.

Helzer, J. E., Robins, L. N., & McEvoy, L. (1987), Post-traumatic stress disorder in the general population: Findings of the Epidemiologic Catchment Area Survey. *New Eng. J. Med.*, 317:1630–1634.

Herman, J. L. (1992a), Complex PTSD: A syndrome in survivors of prolonged and repeated trauma. *J. Traumat. Stress*, 5:377–391.

────── (1992b), *Trauma and Recovery*. New York: Basic Books.

Hobfoll, S. E. (1989), Conservation of resources: A new attempt at conceptualizing stress. *Amer. Psychologist*, 44:513–524.

Horowitz, M. J. (1986), *Stress Response Syndromes*, 2nd ed. Northvale, NJ: Jason Aronson.

────── Wilner, N., & Alvarez, W. (1979), Impact of Events Scale: A measure of subjective stress. *Psychosom. Med.*, 41:209–218.

Janoff-Bulman, R. (1992), *Shattered Assumptions*. New York: Macmillan.

Karson, C. N., Garcia-Rill, E., Biedermann, J., Mrak, R. E., Husain, M. M., & Skinner, R. D. (1991), The brain stem reticular formation in schizophrenia. *Psychiatry Res.*, 40:31–48.

Keane, T. M. (1989), Post-traumatic stress disorder: Current status and future directions. *Behav. Ther.*, 20:149–153.

────── Gerardi, R. J., Lyons, J. A., & Wolfe, J. (1988), The interrelationship of substance abuse and posttraumatic stress disorder. In: *Recent Developments in Alcoholism*, Vol. 6, ed. M. Galanter. New York: Plenum, pp. 27–48.

────── Wolfe, J. (1990), Comorbidity in post-traumatic stress disorder: An analysis on community and clinical studies. *J. Appl. Soc. Psychol.*, 20:1776–1788.

Keehn, R. J. (1980), Follow-up studies of World War II and Korean conflict prisoners: Mortality to January 1, 1976. *Amer. J. Epidemiol.*, 111:194–211.

Kilpatrick, D. G. (1993), Assessment of rape-related posttraumatic stress disorder. Paper presented at the workshop Sexual Trauma in Female Veterans, New Orleans.

────── Edmunds, C. N., & Seymour, A. K. (1992), *Rape in America: A Report to the Nation*. Arlington, VA: National Victim Center and Medical University of South Carolina.

────── Resnick, H. S. (1993), A description of the posttraumatic stress disorder field trial. In: *Posttraumatic Stress Disorder: DSM-IV and Beyond*, ed. J. R.

T. Davidson & E. B. Foa. Washington, DC: American Psychiatric Press, pp. 243–250.

———— Resick, P. A., & Veronen, L. J. (1981), Effects of a rape experience: A longitudinal study. *J. Soc. Issues,* 37:105–122.

———— Saunders, B. E., Amick-McMullan, A., Best, C. L., Veronen, L. J., & Resnick, H. S. (1989), Victim and crime factors associated with the development of crime-related post-traumatic stress disorder. *Behav. Ther.,* 20:199–214.

———— ———— Veronen, L. J., Best, C. L., & Von, J. M. (1987), Criminal victimization: Lifetime prevalence, reporting to police, and psychological impact. *Crime & Delinquency,* 33:479–489.

Kinzie, J. D., Sack, W., Angell, R., Clarke, G., & Ben, R. (1989), A three-year follow-up of Cambodian young people traumatized as children. *J. Amer. Acad. Child & Adol. Psychiatry,* 28:501–504.

Kiser, L., Ackerman, B., & Brown, E. (1988), Post-traumatic stress disorder in young children: A reaction to purported sexual abuse. *J. Amer. Acad. Child & Adol. Psychiatry,* 27:645–649.

Klonoff, H., McDougall, G., Clark, C., Kramer, P., & Horgan, J. (1976), The neuropsychological, psychiatric, and physical effects of prolonged and severe stress: 30 years later. *J. Nerv. & Ment. Dis.,* 163:246–252.

Kluznik, J. C., Speed, N., Van Valkenburg, C., & Magraw, R. (1986), Forty-year follow-up of United States prisoners of war. *Amer. J. Psychiatry,* 143:1443–1446.

Kolb, L. C. (1987), A neuropsychological hypothesis explaining posttraumatic stress disorder. *Amer. J. Psychiatry,* 144:989–995.

Kosten, T. R., Krystal, J. H., Giller, E. L., Frank, J., & Dan, E. (1992), Alexythymia as a predictor of treatment response in post-traumatic stress disorder. *J. Traumat. Stress,* 5:563–573.

Kulka, R. A., Schlenger, W. E., Fairbank, J. A., Hough, R. L., Jordan, B. K., Marmar, C. R., & Weiss, D. S. (1990), *Trauma and the Vietnam War Generation: Report of Findings from the National Vietnam Veterans Readjustment Study.* New York: Brunner/Mazel.

Lazarus, R. S., DeLongis, A., Folkman, S., & Gruen, R. (1985), Stress and adaptional outcomes: The problem of confounded measures. *Amer. Psychologist,* 40:770–777.

Litz, B. T., Keane, T. M., Fisher, L., Marx, B., & Monaco, V. (1992), Physical health complaints in combat-related post-traumatic stress disorder: A preliminary report. *J. Traumat. Stress,* 5:131–141.

———— Penk, W. E., Gerardi, R. J., & Keane, T. M. (in press), The assessment of post-traumatic stress disorder. In: *Post-traumatic Stress Disorder: A Behavioral Approach to Assessment and Treatment,* ed. P. A. Saigh. New York: Pergamon.

March, J. S. (1993), What constitutes a stress? The "criterion A" issue. In: *Posttraumatic Stress Disorder: DSM-IV and Beyond,* ed. J. R. T. Davidson & E. B. Foa. Washington, DC: American Psychiatric Press, pp. 37–54.

McFarlane, A. C. (1988), The phenomenology of posttraumatic stress disorders following a natural disaster. *J. Nerv. & Ment. Dis.,* 176:22–29.

McNally, R. J., Luedke, D. L., Beysyner, J. K., Peterson, R. A., Bohm, K., & Lipps, O. J. (1987), Sensitivity to stress-relevant stimuli in posttraumatic stress disorder. *J. Anxiety Disord.,* 1:105–116.

Melick, M. E., Logue, J. N., & Frederick, C. J. (1982), Stress and disaster. In: *Handbook of Stress: Theoretical and Clinical Aspects*, ed. L. Goldberger & S. Breznitz. New York: Free Press, pp. 613–620.

Mellman, T. A., Randolph, C. A., Brawman-Mintzer, O., Flores, L. P., & Milanes, F. J. (1992), Phenomenology and course of psychiatric disorders associated with combat-related posttraumatic stress disorder. *Amer. J. Psychiatry*, 149:1568–1574.

Mollica, R. F., Wyshak, G., & Lavelle, J. (1987), The psychosocial impact of war trauma and torture on Southeast Asian refugees. *Amer. J. Psychiatry*, 144:1567–1572.

———— Wyshak, G., Lavelle, J., Truong, T., & Yang, T. (1990), Assessing symptom change in Southeast Asian refugee survivors of mass violence and torture. *Amer. J. Psychiatry*, 147:83–88.

Nader, K., Pynoos, R., Fairbank, L., & Frederick, C. (1990), Children's PTSD reactions one year after a sniper attack at their school. *Amer. J. Psychiatry*, 147:1526–1530.

Norris, J., & Feldman-Summers, S. (1981), Factors related to the psychological impacts of rape on the victim. *J. Abnorm. Psychol.*, 90:562–567.

Pitman, R. K. (1989), Post-traumatic stress disorder, hormones, and memory. *Biolog. Psychiatry*, 26:221–223.

———— Altman, B., & Macklin, M. L. (1989), Prevalence of posttraumatic stress disorder in wounded Vietnam veterans. *Amer. J. Psychiatry*, 146:667–669.

Resnick, H. S., Kilpatrick, D. G., Best, C. L., & Kramer, T. L. (1992), Vulnerability-stress factors in development of posttraumatic stress disorder. *J. Nerv. & Ment. Dis.*, 180:424–430.

———— Kilpatrick, D. G., & Lipovsky, J. A. (1991), Assessment of rape-related posttraumatic stress disorder: Stressor and symptom dimensions. *Psycholog. Assess.: J. Consult. & Clin. Psychol.*, 3:561–572.

Roth, S., & Cohen, L. J. (1986), Approach, avoidance, and coping with stress. *Amer. Psychologist*, 41:813–819.

Sack, W. H., Clarke, G., Him, C., Dickason, D., Goff, B., Lanham, K., & Kinzie, J. D. (1993), A 6-year follow-up study of Cambodian refugee adolescents traumatized as children. *J. Amer. Acad. Child & Adol. Psychiatry*, 32:431–437.

Saigh, P. A. (1989), The validity of the DSM-III posttraumatic stress disorder classification as applied to children. *J. Abnorm. Psychol.*, 98:189–192.

Sedney, M. A., & Brooks, B. (1984), Factors associated with a history of childhood sexual experience in a nonclinical female population. *J. Amer. Acad. Child Psychiatry*, 23:215–218.

Shalev, A., Bliech, A., & Ursano, R. J. (1990), Posttraumatic stress disorder: Somatic comorbidity and effort tolerance. *Psychosomatics*, 31:197–203.

Shore, J. H., Tatum, E. L., & Vollmer, W. M. (1986), Psychiatric reaction to disaster: The Mt. St. Helens experience. *Amer. J. Psychiatry*, 140:590–595.

———— Vollmer, W. M., & Tatum, E. L. (1989), Community patterns of post-traumatic stress disorders. *J. Nerv. & Ment. Dis.*, 177:681–685.

Sierles, F. S., Chen, J. J., McFarland, R. E., & Taylor, M. A. (1983), Posttraumatic stress disorder and concurrent psychiatric illness: A preliminary report. *Amer. J. Psychiatry*, 140:1177–1179.

———— ———— Messing, M. L., Besyner, J. K., & Taylor, M. A. (1986), Concurrent psychiatric illness in non-Hispanic outpatients diagnosed as having post-traumatic stress disorder. *J. Nerv. & Ment. Dis.*, 17:171–173.

Solomon, S. D. (1989), Research issues in assessing disaster's effects. In: *Psychological Aspects of Disaster*, ed. R. Gist & B. Lubin. New York: John Wiley, pp. 308–340.

———— Canino, G. J. (1990), Appropriateness of DSM-III-R criteria for posttraumatic stress disorder. *Comprehen. Psychiatry*, 31:227–237.

Solomon, Z., & Mikulincer, M. (1987), Combat stress reactions, PTSD, and somatic complaints among Israeli soldiers. *J. Psychosom. Res.*, 31:131–137.

———— ———— (1988), Psychological sequelae of war: A two-year follow-up study of Israeli combat stress reaction (CSR) casualties. *J. Nerv. & Ment. Dis.*, 176:264–269.

———— ———— Kotler, M. (1987), A two-year follow-up of somatic complaints among Israeli combat stress reaction casualties. *J. Psychosom. Res.*, 31:463–469.

Southwick, S. M., Yehuda, R., & Giller, E. L. (1993), Personality disorders in treatment-seeking combat veterans with posttraumatic stress disorder. *Amer. J. Psychiatry*, 150:1020–1023.

Speed, N., Engdahl, B., Schwartz, J., & Eberly, R. (1989), Posttraumatic stress disorder as a consequence of the POW experience. *J. Nerv. & Ment. Dis.*, 177:147–153.

Stenger, C. A. (1993), *American Prisoners of War in WWI, WWII, Korea and Vietnam: Statistical Data Concerning Numbers Captured, Repatriated and Still Alive as of January 1, 1993.* Washington, DC: American Ex-Prisoners of War.

Sutker, P. B. (1991), Special series on issues and methods in assessment of posttraumatic stress disorder. *Psycholog. Assess.: J. Consult. & Clin. Psychol.*, 3:517–587.

———— Allain, A. N. (1991), MMPI profiles of veterans of WWII and Korea: Former POW and combat survivors. *Psycholog. Rep.*, 68:279–284.

———— ———— Motsinger, P. A. (1988), Minnesota Multiphasic Personality Inventory (MMPI)-derived psychopathology prototypes among former prisoners of war (POWs): Replication and extension. *J. Psychopathol. & Behav. Assess.*, 10:129–140.

———— ———— Winstead, D. K. (1993), Psychopathology and psychiatric diagnoses of World War II Pacific theater prisoner of war survivors and combat veterans. *Amer. J. Psychiatry*, 150:240–245.

———— Bugg, F., & Allain, A. N. (1990), Person and situation correlates of posttraumatic stress disorder among POW survivors. *Psycholog. Rep.*, 66:912–914.

———— ———— ———— (1991), Psychometric prediction of PTSD among POW survivors. *Psycholog. Assess.: J. Consult. & Clin. Psychol.*, 3:105–110.

———— Davis, J. M., Uddo, M., & Ditta (in press), War-zone stress, personal resources, and PTSD in Persian Gulf War returnees. *J. Abnorm. Psychol.*

———— Galina, Z. H., West, J. A., & Allain, A. N. (1990), Trauma-induced weight loss and cognitive deficits among former prisoners of war. *J. Consult. & Clin. Psychol.*, 58:323–328.

—————— Uddo, M., Brailey, K., & Allain, A. N. (1993), War zone trauma and stress-related symptoms in Operation Desert Storm (ODS) returnees. *J. Soc. Issues*, 49:33–50.

—————— —————— —————— —————— Errera, P. (1994), Psychological symptoms and psychiatric diagnosis in Operation Desert Storm troops serving graves registration duty. *J. Traum. Stress.*, 159–171.

—————— —————— —————— Vasterling, J. J., & Errera, P. (in press), Psychopathology in war-zone deployed and non-deployed Operation Desert Storm troops assigned graves registration duties. *J. Abnorm. Psychol.*

—————— Uddo-Crane, M., & Allain, A. N. (1991), Clinical and research assessment of posttraumatic stress disorder: A conceptual overview. *Psycholog. Assess.: J. Consult. & Clin. Psychol.*, 3:520–530.

—————— Winstead, D. K., & Allain, A. N. (1987), Cognitive performances in former WWII and Korean-Conflict POWs. *VA Practitioner*, 4:77, 78, 81, 85.

—————— —————— Galina, Z. H., & Allain, A. N. (1990), Assessment of long-term psychosocial sequelae among POW survivors of the Korean conflict. *Personal. Assess.*, 54:170–180.

—————— —————— —————— —————— (1991), Cognitive deficits and psychopathology among former prisoners of war and combat veterans of the Korean conflict. *Amer. J. Psychiatry*, 148:67–72.

—————— —————— Goist, K. C., Malow, R. M., & Allain, A. N. (1986), Psychopathology subtypes and correlates among former prisoners of war. *J. Psychopathol. & Behav. Assess.*, 8:89–101.

Tennant, C. C., Goulston, K. J., & Dent, O. F. (1986), The psychological effects of being a prisoner of war: 40 years after release. *Amer. J. Psychiatry*, 143:618–621.

Terr, L. C. (1983), Chowchilla revisited: The effects of psychic trauma four years after a school-bus kidnapping. *Amer. J. Psychiatry*, 140:1543–1550.

—————— (1991), Childhood trauma: An outline and overview. *Amer. J. Psychiatry*, 148:10–20.

Thygesen, P., Hermann, K., & Willanger, R. (1970), Concentration camp survivors in Denmark: Persecution, disease, disability, compensation. *Dan. Med. Bull.*, 17:65–108.

Trandel, D. E., & McNally, R. J. (1987), Perception of threat cues in posttraumatic stress disorder: Semantic processing without awareness. *Behav. Res. & Ther.*, 25:469–476.

Uddo, M., Vasterling, J. J., Brailey, K., & Sutker, P. B. (1993), Memory and attention in combat-related post-traumatic stress disorder. *J. Psychopathol. & Behav. Assess.*, 15:43–52.

Ursano, R. J. (1981), The Viet Nam Era prisoner of war: Precaptivity personality and the development of psychiatric illness. *Amer. J. Psychiatry*, 138:315–318.

—————— (1987), Commentary: Posttraumatic stress disorder: The stressor criterion. *J. Nerv. & Ment. Dis.*, 175:273–274.

U.S. Department of Veterans Affairs (1992), *The Veteran: Annual Report*. Washington, DC: Secretary of Veterans Affairs.

van der Kolk, B. A. (1987), *Psychological Trauma*. Washington, DC: American Psychiatric Press.

Weiss, D. S., Marmar, C. R., Schlenger, W. E., Fairbank, J. A., Jordan, B. K., Hough, R. L., & Kulka, R. A. (1992), The prevalence of lifetime and partial post-traumatic stress disorder in Vietnam theater veterans. *J. Traum. Stress,* 5:365–376.

Wilson, J. P., & Krauss, G. E. (1985), Predicting post-traumatic stress disorders among Vietnam veterans. In: *Post-Traumatic Stress Disorder and the War Veteran Patient,* ed. W. E. Kelly. New York: International Universities Press, pp. 102–147.

Wolfe, J., & Charney, D. S. (1991), Use of neuropsychological assessment in posttraumatic stress disorder. *J. Psycholog. Assess.,* 3:573–580.

———— Keane, T. M. (1990), Diagnostic validity of post-traumatic stress disorder. In: *Posttraumatic Stress Disorder: Etiology, Phenomenology, and Treatment,* ed. M. E. Wolf & A. D. Monsnaim. Washington, DC: American Psychiatric Press, pp. 48–63.

———— ———— Kaloupek, D. G., Mora, C. A., & Wine, P. (1993), Patterns of positive readjustment in Vietnam veterans. *J. Traum. Stress,* 6:179–193.

World Almanac (1992), New York: Pharos Books.

Yehuda, R., Southwick, S. M., & Giller, E. L. (1992), Exposure to atrocities and severity of chronic posttraumatic stress disorder in Vietnam veterans. *Amer. J. Psychiatry,* 149:333–336.

Zeiss, R. A., & Dickman, H. R. (1989), PTSD 40 years later: Incidence and person-situation correlates in former POWs. *J. Clin. Psychol.,* 45:80–87.

Zeitlin, S. B., & McNally, R. J. (1991), Implicit and explicit memory bias for threat in posttraumatic stress disorder. *Behav. Res. & Ther.,* 29:451–457.

Chapter 8
Current Measures in the Assessment of Stressful Life Events

THOMAS W. MILLER, Ph.D., A.B.P.P.

Innovation in the clinical assessment of the impact of stressful life events on health has encompassed numerous approaches in the evaluation of traumatization and life stress. Among the variety of approaches are measures of self-report, structured clinical interviews, diagnostic interview scales, and specific measures helpful in addressing psychometric and psychophysiological aspects of life stress events. Reviewed are some of the more prominent scales used in the development, standardization, and evaluation of life stress. Consistent across all measures are three basic objectives: (1) the identification of experiences involving traumatization and stress and subsequent symptoms; (2) consideration of the presence of coexisting psychological features; and (3) specificity with respect to the diagnostic and statistical evaluation criteria of the American Psychiatric Association and the international classification of disorders. Summarized, therefore, are measures currently utilized in assessing life stress events, including but not limited to, those hereby defined.

SOCIAL READJUSTMENT RATING SCALE (Holmes and Rahe, 1967)

In 1964, Holmes and Rahe devised the Social Readjustment Rating Questionnaire (SRRQ) to obtain numerical estimates of the average degree of life change and readjustment that subjects assign to life change events. Life changes studied involved those modifications of sleeping, eating and social, recreational, personal, and interpersonal habits that required or indicated varying degrees of adjustment. The result of Holmes and Rahe's revision was the Social Adjustment Rating Scale (SRRS), which assigned magnitudes to each of 42 life change items according to the amount, severity, and duration of adjustment each requires. The scaling instrument was found concordant among various segments of the American population and between American citizens and people of other cultures.

Holmes and Rahe then devised the Schedule of Recent Experience (SRE), a self-administered paper and pencil survey that listed life changes by year of occurrence. Currently known as the Recent Life Changes Questionnaire (RLCQ), this version of the SRE retains the essence of the 42 original life change questions of the SRE, but the wording of questions has been altered for clarity and to allow for specific options of response. Instructions were placed at the end of the RLCQ so the subject could self-scale his own subjective life change scores for each life change he had recently experienced. Patients obtained at least three different life change scores for analyses with various illness criteria. First, subjects obtained a 6-month life change unit (LCU) score for the 42 SRE items. Second, they scored a sum of all recent life changes indicated in a 6-month time period. This was called the unit scaling method and proved to be particularly useful with subjects between 18 and 25 years of age, a group that usually experiences few high LCU life changes. (It is recommended that the investigator use the LCU scoring system when dealing with samples of older subjects who may have experienced more life

changes, such as marriage, childbirth, divorce, business readjustment, illnesses of family members, death in the family, and so
on.) Finally, a subjective life change unit (SLCU) score was obtained and yielded a 6-month SLCU total for the original 42 SRE
life change questions permitted SLCU scores to be subtracted
from the standard LCU scores for those 42 questions.

Coddington (1972) modified the Social Readjustment Rating
Questionnaire to assess stressful life events related to childhood.
Using the method in the Social Readjustment Rating Scale, he
constructed a different list of experiences for each of the following groups: preschool age, elementary school age, junior high
school age, and senior high school age. The 250 people who did
the rating included teachers, pediatricians, and mental health
workers. Interrater agreement was high, with rank order correlations or $R \leqslant / = .90$.

Ruben, Gunderson, and Arthur (1971) assessed the predictive
validity of the SRE. A stepwise regression analysis was used with
favorable results to predict the onset of emotional disturbance
for Navy personnel. In another study, Rahe, Mahan, and Arthur
(1970) demonstrated a linear relationship between the mean illness rate of shipboard personnel and the magnitude of life
change.

Skinner and Lei (1980) conducted a factor analysis using an
interactive principal factor model with least squares estimate. The
results suggest that a relatively homogeneous subset of life events
can be identified among the SRE items. The six factors isolated
by Skinner and Lei are: (1) personal and social activities; (2) work
changes; (3) marital problems; (4) residence changes; (5) family
issues; and (6) school changes. The clinical population used by
Skinner and Lei consisted of 353 individuals who voluntarily
sought help for alcohol or substance abuse, or both.

Lei and Skinner found an internal consistency reliability esti-
mate of $r = .80$ for the SRE with this clinical population. Often,
the 43 life events are scaled by social readjustment weights (the
SRRs) to yield a weighted total score in life change units (LCU).
However, Lei and Skinner found overlap between the SRE and
LCU scores, a correlation of $r = .97$. Also, the reliability estimate,

$r = .72$ for the LCU scores was lower than the SRE. Reliability and validity studies with SRE show variable results. Three reliability estimates of the SRE that used college subjects and allowed only a week between test and retest had high correlations between $r = .87$ and $r = .90$ (Hawkins, 1957; Rahe, 1974). Rahe (1980) and Rahe, Floistad, and Bergan (1974) reported that when the interval between test and retest was extended to 6 to 9 months, resident physicians obtained correlations around $r = .70$, and the U.S. Navy enlisted men obtained correlations of $r = .55$.

The potential user of the most recent version of the SRE can consider a number of issues before applying the instrument to clinical or research use. The SRE instructions are limited and nonspecific, and not having carefully worked out pretested instructions is a concern when working with people who are experiencing stressful life events. Furthermore, the issue of social desirability and response sets must be assessed, since this issue is not addressed satisfactorily. The SRE could also be enhanced if it employed a Likert-type scale for items. The degree of severity must be assessed for individual items before valid comparability purposes; validity and reliability data might better be presented in tables rather than in the text of articles. Disappointingly little information is available on the application of the SRE to both clinical and normal samples. Until more information is available, the SRE has limited application in clinical settings. While the SRE has done much to identify the importance of assessing stressful life events, it has not kept pace with the most recent measures available to be considered. The SRE requires more sophisticated measurement technology; however, it stands as an interesting and promising clinical and research tool.

Structured Event Probe and Narrative Rating (SEPRATE) (Dohrenwend, Raphael, Schwartz, Stueve, and Skodol, 1993)

The Structured Event Probe and Narrative Rating (SEPRATE) consists of a clinical interview and a rating component. The interview includes an events checklist and probes to obtain detailed information on the number, dates, and types of events experienced by each respondent. Emphasis is placed on obtaining a descriptive narrative about what led to the occurrence of each event and what took place when the event occurred. The interviewer is instructed to use different probes for different checklists. Event descriptions are then abstracted from the interview material and rated by two or more judges appropriately trained on the dimensions of theoretical interest. Judges are kept blind to the information about other components in the life stress process by carefully stripping such information from the event descriptions to be rated. Respondents' subjective appraisals of events are also separately elicited and quantified during the interview.

The measure reflects the theoretical framework espousing to three main structural components of life stress: the stimulus component, ranging from extreme situations such as man-made or natural disasters, to more unusual events such as marriage; a second component being the ongoing social situation that existed before the occurrence of life stress events; and the third component consisting of the personal characteristics or disposition of the individual exposed to the stressful life experience. The SEPRATE approach to measurement of life stress continues to be in its developmental form; however, it has clearly defined an effective means of assessing the essential features of stressful life events. Initial validity and reliability estimates with specific attention to construct validity are promising. Tests in the New York Risk Factor Study suggest the interrater reliability was quite satisfactory. However, the SEPRATE approach to life events measurement continues to need a broader base to assess its validity and reliability factors and to examine the impact of cultural differences which may be an important ingredient in its potential use.

HASSLES SCALE (Kanner, Coyne, Schaefer, and Lazarus, 1981)

This scale consists of 117 hassles addressing areas of work, health, family, friends, environment, practical considerations, and chance occurrences. Examples include misplacing and losing things, declining physical abilities, not enough time for family, concerns about owing money, and pollution. An earlier version of the scale was used in a study of Kaiser Permanente patients with high life events scores. Subjects were encouraged to suggest hassles that they experienced that were not included in the original scale, and a number of these were incorporated in the scale used currently.

The Hassles Scale yields three summary scores, including: (1) Frequency, a simple count of the number of items checked, which could range from 0 to 117; (2) Cumulated Severity, the sum of the 3-point severity ratings, which ranged from 0 to 351 (3 × 117); and (3) Intensity, the Cumulated Severity divided by the Frequency, which ranged from 0 to 3. The latter score is an index of how strongly or intensely the average hassle is experienced, regardless of the number (frequency) of hassles checked. The correlations between frequency and cumulated severity are extremely high ($R \leqslant / = 0.95$).

The Uplifts Scale is constructed in a fashion similar to that of the Hassles Scale. The Uplifts Scale consists of a list of 135 uplifts that was generated using the content areas of the Hassles Scale as guidelines. Examples include relaxing, spending time with family, using skills well at work, praying, and nature.

Results with the Hassles Scale suggest that the pattern supports the hypothesis that hassles are more strongly associated with adaptational outcomes than are life events. The variance in symptoms that can be accounted for by life events can also be accounted for by hassles. Thus, major life events had little effect independent of daily hassles.

The results further suggest that hassles contribute to symptoms independent of major life events. In predicting symptoms, a substantial relationship remained for hassles even after the effect due to life events had been removed. Moreover, the remaining relationship between hassles and psychological symptoms was generally greater than between life events and symptoms.

Questionnaire on Resources and Stress for Families with Chronically Ill or Handicapped Members (Holroyd, 1988)

The QRS (Holroyd, 1988) measures stress in families who are caring for ill or disabled members. It assesses the impact of an illness or handicap on the responder and on other family members and provides information about a variety of problem areas for the responder, the family, and the disabled family member. Clinical cases used in the development of the QRS included developmental disabilities, psychiatric problems, renal disease, cystic fibrosis, neuromuscular disease, and cerebral palsy.

The QRS consists of 285 self-administered true–false items in 15 subtests, each designed to provide a maximum amount of information about family stress: Poor Health / Mood, Excess Time Demands, Negative Attitude, Overprotective / Dependency, Lack of Social Support, Overcommitment / Martyrdom, Pessimism, Lack of Family Integration, Limits on Family Opportunity, Financial Problems, Physical Incapacitation, Lack of Activities, Occupational Limitations, Social Obtrusiveness, and Difficult Personality Characteristics.

The QRS was normed on parents of 107 normal children and parents of 329 clinical cases, including children with developmental disabilities, psychiatric problems, and medical illnesses. Results are reported in standard scores, and the overall internal consistency reliability for the 285 items is .96. An extensive rationale for content, criterion, construct, and discriminant validity is available in the test manual.

Psychiatric Epidemiological Research Interview—Life Events Scale (Dohrenwend and Dohrenwend, 1978)

The Psychiatric Epidemiological Research Interview—Life Events Scale (PERI-LES) was developed by Dohrenwend, Krasnoff,

Askenasy, and Dohrenwend in 1978 to measure such life events as divorce, loss of job, and other more minor events. A number of these life events have been shown to correlate with the onset of medical and psychiatric illness. PERI-LES was constructed as part of a New York City study designed to develop methods for psychiatric epidemiological research in community populations, during which a sample of life events characteristic of New York City was drawn from the experience of the local population. The list of 102 events was constructed from previous lists, the researcher's own experiences, and the events reported to the Washington Heights series of studies on stressful life events. Excluded from the list were subjective events reported by subjects but not used in the final study.

The Dohrenwend group accorded much research effort to the assessment of the applicability of their scale, and that research suggested that ratings obtained on the PERI-LES yield significant group differences. More of those differences were due to ethnic background rather than social class or sex variation. The PERI-LES has technical weaknesses: (1) There is no reliability data on the frequency of occurrence of individual life events; and (2) the samples that judges used in assessing the ratings of life events were too small to assure that group differences were reliable. The strength of this scale is its potential methodological rigor. Researchers should yield improved revisions of their scale, which will serve to provide clinical researchers more valid and reliable estimates of assessing stressful life events. Multiple measures incorporating lists of stressful life events such as the Dohrenwend group generated must be assessed from a number of perspectives. Estimates of psychological constructs can aid in understanding the interplay of multiple factors involved as the individual perceives and responds to stressful life events.

UNIVERSAL- AND GROUP-SPECIFIC LIFE EVENTS SCALES (Hough, 1980)

The V.A./UCLA Life Change and Illness Research Project has developed universal- and group-specific life change scales, which include weights for their five scales. They include standardized weights derived from latent trait analysis for the qualities of scale items.

Hough (1980) and his colleagues developed the scales of life change events that can be applied to culturally heterogeneous populations. The scales were compiled from a random sampling of adults, ages 21 to 60, from El Paso, Texas, and a multilevel clustered sampling of similar adults from Ciudad Juarez, Mexico. Respondents were asked to rate the seriousness of 95 stressful life events. The specific 95 were chosen after a review of events used in previous life events scales. Assessment criteria included interviewer reports on the respondent's ability to do the task, completeness of the responses, the rating of undesirable versus desirable events, and the correlation of the individual's scores with his or her group's average and case-specific criteria. Several scales were constructed on the basis of latent trait analysis. Scale I, the Universal Scale, contains 51 events seen as essentially alike by the ethnic groups studied.

There is a scale of life events for each ethnic group as well. These scales contain the Universal Scale items and items scaled for each ethnic group. Items in the scales met two criteria: Small mean square error and agreement among groups on the change value due an item. The 51 items in the Universal Scale are those whose response patterns fit the latent trait model and over which there was little disagreement among the ethnic groups sampled. The same criteria were applied within each of the ethnic groups to obtain the group-specific scale items. Statistical analyses suggest that the scales have a ratio quality. Hough and colleagues found ethnic differences similar to the Dohrenwend group. The use of the Hough scales has added a dimension to this early phase of assessing stressful life events and confirmed the importance of distinguishing between universal- and group-specific change variables.

New Haven Life Events Measure (Paykel, Prusoff, and Uhlenhuth, 1971)

The New Haven group (1971) employed a checklist format of 60 items to ascertain events occurring within the 6 months prior to the onset of illness. Events were assessed by activity area—including work, family, and change in health—and whether these life event changes represented entrances or exits to a person's social field. A third rating determined whether these events were socially desirable or undesirable. Weights accommodated degrees of desirability to the average person for comparability purposes. The weighted scores were summed to estimate the life event stress experienced by the subject. Brown's research group (Brown and Birley, 1968) explored criteria for which life events should be regarded as most and least stressful. Identified criteria included changes in life circumstances, role, subject experiences, health changes, and the personality and influence of relatives and members of the immediate living environment—a key ingredient. Circumstances and critical life events were documented, with date, context, and verification by significant others in the subject's environment. In the second state, the research team rated the severity of life events experienced by the subject and compared it with the perceived threat this event might have to the average person. The subject's own reaction to the life event was not weighted in the rating. Brown and colleagues were attempting to reduce or eliminate the bias that confused previous studies. Should the identification and scaling of events be accomplished with satisfactory reliability, then researchers have succeeded in eliminating a key bias and have strengthened the process of life events scaling by accommodating the variability of circumstances and events that comprise our daily life experiences.

Allodi Trauma Scale (Allodi, 1985)

The Allodi is a semistructured interview schedule developed to document traumatization related to torture experiences. This is a 41-item questionnaire which assesses traumatic experiences associated with political persecution, imprisonment, disappearance, and death of individuals and families. It includes seven parts: (1)

Nonviolent persecution; (2) Arrest History; (3) Physical Torture; (4) Deprivation During Imprisonment; (5) Sensory Manipulation; (6) Psychological Torture and Ill Treatment; and (7) Violence to Family Members. The instrument yields a subtotal for each section, as well as a total score measuring the victim's total trauma/torture experience.

HARVARD TRAUMA QUESTIONNAIRE (HTQ) (Mollica, Wyshak, de Marneffe, Khuon, and Lavelle, 1987)

The Harvard Trauma Questionnaire is designed to empirically measure the trauma events and trauma syndromes of individuals who have survived torture and other trauma of mass violence. It is modeled in three Indochinese languages, as well as English, after the successful validation of the Hopkins Symptom Checklist 25 for anxiety and depression. The HTQ has three sections. The first section includes 17 specific trauma events, historically accurate for assessing the Indochinese refugee experience. Events range from starvation to killing of family members. The second section consists of an open-ended question which asks the respondent to describe the most terrifying events that have happened. The third section elicits 30 symptoms related to torture–trauma experience. Sixteen of these symptoms are derived from the DSM-III-R criteria for posttraumatic stress disorder (PTSD; APA, 1987). Initial validation of the HTQ has revealed interrater reliability of .93. Preliminary analysis suggests that highly symptomatic respondents have the best test–retest concordance.

VIETNAM EXPERIENCES QUESTIONNAIRE (VEQ) (Miller and Buchbinder, 1982)

The Vietnam Experiences Questionnaire is a 70-item measure that has been factor-analyzed into six distinct scale descriptions.

Scales include: (1) Disturbance in Interpersonal Relationships; (2) Sleep Disturbance; (3) Hypersensitivity; (4) Psychoticlike Symptomatology; (5) Perceived Capacity for Violence; and (6) Motivational Disturbances. The VEQ assesses the impact of stressful life events utilizing symptoms associated with PTSD, as well as items similar to the critical items of the MMPI. Kuder Richardson - 20 reliabilities for the six subscales of the VEQ are: (1) Disturbances in Interpersonal Relationships (R = .68); Sleep Disturbance (R = .75); Hypersensitivity to Sound (R = .74); Psychoticlike Symptomatology (R = .79); Perceived Capacity for Violence (R = .91); and Motivational Disturbances (R = .75). While the Vietnam Experiences Questionnaire was developed primarily for use with veterans from the Vietnam War, its applicability to other populations who have been traumatized through combat or war-type experiences is recognized.

THE BOSTON CLINICAL INTERVIEW FOR PTSD
(Gerardi and Wolfe, 1989)

The Boston Clinical Interview for PTSD is a 122-item structured clinical interview which includes demographic information and background, a family diagram, and pre-military history, and addresses such factors as home life and school situation, legal problems prior to the military service, involvement in substance abuse, and an evaluation of stressful experiences or significant losses prior to military experience. A third section deals with the military history, carefully evaluating specific stressful life events and patterns of coping. The fourth section of this instrument looks at postmilitary experience and adjustment, including postmilitary stressful experiences or significant losses. The fifth section addresses family and social relationships, which is followed by a sixth section addressing psychiatric treatment history, including prescription medications utilized and history of hospitalization. A medical history section, as well as a section addressing veterans' perceived problem areas which need treatment and clinician's observations, is included in this measure.

CLINICIAN-ADMINISTERED PTSD SCALE (CAPS) (Blake, Weathers, and Nagy, 1990)

The CAPS is a structured clinical interview designed to assess the 17 symptoms for PTSD outlined in DSM-III-R (APA, 1987). In addition, it also assesses eight associated features. The CAPS provides a means toward evaluation of the frequency and intensity of dimensions of each symptom, the impact of the symptoms on patients' social and occupational functioning, the overall severity of the symptom complex, the patient's global improvement since baseline, and validity of ratings obtained. The time frame for each symptom measured is 1 month. A frequency rating of 1 or greater and an intensity rating of 2 or greater reflect significant problems with a particular symptom and should be considered a symptom endorsement.

STRUCTURED CLINICAL INTERVIEW FOR DSM-III-R (SCID-R) (Spitzer and Williams, 1987)

The structured clinical interview (SCID-R) for PTSD is an instrument that provides operational criteria for assessing the 17 symptoms of PTSD within the criterion categories of reexperiencing, numbing–avoidance, and physiological arousal. The SCID instructs the clinician to ask specific questions, the answers to which determine whether a patient satisfies the diagnostic criteria for major Axis I disorders. For the patient, the number of symptoms positively endorsed is summed to arrive at an index of PTSD symptom severity.

PTSD Subscale of the Minnesota Multiphasic Personality Inventory (MMPI) and Minnesota Multiphasic Personality Inventory-2 (MMPI-2) (Hathaway and McKinly, 1967)

The MMPI and MMPI-2 are two of the most standardized measures utilized for the assessment of psychopathology. The MMPI and MMPI-2 PTSD subscales have been used extensively in the study of traumatization and stress. The PTSD subscale of the MMPI consists of 49 items from the MMPI found to discriminate psychiatric patients with mixed diagnoses, but no PTSD< from patients with a PTSD diagnosis. A minimum subscale score of 30 has been used as a criterion indicating the presence of PTSD. Correct classification of PTSD and non-PTSD patients has ranged from 66 to 82 percent in a variety of studies.

State-Trait Anxiety Inventory (STAI) (Spielberger, Gorsuch, and Lusbene, 1970)

This measure, used to assess anxiety in two modes, both state and trait, has been utilized extensively in the evaluation of anxiety and stress. It is found that PTSD subjects reported significantly more state and trait anxiety than did normal controls on the State-Trait Anxiety Inventory and that there was a trend in some directions for PTSD patients, compared to diagnostically heterogeneous psychiatric controls.

Impact of Events Scale (Horowitz, Wilner, and Aldarez, 1979)

The Impact of Events Scale is a 15-item scale measuring two core phenomena of traumatizing stress: (1) ideational and affective reexperiencing of the traumatic events; and (2) defensive avoidance or denial of trauma-related memories and emotions. Zilberg, Weiss, and Horowitz (1982) report that interscale correlations at .42 indicate that these dimensions assess separate but related phenomena. Several studies have demonstrated excellent discriminant validity for the Impact of Events Scale in patients with PTSD symptoms as distinguished from traumatized, asymptomatic control subjects in military and nonmilitary populations. Mean scores for veterans of combat have been reported to be 25.6 for the Intrusion subscale and 27.7 for the Avoidance subscale. In terms of the relative severity of life events, the Impact of Events Scale permits events to be compared according to the degree of subjective distress engendered by them.

This instrument, as it is focused on the formal properties of thought, permits comparison of the impact of different kinds of stressful life experiences and individual differences in response to them. Empirical investigations of subjective stress in response to stressful life events and the use of the Impact of Events Scale is discussed in detail elsewhere (Goldberger and Breznitz, 1993).

BECK DEPRESSION SCALE (Beck, Ward, Mendelson, Mock, and Erbaug, 1961)

This substantially used screening device has been utilized primarily for the assessment of depression and depressive symptoms, but it has been applied to the study of stress as well, as it is helpful in distinguishing the incidence of traumatizing stress from other groups, including nonpsychotic, psychiatric controls. Many of the symptomatology associated with traumatizing stress is related, both theoretically and descriptively, to psychiatric depression. Fairbank, Malloy, and Keane (1983) applied the Beck Depression Scale to assess depression associated with PTSD and found that PTSD subjects reported significantly more depression than both normals and psychiatric controls, as measured on the Beck Depression Inventory and greater depression than normal controls on other measures, such as the Zung. Depression scores for PTSD groups were greater than those of psychiatric controls. The Beck Depression Inventory addresses both cognitive and behavioral features thought to be associated with Major Depression and is considered to be an important diagnostic screening measure in the study of posttraumatic stress.

MISSISSIPPI SCALE FOR COMBAT-RELATED PTSD (M-PTSD) (Keane, Caddell, and Taylor, 1988)

The Mississippi Scale for Combat-Related PTSD is a 35-item Likert scale questionnaire originally developed to assess DSM-III-R symptoms and various associated features in Vietnam veterans who have been exposed to combat. The Mississippi Scale has high internal consistency (alpha = 0.94). A score above 106 has been shown to have high sensitivity (93%) and specificity (89%) in discriminating combat veteran patients with PTSD from various non-PTSD control subjects. The factor structure for this instrument is stable, and the six factors could be labeled as reexperiencing the traumatic, affective interpersonal problems, depression, memory–concentration problems, aggression and sleep disturbance.

THE CIVILIAN MISSISSIPPI (Keane et al., 1988)

This is a 39-item inventory based on the Mississippi Scale for Combat-Related PTSD adapted to civilian experiences independent of cambat or wartime. Its applicability and utilization includes natural structure for this instrument attempts to measure symptomatology consistent with traumatic stress, including sleep disturbance, memory and concentration difficulties, depression, interpersonal problems, affective disturbance, and the reexperiencing of the traumatic event.

THE MISSISSIPPI SCALE—HOSTAGE VERSION (Keane et al., 1988)

This is a 39-item inventory adapted from the original Mississippi Scale for Combat-Related PTSD. It assesses DSM-III-R criteria, including symptoms and associated features of victims of hostage-taking experiences (APA, 1987). As in the case of the Civilian Mississippi, it is adapted specifically for the assessment of posthostage adaptation, focusing on difficulties in memory and concentration, aggression and sleep disturbance, interpersonal difficulties and reexperiencing the trauma.

THE MISSISSIPPI SCALE FOR PERSIAN GULF WAR ZONE PERSONNEL (Keane, Caddell, and Taylor, 1988)

This is a 38-item measure adapted from the Mississippi Scale for Combat-Related PTSD. It is designed to assess the impact of being in the Persian Gulf war zone, as related to symptomatology consistent with DSM-III-R criteria for PTSD (APA, 1987). Validation studies of the original Mississippi Scale for Combat-Related PTSD, normed on Vietnam-era veterans, showed high levels of sensitivity and specificity in discriminating patients with PTSD from various non-PTSD control subjects. Factors measured on the Mississippi Scale for Persian Gulf War Zone Personnel include the six factors labeled Reexperiencing the Trauma, Affective and Interpersonal Problems, Depression, Memory–Concentration Difficulties, Aggression, and Sleep Disturbance. The scoring procedures for this measure are consistent with those for the Mississippi PTSD Scale, spouse, hostage, and civilian versions of the Mississippi Scale.

VIETNAM ERA STRESS INVENTORY
(Wilson and Krauss, 1984)

This is a 44-item inventory developed for use with patients who have had specific exposure to war conflict. Forty items of the 44-item inventory have demonstrated, through factor analysis, to divine dimensions of injury or death and exposure to ecological stresses. Reliability analysis has demonstrated high internal consistency for the total scale (alpha = 0.94) and corrected correlations between items and total score averaged $R = .50$.

MILLON CLINICAL MULTIAXIAL INVENTORY (MCMI)
(Millon, 1982)

This 175-item inventory is specifically designed to assess the DSM-III-R categories of personality disorders and clinical syndromes. Many of these are often associated with traumatizing, stressful experience and address the etiology and onset potential of the patient for symptoms consistent with traumatizing stress and anxiety. Theory-derived constructs are quantitatively measured to suggest diagnoses and psychodynamics, as well as testable hypotheses about patient history and current behavior. The clinical interpretive report includes a profile and provides a detailed narrative explanation of the psychodynamic relationships between the patient's personality patterns of behavior and feelings and accurate clinical symptoms exhibited.

PSYCHOPHYSIOLOGICAL AND BIOCHEMICALLY RELATED MEASURES

Clinicians and researchers alike have been interested in the assessment of stressful life events through biochemical markers of psychological disorders as well as through other psychophysiological phenomena. The use of psychophysiological measures including EMG and electrothermal biofeedback has shown considerable strength in assessing the psychophysiological aspects of traumatization. This diagnostic technique is based on the fact that traumatization and the stimuli therefrom elicit sympathetic hyperarousal. Techniques utilized in psychophysiology are sensitive and powerful when one uses general stimuli of either a visual or auditory nature related to the focused traumatization. It has been found to be even more discriminatory when the provocative stimulus is an individual autobiographical traumatic anecdote. Reactivity to the traumatization can predict certain elements of traumatic stress, and its impact can be measured utilizing the reactivity measured from the traumatization. The presentation of a physiologically meaningful cue while measuring psychologically and psychophysiologically relevant responses, appears to have significant potential for addressing key dimensions of traumatization and stress.

Likewise, the dexamethasone suppression test (DST) has been well recognized for its use in diagnosing major depressive disorders. Some clinical researchers are also finding that patients with traumatization and stress tend to have normal DSTs and could therefore be classified as suppressors, whereas patients with traumatic stress disorder and major depressive disorders may well be seen as nonsuppressors. Sodium lactate, or yohimbine, infusion and sodium amytal interviews have also been recognized as potentially helpful in assessing traumatic stress in patients.

DISCUSSION

There is a growing body of evidence that specific environmental factors can have traumatic and long-lasting psychological consequences. The issue of diagnostic assessment of such traumatizing experiences, however, is being addressed through three basic organizational formats of assessment. These three areas include: (1)

structured clinical interviews; (2) psychological testing; and (3) psychophysiological evaluations. Krystal and others have well defined and summarized the development of both unstructured and semistructured clinical interviews when examining trauma-related disorders. These interviews often were structured with a chronological perspective in mind and surveyed a developmental history, as well as situational-specific traumatic factors.

The development of the structured clinical interview for diagnosis of the DSM-III-R, as well as the Jackson Structured Clinical Interview, has helped to organize relevant and important material necessary in the assessment and diagnosis of patients. Such factors as current status, including relevant background demographics, current living, educational, vocational, and social situations; factors leading up to treatment, including important antecedent events and their consequences; and the formation of symptom clusters, with specific attention to the presence of clinical features that reflect cardinal symptoms of traumatizing stress, have emerged.

There is a growing body of multiple independent assessment techniques available for providing helpful diagnostic information about patients with stress-related disorders and traumatization. Such instruments yield information ranging from background factors to specific response measures. The advantages of such instruments include: (1) the validity and reliability of diagnosis may reach greater assurety; (2) multiaxial models provide for a greater understanding of patient adaptability and psychopathology; and (3) multiple sources can provide the necessary ingredients for a convergence of the data obtained. There remain numerous areas in need of systematic research and development, including those dealing with the following:

1. It is important to understand the individual's personality within the context of life events. Biological and intellectual variables limit adaptation.
2. Life events are mediated by several variables, including psychological, social, biological, and physical characteristics of the individual and their interface with the environment.

3. Cultural factors become an important influence in the individual's perception of both life stress and the adaptation process. In the development of life events scaling, it is essential to consider social and cross-cultural differences in weighing the impact of life stress events.

4. Clear differentiation must be made with respect to the processing and impact of traumatization from man-made versus natural traumas, physical versus psychological traumas and traumas associated with domestic violence.

5. Age and gender issues become an important ingredient in understanding differential adaptation process, and assessment measures to effectively differentiate for age and gender must be developed.

6. Clustering of life events impacts adjustment. Individuals, it is known, adapt well to given life events, such as retirement, departure of a last child from home, widowhood or illness, unless two or more such events occur simultaneously.

7. Beyond the structured clinical interview, better measures to assess variables that affect life events, such as socioeconomic status and interpersonal support systems, must be developed.

Miller and Basoglu (1991) have argued that the assessment of life stress events must include more research studies addressing the following: (1) the exploration of how life events contribute to the etiology and onset of illness; (2) the assessment of the full range of psychological components that account for adjusted persons; and (3) the study of the range of effects each stressful life event produces on the range of different types of people. In addition to this, biosocial approaches to understanding stress life event and the individual differences among human beings must be explored. Within the context of each of these charges is the essential need to have instruments that validly and reliably measure this most important area of psychopathology. The scientific community must appreciate efforts made so far to identify and analyze the impact of life stress on psychological and physical adjustment and must continue to support further efforts in our refinement and understanding of the impact of life stress events on our lives.

SUMMARY

Several approaches have been identified and utilized in the assessment of traumatization and life stress. Among these are stressful life events self-report scales that include measures of social readjustment, hassles and uplift, and various forms of rating stressful life experiences. A second level of measurement has been the emergence of the structured clinical interview. This has included efforts to match specific criteria developed by the International Classification of Diseases (ICD) and DSM-III-R (APA, 1987). The third are well standardized measures of psychological phenomena which carefully assess psychopathology through construct validity. The measures available can address issues on both Axis I and Axis II of the DSM series. Also present are scales for related psychopathology that can include state–trait anxiety, various measures of depression, and specific scales that assess trauma events and trauma syndromes of individuals who have survived torture and mass violence. The development and implementation of the structured event probe and narrative event rating method for assessing stressful life events has gained considerable attention as have psychobiological and psychophysiological measures in the assessment of stressful life experiences.

Areas for future consideration in clinical and research studies include, but are not limited to, the following: (1) a systematic assessment of stressful life events that are mediated by variables such as the individual's social, biological, and psychological characteristics; (2) cultural and individual differences which may influence an individual's perception of both life stress and the adaptation process; (3) personality characteristics of the individual that include intellectual variables that aid in adaptation and accommodation to traumatization; (4) issues related to age and gender which may help in understanding the adaptation process and measures that can effectively differentiate for age and gender; (5) models that will help in understanding the processing of traumatization and the subsequent impact from environment and natural disasters; and (6) research efforts that compare and contrast the effectiveness of such measures as structured clinical interviews, psychophysiological measures, and self-report indices as helpful in addressing diagnostic and clinical issues in assessment of stressful life experiences.

REFERENCES

Allodi, F. (1985), Physical and psychiatric effects of torture: Canadian study. In: *The Breaking of Bodies and Minds: Torture, Psychiatric Abuses and the Health Professions*, ed. E. Stover & E. O. Nightingale. New York: W. H. Freeman, pp. 66–78.

American Psychiatric Association (1987), *Diagnostic and Statistical Manual of Mental Disorders*, 3rd ed. rev. (DSM-III-R). Washington, DC: American Psychiatric Press.

Beck, A. T., Ward, C. H., Mendelson, M., Mock, J., & Erbaug, J. (1961), An inventory for measuring depression. *Arch. Gen. Psychiatry*, 12:63–70.

Blake, W., Weathers, P., & Nagy, R. (1990), *Clinician-Administered PTSD Scale (CAPS)*. Boston: National Center for PTSD, Behavioral Sciences Division.

Brown, G. W., & Birley, J. L. (1968), Crisis and life changes and the onset of schizophrenia. *J. Health & Soc. Behav.*, 9:203–214.

Coddington, R. D. (1972), The significance of life events as etiological factors in the diseases of children, Part 1: A survey of professional workers. *J. Psychosom. Res.*, 16:7–18.

Dohrenwend, B. P., Raphael, K. G., Schwartz, S., Stueve, A., & Skodol, A. (1993), Structured event probe and narrative rating method for measuring stressful life events. In: *Handbook of Stress*, 2nd ed., ed. L. Goldberger & S. Breznitz. New York: Free Press, pp. 174–199.

Dohrenwend, B. S., & Dohrenwend, B. P. (1978), Some issues in research on stressful life events. *J. Nerv. & Ment. Disord.*, 153:207–234.

Fairbank, J. A., Malloy, P. F., & Keane, T. M. (1983), Validation of multimethod assessment of posttraumatic stress disorders in Vietnam veterans. *J. Consult. & Clin. Psychol.*, 51:488–494.

Gerardi, R., & Wolfe, J. (1989), *Boston Clinical Interview for PTSD*. Boston: National Center for PTSD, Behavioral Science Division.

Goldberger, L., & Breznitz, S., Eds. (1993), *Handbook of Stress*. New York: Free Press.

Hathaway, S. R., & McKinley, J. C. (1967), *Minnesota Multiphasic Personality Inventory: Manual for Administration and Scoring.* New York: Psychological Corporation.

Hawkins, N. G. (1957), Evidence of psychosocial factors in the development of pulmonary tuberculosis. *Amer. Rev. Tuberc. & Pulmon. Dis.*, 75:768–780.

Holmes, T. H., & Rahe, R. H. (1967), The Social Readjustment Rating Scale. *J. Psychosomat. Res.*, 11:213–218.

Holroyd, J. (1988), Questionnaire on resources and stress. *Manual for ORS.* Los Angeles: CPPS.

Horowitz, M. J., Wilner, N., & Alvarez, W. (1979), The Impact of Events Scale: A measure of subjective stress. *Psychosom. Med.*, 41:209–218.

Hough, R. L. (1980), *Universal- and Group-Specific Life Change Scales.* Los Angeles, Life Change and Illness Research Project, University of California. Typescript.

Kanner, A. D., Coyne, J. C., Schaefer, C., & Lazarus, R. S. (1981), Comparison of two modes of stress measurement: Daily hassles and uplifts versus major life events. *J. Behav. Med.*, 4:1–39.

Keane, T. M., Caddell, J. M., & Taylor, K. L. (1988), Mississippi Scale for combat-related post-traumatic stress disorder: Three studies in reliability and validity. *J. Consult. & Clin. Psychol.*, 56:85–90.

Miller, T. W., & Basoglu, M. (1991), Posttraumatic stress disorder: Impact of life stress events on adjustment. *Integr. Psychiatry*, 7:209–217.

———— Buchbinder, J. (1982), Vietnam Experiences Questionnaire (VEQ), an experimental measure for assessing stress in veterans. Lexington, KY: Department of Psychiatry, College of Medicine, University of Kentucky.

Millon, T. (1982), *Millon Clinical Multiaxial Inventory Manual,* 2nd ed. Minneapolis: National Computer Systems.

Mollica, R. F., Wyshak, G., de Marneffe, D., Khuon, F., & Lavelle, J. (1987), Indochinese versions of the Hopkins Symptom Checklist-25: A screening instrument for the psychiatric care of refugees. *Amer. J. Psychiatry*, 144:497–500.

Paykel, E. S., Prusoff, B. A., & Uhlenhuth, E. H. (1971), Scaling of life events. *Arch. Gen. Psychiatry*, 25:340–347.

Rahe, R. H. (1974), A model for life changes and illness research. Cross-cultural data from the Norwegian Navy. *Arch. Gen. Psychiatry*, 31:172–177.

———— (1980), Recent life change stress and psychological depression. In: *Stressful Life Events*, ed. T. Miller. Madison, CT: International Universities Press, pp. 5–11, 1989.

———— Floistad, R. L., & Bergan, C. (1974), A model for life changes and illness research. Cross-cultural data from the Norwegian Navy. *Arch. Gen. Psychiatry*, 31:172–177.

Ruben, R. T., Gunderson, E. K. E., & Arthur, R. J. (1971), Life stress and illness patterns in the U.S. Navy, IV: Environmental and demographic variations in relation to illness onset in a battleship's crew. *J. Psychosom. Res.*, 15:221–227.

Skinner, H. A., & Lei, H. (1980), The multidimensional assessment of stressful life events. *J. Nerv. & Ment. Disord.*, 168:535–541.

Spielberger, C. D., Gorsuch, R. L., & Lusbene, R. E. (1970), *Manual for the State-Trait Anxiety Inventory (Self-Evaluation Questionnaire)*. Palo Alto, CA: Consultant Psychologists Press.

Spitzer, R. J., & Williams, J. B. W. (1987), *Structured Clinical Interview for DSM-III (SCID 3/15/83)*. New York: Biometrics Research Department, NY State Psychiatric Institute.

Wilson, J., & Krauss, R. F. (1984), *Vietnam Era Stress Inventory*. Typescript.

Zilberg, N. J., Weiss, D. S., & Horowitz, M. J. (1982), Impact of Event Scale: A cross-validation study and some empirical evidence supporting a conceptual model of stress response syndromes. *J. Consult. & Clin. Psychol.*, 50:407–414.

Chapter 9
Assessment of Rape and Other Civilian Trauma-Related PTSD: Emphasis on Assessment of Potentially Traumatic Events

HEIDI S. RESNICK, Ph.D., SHERRY A. FALSETTI, Ph.D., DEAN G. KILPATRICK, Ph.D., AND JOHN R. FREEDY, Ph.D.

This chapter focuses primarily on the assessment of civilian stressor events that would be included in criteria for PTSD (APA, 1987; Kilpatrick and Resnick, 1993). The initial necessary criterion for PTSD (Criterion A) requires that an individual has experienced an event that is perceived as highly threatening and which may include threat to life or physical integrity or actual injury to that individual or serious harm or death of a loved one. Events described as typical exemplars of Criterion A stressors have included combat, direct personal assaults, and rape in particular, as well as accidents and disaster experiences. In addition to the stressor experience an individual must display specific symptom criteria

Acknowledgments. The preparation of this manuscript was partially supported by NIDA Grant No: DA 05220-01A2.

that reflect: reexperiencing of the event in thoughts/memories, physiological reactions, emotions, or dreams (Criterion B); avoidance of reminders of the stressor event (Criterion C); and indices of increased arousal, including sleep disturbance and concentration difficulties (Criterion D). Results of several recent epidemiological studies indicate that rates of rape and other civilian trauma and related posttraumatic stress disorder are significant. These reports indicate high rates of exposure to a wide variety of events, ranging from 40 to 70 percent of populations studied (Kilpatrick, Saunders, Veronen, Best, and Von, 1987; Breslau, Davis, Andreski, and Peterson, 1991; Resnick, Kilpatrick, Dansky, Saunders, and Best, 1993). Furthermore, results of several studies indicated high rates of history of multiple events, reported by 30 to 50 percent of those exposed to any type of Criterion A event (Resnick et al., 1993). Rates of PTSD observed in these studies ranged from approximately 18 to 28 percent among those identified with some type of civilian trauma history. The consistency of these findings suggests that earlier reports of very low PTSD prevalence rates (George and Winfield-Laird, 1986; Helzer, Robins, and McEvoy, 1987) reflected underestimates of true population rates. It has been suggested that these underestimates may have been due primarily to methodological factors related to failure to adequately assess a broad range of Criterion A (APA, 1987) civilian stressor events (Kilpatrick and Resnick, 1993; Resnick et al., 1993). Results of these studies indicated that rape and sexual assault are associated with high rates of PTSD relative to other events (Resnick et al., 1993). Finally, data indicate that qualities of traumatic events, including fear of death or serious injury and receipt of injury are risk factors for PTSD among civilian samples (Kilpatrick et al., 1987; Resnick et al. 1993). Substantial rates of stressor events and PTSD observed in these studies highlight the need for sound assessment strategies and instruments to adequately assess a broad range of potentially traumatic events, and sexual assault events in particular, as well as related symptoms and diagnoses.

As reviewed by Resnick, Kilpatrick, and Lipovsky (1991) considerable progress has been made in development of sound strategies, and reliable and valid instruments for the assessment of

PTSD *symptomatology* related to rape, other types of sexual assault, physical abuse/assault, and secondary victimization due to homicide. Many such measures have been adapted, with little or no modification, from structured interview and self-report instruments developed in the study of combat-related PTSD. In addition, some new self-report diagnostic instruments have been developed within civilian trauma samples that have concurrent validity with structured diagnostic interview measures (Saunders, Mandoki, and Kilpatrick, 1990); and some data from longitudinal research on chronic postrape PTSD are available on predictive utility of some self-report instruments administered within a few weeks postrape (Rothbaum, Foa, Riggs, Murdock, and Walsh, 1992). Replication of these general symptom and diagnostic assessment findings is needed. Future research also needs to focus on comorbidity of other diagnoses with PTSD and corresponding patterns on self-report instruments. An additional area in need of further development is the identification of new methods for multimodal assessment of distress. The critical component of sophisticated assessment of civilian trauma (the stressor criterion itself) is much less well developed at present. Sensitive, reliable, and valid instruments for the assessment of potentially traumatic events are critical because these events have a gatekeeping role in the diagnostic criteria for PTSD as the necessary but not sufficient stressor criterion (Davidson and Foa, 1991). Thus, typically if critical event incidents are not identified, symptoms of PTSD are not assessed. In addition, lack of inclusion of stressor event assessment measures in studies of major depression, substance abuse, other anxiety disorders, and other mental and physical health variables limits our current knowledge of the role of stressor events in influencing other areas of functioning. The emphasis in this chapter on assessment of these potentially traumatic events reflects the notion that this assessment should have at least equal weight in terms of sophisticated assessment strategies as that placed on symptom assessment.

The goal of this chapter is to focus primarily on issues related to assessment of potential traumatic stressor events, and to provide information about existing and newly developed instruments to

assess the history of civilian trauma as distinct from PTSD symptom assessment. In addition to provision of data related to psychometric properties of instruments, these measures will be described
in reference to several qualitative characteristics described below
that may be important to consider when choosing a particular
instrument. In cases in which specific stressor event interviews
have been paired with specific PTSD interview or self-report measures, the symptom assessment instrument will also be described briefly.

Issues in the Assessment of History of Potentially Traumatic Events

As noted by Resnick, Kilpatrick, and Lipovsky (1991) in the earlier
assessment review, there are several major factors to be considered and addressed for sensitive, reliable, and valid assessment of
potentially traumatic events.

Opening Preface

First, the use of a preface or opening statements prior to assessment of potentially sensitive traumatic event history material is
important. This provides a context for the subsequent assessment
and demonstrates knowledge and sensitivity on the part of the
interviewer about the prevalence of such events. It also provides
information about the circumstances under which they may occur, and the variety of mental health outcomes that might be
associated with traumatic events. Providing information that Criterion A events are not rare, in addition to being accurate, may
also be therapeutic for those respondents who have experienced
such events rather than promoting the view that they are highly
unusual occurrences.

Use of Behaviorally Specific Questions

Second, the use of behaviorally specific terms in questions designed to assess events such as rape and other sexual assault is an important component of assessment. This strategy is essential in reference to events for which respondents are likely to hold stereotypes about the meaning of the term. For example, it has been demonstrated that use of legal terms such as *rape* have led to vast underestimates of the true rates of rape defined behaviorally as forced anal, oral, or vaginal penetration by a penis, finger, or other object (Koss, 1985; Kilpatrick et al., 1987). As noted by Resnick et al. (1993) reports of trauma-specific PTSD rates across epidemiological studies have consistently indicated that rape and sexual assault are associated with some of the highest rates of PTSD. However, the assessed rates of rape and other sexual assault noted in these studies vary widely. Resnick et al. suggested that it would be critical to adequately assess rape and other sexual assault, because the failure to do so might alter observed general PTSD prevalence rates and/or might influence rates observed in response to other specific traumatic events under study. For example, someone identified as having accident-related PTSD might have a "hidden" history of rape that could have affected the outcome to a subsequent accident incident. A more detailed discussion of clinical strategies to assess sensitive history of sexual assault is included in Kilpatrick (1983) and Resnick, Kilpatrick, and Lipovsky (1991).

Assessment of Multiple Stressor Events

Third, the breadth of coverage of a variety of relevant potentially traumatic events that may occur within a person's lifetime and provision for assessment of multiple incidents or types of occurrence is important for proper assessment. Those with complex histories of multiple traumatic events or those with events occurring at critical developmental stages might have specialized treatment needs. In addition, as with the accurate identification of sexual assault incidents, if one is assessing PTSD in relation to a particular traumatic event such as combat it would be critical to know about all other potentially traumatic events that could in themselves lead to PTSD.

QUALITATIVE CHARACTERISTICS OF EVENTS

Finally, specific trauma-related variables, including degree of perceived life threat and experience of injury, that have been identified to increase risk of PTSD across a variety of event types (Green, 1990) should be an integral part of trauma assessment. Foy, Carroll, and Donahoe (1987) found that degree of combat exposure based on a continuous sum of experiences that included injury and witnessing death was the best predictor of PTSD outcome among Vietnam veterans. Within a civilian community sample, Kilpatrick, Saunders, Amick-McMullan, Best, Veronen, and Resnick (1989) found that perceptions of life threat and actual physical injury were significant predictors of PTSD outcome, whereas specific crime types (with the exception of rape) were not in themselves significant predictors of PTSD after these factors were statistically controlled. These findings indicate that there is likely heterogeneity within broad categories of traumatic events. Thus, more detailed information about a range of experiences within broader event categories needs to be assessed to more clearly identify PTSD risk factors.

RULES FOR INTEGRATING INFORMATION ABOUT STRESSOR HISTORY WITH SYMPTOM AND DIAGNOSTIC ASSESSMENT

Instruments vary in terms of approaches for integrating information obtained about potentially complex trauma history with existing approaches for PTSD symptom and diagnostic assessment. For example, in cases in which there are several relevant Criterion A events identified, there are varying policies across measures for conducting PTSD diagnostic interviews and for instructing respondents in the completion of self-report instruments. Specific guidelines for related symptom assessment are less relevant in cases in which the symptom or diagnostic measure is not event-specific, such as with measures of general symptom distress. Many instruments used in lifetime PTSD assessment, however, require the identification of index events for subsequent establishment of symptom content specific to a given event or symptom onset subsequent to that event. Typically these instruments specify at the beginning that the respondent is being asked about reactions or symptoms that are due to the event or that relate to the event (i.e., nightmares). Similarly, some self-report measures designed to tap PTSD such as the Impact of Events Scale (IES; Horowitz, Wilner, and Alvarez, 1979) refer to specific events to which current symptoms relate. This may not be realistic in cases in which multiple events have been experienced. In such cases it may be optimal to evaluate current distress related to any Criterion A event that has been experienced.

OTHER PSYCHOMETRIC EVALUATION CRITERIA

In addition to the five trauma assessment measure characteristics identified above, there are a number of other important features related to psychometric and practical issues to be considered. Following the format used by Watson (1990) to evaluate PTSD symptom and diagnostic measures, we applied Watson's set of criteria to evaluate existing or newly developed instruments for the assessment of traumatic event history. These include: (1) correspondence with DSM-III-R PTSD Criterion A; (2) reliability; (3) established empirical validity; (4) availability of both dichotomous and continuous output; (5) mode of administration and ease of use by trained subprofessionals. A sixth feature related to stressor assessment coverage was the inclusion in the measure of "lower level" or non-Criterion A stressor events in the instrument, that would include recent instances of financial difficulties and relationship problems. These events, which are currently excluded from Criterion A, need further empirical evaluation in terms of potential role in leading to psychological distress either by themselves or in conjunction with a Criterion A trauma history. We include information on these features in a summary table (Table

9.1) to be referred to in reference to the specific lifetime trauma assessment instruments described below.

Typically the psychometric characteristics outlined by Watson have been applied to symptom rather than stressor event assessment. Therefore we discuss relevant characteristics as they may relate specifically to stressor event assessment. Several types of reliability are relevant with regard to symptom or diagnostic level assessment including test–retest, interrater, and internal consistency. In terms of stressor event assessment measures, high test–retest reliability would reflect consistency over time in identification of trauma history. There may be several factors which could artificially lower test–retest reliability in relation to traumatic experiences, however. For instance, it is possible that more events may be remembered at the second testing because memory has been cued by inquiry during the first assessment or the individual is more willing to disclose a particular incident after additional contact with the interviewer. Conversely, if PTSD avoidance is strong, it is also possible that an individual might purposely avoid disclosure of an event at a second assessment. It is also possible that many people may not label certain experiences as sexual assault or physical assault on a consistent basis because they are struggling with the meaning of their experiences. If events are behaviorally defined, error due to this factor would be reduced. Interrater reliability issues would be similar for both symptom and stressor event assessment measures. Finally, although internal consistency is certainly important with symptom measures, it is not really applicable to stressor event assessment measures because there is no conceptual reason to expect discrete types of stressor events (i.e., disaster, accident, assault) to be correlated.

As with reliability, establishment of validity of trauma assessment measures may be difficult due to some unique aspects related to stressor event reporting and documentation. For example, police and hospital records that are usually obtained close in time to the actual event are very helpful for collateral information such as time of event, injury, and other descriptive characteristics. Often, however, these documents are not available because many crimes are not reported to the police and many serious crime incidents such as sexual assaults do not typically involve high degrees of actual physical injury (Kilpatrick, 1983). Thus, the presence or absence of such documentation cannot be used generally to establish the validity of self-reported incidents. Instead, to establish validity, other trauma assessment instruments must be relied upon. The instrument under investigation can either be compared to other trauma instruments in the same study, or to results of other studies to determine if similar prevalence rates for traumatic events are reported.

Several researchers have noted the importance of providing continuous as well as dichotomous outputs for PTSD symptom measures (Watson, 1990; Falsetti, Resnick, Resick, and Kilpatrick, 1993). We would extend the importance of such data to trauma assessment measures as well. Simple occurrence of an event is by nature dichotomous data. However, the number of times an event occurred, or qualitative characteristics related to events such as perceived life threat, can be assessed as continuous data. In addition, open-ended questions can provide descriptive data about aspects of trauma which are salient to the individual that may be missed with closed-ended questions. These data can provide additional information about stressor events and their relationship to PTSD symptomatology and other indices of psychological functioning. In clinical settings, descriptive data would also be helpful in identifying treatment issues. For example, it is often in the answers to open-ended questions that issues regarding self-blame arise.

Finally, Watson (1990) recommended that PTSD instruments be designed for administration by subprofessionals. Such a recommendation is equally applicable for trauma assessment measures. Self-report measures are also another viable option. Financially and in terms of time efficiency, the use of these types of instruments would lessen the burden for clinicians, researchers, and clients. The required level of standardization of such instruments and reduced cost of administration would also increase the probability that stressor event data would be reliably collected.

TABLE 9.1

Criteria, Administration Methods, Validity, and Reliability Data on Measures of Trauma

Instruments	DSM-III-R Criteria on A Trauma	Type of Output	Administration Method	Low Level Stressors Assessed	Reliability Data	Validity Data
IRI (Kilpatrick, Saunders, Veronen, et al., 1987)	Crime only	Dichotomous & descriptive	Interview by subprofessionals	No	None	Prevalence rates comparable to other studies
NIDA (Kilpatrick, 1990)	All Criterion A events, except combat	Dichotomous & descriptive	Interview by subprofessionals	No	None	Comparable to other studies
PSEI (Kilpatrick, Resnick, Freedy, et al., 1992)	All Criterion A events	Continuous, dichotomous & descriptive	Combination interview & self-report by subprofessionals	Yes: low magnitude events	None	None

TABLE 9.1
Criteria, Administration Methods, Validity, and Reliability Data on Measures of Trauma

Instruments	DSM-III-R Criteria on A Trauma	Type of Output	Administration Method	Low Level Stressors Assessed	Reliability Data	Validity Data
TSS (Norris, 1990)	All Criterion A events	Dichotomous only	Combination interview & self-report by subprofessionals	Yes	Test–retest .88	Comparable to other studies
THQ (Green, 1992)	All Criterion A Events	Dichotomous & descriptive	Self-report	No	Test–retest	None
Brief Screening Questionnaire (Saunders, Kilpatrick, et al., 1989)	Physical & sexual assault; Homicide	Dichotomous & descriptive	Interview by subprofessionals	No	None	Comparisons to chart reviews
SES (Koss & Gidycz, 1985)	Rape & sexual assault only	Dichotomous only	Self-report	Other sexual experience	Test–retest .93	r = .73 with clinical interview

Descriptions of Specific Traumatic Event Assessment Measures

Eight main instruments were chosen for review in this section based on their inclusion of a fairly broad array of civilian traumatic events (either multiple types of crime events or crime and other Criterion A events) as well as their use within civilian trauma populations or clinical samples. First, we describe the stressor event assessment section of the two structured interviews that have been most widely used in assessment of civilian trauma–related PTSD: The Diagnostic Interview Schedule (DIS; Helzer et al., 1987) and the Structured Clinical Interview for DSM-III-R (SCID; Spitzer, Williams, and Gibbon, 1987). Several of the remaining six measures were modified from instruments originally developed by Kilpatrick and his colleagues. New measures for assessment of traumatic events have also been developed by Norris and Green. We also cite some measures designed to assess more limited types of events where relevant, and some measures still under development. This review of this subset of instruments is intended to highlight critical areas for ongoing research focused on development and evaluation of new and existing measures to assess the history of potentially traumatic events.

Diagnostic Interview Schedule (DIS; Robins, Helzer, Croughan, and Ratcliff, 1981)

In the earliest version of the DIS PTSD assessment section reported on by Helzer, Robins, and McEvoy (1987) only two general types of events were routinely assessed. All interviewees were asked about lifetime military service, and were asked whether they had been "mugged or beaten" within the 6 months prior to interview. Qualitative event characteristics were asked of those who had military service during the Vietnam era. Those veterans were asked if they had experienced combat or had been wounded. Aside from these two major probe questions traumatic event history was not assessed independently from PTSD symptom occurrence. The traumatic event assessment was described as asking respondents "whether they had experienced an event that frightened them so much that they had one or more of the symptoms . . ." that were included in DSM-III (APA, 1980) PTSD criteria. Only those events reported as being associated with critical symptom items were documented. Clearly, this strategy for trauma assessment does not allow for determination of either population rates of traumatic events or event specific PTSD rates as noted elsewhere (Breslau et al. 1991; Kilpatrick and Resnick, 1993).

A revised PTSD module of the DIS separates out the event assessment from the symptom assessment (Robins, Helzer, Cottler, and Goldring, 1988). Rather than employing separate questions to assess specific types of events, a summary of qualifying event types is included in a global preface/question at the beginning of the PTSD section as follows: "A few people have terrible experiences that most people never go through—things like being attacked (if female: or raped), being in a fire or flood or bad traffic accident, being threatened with a weapon, or seeing someone being badly injured or killed. Did something like this ever happen to you?" (p. 22). If a respondent has not directly experienced such an event, he or she is asked whether this type of event has occurred to someone close to them. The interview addresses the possibility of multiple Criterion A events among those who report at least one such event. The questions used to assess two additional stressor events are "Have you had any other terrible or shocking experience?" (pp. 23–24). In terms of qualitative event characteristics, the DIS symptom assessment includes a question about the experience of injury during directly experienced Criterion A events. Questions about sustained head injury or loss of consciousness also allow for evaluation of memory deficits due to these causes. Specific and clear instructions are provided for assessment of all PTSD symptoms specific to up to three Criterion A events. The procedure is to ask about presence of all

17 PTSD symptom items in reference to the first identified event, then to go through all symptom items for the second and third events.

In terms of the evaluative criteria specified above, the recent version of the DIS has some positive characteristics that include the provision for multiple event assessment and clear rules for PTSD assessment in reference to up to three events. In addition, the interview is designed to be administered by trained nonclinicians which makes it convenient. There are several problems with the interview, however. First, the preface specifying that these Criterion A events are rare is not consistent with current data. Perhaps the greatest limitation of the trauma assessment section is the lack of behaviorally specific questions to assess sexual assault and rape. As noted earlier and in other reviews (Kilpatrick, 1983; Resnick et al., 1991) use of legal terms like *rape* is likely to elicit vast underestimates of true rates. Thus, it is not surprising that using this term Breslau et al. (1991) observed a 2.6 percent rate of rape (not operationally defined) among a subsample of adult women, while Kilpatrick et al. (1987) and Resnick et al. (1993) reported rates of 23.3 and 12.7 percent among general population samples of women based on questions that allowed for operational definitions of completed rape. An example of the type of screening approach designed to sensitively assess history of rape is presented within this section of the paper in the description of the National Women's Study Interview.

STRUCTURED CLINICAL INTERVIEW FOR DSM-III-R (SCID-NP; Spitzer, Williams, and Gibbon, 1987)

The nonpatient version of the SCID PTSD section contains a specific set of questions to assess military experience and several important qualitative characteristics of that experience. The assessment of other lifetime traumatic events history, however, is quite brief and limited. Similar to the DIS measure a variety of experiences are listed in an opening preface-question as follows:

Sometimes things happen to people that are very stressful or disturbing —things that do not happen to most people and are so bad that they would be distressing, upsetting, or frightening to almost everyone. By that I mean things like major earthquakes or floods, very serious accidents or fires, physical assault or rape, seeing other people killed or dead, being in a war or heavy combat, or some other type of disaster. At any time during your life—that is, before, during, or after you were in the military—have any of these kinds of things happened to you? [p. 52].

The PTSD section allows for assessment and recording of multiple potentially traumatic events. The interviewer is instructed to record all such events reported in response to the opening question on an allocated page with headings for specification of assigned event number, date(s) of occurrence, and brief description(s) of each event. Instructions are provided for assessment of PTSD specific to identified Criterion A events. Following determination of lifetime event history, the individual is asked to identify the event that was or is most stressful or upsetting. Symptom-specific questions are then asked in reference to this "worst" event.

In terms of the evaluative criteria for assessment of potentially traumatic events, the SCID assessment section is very similar to the DIS in phrasing. In contrast to the DIS, the SCID instructions do specify that all such events within a person's lifetime be recorded, rather than restricting the event assessment to three events. However, the restriction in the SCID to assessment of PTSD in reference to one "worst" event may be a limitation in terms of gaining a full understanding of how a complex traumatic event history may influence the course of PTSD to a single identified event. Another difference between the two interview measures is that the SCID was designed to be used by clinicians employing a degree of clinical judgment. Like the DIS, there are no behaviorally defined questions to assess rape or other sexual assault, and the preface does not provide information about the true rates of occurrence or the variety of circumstances under which these Criterion A events occur. No qualitative characteristics of specific noncombat events are assessed in a structured way.

In summary, the current SCID and DIS trauma assessment sections do not meet the majority of criteria that would be critical for a useful stressor event assessment instrument. We recommend that these diagnostic interviews be used with more comprehensive and sensitive stressor event assessment instruments like the ones described in the remainder of this section.

INCIDENT REPORT INTERVIEW (IRI; Kilpatrick et al., 1987)

The IRI interview was designed to comprehensively assess lifetime history of civilian crime events included in the DSM-III-R (APA, 1987) stressor criterion for PTSD. To orient the respondent to the assessment of traumatic event history, the IRI begins with statements that give an overview of the interview procedure indicating that questions will be asked about crime incidents in several different ways and specifying that the incidents asked about need not have been reported to police or identified by the respondent as a "crime." A separate and more detailed preface is provided prior to the assessment of sexual assault incidents. This overview again emphasizes that these types of incidents need not have been reported to police or others, and provides factual information about the variety of circumstances under which sexual assault incidents may occur and the general frequency with which they occur. The opening preface for the overall crime section is worded as follows: "Although there is a lot of talk about crime, no one really knows how many people are victimized. People sometimes disagree about whether certain experiences are crimes or not. In addition, many people don't report certain experiences to the police even if they think they have been victimized."

The IRI includes questions for assessment of eight types of major crimes including attempted rape, attempted or completed molestation, other sexual assault, aggravated assault, robbery, and burglary. Each of these crimes is specifically behaviorally defined as described in Kilpatrick et al., (1987). Sufficient questions for the assessment of sexual assault incidents are included to behaviorally define and classify cases of completed rape, molestation, and attempted rape incidents. For example, these questions focused on determination of incidents of completed penetration, contact with breasts or genitals, and sexual assault attempts that involved the use of force or the threat of force. Detailed examples of such behaviorally defined questions for assessment of sexual assault and other incidents and corresponding classification rules are included in the description of the next instrument developed for the National Women's Study described below.

The IRI includes comprehensive instructions for a somewhat complex procedure for reducing information about multiple crime history into a final classification of up to three major index events. These events include the first, most recent, and worst (if different from first or most recent) crime within a person's history. Following this summary classification, the IRI includes probes to assess characteristics of the index crime incidents. These specific crime characteristics include age of onset, brief open-ended description, reporting to police, serial versus single incident occurrence, relationship to perpetrator, presence of a weapon, and reported fear of death or serious injury during an incident.

Finally, in their use of the IRI in conjunction with a structured diagnostic interview for assessment of PTSD, Kilpatrick et al. (1989) assessed all symptoms of DSM-III defined PTSD in reference to a respondent's "only" or subjectively defined "worst" event. The complexity of the design and the inclusion of so many potentially critical predictor variables, allowed for empirical evaluation of risk factors for PTSD among a population exposed to civilian trauma events. The results of multivariate analyses to predict PTSD that were conducted by Kilpatrick et al. (1989) provide extremely useful data about which variables continue to be important to emphasize in newly developed instruments. Specifically, their results indicated that the only variables that were significant predictors of PTSD in multivariate regression analyses were: fear of death or serious injury during an incident; actual receipt of some degree of injury during an incident; and the experience of completed rape.

The finding of consistent rates of civilian trauma identified across studies using general population samples supports the validity of the IRI. For example, the overall rate of crime identified within the sample of 75 percent is very similar to that obtained by Norris (1992) for general trauma within a civilian sample (69%) and the 69 percent general trauma prevalence rate obtained in a larger representative sample of 4009 women (Resnick et al., 1993). In addition, rates of PTSD specific to particular traumatic event history profiles are similar to those found in other studies, which is supportive of IRI validity. Thus, the 78 percent rate of lifetime PTSD among rape victims whose histories included life threat and injury observed by Kilpatrick et al. (1989) is similar to the extremely high rates of PTSD observed among rape victims in other studies in which these characteristics were likely to be present (Breslau et al., 1991; Rothbaum et al., 1992). The rate of PTSD among those exposed to any type of traumatic event (27.8%) was similar to that observed by Breslau et al. of 23.6 percent. In terms of the evaluative criteria specified, the IRI is in many ways groundbreaking in the area of assessment of critical traumatic events for several reasons already outlined: breadth of coverage; helpful prefaces to interview sections; use of sensitive behaviorally defined questions; and inclusion of critical event characteristics. In addition, qualitative characteristics of events are included. Other strengths are the clear instructions for assessment and classification of multiple crime events and the related PTSD assessment. A limitation of the instrument is the restriction to crime events. Thus, in terms of DSM-III-R Criterion A some event types would not be captured. Finally, while the IRI can be used by trained non-clinicians, some of the instructions for event classification are complex requiring more extensive training.

National Women's Study PTSD Module
(Kilpatrick, Resnick, Saunders, and Best, 1989)

The interview currently being used in the National Institute of Drug Abuse (NIDA) funded study of risk factors for substance abuse among women (Kilpatrick, 1990) contains separate stressor event assessment and PTSD components. We describe the development and evaluation of psychometric properties of these components separately as follows.

The stressor event section of the PTSD Module contains comprehensive assessment of crime and direct assault events adapted from the IRI. In addition, the stressor event section was expanded to include lifetime history of noncrime traumatic events. Thus, this interview also contains questions to assess multiple exposure(s) to serious accident, natural disaster, witnessing serious injury or death, other incidents in which the subject suffered serious injury or feared that she might be killed or seriously injured, and secondary victimization due to homicide of a close friend or family member. This expanded component of the stressor event section was adapted primarily from the "Stressful and Traumatic Life Events" interview developed by researchers at Research Triangle Institute in conjunction with Louis Harris and Associates for use in the National Vietnam Veterans Readjustment Study (NVVRS; Kulka, Schlenger, Fairbank, Hough, Jordan, Marmar, and Weiss, 1990). A major difference between the National Women's Study PTSD Module and the NVVRS instrument is that the National Women's Study measure contains the detailed assessment sections devoted to identification of all types of sexual assault and aggravated assault adapted from the IRI, whereas the NVVRS measure does not assess these types of events comprehensively.

Like the IRI, prefaces are included at the beginning of each trauma assessment section, including the sections for assessment of completed rape, completed molestation, attempted sexual assault, aggravated assault with or without a weapon, and a separate section covering other Criterion A events including homicide death, disaster, accident, witnessing violence, and other events that were perceived as life threatening or that led to physical injury or damage. In addition to assessment of Criterion A stressor events, past year occurrence of illness, bereavement, marital discord, and financial difficulties is assessed in a separate section of the interview. As an example of the type of preface and behaviorally specific terms recommended for valid assessment of history of sexual assault events, these components of the National Women's Study interview for assessment of completed rape are presented here:

Another type of stressful event that many women have experienced is unwanted sexual advances. Women do not always report such experiences to the police or other authorities or discuss them with family or friends. The person making the advances isn't always a stranger, but can be a friend, boyfriend, or even a family member. Such experiences can occur anytime in a woman's life, even as a child. Regardless of how long ago it happened or who made the advances ...

Has a man or boy ever made you have sex by *using force* or threatening to harm you or someone close to you? Just so there is no mistake, by sex we mean putting a penis in your vagina.

Has anyone ever made you have oral sex by force or threat of harm. Just so there is no mistake, by oral sex we mean that a man or a boy put his penis in your mouth or someone penetrated your vagina or anus with their mouth or tongue?

Has anyone ever made you have anal sex by force or threat of harm? Has anyone ever put fingers or objects in your vagina or anus against your will by using force or threats?

As noted by Resnick, Kilpatrick, and Lipovsky (1991) the use of the type of preface included in the National Women's Study instrument allows the clinician or researcher to orient the woman to the topic of sexual assault, and displays sensitivity and knowledge on the part of the interviewer. There is no mention of the term *rape* despite the fact that this section is designed to assess rape history. Rather than presenting a term that may hold varied meaning for individuals, simple behavioral terms are used to elicit history of specific experiences. The use of these questions allows for identification of behaviorally defined experiences that meet the legal definition of rape. Incidents are defined as *completed rape* if they include actual penile, digital, or foreign object penetration of the victim's mouth, anus, or vagina by the assailant; occur without the victim's consent; and involve the use or threat of force.

The National Women' Study PTSD Module provides for assessment of multiple traumatic events and detailed information is gathered about a subset of these events. For completed rape incidents, qualitative characteristic data including perceived life threat, injury, frequency of occurrence, relationship to perpetrator, and reporting to authorities are gathered in reference to an individual's first, most recent, and worst incident. For other types of sexual assault and aggravated assault incidents, data are gathered about number of such incidents within a person's lifetime, age at first or only incident of a given type, and the most serious incident of a given type. To reduce the length of the interview other qualitative characteristic information is then gathered about a single incident of each additional type of direct assault event (completed molestation, attempted sexual assault, and aggravated assault). For other Criterion A events including accident or disaster, information is gathered about age, life threat, and injury for the first and most recent instance of each type of incident.

As discussed in reference to the IRI above, the findings of consistent rates of specific traumatic events and event specific PTSD rates across civilian population samples support the validity of this trauma assessment instrument. The 69 percent rate of any type of Criterion A event identified in the National Women's Study (Resnick et al., 1993) is the exact rate obtained by Norris (1992). The rates of crime events identified were also very similar. In the National Women's Study we observed a rate of 36 percent among women (Resnick et al., 1993), while Norris found a rate of 33 percent. These rates are similar to the proportion of Breslau et al.'s sample that had been exposed to any type of traumatic event (39%). Similar proportions of this and other samples have also been identified as having experienced histories of multiple potentially traumatic events. In the National Women's Study 52 percent of women who reported at least one event had experienced multiple Criterion A events. The rate observed using the IRI was 54 percent (Kilpatrick et al., 1987), while Breslau et al. (1991) found that 33 percent of those with some trauma history had experienced multiple events.

The PTSD assessment component of the PTSD Module was altered from a specially developed Diagnostic Interview Schedule (DIS) used in the NVVRS. It should be noted that the NVVRS DIS instrument and the National Women's Study Module differ significantly from the standard DIS used with civilians (Helzer et al., 1987). As opposed to that version of the DIS, these instruments were used in conjunction with sensitive traumatic event assessment instruments to determine Criterion A event history. Our PTSD Module differs from the NVVRS measure in the following ways. First, several symptom items were added to allow for evaluation of all DSM-III-R PTSD criteria. Second, we eliminated DIS follow-up probes including determination of treatment seeking or prescribed medication use due to symptom presence that may reduce sensitivity of assessment. The PTSD symptom assessment section of the Module is administered after the stressor event section, but uses a nonevent specific approach to assessment of PTSD symptoms. Full lifetime trauma history data are meant to be empirically linked with presence of PTSD symptoms sufficient to meet diagnostic criteria rather than requiring the individual to link a set of symptoms with a subset of events. In the most recent version of the PTSD Module, respondents are asked about presence of symptoms that persisted for at least two weeks, followed by open-ended probes to assess symptom content. For example, if an individual reports a period of two weeks during which repeated bad dreams or nightmares were present, they are asked what those nightmares were about. Information obtained about age of onset of stressor events and symptoms can also be used to establish chronology.

General and trauma related PTSD prevalence rates obtained

using the PTSD Module are compatible with those obtained in other population studies, supporting the validity of the instrument. The crime specific lifetime PTSD rate of 25.8 percent (Resnick et al., 1993) was highly similar to the crime specific lifetime PTSD rate identified using the IRI (27.8%) and the trauma specific rate of 23.6 percent observed by Breslau et al. (1991). Current PTSD rates associated with history of any type of traumatic event were also similar across studies. For example, Resnick et al. (1993) observed a 6.7 percent rate of current PTSD using the National Women's Study Interview, while Norris obtained a rate of 7.0 percent and Kilpatrick et al. (1987) found a current rate of PTSD among crime victims of 7.5 percent.

Kilpatrick et al. (in press) reported data from the PTSD Field Trial Study indicating good correspondence between the National Women's Study PTSD Module and the Structured Clinical Interview for DSM-III-R (Spitzer, Williams, and Gibbon, 1987). Kappa coefficients of agreement between the two measures were .77 for lifetime PTSD and .71 for current PTSD. A more thorough description of the psychometric properties of this interview is contained in Resnick et al. (1993).

In terms of evaluative criteria, the stressor event component of the National Women's Study PTSD Module shares many important features of the IRI and also includes secondary victimization due to homicide of a friend or relative as well as other Criterion A events. In addition, this interview is briefer than the IRI and has been used by trained nonclinicians with ease due to simple and comprehensive instructions that guide the interviewer with skip patterns and probes. A disadvantage to the interview is that like the IRI, the phrasing in the prefaces and screening questions was designed for adult women. However, the phrasing could be adapted for men and other age groups as was done in the Potential Stressful Events Interview (described below). A potential disadvantage with the interview is that some additional instructions would be required for use with event-specific PTSD measures such as the SCID or DIS interviews to specify only a subset of events in cases with multiple trauma history.

Finally, the PTSD component of the interview appears to be a psychometrically sound instrument based on comparison of PTSD rates obtained across similar populations as well as agreement with the SCID interview. Previously the NVVRS version of the DIS interview from which the PTSD Module was adapted was found to have unacceptably low sensitivity (Kulka, Schlenger, Fairbank, Jordan, Hough, Marmar, and Weiss, 1991). We suggest that the higher concordance observed between the National Women's Study PTSD Module and the SCID interview may be due either to the modifications in the structure of the interview described earlier, or to the greater comprehensiveness with which some critical major traumatic events are assessed. Thus, even though the module assesses symptoms in a non-event-specific way, it could be argued that the sensitive assessment of incidents such as sexual assault and rape within an individual's history may be critical to cueing the individual to consider and report PTSD symptoms.

POTENTIAL STRESSFUL EVENTS INTERVIEW (PSE; Kilpatrick, Resnick, and Freedy, 1991)

The PSE interview was developed for use in the DSM-IV PTSD Field Trial by combining useful features of both the IRI and the National Women's Study Interview along with new components designed to assess major questions about Criterion A addressed in the Field Trial. In addition, a subset of detailed questions about military combat history were adapted from the SCID-NP (Spitzer, Williams, and Gibbon, 1987) and the Vietnam History Question-naire (Foy, 1987). The Field Trial methods were described by Kilpatrick and Resnick (1993). The study required an in-depth description of potential stressor events, qualities of such events, and subjective reactions to the events to empirically evaluate the breadth of Criterion A. The interview consists of five components, the first of which includes ten questions regarding *Demographic*

Characteristics. The second component is the assessment of *Low Magnitude Stressors* which occurred in the past year. These are events which are potentially stressful, but are not of the magnitude to meet PTSD Criterion A as defined in DSM-III-R including: job loss, financial difficulties, trouble with bill collectors, marital difficulties, breaking up with a significant other, divorce or separation, serious illness of self, serious illness of household member, death of someone in the household due to natural causes, illness or death of other relatives or close friends due to natural causes, or a close relative or significant other sent to the Persian Gulf

The third section of the interview assesses for *High Magnitude Stressors* that currently meet diagnostic criteria for Criterion A of PTSD (DSM-III-R). Each set of questions in this section is prefaced by a detailed statement regarding the nature of the questions to be asked. Combat–military experience, physical abuse and assault, sexual assault, homicide of close friend or family member, disaster, serious accidents, exposure to health threatening chemicals, witnessing someone being seriously injured or killed, and other situations that involved fear of being killed or seriously injured, or in which serious injury did take place are assessed. All events are defined in behaviorally specific terms, and there are specific probes that are intended to increase accurate reporting rates of such events. This section also includes questions to determine whether particular events occurred repeatedly over time (chronicity) or were single incidents. A detailed summary section provides instructions for listing High Magnitude events in chronological order to yield a codable summary of up to three High Magnitude Events: First, Most Recent, and Worst (if different from first and most recent). In addition, if more than one Low Magnitude event is reported, the respondent is required to identify the worst such event. This summary of event history can be easily used with a variety of interview and self-report measures that require identification of a single or limited set of stressor events to allow for event-specific symptom assessment.

The fourth and fifth sections of the interview assess objective and subjective characteristics of the first (only), most recent and worst high magnitude events, as well as these characteristics for the worst low magnitude event in the past year. For the *Objective Characteristics Section*, injury of self and others, perceived causal factors (human vs. act of nature), perception of perpetrator's intent to harm (if human), suddenness, expectedness, and warning received are assessed. These characteristics are assessed separately for up to four events (first, most recent, and worst high magnitude, and worst low magnitude past year).

The final section of the interview, *Subjective Reactions,* is actually a self-report measure of emotional and physical responses which occurred at the time of each event. Fifteen different emotional responses are assessed. Included are items such as surprised, felt it really wasn't happening, angry, disgusted, sadness, detached as if in a dream, and embarrassed or ashamed. Physical reactions which are assessed include symptoms common during a panic attack. Ten different symptoms are assessed including: shortness of breath, dizziness or feeling faint, rapid heart rate, and chest pain or discomfort. This section of the interview may yield useful information in terms of reactions that may have become persistent learned responses subsequent to stressor event exposure that may be an important focus of treatment and research. For the Field Trial, the PSE interview was used in conjunction with the SCID PTSD Module and the PTSD interview schedule from the National Women's Study. Data indicate similar proportions of specific types of stressor events were assessed in two community comparison samples that participated in the Field Trial study. Rates of identified history of sexual assault, aggravated assault, homicide of a significant other, and accident did not differ across the Charleston, South Carolina and St. Louis, Mo. community sites. This finding supports the reliability of the instrument. Reported disaster exposure was significantly higher at the Charleston site, which had been affected by hurricane Hugo the previous year. A more thorough description of the PSE is provided in Falsetti, Resnick, Kilpatrick, and Freedy (1994).

One disadvantage of the PSE is that it can take a considerable amount of time to administer, particularly if the person being assessed has an extensive trauma history. Thus, we have developed a more streamlined version for use in interview or self-report format called the *Trauma Assessment for Adults* (TAA; Resnick, Best, Freedy, Kilpatrick, and Falsetti, 1993). This interview designed for clinical and research use with adults maintains many of the features of the PSE, but is less lengthy. It contains an opening preface, followed by questions that assess for lifetime history of Criterion A events. There is an additional preface before the sexual assault screening questions that clarifies that the respondent is being asked about unwanted sexual experiences that may not have been reported previously, that can occur throughout the life span, and that may be perpetrated by someone the respondent knows (i.e. family member, friend) as well as by strangers. Age of first and most recent occurrence is determined for multiple incidents of a given type and follow-up questions are included to assess perceived life threat as well as receipt of injury during each type of Criterion A event reported within a person's history. For those reporting incidents of sexual assault a question is asked to determine whether the incident(s) included forced sexual penetration of some type to determine whether the incident was a completed rape. The follow-up probes to assess threat, injury, and penetration allow for an evaluation of severity of incidents, with presence of these characteristics associated with increased risk of PTSD. In addition, positive responses to probes about fear of death or serious injury during incidents can be used as a brief indicator of subjective distress during exposure that has been proposed for DSM-IV. The instrument can be scored to get a continuous count of stressor events experienced and counts can be summed for events that were characterized by threat or injury as well. At the present time there are no reliability and validity data available on the TAA.

THE TRAUMATIC STRESS SCHEDULE
(TSS; Norris, 1990)

The TSS is a brief screening instrument designed to provide basic information regarding the occurrence of traumatic events. The

RESNICK, FALSETTI, KILPATRICK, AND FREEDY

following events are assessed: robbery, physical assault, sexual assault, tragic death of a close friend or family member, motor vehicle crash, combat, fire, other disaster, and other hazard. Norris (1992) used this scale in a large epidemiological study (n = 1000) and reported that 69 percent of the sample disclosed the experience of at least one traumatic event in their lifetime and 21 percent reported a traumatic experience in the past year. More recently, Norris (personal communication, April 13, 1993) has combined this scale with the Civilian Mississippi Scale (Keane, Caddell, and Taylor, 1988), and has also developed English and Spanish self-report versions of the combined instruments. The symptom items on the Mississippi Scale are not tied to particular traumatic events assessed, and are thus compatible with general trauma information obtained. The use of the Mississippi Scale will allow for development of norms within a civilian population. Information is not provided for organizing trauma history information that might be used in conjunction with some structured interview or other self-report measures that may require a specific event focus.

The reliability of the instrument appears quite good. Pretest results by Norris indicate a test-retest correlation of .88 for the ten trauma items, with a tendency for people to report more events in the first session than the second session. Alphas for the PTSD items were also quite good; ranging from .74 for nonanchored items to .86 for anchored items.

One disadvantage of this scale is that there is not a detailed preface to trauma questions. Another weakness of this scale is that sexual assault is not behaviorally defined in very detailed manner, thus many assault victims may not report events such as date rapes.

TRAUMA HISTORY QUESTIONNAIRE
(THQ; Green, 1992)

The THQ is an experimental research instrument which was created from the DSM-IV PTSD Field Trial *Potential Stressful Events*

Interview, previously reviewed in this chapter. The THQ, however, is a self-report measure and consists of 24 items, thus administration time is relatively shorter than with the PSEI. The THQ begins with an introductory paragraph that normalizes the occurrence of traumatic events. It also assesses a range of traumatic events including crime related events (e.g. robbery, mugging), general disaster and trauma (e.g. injury, disaster, witnessing death), and physical and sexual assault. The questions are sensitive, behaviorally specific, and continuous data is collected in terms of the number of times each event occurred. This instrument is intended to be used with a followup instrument developed by Norris (1990) to assess details regarding life threat, extent of injury, and other details about traumatic events. There are no instructions regarding classification of multiple events to transition to PTSD symptom questions.

There has been some psychometric investigation of this scale (Green, personal communication, April 13, 1992) that indicates good test–retest reliability of the items of this scale. Test–retest correlations for items that assessed seeing dead bodies ($r = 1.00$), robbery ($r = .91$), and attack with a weapon ($r = .90$) were highest. The lowest reliabilities were reported for more general categories. For instance "other unwanted sex" has a correlation of .47. Green hypothesizes that differences reported from Time 1 to Time 2 are probably a result of individuals knowing the second time that their experiences may fit a specific category or that they may remember additional experiences.

HISTORY OF PSYCHOSOCIAL STRESSORS (HPS; Saunders, Kilpatrick, Resnick, and Tidwell, 1989)

The HPS was developed as a trauma screening instrument for use within a mental health center population. It begins with a preface that states that sometimes distressing or disturbing things happen to people, gives some examples of such events (e.g., physical or sexual assault), and then asks respondents to consider their whole lifetimes when answering. There is also a separate preface before questions about sexual assault that dispells many stereotypes by stating that this type of event happens to men as well as women, and that the perpetrator may be someone the person knows. The interview itself consists of three questions about physical abuse, two about homicide, and five about sexual assault. The questions appear to be sensitive for secondary victimization due to homicide, physical abuse, and sexual assault in general. Saunders et al. (1989) evaluated the use of this measure in a mental health center setting. They compared data obtained using the interview versus that obtained from chart records based on standard staff intake interviews completed prior to the use of the HPS. They suggested that the data supported the construct validity of the measure because when compared to chart reviews, the proportion of identified cases of criminal victimization (72%) was increased significantly and was comparable to high rates of trauma identified within other clinical populations. Importantly, the study demonstrated the feasibility of using this type of structured interview in the mental health center setting.

Although this instrument is certainly a helpful improvement over the failure to use a structured instrument to assess for trauma history there are some disadvantages as well. First, this instrument does not assess for all Criterion A events and does not include behaviorally specific items to allow for identification of completed rape. In addition, there are no instructions for transitioning into screening for the symptoms of PTSD.

This review of traumatic event assessment instruments was restricted to a subset of instruments developed to comprehensively assess civilian trauma and PTSD within general population samples. Other instruments have been developed using other types of trauma populations. In addition, there are useful instruments that have been developed to assess very specific traumatic event histories that were not reviewed above. Some of these measures are noted here briefly. A new instrument is currently being developed and evaluated by Dr. Karen Krinsley and colleagues at the Boston VAMC for the identification of comprehensive lifetime traumatic event history (including detailed questions for assessment of sexual assault) and military combat event history among men and women who have been in the military. The development of such an instrument recognizes the importance of a thorough lifetime traumatic event history assessment to the understanding of PTSD in reference to combat trauma or any other specific traumatic event category under study. Data obtained by Krinsley et al. will also be extremely useful in development of sexual assault and other event history measures for use with men.

Examination of existing instruments designed to assess very specific histories of trauma within any type of population may also be useful for ongoing development of more comprehensive traumatic event history measures. These measures focus in a more in-depth way on a single type of traumatic event and contain some unique questions that may assess subtle but important characteristics of a given type of event. Examples of such instruments are the Sexual Experiences Survey (SES; Koss and Gidycz, 1985) and the Conflict Tactics (CT) Scales (Straus, 1979). The SES is a 10-item self-report instrument that assesses a range of sexual assault types including molestation and rape. In contrast to the measures described above for assessment of sexual assault, the SES includes assessment of a variety of types of coercion that may occur as part of sexual assault including verbal pressure, use of authority, as well as use of physical force or threat. Koss and Gidycz found that the SES had high internal consistency reliability (.74) and one week test–retest reliability (.93) within a sample of 305 college women. There was also good correspondence between classification of sexual assault victimization based on self-report and interview modes of administration of the measure (.73). The CT Scales contain a list of items that assess various forms of familial interpersonal violence and conflict a well as more adaptive means of conflict resolution such as calm discussion. The respondent evaluates a family member by noting the frequency (with 6 categories ranging from once, to more than 20 times) with which they engage in specific behaviors to settle conflicts. Such behaviors include verbal insults, refusal to discuss an issue, and physical violence. The time frame used is the past 12 months. This measure provides rich information about positive and negative conflict resolution which includes psychological as well as physical abuse/violence, and continuous frequency information to assess intrafamilial violence.

SYMPTOM AND DIAGNOSTIC ASSESSMENT

Due to the focus in this chapter on stressor event assessment we are not providing a review of psychometric properties of interview and self-report measures designed to assess PTSD that were discussed in a previous paper (Resnick, Kilpatrick, and Lipovsky, 1991). That paper is contained within the Special Section addressing assessment of PTSD in the third volume of *Psychological Assessment* (1991) which includes several articles that review psychometric properties of self-report and interview measures. A discussion of findings from the National Vietnam Veterans Readjustment Study evaluating the validity and reliability of the DIS and SCID PTSD interviews is also included in this issue (Kulka et al., 1991). The Clinician Administered PTSD Scale (CAPS), a more recently developed PTSD interview that includes assessment of symptom frequency and intensity, is described in Blake, Weathers, Nagy, Kaloupek, Klauminzer, Charney, and Keane (1990). With regard to self-report instruments, there are limited data available on use of such measures as indicators of PTSD as designated by clinical interview. We note here several reports of measures for which such scoring rules and cutoff scores are available. Rothbaum et al. (1992) reported data on predictive utility of cutoff scores obtained within the first few weeks post-trauma on the Impact of Events (IES; Horowitz et al., 1979) and Rape Aftermath Symptom (RAST; Kilpatrick, 1988) in predicting chronic PTSD among rape victims. It should be noted that the RAST which contains items from the Symptom Checklist 90-Revised (SCL-90-R; Derogatis, 1977) and the Modified Fear Survey (MFS; Seidner and Kilpatrick, 1988) is relevant for administration to those who have experienced a wide variety of stressor events, not just rape. Saunders et al. (1990) reported results of a second scale derived from the SCL-90-R that discriminated between current PTSD positive and negative cases identified using structured diagnostic interviews within a large community sample. More recently developed self-report measures have been evaluated in terms of reliability and validity based on convergence with the SCID (Spitzer et al., 1987) within civilian populations exposed to traumatic stressors. These measures include all 17 PTSD symptom items and use continuous ratings to assess past two week symptom frequency as in the PTSD Symptom Scale (PSS; Foa, Riggs, Dancu, and Rothbaum, 1993) or the Modified PTSD Symptom Scale (MPSS-SR; Resick, Falsetti, Resnick, and Kilpatrick, 1991; Falsetti, Resick, Resnick, and Kilpatrick, 1992) which assesses both frequency and severity of PTSD symptoms within the past two weeks. These measures may be useful as quick and valid tools for initial and ongoing assessment of PTSD that may be more sensitive to changes occurring over time or during treatment than dichotomous symptom measures.

This review of stressor event assessment measures indicates a wide range of opening prefaces used that are likely to affect the response sets of those being interviewed. It is likely that phrasing suggesting that Criterion A events are rare and that include legal terms to define typical events are misleading and lead to underreporting of events. Contextual information that acknowledges that such events are not rare, along with behavioral level description of a variety of circumstances in which these events may occur is more accurate and may increase sensitivity rates. Data indicate that stressor event measures must include specific behaviorally defined questions to assess history of rape and other sexual assault in particular, as well as other Criterion A events. The terms *rape* or *sexual assault* may hold varied meaning for different individuals and information obtained using these terms has limited value. Given findings that rape is a significant risk factor for PTSD, it is critical that sensitive screening approaches be used to assess for lifetime history of rape.

In addition to broad assessment of event categories these measures should also include assessment of characteristics that may increase risk of PTSD across event categories. Some factors that have been identified include perceived life threat and receipt of injury. Data should be gathered on these and other as yet unidentified event-related factors that may be risk factors for PTSD. Finally, based on findings that many people have experienced multiple traumatic events such instruments must include questions to identify these complex histories and to organize this information in ways that will be compatible with PTSD symptom assessment instruments that require the evaluation of symptoms in reference to a limited specified set of events. To be compatible with these approaches stressor event history information can be organized into a set of index events as in the IRI and PSE approaches (i.e., first, most recent, worst) for assessment of related PTSD symptoms. Many PTSD symptom assessment approaches as well as the interview used in the National Women's Study described earlier do not require specific linkage between report of a symptom(s) and a single identified stressor event. In these cases stressor event history information and information about symptoms can be used empirically to evaluate associations between complex event histories and PTSD. This approach can also be used to study associations between stressor event history and other potential outcomes including major depressive disorder, and other anxiety disorders. Regardless of symptom assessment approach, thorough knowledge of lifetime Criterion A stressor event history is critical to gaining a better understanding of PTSD and other significant mental or physical health outcomes that may relate to these types of stressor events. Thus, we recommend thorough lifetime assessment of stressor event history be conducted routinely in conjunction with administration of PTSD and other outcome measures to further our understanding of the role of stressful life events.

REFERENCES

American Psychiatric Association (1980), *Diagnostic and Statistical Manual of Mental Disorders* 3rd ed. (DSM-III). Washington, DC: American Psychiatric Press.

—— (1987), *Diagnostic and Statistical Manual of Mental Disordrs*, 3rd ed. rev. (DSM-III-R), Washington, DC: American Psychiatric Press.

Blake, D. D., Weathers, F. W., Nagy, L. M., Kaloupek, D. G., Klauminzer, G., Charney, D., & Keane, T. M. (1990), A clinician rating scale for assessing current and lifetime PTSD: The CAPS-1. *Behav. Therapist*, 13:187–188.

Breslau, N., Davis, G. C., Andreski, P., & Peterson, E. (1991), Traumatic events and posttraumatic stress disorder in an urban population of young adults. *Arch. Gen. Psychiatry*, 48:216–222.

Davidson, J. R. T., & Foa, E. B. (1991), Diagnostic issues in posttraumatic stress disorder: Considerations for the DSM-IV. *J. Abnorm. Psychol.*, 100:346–355.

Derogatis, L. R. (1977), *SCL-90: Administration, Scoring and Procedure Manual-I for the R(revised) Version*. Baltimore: Johns Hopkins University School of Medicine.

Falsetti, S. A., Resnick, H. S., Kilpatrick, D. G., & Freedy, J. R. (1994), A review of the "Potential Stressful Events Interview": A comprehensive assessment instrument of high and low magnitude stressors. *Behav. Therapist*, 7:66–67.

—— —— Resick, P. A., & Kilpatrick, D. G. (1993), The Modified PTSD Symptom Scale: A brief self-report measure of posttraumatic stress disorder. *Behav. Therapist*, 16:161–162.

—— Resick, P. A., Resnick, H. S., & Kilpatrick, D. G. (1992), Post-traumatic stress disorder: The assessment of frequency and severity of symptoms in clinical and nonclinical samples. Paper presented at the 26th Annual Meeting of the Association for the Advancement of Behavior Therapy, Boston.

Foa, E. B., Riggs, D. S., Dancu, C. V., & Rothbaum, B. O. (in press), Reliability and validity of a brief instrument for assessing posttraumatic stress disorder. *J. Traum. Stress*.

Foy, D. W. (1987), Vietnam History Questionnaire (VHQ). Unpublished Assessment Interview.

—— Carroll, E. M., & Donahoe, C. P. (1987), Etiological factors in the development of PTSD in clinical samples of Vietnam combat veterans. *J. Clin. Psychol.*, 43:17–27.

George, L. K., & Winfield-Laird, I. (1986), *Sexual Assault: Prevalence and Mental Health Consequences*. Final report submitted to NIMH.

Green, B. L. (1990), Defining trauma: Terminology and generic stressor dimensions. *J. Appl. Soc. Psychol.*, 20:1632–1642.

—— (1992), *Traumatic History Questionnaire*. Washington, DC: Georgetown University. Unpublished instrument.

Helzer, J. E., Robins, L. N., & McEvoy, L. (1987), Post-traumatic stress disorder in the general population. *New Eng. J. Med.*, 317:1630–1634.

Horowitz, M., Wilner, N., & Alvarez, W. (1979), Impact of Event scale: Measure of subjective stress. *Psychosom. Med.*, 41:209–218.

Keane, T. M., Caddell, J. M., & Taylor, K. L. (1988), The Mississippi scale for combat-related PTSD: Studies in reliability and validity. *J. Consult. & Clin. Psychol.*, 56:85–90.

Kilpatrick, D. G. (1983), Rape victims: Detection, assessment, and treatment. *Clin. Psychologist*, 36:92–95.

———— (1988), Rape Aftermath Symptom Test. In: *Dictionary of Behavioral Assessment Techniques*, ed. M. Hersen & A. S. Bellack. New York: Pergamon Press, pp. 366–367.

———— (1990), The epidemiology of potentially stressful events and their traumatic impact: Implications for prevention. In: *Trauma Studies: Contributions to Prevention*, chair, C. Dunning. Plenary session conducted at the 6th Annual Meeting of the International Society for Traumatic Stress Studies, New Orleans, LA.

———— Resnick, H. S. (1993), PTSD associated with exposure to criminal victimization in clinical and community populations. In: *PTSD in Review: Recent Research and Future Directions*, ed. J. R. T. Davidson & E. B. Foa. Washington, DC: American Psychiatric Press, pp. 113–143.

———— ———— Freedy, J. R. (1991), *The Potential Stressful Events Interview*. Charleston, SC: Crime Victims Research and Treatment Center, Department of Psychiatry, Medical University of South Carolina. Unpublished instrument.

———— ———— ———— Pelcovitz, D., Resick, P., Roth, S., & van der Kolk, B. (1992), *The Posttraumatic Stress Disorder Field Trial: Emphasis on Criterion A and Overall PTSD Diagnosis*. Unpublished manuscript.

———— ———— Saunders, B. E., & Best, C. L. (1989), *The National Women's Study PTSD Module*. Charleston, SC: Crime Victims Research and Treatment Center, Department of Psychiatry, Medical University of South Carolina. Unpublished instrument.

———— Saunders, B. E., Amick-McMullan, A., Best, C. L., Veronen, L. J., & Resnick, H. S. (1989), Victim and crime factors associated with the development of crime-related post-traumatic stress disorder. *Behav. Ther.*, 20:199–214.

———— ———— Veronen, L. J., Best, C. L., & Von, J. M. (1987), Criminal victimization: Lifetime prevalence, reporting to police, and psychological impact. *Crime & Delinquency*, 33:479–489.

Koss, M. P. (1985), The hidden rape victim: Personality, attitudinal, and situational characteristics. *Psychol. Women Quart.*, 9:193–212.

———— Gidycz, C. A. (1985), Sexual Experiences Survey: Reliability and validity. *J. Consult. & Clin. Psychol.*, 53:422–423.

Krinsley, K., Weathers, F. W., Young, L. S., Kimerling, R. & Newman, E. (1993), *Lifetime Stressors Inventory—Interview*. Unpublished assessment interview.

Kulka, R. A., Schlenger, W. E., Fairbank, J. A., Hough, R. L., Jordan, B. K., Marmar, C. R., & Weiss, D. S. (1990), *Trauma and the Vietnam War Generation*. New York: Brunner/Mazel.

———— ———— Jordan, K. B., Hough, R. L., Marmar, C. R., & Weiss, D. S. (1991), Assessment of posttraumatic stress disorder in the community: Prospects and pitfalls from recent studies of Vietnam veterans. *Psychol. Assess.*, 3:547–560.

Norris, F. H. (1990), Screening for traumatic stress: A scale for use in the general population. *J. Appl. Soc. Psychol.*, 20:1704–1718.

———— (1992), Epidemiology of trauma: Frequency and impact of different potentially traumatic events on different demographic events. *J. Consult. & Clin. Psychol.*, 60:409–418.

Resick, P. A., Falsetti, S. A., Resnick, H. S., & Kilpatrick, D. G. (1991), *The Modified PTSD Symptom Scale—Self Report*. St. Louis, MO: University of Missouri & Charleston, SC, Crime Victims Treatment and Research Center, Medical University of South Carolina.

Resnick, H. S., Best, C. L., Freedy, J. R., & Kilpatrick, D. G. (1992), *Clinician Administered Traumatic Events Interview*. Unpublished assessment interview.

—— —— —— Falsetti, S. A. (1993), *Trauma Assessment for Adults (TAA)*. Unpublished Assessment Interview.

—— Kilpatrick, D. G., Dansky, B. S., Saunders, B. E., & Best, C. L. (1993), Prevalence of civilian trauma and PTSD in a representative national sample of women. *J. Consult. & Clin. Psychol.*

—— —— Lipvosky, J. A. (1991), Assessment of rape-related posttraumatic stress disorder: Stressor and symptom dimensions. *Psycholog. Assess.*, 3:561–572.

Robins, L., Helzer, J., Cottler, L., & Goldring, E. (1988), *NIMH Diagnostic Interview Schedule Version III Revised (DIS-III-R)*. St. Louis: Washington University Press.

—— —— Croughan, J., & Ratcliff, K. S. (1981), National Institute of Mental Health Diagnostic Interview Schedule. Its history, characteristics, and validity. *Arch. Gen. Psychiatry*, 38:381–389.

Rothbaum, B. O., Foa, E. B., Riggs, D. S., Murdock, T., & Walsh, W. (1992), A prospective examination of posttraumatic stress disorder in rape victims. *J. Traum. Stress*, 5:455–475.

Saunders, B. E., Kilpatrick, D. G., Resnick, H. S., & Tidwell, R. P. (1989), Brief screening for lifetime history of criminal victimization at mental health intake: A preliminary study. *J. Interpers. Viol.*, 4:267–277.

—— Mandoki, K. A., & Kilpatrick, D. G. (1990), Development of a crime-related post-traumatic stress disorder scale within the Symptom Checklist-90-Revised. *J. Traum. Stress*, 3:439–448.

Seider, A. L., & Kilpatrick, D. G. (1988), Modified fear survey. In: *Dictionary of Behavioral Assessment Techniques*, ed. M. Hersen & A. S. Bellack. New York: Pergamon Press, pp. 307–309.

Spitzer, R. L., Williams, J. B., & Gibbon, M. (1987), *Structured Clinical Interview for DSM-III-R—Non-patient Version* (SCID-NP-V). New York: New York State Psychiatric Institute, Biometrics Research Department.

Straus, M. A. (1979), Measuring intrafamily conflict and violence: The Conflict Tactics (CT) scales. *J. Marr. & Fam.*, 41:75–88.

Watson, C. G. (1990), Psychometric posttraumatic stress disorder measurement techniques: A review. *Psycholog. Assess.*, 2:460–469.

Chapter 10
The Assessment of Events and Their Related Symptoms in Torture and Refugee Trauma

RICHARD F. MOLLICA, M.D., AND
YAEL CASPI-YAVIN, M.A., M.P.H.

The medical and psychiatric assessment and treatment of survivors of torture and mass trauma is a unique field of study that is concerned with the impact of trauma experiences of an extreme nature that occur within diverse political and cultural settings.

The influx of refugees from Southeast Asia into the United States since 1975, and the documentation of the extent and severity of the trauma they experienced, stimulated psychiatrists and other health care providers to address the problems and needs of these populations. Since migrants in general have been observed to have a higher rate of psychiatric disorders (Odegaard, 1932), initial reports focused on the refugees' psychological adaptation to U.S. society (Vignes and Hall, 1979; Hull, 1979; Lin, Tazuma, and Masuda, 1979; Westermeyer, Vang, and Neider, 1983). Clinical descriptions varied in terms of the diagnostic categories observed, yet all indicated the importance of major affective disorders. The 1984 report of Kinzie et al. was the first to apply the diagnosis of posttraumatic stress disorder (PTSD) to refugees (Kinzie, Fredrickson, Ben, Fleck, and Karls, 1984).

Historically, the study of torture has been part of the human rights field rather than psychiatry. The United Nations definition of torture (1987) primarily emphasizes violence directed unjustly at individuals for political purposes. It is unclear whether this definition applies to entire populations that have experienced unimaginable suffering through economic oppression, starvation, and humiliating life experiences, such as the millions of Cambodians who experienced forced dislocation, slave labor, starvation, and ill health under the Khmer Rouge regime (Mollica and Jalbert, 1989).

Early studies of torture survivors consisted of phenomenological descriptions of patient demographic characteristics, torture experiences, and the immediate medical and personal needs of the survivor. The objectives of these studies were to examine persons who had allegedly been tortured in order to document the medical impact of the torture experience as well as to prove that the torture had actually occurred. The human rights field has not considered the problems of torture survivors as the legitimate domain of medicine, especially psychiatry. Attempts at empirically measuring torture and its psychiatric sequelae have encountered resistance from advocacy groups (Mollica, 1992). It was argued that if torture survivors do not have "diseases" but "normal" psychological responses to their life-threatening situations, then the medicalization of the field will only lead to highly stigmatizing medical and psychiatric labeling, and shift the focus from the political situation to the individual victim. Scientists who specialize in understanding the impact of stressful life events on human well-being have also been reluctant to investigate the torture experience. George Brown, England's foremost medical sociologist, once stated (private communication) that studying refugees and other torture survivors was like contrasting the life of King Lear to the lives of ordinary men and women. Unfortunately, most survivors are ordinary people who have had the misfortune of having "Lear-ian" experiences. It is also becoming apparent that the fields of torture and refugee trauma are not truly two separate domains, but rather that they share many similar concerns regarding the assessment and treatment of survivors.

The large numbers of individuals world-wide who are affected by torture and mass trauma, and their associated medical and social impairment, have encouraged the development of empirical research in these fields. While it is assumed that the development of measures must adhere to those scientific standards that exist for establishing standardized psychological instruments with acceptable psychometric properties, there are certain features unique to the study of torture and refugee trauma that should be considered.

The relationship of stressful life events to the etiology, onset, course, and outcome of various psychiatric conditions, such as schizophrenia, depression, and anxiety, has been the focus of significant empirical research (Miller, 1988). The process of developing a clinical instrument for the assessment of traumatic events and their related symptoms encounters special problems that are inherent to the evaluation, diagnosis, and treatment of trauma and torture survivors. Clinicians are often faced with the changing nature of the trauma story, the gaps and lapses in the patient's memory; the emotional upset shared by both therapist and patient as personal accounts of horrific life experiences unfold; and the complex task of assigning a diagnosis to the diversity of symptoms reported by trauma survivors. These issues are often augmented by the impact of cultural beliefs and attitudes on the reactions to trauma and require special attention in clinical settings that treat survivors from diverse cultural backgrounds.

The magnitude and importance of this new field demands the rapid introduction of valid methods of assessment that are simple, culturally sensitive, and capable of providing proper guidelines for effective diagnosis, treatment, and policy recommendations. The major goal of this chapter, therefore, is to review the factors which influence the development of measures suitable for empirically evaluating refugee trauma and torture and their related symptoms. Since survivors of traumatic human rights abuses represent a myriad of cultural and political backgrounds, the important impact of culture on the trauma experience will be discussed. Similarities and differences between the psychological assessment of the trauma–torture survivor and American combat veterans will be presented in light of the progress in the development of assessment tools in the field of combat-related trauma diagnostic categories of the Vietnam War veterans. Finally, the adaptation of instruments developed in one culture for use in another culture is illustrated in a discussion of the modifications suggested for using the Harvard Trauma Questionnaire (HTQ) in non-Indochinese populations.

ELICITING INFORMATION ABOUT THE TRAUMA AND TORTURE EVENT

Any attempt to measure mass trauma and torture should begin with a comprehensive review of the historical context and an elucidation of the types of events experienced by individuals within their unique sociopolitical setting. If a complete and accurate list of possible experiences is offered immediately to the patient, it will cue the survivor that the interviewer knows something of his or her situation. This knowledge initiates a process of revelation which often does not occur through the use of open-ended interviews or the recitation of a list of general experiences. Many survivors appreciate knowing that the medical professional is aware of what they have suffered and interested in eliciting information about the specific details of the trauma as part of the health-seeking process.

Life history research is replete with methodological concern for evaluating the psychological impact of a life experience as measured by its intensity, duration, frequency, and meaning. The process of giving meaning to the experience is mediated by language and culture and is likely to differ for each generic class of trauma and torture. Although *torture* is a commonly used term (Peters, 1985), recent investigations reveal the major differences in the cultural meaning of torture in Western and Asian societies (Mollica, 1988b). The impact on the overall well-being of the survivor of cultural and personal beliefs such as the Cambodian belief in karma—that actions or thoughts (often of an evil nature) in a prior life produce effects in the current life—has not been adequately explored. Furthermore, the psychological impact of different types of trauma is unknown. It is possible that specific experiences are associated with specific symptoms and psychological reactions. For example, the unique reactions of Indochinese women to rape trauma are just being demonstrated (Mollica and Son, 1989). These women keep knowledge of their rape a secret unknown to all, especially their husbands and parents. Community awareness of the rape trauma will negatively stigmatize the victim and her entire extended family, causing all family members to suffer from severe social ostracization. In contrast, Sandinista Nicaraguan women publicly shared their rape trauma as a symbol of their sacrifice and commitment to what they considered a new society. Little is known of the psychological reactions of the families of the "missing and disappeared" in Argentina, physically abused black children who have been tortured in South African prisons, or Ethiopian refugees who have suffered from politically motivated starvation. Due to this lack of information, case reports from Amnesty International, the published clinical experiences of refugee and torture treatment centers, and the literary biographies and testimonies of survivors are irreplaceable resources for developing measures capable of accurately capturing the trauma experience.

ACCURACY OF REPORTING

Survivors of trauma and torture constantly change the details of their reports (Mollica and Lavelle, 1988). Changes in the reporting of trauma and torture events may be due to (1) high emotional arousal with associated hyperbole or defensiveness for some individuals in reporting the torture events; (2) impaired memory secondary to psychiatric and neurologic impairments (e.g., beatings to the head and subsequent head injury); (3) culturally prescribed sanctions that allow the trauma experience to be revealed only in highly confidential settings (e.g., rape trauma for Indochinese women); (4) coping mechanisms that utilize denial and the avoidance of memories or situations associated with the trauma.

Obtaining accurate information of a trauma survivor's life experience and symptoms is necessary for properly diagnosing patients and providing effective treatment and good therapeutic outcome. The employment of open-ended interviewing methods requires that trauma survivors disclose their experiences in their own words, using free recall, a method that appears to generate limited reporting and the greatest emotional distress. Memory is best enhanced by using neutral methods such as checklists of specific questions that help "put words around" the trauma events and symptoms while signaling to patients that the therapist is well aware of the type of experiences they might have endured (Cienfuegos and Monelli, 1983; Mollica and Lavelle, 1988). While events and symptoms can be successfully measured by a checklist format, the stability of these events and symptoms over even brief periods of time is unknown (Mollica, Wyshak, de Marneffe, Khuon, and Lavelle, 1987; Mollica, Wyshak, and Lavelle, 1987). Furthermore, since almost all research has been conducted in clinic settings, the problems of measurement in population-based surveys of highly traumatized communities could reveal a significant spectrum effect (Sackett, Haynes, and Tugwell, 1985). Respondents in the general population who have been traumatized but have not sought treatment may exhibit differences in measurement responses from their clinical counterparts. Before large epidemiologic surveys are conducted, the spectrum effect will need to be clarified.

Clinical experience and research findings indicate that once an account is given both an increase in memory and an intensification of symptoms is likely to occur (Mollica, Caspi-Yavin, Bollini, Truong, Tor, and Lavelle, 1991). Special attention should be given to variations in reporting during the course of therapy as these may indicate an increase in emotional distress associated with attempts to reveal more severely traumatizing experiences. For example, it is not uncommon that the experience of sexual trauma in Indochinese women is denied during initial phases of therapy, and is revealed only when trust and therapeutic alliance are well established.

THERAPIST–PATIENT INTERACTION

Impact of the spectrum effect on the assessment of torture survivors may be great because of the many complex distortions that occur in the interaction between interviewer and respondent. The therapist must elicit from the trauma and torture survivor accounts of an individual's tragic life experience (Mollica, 1988b). The clinician is called upon to abandon his or her clinical neutrality and acknowledge and condemn the injustice and brutality of the experience. This level of involvement provides only one explanation for the numerous barriers that may inhibit the clinician from obtaining accurate and comprehensive history of the trauma experience. Clinicians who treat trauma and torture survivors are frequently concerned that their interview will trigger off severe emotional upset and possibly retraumatize the patient. For some, asking personal and direct questions at the onset of therapy may represent a radical shift from their understanding of the traditional therapeutic process. These questions may appear too intrusive, impersonal, and insensitive. In addition, numerous clinic reports have revealed the horror that is often confronted by the clinician-interviewer (Kinzie, Boehnlein, Leung, Moore, Riley, and Smith, 1990). In bicultural settings, the bicultural worker (who might have survived experiences similar to those of the patient) must mediate between the torture survivor and the English-speaking professional (Mollica and Lavelle, 1988). The measurement of torture–trauma events and symptoms is seriously affected by both the ability of English-speaking or bicultural workers to objectively elicit information from the torture survivor. Often interviewers are reluctant to ask any, if not all, of the questions on the standardized interview especially if the respondent exhibits emotional distress. Often, the interviewer will experience nightmares and depressive feelings following the interview. Similarly, psychiatrically impaired torture survivors will have a wide range of reactions to the measurement interview. Over the past decade, however, the general clinical impression has emerged that survivors appreciate giving information about their experience as a "testimony" of their traumatic life history and value the recognition (often for the first time) by the health professional. Investigators working with Indochinese patients in both clinical and community settings have often been "thanked" by the respondents for documenting and validating their torture–trauma experiences. Under favorable conditions where confidentiality, informed consent, and respect for the torture survivor is obvious, it is possible that the interviewer has more difficulty in "documenting" the trauma history than the survivor has in "telling" it. The latter phenomenon may account for the widespread interest of clinicians working in this field in adapting and using symptom checklists.

Clinicians using assessment instruments in a cross-cultural setting should also be aware of possible biases such as the "courtesy bias" that has been detected in many Asian populations (Jones, 1963). Respondents may provide information they feel will please the interviewer, and omit information they feel might not be interesting or cause embarrassment. As a corollary, Western interviewers need also be aware of their own cultural bias that could emerge when judging the appropriateness of the affective presentation of torture and trauma survivors.

CATEGORIZING THE TRAUMA RESPONSE

Empirical phenomenological descriptions of torture survivors have failed to reveal a unique torture treatment syndrome (Goldfeld, Mollica, Pesavento, and Faraone, 1988). Similarly, it is unknown whether a culture-specific illness associated with trauma exists in any of the refugee groups studied. In fact, there appears to be considerable overlap between symptoms manifested by refugees and other torture survivors and the DSM-III-R (APA, 1987) diagnosis of PTSD. Unfortunately, studies have not been conducted which have demonstrated whether the same underlying cultural constructs for PTSD in Western societies exist in non-Western societies. In contrast, considerable cross-cultural research has revealed the folk diagnoses in non-Western cultures associated with depression (Boehnlein, 1987; Dhadphale, Cooper, and Cartwright-Taylor, 1989). The World Health Organization (WHO) collaborative study of depression, in fact, revealed an important general principle, namely, that while core symptoms for depression exist across cultures, these core symptoms may not be those that are emphasized by depressed patients within their unique cultural settings (Sartorious, 1987). It, therefore, follows from the WHO study that while the DSM-III-R criteria for PTSD may be present across cultures, none of the DSM-III-R PTSD symptoms may be the most culturally relevant. The core symptoms of PTSD common to all cultures still need to be identified.

Unfortunately, the recent nondiscriminating use of the DSM-III-R criteria for eliciting the presence of PTSD in survivors of torture and mass trauma has led to a lack of definition of the culture-specific constructs for PTSD, as well as their relative overlap with DSM-III-R criteria. This fact has important implications for evaluating the validity of translated instruments. Recent advances in cross-cultural research have resulted in translation methods for generating linguistic equivalents and obtaining item by item validity for individual symptoms in standardized American checklists (Westermeyer, 1985). Yet, anthropological and epidemiologic methods for determining the overall construct validity of the diagnoses given by assembling the symptom items of the checklists are in their preliminary stages of development. For example, while evidence suggests that high rates of PTSD symptoms are experienced by both patient and nonpatient refugee groups, recent investigations using the HTQ, a cross-cultural instrument for the assessment of trauma and PTSD in Indochinese refugees, indicate that not all PTSD criteria, as determined by the DSM-III-R, is present in this population (Mollica et al., 1991).

In addition to the questionable cultural validity of Western psychiatric disease constructs, the diagnosis of survivors of human rights abuses of such magnitude is further complicated by the frequent comorbid presence of a history of head injury and symptoms identified with extensive neuropsychiatric and organic impairment. There is an urgent need for the development and validation of culturally sensitive instruments that would assess neuropsychiatric symptoms and examine their related social impairment.

MEASURING TORTURE AND TRAUMA EVENTS

Until recently few systematic efforts have been made to standardize instruments for assessing the traumatic experiences of torture survivors. In October 1974, the Danes created the first medical group within Amnesty International and initiated the first comprehensive medical assessment of torture victims. In a comprehensive monograph published in 1990 by O. V. Rasmussen in the *Danish Medical Bulletin.* A review of their methods and findings on 200 torture victims examined between April 1975 to May 1982 is presented (Table 10.1). Until 1980, their initial evaluation of the torture experience consisted of an examination procedure which utilized open-ended questions. For example, direct questions such as "Have you been tortured by electricity?" were not used. The Danish investigators attempted to obtain the history of the person who had been tortured by having the patient state it in their own words. When it came to torture methods, all details were requested from the patient. Eventually, patients were asked to pantomime the torture sessions. By 1980, the Danish group had abandoned this open-ended approach and adapted a standardized method using the instruments of Allodi and his colleagues in Toronto.

TABLE 10.1
Types of Torture Reported by 200 Torture Survivors

Type	n	Type	n
Beating	198	Suspension ("*la barra*")	20
Severe beating	195	Physical exhaustion	68
Severe beating to head	146	"Standing"	35
Severe beatings in genitals	41	Maintain abnormal	
Falanga	59	body position	26
Telefono	19	Forced gymnastic	22
Banging the head against		Climatic Stress	67
the wall or floor	31	Asphyxiation	59
Pushed down stairs, out of		Wet *submarino*	
windows, etc.	3	("La bañera")	39
Torture by heat	27	Dry *submarino*	13
Electric torture	109	Strangulation	6
Nail torture	5	Light torture	3
Tearing out hairs	6	Sexual violation: rape	7
"Finger" torture	13	Sexual violation:	
Suspension by arms or		instruments	20
legs	33	Other physical torture	44

Source: Rasmussen and Lunde (1980).

The Allodi trauma scale (Allodi, 1985) is one of the first semi-structured interview schedules developed to document the torture experience. It is a 41-item questionnaire which assesses traumatic experiences associated with political persecution, imprisonment, disappearance, and death of individuals and families. It includes seven parts: (1) nonviolent persecution; (2) arrest history; (3) physical torture; (4) deprivation during imprisonment; (5) sensory manipulation; (6) psychological torture and ill treatment; and (7) violence to family members. A respondent can receive a subtotal for each section (except for trauma to family which is not graded) as well as a total score between 0 and 40 measuring his or her total trauma–torture experience.

These initial attempts in the field to assess exposure to torture rely heavily on the respondent's memory and ability to recall horrific life events, often many years after their actual occurrence.

The accuracy and completeness of the information given based upon these instruments is unknown. Of course, validating the torture event may be a methodological problem impossible to solve since more objective sources than the individual's self-report, such as prison and military records (if any exist), are not available and the evaluation often takes place outside the survivor's country of origin. Stability of reporting over time, test–retest, and interrater reliability is unknown for almost all studies utilizing the above assessment methods.

The field of refugee trauma has witnessed in recent years the development and adaptation of several assessment tools for depression such as the Vietnamese Depression Scale (Kinzie, Manson, Vinh, Tolan, Anh, and Fo, 1982), the Lao Depression Inventory (Davidson-Muskin and Golden, 1989), and the Hmong adaptation of the Beck Depression Inventory (Mouanoutoua, Brown, Cappelletty, and Levine, 1991).

The HTQ was designed to empirically measure trauma events and PTSD in Indochinese refugees, most of whom had survived torture and the trauma of mass violence (Mollica et al., 1991). This instrument was modeled in three Indochinese languages after the successful validation of the Hopkins Symptom Checklist-25 for anxiety and depression (Mollica, Wyshak, and de Marneffe, 1987). The questionnaire has four sections: The first section includes 17 specific trauma events historically accurate for assessing the Indochinese refugee experience (Table 10.2). The choice of items for part I was based upon the extensive clinical experience of the Indochinese Psychiatry Clinic (IPC), the consultation of bicultural mental health specialists, and an initial outcome study conducted by the Indochinese Psychiatry Clinic (Mollica, Wyshak, and Lavelle, 1987). The respondent is asked to answer whether he or she witnessed, experienced, or heard about any of the 17 trauma events listed. The second section consists of an open-ended question which asks the respondent to describe the most terrifying event(s) that have happened to him or her. The third section elicits information related to the occurrence of head injury. Part IV elicits 30 symptoms related to the torture–trauma

TABLE 10.2
List of Trauma Events from Part I of the Indochinese Versions of the Harvard Trauma Questionnaire

1. Lack of Food or Water
2. Ill Health Without Access to Medical Care
3. Lack of Shelter
4. Imprisonment
5. Serious Injury
6. Torture
7. Brainwashing
8. Rape or Sexual Abuse
9. Forced Isolation from Others
10. Being Close to Death
11. Forced Separation from Family Members
12. Murder of Family or Friend
13. Unnatural Death of Family or Friend
14. Murder of Stranger or Strangers
15. Lost or Kidnapped
16. Combat Situation
17. Any Other Situation that Was Very Frightening or You Felt Your Life Was in Danger (Please Specify)

Source: Mollica, Caspi-Yavin, Bollini, Truong, Tor, and Lavelle (1991).

experiences recalled in the previous sections. The first 16 symptoms were derived from the DSM-III-R criteria for PTSD; 14 additional symptoms were derived from IPC's clinical experience with Indochinese torture survivors. Examples of symptoms from the latter category include: (1) feeling ashamed of the traumatic or hurtful things that have happened to you; (2) feeling as if you are going crazy; (3) feeling that someone you trusted has betrayed you; (4) feeling that you have no one to rely upon. Linguistic equivalents for the individual items of all three sections were obtained in each of the three Indochinese languages using the rigorous translation/back-translation methods of cross-cultural instrument development (Westermeyer, 1985).

Initial validation of the HTQ has revealed high rates of interrater reliability for both the trauma events and the trauma symptoms. Test–retest reliability over a 1-week period for individual trauma events varied, and a significant degree of change in reporting of torture–trauma events over a 1-week period was evident. There was a higher consistency found over a 1-week period for personal trauma items (such as torture) than for more general items (such as lack of food or water). It is interesting that more events were remembered during the second interview. Preliminary analyses suggest that highly symptomatic respondents had the best test–retest concordance. While this increase in memory is consistent with clinical experience, these findings suggest the ongoing importance of studying the stability of memory over time, and the associated correlates of high consistency (for example, possible "fixation" on the trauma–torture experience in more symptomatic individuals).

Preliminary validation studies of section IV, the trauma symptoms, revealed medium sensitivity and specificity rates against a blind diagnosis of PTSD given by experienced clinicians. One of the more interesting findings was that the HTQ's sensitivity for PTSD based upon the first 16 items derived from the DSM-III-R alone was increased by the addition of the 14 culture dependent items. This is the first demonstration of cultural symptoms being associated with the PTSD criteria.

Some similarities and differences can be seen between instruments being developed to measure torture and mass trauma and those that have already been developed to measure the experiences of American combat veterans. For example, the Combat Exposure Scale (Foy, Lund, Sipprelle, and Strachan, 1984; Foy, Sipprelle, Rueger, and Carroll, 1984) is a 7-item cumulative scale for measuring stressful events that were generated out of the premilitary and military history of Vietnam era veterans. This scale has been found to be reliable and to have excellent psychometric properties. Comparison of methods for assessing torture events, the experiences of mass violence, and the trauma experiences of American combat veterans might illuminate the impact of the nature and type of event on the psychometric properties of the assessment tools.

Results of the validation studies on various standardized instruments for measuring PTSD, evaluated by the National Vietnam

Veterans Readjustment Study (NVVRS) (Kulka, Schlenger, Fairbank, et al., 1988), reveal sensitivity scores higher than the HTQ (see Table 10.3). Again, differences in sensitivity between the Indochinese versions of the HTQ and the American combat veteran assessment instruments for PTSD raise numerous possibilities.

The most culturally important torture–trauma related symptoms for Indochinese refugees may still need to be determined. Research is necessary to identify those cultural factors which when added to the "core" PTSD symptoms will increase the sensitivity of the HTQ. In contrast, future validation studies using the HTQ may continue to show that it is not as sensitive an instrument as the Mississippi Scale for combat-related PTSD (Keane, Caddell, and Taylor, 1988), or the PTSD checklist. This could occur due to the HTQ's lack of sampling content validity because of the widespread presence of culture-specific trauma-related symptoms that have no relationship at all to Western-based PTSD criteria.

TABLE 10.3

Measure	% Correctly Classified	Kappa*	Sensitivity	Specificity
Mississippi Scale	88.9	.753	94.0	79.7
DIS	87.5	.714	95.5	72.6
Checklist of PTSD	84.9	.672	88.3	78.9
MMPI	81.5	.605	90.1	68.8
Impact of Event	81.6	.565	91.7	61.8*

Kappa above .75—excellent agreement; between .40 & .75—fair

Adaptation of the HTQ for use with non-Indochinese survivors of torture and mass trauma requires the development of a new questionnaire. First, the specific political and sociocultural history of trauma should be studied by means of historical analysis, oral histories, reports from key informants, and patient focus groups. Second, the DSM-III-R items of PTSD should be translated and back-translated and tested for semantic equivalence (APA, 1987). New culture-specific symptoms related to the trauma should be identified by means of ethnographic studies, clinical experience, key informants, traditional healers, and primary care settings.

Once the new questionnaire is developed, its reliability and criterion validity against a gold standard, such as the Structured Clinical Interview for DSM-III-R (SCID; Spitzer and Williams, 1983), should be established with the associated sensitivity and specificity rates. The construct validity of the new questionnaire should be examined by establishing a relationship between PTSD symptoms and trauma experiences, social disability, health status, and other psychological markers. Longitudinal and ethnographic studies can clarify the nature of a trauma and torture-related illness in non-Western populations. The HTQ is wedded to the construct of PTSD and does not attempt to define a culture-specific disease entity. Only when culture-specific symptoms that are related to trauma and torture can be identified and their relationship to the symptoms of PTSD established, will it be possible to modify the DSM-III-R criteria and develop an instrument that is truly culture specific.

CONCLUSIONS

Measuring torture and mass trauma and their related symptoms is an extremely difficult task. In the torture field, until recent studies, scientific investigations of the psychological symptoms of torture survivors consisted primarily of the recording of symptoms without any systematic reference to standardized psychiatric diagnostic criteria (Goldfeld et al., 1988). Although recognition of the psychosocial impact of trauma has been manifested already in early studies of refugee populations, the field has yet to resolve the conceptual problems associated with determining the cultural constructs for trauma-related disease states in the survivors studied.

Over the past 15 years, investigators in the torture field have shifted from reliance upon open-ended interviews to the introduction of semistructured interview schedules. The psychometric properties of these new instruments are just being explored. Acceptance of checklists and standardized interview methods now exist only after extensive clinical experience with torture survivors proved that empirical methods could systematically be applied to facilitate the care of torture survivors (Mollica and Lavelle, 1988; Mollica, Wyshak, Lavelle, Truon, Tor, and Yang, 1990).

The developers of assessment instruments with acceptable psychometric properties have many methodological problems to solve (Helzer, Robins, and McEvoy, 1987; Helzer and Robins, 1988; Haber-Schaim, Solomon, Bleich, and Kottler, 1988; Keane and Penk, 1988). First, clinical concern for the potential emotional upset that may follow an assessment of torture and trauma survivors raises major ethical issues of when these instruments should be utilized (e.g., first evaluation interview), where (e.g., patient sample versus community sample), and the nature of obtaining informed consent and the follow-up process. The HTQ, one of the first attempts to develop a culturally valid and reliable instrument for assessing torture–trauma survivors, was not allowed to be administered to new patients during the initial evaluation interviews because of the potentially negative impact of the instrument's questions on the patient's clinical state. This limitation most likely contributed to the HTQ's lower sensitivity as compared to similar instruments for American combat veterans, since the HTQ was given only after treatment had a chance to reduce acute PTSD symptomatology. Yet, these restrictions placed upon the HTQ may have been overly cautious since it is not known whether clinical patients are incapable of completing the HTQ in the first interview. Using the HTQ in the Khmer camps in our large population-based study in Thailand (n = 1500) did not precipitate a single distraught respondent who needed acute psychiatric care (Mollica, Donelan, Tor, Lavelle, Elias, Frankel, and Blendon, 1993). Again, the spectrum effect is unknown; that is, differences between acutely symptomatic clinical patients and community members. Investigations exploring the possible negative or positive clinical impact of standardized interview schedules on acute patients could contribute considerably to our knowledge of the diagnostic and therapeutic efficacy of eliciting trauma events and symptoms early in the treatment process.

Second, the development of useful measurements in the torture–trauma field can profit from a thorough evaluation of the problems of measurement reliability. Test–retest methods to assess measurement reliability for torture–trauma related events and symptoms raise crucial concerns regarding the influence of repeated testing on the stability of item by item responses versus disease related fluctuations in memory recall and symptom intensity. Clarifying the latter could contribute to a better understanding of the disease process.

Third, the construct validity of PTSD in non-Western cultures remains elusive (Guarnaccia, Good, and Kleinman, 1990). Identification of core trauma-related symptoms which may exist across cultures would considerably increase our knowledge of the biological and sociocultural dimensions of traumatic disorders. The initial results of the HTQ have already indicated that it is highly probable that symptoms exist in Indochinese cultures which are strongly associated with the DSM-III-R criteria for PTSD. As yet, neither unique folk diagnoses nor culture-bound syndromes specific for trauma-related disease states have been identified. Similarly, the search for a "torture syndrome" continues but with little supporting evidence. The methodological problems inherent in establishing the construct validity of cultural equivalents of PTSD, as well as those unique psychological states associated with specific torture experiences, remain to be overcome. While extensive phenomenological descriptions of the torture response in survivors from diverse cultural and geopolitical backgrounds now exist, attempts to organize these phenomena into useful disease concepts or psychological syndromes that can be reliably measured have not occurred.

Fourth, the development of valid measurements in the torture–trauma field can profit considerably from PTSD research on American combat veterans. Yet, even in this more advanced area, many validity issues remain unresolved. For example, the striking contrast between prevalence rates for PTSD found in Vietnam veterans in the National Vietnam Veterans Readjustment Study (NVVRS) (Kulka et al., 1988) (current prevalence rates for the PTSD = 15.2%) and in the earlier Vietnam Experience Study (VES) (current prevalence rates for PTSD = 2.2%) (Center for

Disease Control, 1988) is partially due to methodological differences. In the VES, prevalence estimates were based upon a lay-administered DIS, an instrument whose sensitivity for detecting PTSD is only 25 percent (Kulka et al., 1988). In contrast, the NVVRS based its prevalence upon multiple scales, including a clinician-administered SCID (Spitzer and Williams, 1983). Cross-validation and cross-national studies remain central to the methodological advances necessary in both fields (Keane and Penk, 1988).

Finally, research that focuses on torture and refugee trauma must be socially useful. Because of the extreme victimization and exploitation experienced by the survivor, it is ethically correct to assume, as top priority, a research position which protects the patient from further exploitation and harm as well as provides the patient with the maximum benefits of the research process (Hellman and Hellman, 1991). To achieve protection of the survivor from further exploitation and from the well-documented aspects of Western medicine's care of poor, minority, the seriously disabled, and other emarginated social groups (Mollica, 1983), the researcher-clinician must form a working partnership with the survivor and the community he or she represents, as well as a contract to share any new knowledge discovered (Mollica, 1992).

In order to advance the special insight and methods of the study of torture and mass trauma, the uncritical use of ready-made constructs such as the DSM-III-R diagnosis of PTSD must be avoided. The problem of establishing reliable and valid measurements which "capture" the reality of the torture and trauma experience and related disease processes, reveals the complex relationship between concept (e.g., torture, trauma) and indicators (e.g., events and symptoms). It also reveals the many human reactions and limitations which affect our ability to assess the "horror" experienced by the survivors.

REFERENCES

Allodi, F. (1985), Physical and psychiatric effects of torture: Canadian study. In: *The Breaking of Bodies and Minds: Torture, Psychiatric Abuses and the Health*

Professions, ed. E. Stover & E. O. Nightingale. New York: W. H. Freeman, pp. 66–78.

American Psychiatric Association (1987), *Diagnostic and Statistical Manual of Mental Disorders* (DSM-III-R), 3rd ed. rev. Washington, DC: American Psychiatric Press.

Boehnlein, J. K. (1987), Clinical relevance of grief and mourning among Cambodian refugees. *Soc. Sci. & Med.*, 25:765–772.

Center for Disease Control (1988), Health status of Vietnam veterans: I. Psychosocial characteristics. *JAMA*, 259:2701–2707.

Cienfuegos, A. J., & Monelli, C. (1983), The testimony of political repression as a therapeutic instrument. *Amer. J. Orthopsychiatry*, 53:43–51.

Davidson-Muskin, M., & Golden, C. (1989), Lao Depression Inventory. *J. Personal. Assess.*, 53:161–168.

Dhadphale, M., Cooper, G., & Cartwright-Taylor, L. (1989), Prevalence and presentation of depressive illness in a primary health care setting in Kenya. *Amer. J. Psychiatry*, 146:659–661.

Foy, D., Lund, M., Sipprelle, C., & Strachan, A. (1984), The Combat Exposure Scale: A systematic assessment of trauma in the Vietnam war. *J. Consult. & Clin. Psychol.*, 40:1323–1328.

———— Sipprelle, R. C., Rueger, D. B., & Carroll, E. M. (1984), Etiology of posttraumatic stress disorder in Vietnam veterans: Analysis of premilitary, military and combat exposure influences. *J. Consult. & Clin. Psychol.*, 52:79–87.

Goldfeld, A. E., Mollica, R. F., Pesavento, B., & Faraone, S. (1988), The physical and psychological sequelae of torture: Symptomatology and diagnosis. *JAMA*, 259:2725–2729.

Guarnaccia, P. M., Good, B. J., & Kleinman, A. (1990), A critical review of epidemiological studies of Puerto Rican mental health. *Amer. J. Psychiatry*, 147:1449–1456.

Haber-Schaim, N., Solomon, Z., Bleich, M., & Kottler, A. (1988), Letter to the editor. *New Eng. J. Med.*, 318:1691.

Hellman, S., & Hellman, D. S. (1991), Of mice but not men: Problems of the randomized clinical trial. *New Eng. J. Med.*, 324:1585–1589.

Helzer, E. J., & Robins, L. N. (1988), Letter to the editor. *New Eng. J. Med.*, 318:1692.

———— ———— McEvoy, L. (1987), Post-traumatic stress disorder in the general population. *New Eng. J. Med.*, 317:1630–1634.

Hull, D. (1979), Migration, adaptation and illness: A review. *Soc. Sci. Med.*, 10:25–36.

Jones, E. L. (1963), The courtesy bias in Southeast Asian surveys. *Internat. Soc. Sci. J.*, 15:70–76.

Keane, T. M., Caddell, J. M., & Taylor, K. L. (1988), Mississippi Scale for combat-related posttraumatic stress disorder: Three studies in reliability and validity. *J. Consult. & Clin. Psychol.*, 56:85–90.

———— Penk, W. E. (1988), Letter to the editor: The prevalence of post-traumatic stress disorder. *New Eng. J. Med.*, 318:1692.

Kinzie, J. D., Boehnlein, J. K., Leung, P., Moore, L. J., Riley, C., & Smith, D. (1990), The prevalence of posttraumatic stress disorder and its clinical significance among Southeast Asian refugees. *Amer. J. Psychiatry,* 147:913–917.

————— Fredrickson, R. H., Ben, R., Fleck, J., & Karls, W. (1984), Posttraumatic stress disorder in Cambodian concentration camp survivors. *Amer. J. Psychiatry,* 141:654–650.

————— Manson, S. M., Vinh, D. T., Tolan, N. T., Anh, B., & Pho, T. N. (1982), Development and validation of a Vietnamese-language depression rating scale. *Amer. J. Psychiatry,* 130:1276–1281.

Kulka, R. A., Schlenger, W., Fairbank, et al. (1988), *National Vietnam Veterans Readjustment Study (NVVRS): Description, Current Status, and Initial PTSD Prevalence Estimates.* Washington, DC: Veterans Administration.

Lin, K. M., Tazuma, L., & Masuda, M. (1979), Adaptational problems of Vietnamese refugees, part I: Health and mental status. *Arch. Gen. Psychiatry,* 36:955–961.

Miller, T. W. (1988), Advances in understanding the impact of stressful life events on health. *Hosp. & Commun. Psychiatry,* 39:615–622.

Mollica, R. F. (1983), From asylum to community: The threatened disintegration of public psychiatry. *New Eng. J. Med.,* 308:367–373.

————— (1988a), What is a case? In: *Refugee Resettlement and Well Being,* ed. M. Abbott. Auckland, New Zealand: Mental Health Foundation of New Zealand, pp. 87–99.

————— (1988b), The trauma story: The psychiatric care of refugee survivors of violence and torture. In: *Post-Traumatic Therapy and Victims of Violence,* ed. F. M. Ochberg. New York: Brunner/Mazel, pp. 295–314.

————— (1992), The prevention of torture and the clinical care of survivors: A field in need of a new science. In: *Torture and Its Consequences,* ed. M. B. Basoglu. Cambridge, U.K.: Cambridge University Press.

————— Caspi-Yavin, Y., Bollini, P., Truong, T., Tor, S., & Lavelle, J. (1991), The Harvard Trauma Questionnaire: Validating a cross-cultural instrument for measuring torture, trauma and posttraumatic stress disorder in Indochinese refugees. *J. Nerv. & Ment. Dis.,* 180:110–115.

————— Donelan, K., Tor, S., Lavelle, J., Elias, C., Frankel, M., & Blendon, R. J. (1993), The effect of trauma and confinement on functional health and mental health status of Cambodians living in Thailand-Cambodia border camps. *JAMA,* 270:581–586.

————— Jalbert, R. R. (1989), Community of confinement: The mental health crisis in site two (displaced persons camp on the Thai-Kampuchean border). World Federation for Mental Health. Unpublished.

————— Lavelle, J. (1988), Southeast Asian refugees. In: *Clinical Guidelines in Cross-Cultural Mental Health,* ed. L. Comas-Diaz & E. E. H. Griffith. New York: John Wiley, pp. 262–303.

————— Son, L. (1989), Cultural dimensions in the evaluation and treatment of sexual trauma: An overview. *Psychiat. Clin. N. Amer.,* 12:363–379.

————— Wyshak, G., Lavelle, J., Truon, T., Tor, S., & Yang, T. (1990), Assessing symptom change in Southeast Asian refugee survivors of mass violence and torture. *Amer. J. Psychiatry,* 147:83–88.

————— ————— Lavelle, J. (1987), The psychosocial impact of war trauma and torture on Southeast Asian refugees. *Amer. J. Psychiatry,* 144:1567–1572.

———— ———— de Marneffe, D., Khuon, F., & Lavelle, J. (1987), Indochinese versions of the Hopkins Symptom Checklist-25: A screening instrument for the psychiatric care of refugees. *Amer. J. Psychiatry*, 144:497–500.

Mouanoutoua, V. L., Brown, L. G., Cappelletty, G. G., & Levine, R. V. (1991), A Hmong adaptation of the Beck Depression Inventory. *J. Personal. Assess.*, 57:309–332.

Odegaard, O. (1932), Emigration and insanity. *Acta Psychiat. Scand., Suppl.*, 4:9–206.

Peters, E. (1985), *Torture.* Oxford: Basil Blackwell.

Rasmussen, O. V. (1990), Medical aspects of torture: A monograph. *Dan. Med. Bull.*, 37:1–88.

———— Lunde, I. (1980), Evaluation of investigation of 200 torture victims. *Dan. Med. Bull.*, 27:215–217.

Sackett, D. L., Haynes, R. B., & Tugwell, P. (1985), *Clinical Epidemiology* Boston, MA: Little Brown

Sartorious, N. (1987), Cross-cultural research on depression. *Psychopathol.*, 19:6–11.

Spitzer, R. J., & Williams, J. B. W. (1983), *Structured Clinical Interview for DSM-III (SCID 3/15/83).* New York: Biometrics Research Department, New York State Psychiatric Institute.

United Nations Convention Against Torture and Other Cruel, Inhuman or Degrading Treatment or Punishment (1985), GA Res. 39/46, 39 GAOR Supp. (No. 51) at 197, U.N. Doc. A/39/51, opened for signature February 4, 1985, entered into force, June 26, 1987.

Vignes, A. J., & Hall, R. C. W. (1979), Adjustment of a group of Vietnamese people to the United States. *Amer. J. Psychiatry*, 136:442–444.

Westermeyer, J. (1985), Psychiatric diagnosis across culture boundaries. *Amer. J. Psychiatry*, 142:798–805.

———— Vang, T. F., & Neider, J. (1983), Migration and mental health among Hmong refugees. *J. Nerv. & Ment. Dis.*, 171:92–96.

Chapter 11
Quick-Response Disaster Study: Sampling Methods and Practical Issues in the Field

CAROL S. NORTH, M.D., AND ELIZABETH M. SMITH, Ph.D.

The study of the effects of disaster on mental health has evolved in much the same way as any new area of research: the initial studies were limited methodologically yet provided groundbreaking and revealing findings leading to further investigation with more advanced methods. Only in the last decade has the area of disaster research become organized and systematic.

Research into disaster was almost nonexistent prior to World War II, and it grew out of a broader body of study of collective stress situations such as war (Quarantelli, 1985; Warheit, 1988). In the beginning, disaster research consisted of limited, often unsystematic observation of small samples of convenience, case reports, and anecdotal findings (Green, 1985). Theorizing was abundant, and empirical data wanting.

Rapidly advancing scientific technology has created an accelerating potential for severe and potentially large-scale catastrophes, resulting in new waves of technological disasters (Smith, North, and Price, 1988). These have provided increasing opportunities for disaster research studies, which have contributed significant advances in disaster research methodology. For example, the importance of achieving a high response rate in a cirumscribed, representative sample (or randomly selected subsample) is now widely appreciated (Weisaeth, 1989b). This has not been the only methodologic advancement. Systematic data are now routinely obtained with structured or standardized instruments, and specific disorders such as posttraumatic stress disorder (PTSD) are studied with specified diagnostic criteria. In addition, many recent researchers have attempted to utilize control or comparison groups. Methods of data collection relating to sampling, instruments of measure, and timing of interviews have a significant influence on the findings in disaster research (Green, 1985; Smith et al., 1988; Weisaeth, 1989b).

Different responses and reactions evolve over time in individuals and communities affected by disasters (Horowitz, 1985; North, Smith, McCool, and Shea, 1989). Several investigators have explored timing for assessment of mental health after a disaster (Gleser, Green, and Winget, 1981; Green, Grace, Lindy, Titchener, and Lindy, 1983; Baum, Solomon, and Ursano, 1987; Steinglass and Gerrity, 1990; Rubonis and Bickman, 1991). Only systematic longitudinal studies of the course and patterns of mental health responses after disasters will provide the best information on appropriate timing of interviews (Green, 1985), which may vary depending on the purpose of a particular research project.

While retrospective studies have provided important basic information about the welfare of survivors, in the long run they present serious problems with distortion of memory over time (Green, 1985; Rubonis and Bickman, 1991). As a result, retrospective data obtained about acute postdisaster experience may be muddied, and as additional life events accrue over time it becomes difficult to sort out which responses are related to which events. In particular, cases of PTSD identified long after the event may not be representative, and may lead researchers to underestimate the prevalence because many cases of this disorder are brief in duration (Helzer, Robins, and McEvoy, 1987; Solomon, 1989; Breslau and Davis, 1992). Given our current state of knowledge, quick-responses, prospective studies are needed in order to provide accurate information about prevalence rates of symptoms and disorders after disasters, early predictive factors, and the natural history of disaster-related mental health response over time. Acute phase data obtained in quick-response disaster studies are crucial to this effort and can never be regained once the brief opportunity to collect them has passed.

Current trends in some sectors of disaster research are therefore moving toward prospective studies of survivors initially interviewed in the early aftermath of the event (Warheit, 1988) and followed up over time (Solomon, 1989). Research methodology must advance to meet the needs of these kinds of studies. Only recently has funding been available for quick-response prospective studies, and researchers in this area have had to pioneer new methods.

This chapter contains a discussion of innovative methodologic techniques that have been developed from this new line of research experience. Disaster researchers conducting prospective studies will need to get into the field quickly and will benefit from clear direction in methodology in the acute phase. The purpose of this chapter is to describe practical methods of accessing subjects and sampling in quick-response epidemiologic studies of acute disaster effects.

SAMPLING AND PRACTICAL ISSUES IN QUICK-RESPONSE DISASTER RESEARCH

Quick-response disaster studies pose unique difficulties not encountered in traditional research (Solomon, 1989). Weisaeth (1989c) found this to be the case, noting, "The main methodological problems in this study were related to the lack of previous research" (p. 22). Practical problems in acute-phase disaster research that need more than the usual consideration given in more traditional research include factors related to selection of the disaster to be studied, timing of the interviews, access to subjects, and selection of comparison subjects.

Specifics to be considered in choosing a particular disaster event for study include the type of disaster, the extent of the impact of the disaster, characteristics of the study population, and accessibility of subjects.

Obviously, the event needs survivors to provide data. Airplane crashes, for example, often leave no survivors and do not permit study. Or survivors may be so severely injured that they cannot be interviewed.

The size of the event is an additional issue. The available sample must be large enough to provide statistical power in data analysis. For example, our study of a mass shooting episode in Russellville, Arkansas, in 1987 (North, Smith, McCool, and Shea, 1989) sampled only 11 subjects present at the disaster scene and another 7 who were associated but not actually present. Statistical relationships could not be identified from this study, but certain inferences could be suggested, and subsequently these data were combined in a report with data collected systematically from other sites using the same methods (North, Smith, McCool, and Lightcap, 1989; Smith, North, McCool, and Shea, 1990), so that statistical associations could then be drawn (Smith, North, and Spitznagel, 1992).

The location of a disaster will be a limiting factor, depending on financial resources. Locations closer to home are more economical for study. So many disasters occur in modern society that, unless one is studying cross-cultural effects of disaster, there should not be great pressure to pursue events on other continents, particularly when language barriers pose additional logistic problems. Disasters in small towns may be more economical to study than in large metropolitan centers. It is certainly easier and less expensive to conduct a survey of a mass murder in a town such as Russellville, Arkansas, where accommodations are modest and the small community is relatively easy to traverse by automobile, than to pursue a study of, for example, the World Trade Center bombing in New York City, where accommodations are expensive and extensive travel is involved. News in small communities travels fast, however, and information about the research interview may be shared among subjects prior to completion of the interviews—although this same problem can occur in any location. Discussion among subjects before most of them are interviewed can result in biased data due to distortion of answers through forethought or comparison of ideas. Discussion in the community might also result in outright refusals to participate, but on the other hand, in our study of a mass murder in Killeen, Texas, a few subjects we had not yet located heard of our study from others we interviewed and contacted us wishing to participate.

The affected population of a particular disaster may have special characteristics. Depending on the purpose of the study, characteristics of these special groups might cause problems with comparability or generalizability of the findings. These may include a narrow socioeconomic status, as in, for example, survivors of a tornado in a trailer park, or extremes of age as in nursing home resident survivors of a fire or children in a school bus accident. More extreme examples of special groups may be members of an Indian reservation, a Buddhist monk colony, an institution for the blind, or an Alcoholics Anonymous group. The armed standoff between members of a large religious cult in Waco, Texas, and law enforcement authorities is undoubtedly an example of a deviant group. The question to be asked is whether there is something of value to be learned from the atypical group studied, such as, for example, how do religious zealots or recovering alcoholics cope with disaster.

Survivors must be accessible for interview. Individuals who have survived transportation accidents, for example, quickly leave the scene. This is also true of disasters involving commercial airlines and trains. Subway disasters where there are no records of travelers would be least likely to permit identification of a circumscribed sample for study.

One of the main thrusts of disaster research is the study of PTSD. Because this is a relatively uncommon disorder in general populations (Helzer et al., 1987; Breslau, Davis, Andreski, and Peterson, 1991), it is most efficiently studied in survivors of disasters because they produce the highest rates of this disorder. Disaster events thought to evoke the greatest posttraumatic impact are those with an extreme degree of terror and horror (Erikson, 1976; Lifton and Olson, 1976; Parker, 1977; Taylor and Frazer, 1982; Bolin, 1985; Lima, Pai, Santacruz, Lozano, and Luna, 1987; North, Smith, McCool, and Shea, 1989; North and Smith, 1990). For example, in our studies, rates of PTSD following the crash of a jet plane into a hotel (Smith et al., 1990) were much higher than were associated with a tornado in Florida (North, Smith, McCool, and Lightcap, 1989) where the general immediate impact of the disaster agent was milder. The greater pathology following high-impact events may relate to vivid imagery such as is experienced during an explosion, or with seeing people being badly injured and mutilated, or hearing victims scream as they perish—images that provide fertile material for flashbacks and other prominent posttraumatic symptoms (Smith et al., 1988; North and Smith, 1990).

Disasters which can be anticipated to a degree, such as a hurricane (compared to a sudden and unexpected tornado), are also thought to produce more psychopathology, and events that last a long time are thought to result in greater impact (Bolin, 1985). Sudden, brief events which occur without warning may come and go quickly before subjects have a chance to anticipate the danger or even realize what is happening, so that terror and horror do not develop during the event. An example of this was a severe tornado in Florida that blew in suddenly in the middle of the night arousing most people from sleep. Survivors of that storm frequently said that they were not frightened during the tornado; they did not have time for emotion because they were too preoccupied with trying to figure out what was happening (North, Smith, McCool, and Lightcap, 1989).

Events such a toxic leaks would be expected to produce fewer posttraumatic symptoms with their inherent lack of vivid imagery, terror and horror, and lack of opportunity for anticipation (Smith and North, 1993). Anxiety and depressive symptoms (and anger, if there is anyone to blame [Baum, Fleming, and Davidson, 1983; Smith, North, and Price, 1988]) might be more apparent than PTSD symptoms in victims of these events (Baum and Davidson, 1985). More chronic and repeated events such as annual flooding, for which one can prepare, might produce milder pathology and chronic stress, especially given the less dramatic nature of the disaster agent.

Timing of Interviews

Rates of disorders such as PTSD appear to peak early in the post-disaster period and decay over time. For example, Weisaeth (1985) found that 75 percent of high-exposure survivors of a paint factory fire had PTSD when interviewed in the acute phase, but at 7 months the prevalence rate had dropped to 53 percent. Green and colleagues (Green, Grace, Lindy, Gleser, Leonard, and Kramer, 1989; Green, Lindy, Grace, Gleser, Leonard, Korol, and Winget, 1989) found PTSD in 44 percent of victims of a dam break and flood at 18 to 26 months, and by 14 years the rate had dropped to 28 percent. Steinglass and Gerrity (1990) found PTSD in 15 percent of flood victims at 4 months, and rates dropped to 5 percent at 16 months. Krause (1987) found that the psychological impact of a hurricane diminished considerably between interviews at 9 and 16 months following the disaster. He lamented that his study design had not allowed early assessment when the psychological effects of the disaster first developed.

Advantages to making more than one assessment over time are that delayed reactions can be observed, and the course of recovery can be plotted. Early predictive factors can also be investigated. Frequently repeated interviews, however, may introduce extraneous effects into the data either by keeping symptoms alive by frequent reminders or alternatively by providing symptomatic relief through repeated opportunities for ventilation. Repeated interviews of the same subjects may burn them out or may bias responses. If sufficient numbers of subjects are interviewed, these problems could be sidestepped by staggering the timing of interviews among different subgroups (Hartsough, 1985). Krause (1987) has identified as a useful method the *synthetic cohort design* described by Kessler (1983), which is a cross-sectional approach where differences in adjustment among subjects are measured early and at varying time intervals after a common event. One potentially problematic time for follow-up interview is the event's anniversary date (Baum et al., 1987), and it might be best to interview one month before or after this date.

Timing of baseline interviews should be sensitive so as not to interfere with acute rescue operations and activities directed toward securing immediate shelter and food and finding missing loved ones. Researchers would not want to interrupt victims who are actively making funeral arrangements or trying to secure their possessions following a tornado or a fire that had severely damaged their homes. Other important business conducted by survivors during this period, such as notifying insurance companies and applying for benefits, and pursuing medical treatment may make the immediate postdisaster time (especially the first 2–3 weeks) unsuitable for interview. Furthermore, individuals still in the throes of acute emotional turmoil in the postdisaster phase may not be able to make a well-informed decision about participation (Solomon, 1989); more time might also allow some individuals to feel free to cooperate. Even if subjects agree to participate during an acute stressful period, their responses to interview questions may be distorted by acute distress and they may be unable to provide well-thought out answers (Solomon, 1989).

In determining how early to begin interviewing after a disaster, one must first ask what is to be learned from interviews within the first few days after a disaster. Everyone is expected to be upset early in the postdisaster period, and lack of variability will produce uniformity of data from which few predictions can be made.

An advantage to delaying baseline interviewing for a few weeks is that subjects will have had more time to develop their postdisaster psychopathology; for example, PTSD is not diagnosable until the symptoms have been present for more than one month (American Psychiatric Association, 1994, p. 429). In addition, the early "honeymoon phase" of community goodwill and empathy (Beigel and Berren, 1985) will be winding down by the end of the first month, and some of the initial numbness that seems to protect people in the very early postdisaster phase will have worn off. A disadvantage to waiting is that subjects may become tired of talking about the disaster after repeated interviews with reporters and repeated discussions of the event with others, and hence may be unwilling to talk about it any further.

Waiting much more than a couple of months risks distortion of memory through reconstruction of experiences over time and repetition of the account to others. Continued "rehearsal" of stories by subjects who have retold them over and over may cement or embellish some recollections in memory and bypass others. By a couple of months postdisaster some individuals may have "moved on," often by conscious decision, having developed an extensive repertoire of denial and avoidance as their dominant coping strategy. Such individuals may be very reluctant to reopen painful memories of the event for the purposes of research.

ACCESS TO SUBJECTS

Gaining access to potential subjects for study is perhaps the biggest practical problem in studies of disaster (Baum et al., 1987; Solomon, 1989). As a result, many studies, particularly earlier studies, have limited their samples to readily available groups. These convenience samples have included victims seeking psychiatric treatment or disaster assistance, subjects sampled at shelters for displaced victims, such as those who have lost their homes in hurricanes and floods, and rescue personnel. These are potentially nonrepresentative samples that may be unusual in many important ways. For example, victims in shelters may be individuals who are special by way of having few personal resources, such as friends or family who could take them in temporarily, or funds to rent a hotel room or apartment. Only a minority of individuals seeks psychiatric treatment after a disaster, and therefore they are not all representative of the community as a whole. Rescue and medical personnel may be special by way of their having selected their field of work, and by preparedness resulting from previous training and experience in the field (Green, 1985; Dunning, 1988). Many rescue personnel, however, are volunteers, such as volunteer firemen, with little or no training or experience. This potentially interesting population has not been well studied in systematic research.

More representative samples of a cross-section of individuals affected by a disaster are challenging to obtain, but the growing consensus is that the effort to sample them is worth the trouble, especially if one is trying to study rates of disorders after disasters (Baum et al., 1987). There is nothing traditional about sampling in quick-response disaster studies, and the usual epidemiologic survey methods may not apply (Baum et al., 1987). A variety of useful techniques may help ease this task.

First, reading local newspaper accounts in advance of entry into the field may help locate key informants, as well as provide additional names of subjects, and further background information about the disaster and the community. These local accounts may help one evaluate the scope of the disaster, providing rough estimates of the number of survivors and the number of fatalities, to help determine whether the event is severe and amenable to study. Conversations with local reporters may yield further information, and occasionally these individuals can be useful in providing personal contacts or names and locating information for potential subjects. Solomon (1989) describes the importance of getting to know the "turf" (local customs, norms, and the setting) in disaster studies. This process begins in the earliest phases of considering a disaster for study, assists in recruiting subjects, and helps one understand the context of the disaster setting that shapes the impact of the event on individuals.

Among the best settings for subject accessibility are businesses affected by disasters. Businesses have circumscribed populations of employees whose whereabouts are usually well known to their employers. A cooperative management may be willing to provide names and addresses for all subjects present at the time of the disaster, and can sometimes be of further benefit by reassuring their employees of the legitimacy of the research. Weisaeth

(1989c) successfully used this method in his study of a paint factory fire in Norway, achieving an impressive 100 percent completion rate for interviews of the company's employees. He apparently accomplished this with the cooperation of colleagues in the company's health department.

If the management is totally uncooperative, however, this may preclude study of the event or at least necessitate other more difficult means of accessing subjects. When gatekeepers such as business owners refuse to cooperate, the investigator must respect this and move on. This was the case in our study of mass murders in Arkansas, where owners of two of the four affected businesses declined to participate, and hence data were collected from only two of the four locations (North, Smith, McCool, and Shea, 1989).

A possible study of a plane crash into a business in the Midwest encountered problems. The business manager was very cautious and requested a copy of the interview, and then insisted the matter be discussed among the executives. He ultimately decided to cooperate with the study, agreeing only to contact the employees himself to recruit them. He did this half-heartedly, and less than half of the potential subjects responded; the project was abandoned. Similarly, a possible study of a mass shooting episode in a public area of a business ran into management concerns about public relations; their representative said too many people from a variety of sources (media, law enforcement, disaster workers, mental health workers, etc.) had already talked to their employees and they didn't want to overload them. Again, their wishes were respected.

Occasions arise where issues of confidentiality prevent organizations such as the Red Cross from disclosing lists of names of victims to researchers (Baum et al., 1987). Owners or managers of businesses may have these same concerns. They may feel very protective of their employees, who often have been intruded on by media, and they may be wary of strangers trying to take advantage of them, and hence unwilling to allow unfamiliar researchers to contact their employees directly. In the authors' study of a plane crash into a hotel in Indianapolis (Smith, North, McCool, and Shea, 1990), the hotel manager came up with the idea of addressing and mailing letters prepared by the researchers inviting employees to participate in the study. He enclosed a self-addressed, stamped return postcard that subjects could use (or, if they preferred, they could call collect) to indicate willingness to participate or decline without having to do so personally. The participation rate in this study was 74 percent. In part, this good response rate was probably related to the conscientiousness of the manager who assisted with employee recruitment.

Because this method worked quite well it was applied in a study of eyewitnesses to a mass shooting incident at a university in the Midwest and for recruitment of control subjects from another department of the same university. The chairmen of the two departments cooperated by sending letters with return postcards inviting potential subjects to participate, according to our description of the parameters for subject selection (i.e., individuals who saw or heard the shooting or saw dead or injured victims, and control subjects matched for gender and academic level). The chairmen also provided us with basic numbers and demographic data about nonparticipants for our records. Rates of cooperation were lower with this method than we have achieved when we have contacted potential subjects personally, especially in the control group. Potential subjects received an unanticipated letter from a distant and unknown researcher, and as a result they were more skeptical and less interested because they did not receive a personal invitation or have an opportunity to ask questions directly. Because there are so many disasters and because high completion rates are crucial, investigators might discard events where they cannot gain direct access to subjects or establish clear enthusiasm on the part of the representative.

In community settings a number of sources of initial contacts may be available. These may include the local newspaper office, mental health providers, and law enforcement officials. These sources may also help to legitimatize researchers in the eyes of potential subjects who may otherwise be doubtful. Initial telephone contact with these key individuals may also provide valuable assistance for additional sources of informants when entering the field.

A surprising means of access to subjects was available in our attempt to sample subjects present at a mass murder in Texas (North, Smith, and Spitznagel, 1994). The research team paid a preliminary visit to the local police department. Once trust was gained, police assistance proved invaluable in our effort to compile a very comprehensive list of survivors; a few additional names were found by sifting through newspapers or by word of mouth.

The initial meeting with potential contacts, especially in the first few moments, is a pivotal time during which they may decide the project is not worthy of their cooperation. This may block access to help which is crucial to the project. Premature requests for assistance may cause a contact to refuse any help. A helpful strategy is to first allow them to talk about the event or their reactions to it, which builds rapport and demonstrates to them that the researcher is sensitive, genuine, and professional. The individual may spontaneously offer assistance, which may be far more comprehensive than cooperation specifically requested. For example, our team has been spontaneously offered the use of telephones, interviewing space, useful materials such as clipping files covering the event, and photographs, additional contacts, and references.

Establishing trust is a key issue upon entering the disaster community. Family members and mental health personnel may be protective of subjects and try to shield them from strangers they feel may exploit them. Those who have had bad media experiences may be especially wary of further interviews. Therefore a helpful issue to clarify at the start of a conversation with a potential informant or subject is that the researcher is not connected with the media and that the interviews will be strictly confidential. Members of small communities, once they are confident of the researchers' legitimacy and professionalism, can be exceedingly trusting and open, and will often go far out of their way to be helpful. They may be stimulated by the novel opportunity to meet researchers who take an interest in them and their community.

Local health professionals, in particular mental health professionals, may be a key source of assistance in gaining access to disaster subjects. In some settings, health professionals routinely see all survivors as part of ongoing health maintenance and have provided systematic or universal subject sources (Henderson and Bostock, 1977; Hoiberg and McCaughey, 1984). In his study of a Norwegian ship disaster, Weisaeth (1989a) achieved his 100 percent completion rate with the apparent assistance of the psychiatrists who treated all the survivors. In other settings, investigators have capitalized on requests by attorneys representing clients to examine all the survivors in order to launch a research project (Leopold and Dillon, 1963).

Local mental health professionals may be sympathetic to the importance of scientific research in their field, and therefore receptive to a research team. In the case of a northern Florida tornado, the local mental health center director proved indispensable to the study (North, Smith, McCool, and Lightcap, 1989). He knew all the survivors in his small community, and he also had counseled a number of them, and led a survivors' support group. He had their confidence as well as considerable knowledge about them and their community.

Another potential means for gaining access to subjects is through directly providing mental health services to them. Black (1987) described his efforts to establish contact with the families of 137 passengers killed in an airplane crash in Dallas. He was initially rejected by the airline, but managed to establish contact by treating medical conditions and providing psychological and emotional support to families, eventually gaining their trust and the gratitude of the airline as well. Another example of mental health professionals providing treatment is Friedman and Linn's study (1957); they were psychiatrists present when the Andrea Doria liner sank. One problem with this means of access is that the intervention by the investigator may affect the results of the study unless this is carefully worked into the study design.

Without providing direct psychiatric services to subjects as part of a research study, one can sometimes elicit the cooperation and assistance of key informants if the interview process is perceived as helpful. Many individuals find the exercise of talking about their experience to an interested listener to be very helpful, and will sometimes even thank interviewers for the interview when it is over. This appreciation of the opportunity to talk about the disaster is consistent with our findings that 69 percent of tornado survivors reported that they coped with the disaster by talking with family and friends (North, Smith, McCool, and Lightcap, 1989), and 9 out of 10 eyewitnesses of mass murders both in Russellville, Arkansas (North, Smith, McCool, and Shea, 1989) and in Killeen, Texas (North et al., 1994) also used this method of coping. Black (1987) noted that family members of deceased airline passengers who had more contact with others (and hence more opportunity to talk about it) coped better with their tragedy. In that sense, a potential selling strategy for a study is that the interview itself may be directly beneficial to subjects. Weisaeth (1989c) found that "to be perceived as a helper as well as a researcher probably improved the quality of the data, and in particular made it possible to reach a 100% response rate" (p. 23).

In our experience, only 2 out of 321 subjects interviewed in our disaster studies to date have exhibited sufficient distress to indicate need for professional help. Neither of these subjects was upset because of the interview and neither required immediate intervention. For those individuals, the interview provided the benefit of recognition of emotional distress and access to psychiatric services that they might not otherwise have obtained. A generally held lay idea is that talking about upsetting events may cause mental harm, and this notion may contribute to problems of nonparticipation in disaster studies. Subjects can be reassured that this is not the experience of disaster interviewers—quite the contrary. Probably the best evidence that participating in a disaster study is a positive, or at least a nonnegative, experience for subjects is the high rate of participation in our follow-up interviews; to date 94 percent of the 294 subjects we located have agreed to participate.

The altruistic nature of research for the purposes of helping future disaster victims may be pointed out to potential subjects (Solomon, 1989). Common public sentiment at present does not fully appreciate the value of research and is somewhat suspicious of it (e.g., ideas that researchers "bend numbers" to suit their biases or needs, or that they prey on disaster victims for prurient reasons). Eliciting cooperation may take time and education. Researchers can stress the importance of the purpose of the research study to help them understand the problems and needs of individuals who have been through severe traumas, so that disaster workers can best tailor intervention programs to help survivors of future disasters.

Reasons should be elicited when someone refuses to participate. Often the problem can be ameliorated by providing more information or clarifying a misunderstanding. Solomon (1989) recommends that even if prospective subjects refuse requests for an interview, they be asked if they may be contacted again later. Some who initially refuse may be willing to participate later when they are less upset or less busy or have found reason to trust the investigator.

Occasionally subjects are reluctant to participate in research studies because they are involved in litigation. Solomon (1989) advises that investigators directly attempt to contact the lawyers representing the subjects, because once the project is explained the lawyers may be of assistance in reassuring subjects and eliciting their participation.

Additional subjects can be obtained by advertising in the media. While the media can cause roadblocks to interviews of potential subjects through negative press and by tiring subjects, and may also contaminate research by reporting information that could bias respondents, they may also be surprisingly useful in legitimating researchers. The essential problem with media-based recruitment of participants lies with selection bias. Volunteer subjects obtained through media advertising may have special characteristics, such as being particularly upset and wanting to talk about it, or wishing to air complaints or praise individuals associated with the event. Volunteer study subjects may have more or less pathology than the average individual in a disaster (Green, 1985).

While large-scale disasters may be particularly attractive events for study, interviewing all survivors may not be feasible or desirable. For example, the Oakland, California, firestorm of 1991 burned in excess of 3000 homes. For such events, a random method of subject selection will yield a representative subsample.

In Oakland, personal property tax records of the damaged area were obtained. From a list of addresses derived from these records, every twentieth geographic household was selected, and a representative member of each household was contacted for interview. Because the firestorm was spotty in its damage, the affected neighborhoods contained properties with all degrees of damage, from total obliteration to only minor damage, to no damage at all. Subjects with different levels of exposure were thus sampled randomly from these neighborhoods, allowing for determination of dose–response relationships.

Krause (1987) randomly sampled from the population of the entire city of Galveston, Texas, to assess the mental health effects of a hurricane there. He obtained a city directory, which was divided into clusters of 50 addresses. He then used a "replicated sampling approach," drawing 10 replicates consisting of 63 clusters at random, and selected one eligible person per household using the Kish grid selection method. He also randomized the scheduling of the interviews. With these methods he completed 351 interviews of randomly selected subjects.

SELECTION OF COMPARISON SUBJECTS

For longitudinal studies of disaster victims, as in most traditional epidemiologic studies, comparison groups are useful if not essential. The objective of a control or comparison group is to sample a group that is like the proband group in every way except that they were unaffected by the disaster (Baum et al., 1987). In selecting a comparison group for victims of a mass murder in a grocery store, for example, one might consider the employees of another store of the same chain in the same city. The problem with this group, however, is that they are likely to have been affected in some way by the event—by personal ties to affected employees, by psychological connections to the affected store chain, and by the general effect on the community. Employees of a store in the same chain in a different city or in a different store chain might be less affected but might also be different in many important ways such as socioeconomic status, racial composition, and the size of the community.

Because of the difficulties in trying to obtain a suitable comparison group, Solomon (1989) has recommended comparison with available standardized population data such as that from the Epidemiologic Catchment Area (ECA) study (Robins and Regier, 1991). This suggestion is not free of problems either. The ECA study did not include data that are specifically useful for the study of disasters, such as disaster-related symptoms, changes in marital status, daily functioning, employment difficulties, and financial problems. Therefore these key variables are left out of any comparisons, and the only really comparable information is rates of psychiatric symptoms. Another problem with the ECA data is that the data conform to the DSM-III standards that were in effect in the early 1980s. The data therefore may not fit data collected with later DSM-III-R, DSM-IV, and future diagnostic versions. This is particularly a problem for the relatively new diagnostic entity of PTSD, which changed considerably after DSM-III. In DSM-III (and hence in the ECA data) interviewers asked for information about traumatic events only if a subject had symptoms associated with it, and therefore a large proportion of trauma history was not obtained.

An interesting comparison group may be those indirectly affected, for example employees of a business affected by a disaster who were not present at the time of the event (Baum et al., 1987) but who undoubtedly experienced some effects of a disaster that may have narrowly missed them. This comparison may allow investigation of dose–response effects. This method has been successfully employed in our studies (North, Smith, McCool, and Shea, 1989; Smith, North, McCool, and Shea, 1990), and has resulted in significant findings (Smith, North, and Spitznagel (1993).

While it may be difficult to persuade survivors of disasters to be interviewed about a painful event, it may be even more difficult, because of lack of motivation, to persuade nonaffected individuals to participate as control subjects. Disaster victims may be invested in supporting research efforts aimed at assisting others who may experience disasters in the future, or may be interested because it is an opportunity to further discuss their experiences with an interested listener. Nonaffected subjects do not share these motivations, as we experienced in a university's control group where we achieved low rates of participants compared to the disaster group. Payment may help promote participation, but this might be a more powerful motivator for affected victims of disasters that have interfered with their livelihood; for example, an explosion that has destroyed the business that employed them.

SOME PRACTICAL MATTERS

Disaster research is like no other area of psychiatric and epidemiologic research; by definition, it is quite novel. It requires flexibility of funding and planning, and depends on rapid assessment and decision making. This is particularly true of quick-response disaster studies where investigators desire to enter the field as early as one month after the event. To maximize on cost savings, airline reservations need to be made in advance. This requires calculating in advance how many interviews can be scheduled and accomplished in a particular period. Length of interview, scheduling of appointments, and details of interview location and transportation logistics need to be worked out in advance (Baum et al., 1987).

Whenever possible, it is most convenient (and cost-effective) to have subjects meet the interviewer in a central location. In some cases, space at the local police department or a local mental health center has been offered and has been very useful. Hotel lobbies and coffee shops are also potential interview locations and can be scouted out to determine their feasibility for a good interview spot. In some cases, it may be advantageous to visit subjects in their homes, particularly if the disaster occurred at home. For example, many interviews for the Oakland firestorm study were conducted at the homes of people whose houses were in heavily burned neighborhoods, but had not been destroyed; this added context and depth to the interview. Interviewing others who had been displaced to temporary apartments also yielded important impressions about their interim living conditions which might be expected to affect their mental health.

No matter where the interview is conducted, privacy is an issue. In hotel lobbies or cafeterias, attention must be paid to finding a private nook. In subjects' homes, one may have to contend with family members who may be listening in or who may want to sit in on the interview and interject their own material, which may compromise the data. The authors have found it necessary to establish a rule that family members be out of earshot if at all possible to avoid potential biasing of information. Family members can generally appreciate this if they are told it's "for the research protocol." Disappointed family members who want to share their own stories can often be successfully managed by being offered their own private interview.

Because of the nature of disaster research, unlike other research, the investigation is usually conducted in places foreign to the investigators and interviewers. Access to telephones may be limited or costly; the FAX machine and the photocopier are not just a moment away. The secretary may be hundreds of thousands of miles away. One has no desk; one's hotel room and the materials one brings constitute one's temporary office and supplies. Even cash (especially pertinent in studies where large numbers of subjects need cash payments) may need to be scouted out. All this requires preplanning, flexibility, and adjustment.

Trips to disaster sites can be intense, due to the need for cost effectiveness and desire to obtain as much data as possible in a limited period of time. With the focus being on the traumas of the study subjects in studies of disaster, the needs of interviewers may be overlooked. The interviewers' task requires a careful balance of attitude: They need to distance themselves enough not to be overwhelmed by the intense emotional nature of the interviews they conduct, often for long and grueling hours, yet they must remain sensitive and open to the human aspects of the experience. In the field they are faced with one subject after another with often overwhelming needs that they can do little to address directly, which can be frustrating and draining. Therefore investigators need to realize the potential for burnout of their interviewers, and potentially of themselves in the field. Long hours of repeated interviews need to be broken up with opportunities to refresh oneself with meals, walks, shopping, exploration, or relaxation. In addition, daily debriefing sessions are helpful to allow interviewers to discuss their reactions to the material being ventilated to them by their interview subjects and to process this intense experience. With skillful debriefing, the resulting experience in the field can be highly stimulating and meaningful as opposed to being a "burn-out" experience.

DISCUSSION

Quick-response studies of disasters are difficult, time-consuming, and demanding; hence, disaster research is not for everyone. Helpful personal attributes in the researcher include inventiveness and creativity, novelty-seeking, poise, on-the-spot problem solving, ability to make quick yet careful decisions, flexibility and adaptability, physical and emotional energy and endurance, and rapport and empathy. Part of what makes this research so difficult is that with each new disaster event to be studied, one must essentially reinvent the wheel. Because each disaster is unique, no two events can be approached in the same way. Therefore there is no "cookbook" approach that can be devised and repeated from one disaster to the next. In this chapter, however, we have identified some commonalities to the approach to the quick-response disaster study, providing specific techniques and generalizations where applicable, and organized ways to think about it.

Data already obtained from quick-response studies will help determine accurate prevalence rates of specific postdisaster psychiatric disorders. Information from quick-response studies may help untangle how disaster-related variables (factors associated with the disaster agent, the individual subjects, and the community) act to contribute to psychopathology, and provide better understanding of the human coping mechanisms. Beyond these immediate uses, however, acute phase data serve as an important database for future prospective follow-up studies to determine the natural course of symptoms over time and predictors of long-term outcome. More longitudinal studies are needed, but these cannot be performed without the baseline study for a starting point.

The traditional concept of a prospective study actually refers to studying subjects prior to the point of interest, and technically in disaster research this would refer to the predisaster period. It is usually not feasible to do these kinds of prospective disaster studies, because of the unexpected nature of disaster events (Baum et al., 1987). A few groups, however, have taken advantage of serendipitous opportunities to restudy after a disaster individuals assessed prior to the disaster for some other purpose, such as following the ECA study in St. Louis where dioxin contamination, flooding, and tornadoes subsequently occurred (Smith, Robins, Przybeck, Goldring, and Solomon, 1986; Robins, Fishbach, Smith, Cottler, Solomon, and Goldring, 1986), and after an ECA-like study in Puerto Rico, the site of a subsequent hurricane (Canino, Bravo, Rubio-Stipec, and Woodbury, 1990; Bravo, Rubio-Stipec, Canino, Woodbury, and Ribera, 1990; Escobar, Canino, Rubio-Stipec, and Bravo, 1992). For the most part, however, we cannot plan such truly prospective studies, but we can be alert to such opportunities when they arise, especially as general population studies become more abundant.

Besides prospective studies, other new areas remain for future disaster research, and increasing sophistication of methods is anticipated. For example, systematic evaluation of children after disasters is virtually nonexistent, and a few anecdotal and observational or otherwise nonsystematic studies suggest that children respond somewhat differently than do adults. Certainly the effects of disaster on developing minds would be a unique and interesting area of investigation lending itself well to longitudinal study. While there is considerable information about effects of disaster on those who survive them, knowledge on how to manage their disaster-related mental health problems is sparse and largely theory-driven. A next logical direction in disaster research is toward intervention studies to document what methods are helpful or not, and for whom. Solomon (1989) recommends controlled clinical trials.

Further research must proceed within a theoretical framework. A theoretical framework already exists and has an extensive literature supporting it, but this framework is largely generated from nonsystematic observational material. Theory must be advanced in a databased manner, with new data generating new hypotheses to be tested in future studies. In this way the field can advance logically, with contributions of both theory and systematic data stimulating and strengthening each other along the way.

REFERENCES

American Psychiatric Association (1994), *American Psychiatric Association: Diagnostic and Statistical Manual of Mental Disorders*, 4th ed. (DSM-IV). Washington, DC: American Psychiatric Press.

Baum, A., & Davidson, L. M. (1985), A suggested framework for studying factors that contribute to trauma in disaster. In: *Disasters and Mental Health: Selected Contemporary Perspectives*, ed. B. J. Sowder. Rockville, MD: National Institute of Mental Health.

——— Fleming, R., & Davidson, L. M. (1983), Natural disaster and technological catastrophe. *Environ. & Behav.*, 15:333–354.

——— Solomon, S. D., & Ursano, R. (1987), Emergency/disaster research issues: A guide to the preparation and evaluation of grant applications dealing with traumatic stress. In: *Proceedings of the Workshop on Research Issues: Emergency, Disaster, and Post-Traumatic Stress*. Bethesda, MD: Uniformed Services University of the Health Sciences.

Beigel, A., & Berren, M. (1985), Human-induced disasters. *Psychiat. Ann.*, 15:143–150.

Black, J. W., Jr. (1987), The libidinal cocoon: A nurturing retreat for the families of plane crash victims. *Hosp. & Commun. Psychiatry*, 38:1322–1326.

Bolin, R. (1985), Disaster characteristics and psychosocial impacts. In: *Disasters and Mental Health: Selected Contemporary Perspectives*, ed. B. J. Sowder. Rockville, MD: National Institute of Mental Health.

Bravo, M., Rubio-Stipec, M., Canino, G. J., Woodbury, M. A., & Ribera, J. C. (1990), The psychological sequelae of disaster stress prospectively and retrospectively evaluated. *Amer. J. Commun. Psychol.*, 18:661–680.

Breslau, N., & Davis, G. C. (1992), Posttraumatic stress disorder in an urban population of young adults: Risk factors for chronicity. *Amer. J. Psychiatry*, 149:671–675.

———— ———— Andreski, P., & Peterson, E. (1991), Traumatic events and post-traumatic stress disorder in an urban population of young adults. *Arch. Gen. Psychiatry*, 48:216–222.

Canino, G., Bravo, M., Rubio-Stipec, M., & Woodbury, M. (1990), The impact of disaster on mental health: Prospective and retrospective analyses. *Internat. J. Ment. Health*, 19:51–69.

Dunning, C. (1988), Intervention strategies for emergency workers. In: *Mental Health Response to Mass Emergencies: Theory and Practice*, ed. M. Lystad. New York: Brunner/Mazel, pp. 284–307.

Erikson, K. T. (1976), Loss of communality at Buffalo Creek. *Amer. J. Psychiatry*, 133:302–305.

Escobar, J. I., Canino, G., Rubio-Stipec, M., & Bravo, M. (1992), Somatic symptoms after a natural disaster: A prospective study. *Amer. J. Psychiatry*, 149:965–967.

Friedman, P., & Linn, L. (1957), Some psychiatric notes on the Andrea Doria disaster. *Amer. J. Psychiatry*, 114:426–432.

Gleser, G. C., Green, B. L., & Winget, C. N. (1981), *Prolonged Psychosocial Effects of Disaster: A Study of Buffalo Creek*. New York: Academic Press.

Green, B. L. (1985), Conceptual and methodological issues in assessing the psychological impact of disaster. In: *Disasters and Mental Health: Selected Contemporary Perspectives*, ed. B. J. Sowder. Rockville, MD: National Institute of Mental Health.

———— Grace, M. C., Lindy, J. D., Gleser, G. C., Leonard, A. C., & Kramer, T. L. (1989), Buffalo Creek survivors in the second decade: Comparison with unexposed and non-litigant groups. Unpublished data.

———— ———— ———— Titchener, J. L., & Lindy, J. G. (1983), Levels of functional impairment following a civilian disaster: The Beverly Hills Supper Club fire. *J. Consult. & Clin. Psychol.*, 51:573–580.

———— Lindy, J. D., Grace, M. C., Gleser, G. C., Leonard, A. C., Korol, M., & Winget, C. (1989), Buffalo Creek survivors in the second decade: Stability and change of stress symptoms over 14 years. Unpublished data.

Hartsough, D. M. (1985), Measurement of the psychological effects of disaster. In: *Perspectives on Disaster Recovery*, ed. J. Laube & S. A. Murphy. Norwalk, CT: Appleton-Century-Crofts, pp. 22–60.

Helzer, J. E., Robins, L. N., & McEvoy, L. (1987), Post-traumatic stress disorder in the general population. *N. Eng. J. Med.*, 317:1630–1634.

Henderson, S., & Bostock, T. (1977), Coping behaviour after shipwreck. *Brit. J. Psychiatry*, 131:15–20.

Hoiberg, A., & McCaughey, B. G. (1984), The traumatic aftereffects of collision at sea. *Amer. J. Psychiatry*, 141:70–73.

Horowitz, M. J. (1985), Disasters and psychological responses to stress. *Psychiat. Ann.*, 15:161–167.

Kessler, R. (1983), Methodological issues in the study of psychosocial stress. In: *Psychosocial Stress: Trends in Theory and Research*, ed. H. Kaplan. New York: Academic Press.

Krause, N. (1987), Exploring the impact of a natural disaster on the health and psychological well-being of older adults. *J. Hum. Stress*, Summer:61–69.

Leopold, R. L., & Dillon, H. (1963), Psychoanatomy of a disaster: A long-term study of post-traumatic neuroses in survivors of a Marine explosion. *Amer. J. Psychiatry*, 119:913–921.

Lifton, R. J., & Olson, E. (1976), The human meaning of total disaster: The Buffalo Creek experience. *Psychiatry*, 39:1–18.

Lima, B. R., Pai, S., Santacruz, H., Lozano, J., & Luna, J. (1987), Screening for the psychological consequences of a major disaster in a developing country: Armero, Colombia. *Acta Psychiat. Scand.*, 76:561–567.

North, C. S., & Smith, E. M. (1990), Post-traumatic stress disorder in disaster survivors. *Comprehen. Ther.*, 16:3–9.

————— ————— McCool, R. E., & Lightcap, P. E. (1989), Acute post-disaster coping and adjustment. *J. Traum. Stress*, 2:353–360.

————— ————— ————— Shea, J. M. (1989), Short-term psychopathology in eyewitnesses to mass murder. *Hosp. & Commun. Psychiatry*, 40:1293–1295.

————— ————— Spitznagel, E. L. (1994), Post-traumatic stress disorder in survivors of a mass shooting episode. *Amer. J. Psychiatry*, 151:82–88.

Parker, G. (1977), Cyclone Tracy and Darwin evacuees: On the restoration of the species. *Brit. J. Psychiatry*, 130:548–555.

Quarantelli, E. L. (1985), An assessment of conflicting views on mental health: The consequences of traumatic events. In: *Trauma and Its Wake. The Study and Treatment of Post-Traumatic Stress Disorder*, ed. C. R. Figley. New York: Brunner/Mazel, pp. 173–215.

Robins, L. N., Fishbach, R. L., Smith, E. M., Cottler, L. B., Solomon, S. D., & Goldring, E. (1986), Impact of disaster on previously assessed mental health. In: *Disaster Stress Studies: New Methods and Findings*, ed. J. H. Shore. Washington, DC: American Psychiatric Press.

————— Regier, D. A. (1991), *Psychiatric Disorders in America: The Epidemiologic Catchment Area Study*. New York: Free Press.

Rubonis, A. V., & Bickman, L. (1991), Psychological impairment in the wake of disaster: The disaster-psychopathology relationship. *Psychol. Bull.*, 109:384–399.

Smith, E. M., & North, C. S. (1993), Post-traumatic stress disorder in natural disasters and technological accidents. In: *International Handbook of Traumatic Stress Syndromes*, ed. J. P. Wilson & B. Raphael. New York: Plenum Press, pp. 405–419.

————— McCool, R. E., & Shea, J. M. (1990), Acute postdisaster psychiatric disorders: Identification of persons at risk. *Amer. J. Psychiatry*, 147:202–206.

————— ————— Price, P. C. (1988), Response to technological accidents. In: *Mental Health Response to Mass Emergencies*, ed. M. Lystad. New York: Brunner/Mazel.

————— ————— Spitznagel, E. L. (1993), Post-traumatic stress in survivors of three disasters. *J. Soc. Behav. & Personal.*, (Special Issue): 8:353–368.

————— Robins, L. N., Przybeck, T. R., Goldring, E., & Solomon, S. D. (1986), Psychosocial consequences of a disaster. In: *Disaster Stress Studies: New Methods and Findings*, ed. J. H. Shore. Washington, DC: American Psychiatric Press, pp. 50–75.

Solomon, S. D. (1989), Research issues in assessing disaster's effects. In: *Psychosocial Aspects of Disaster*, ed. R. Gist & B. Lubin. New York: John Wiley, pp. 308–340.

Steinglass, P., & Gerrity, E. (1990), Natural disasters and posttraumatic stress disorder: Short-term vs. long-term recovery in two disaster-affected communities. *J. Appl. Soc. Psychol.*, 20:1746–1765.

Taylor, A. J. W., & Frazer, A. G. (1982), The stress of post-disaster body handling and identification work. *J. Hum. Stress*, 8:4–12.

Warheit, G. J. (1988), Disasters and their mental health consequences: Issues, findings, and future trends. In: *Mental Health Response to Mass Emergencies. Theory and Practice*, ed. M. Lystad. New York: Brunner/Mazel, pp. 3–21.

Weisaeth, L. (1985), Post-traumatic stress disorder after an industrial disaster. In: *Psychiatry—The State of the Art*, ed. P. Pichot, P. Berner, R. Wolf, & K. Thau. New York: Plenum Press, pp. 299–307.

——— (1989a), Torture of a Norwegian ship's crew. *Acta Psychiat. Scand.*, 80:63–72.

——— (1989b), Importance of high response rates in traumatic stress research. *Acta Psychiat. Scand.*, 80:131–137.

——— (1989c), A study of behavioural responses to an industrial disaster. *Acta Psychiat. Scand.*, 80:13–24.

Name Index

Subject Index

339